Cambridge Studies in Histori

THE TITHE SURVEYS OF ENGLAND AND WALES

Cambridge Studies in Historical Geography

Series editors:
ALAN R. BAKER   J. B. HARLEY   DAVID WARD

Cambridge Studies in Historical Geography encourages exploration of the philosophies, methodologies and techniques of historical geography and publishes the results of new research within all branches of the subject. It endeavours to secure the marriage of traditional scholarship with innovative approaches to problems and to sources, aiming in this way to provide a focus for the discipline and to contribute towards its development. The series is an international forum for publication in historical geography which also promotes contact with workers in cognate disciplines.

1 Period and place: research methods in historical geography. *Edited by* A. R. H. BAKER *and* M. BILLINGE.

2 The historical geography of Scotland since 1707: geographical aspects of modernisation DAVID TURNOCK.

3 Historical understanding in geography: an idealist approach LEONARD T. GUELKE.

4 English industrial cities of the nineteenth century: a social geography R. J. DENNIS.

5 Explorations in historical geography: interpretative essays. *Edited by* A. R. H. BAKER *and* D. J. GREGORY.

6 The tithe surveys of England and Wales ROGER J. P. KAIN *and* HUGH C. PRINCE.

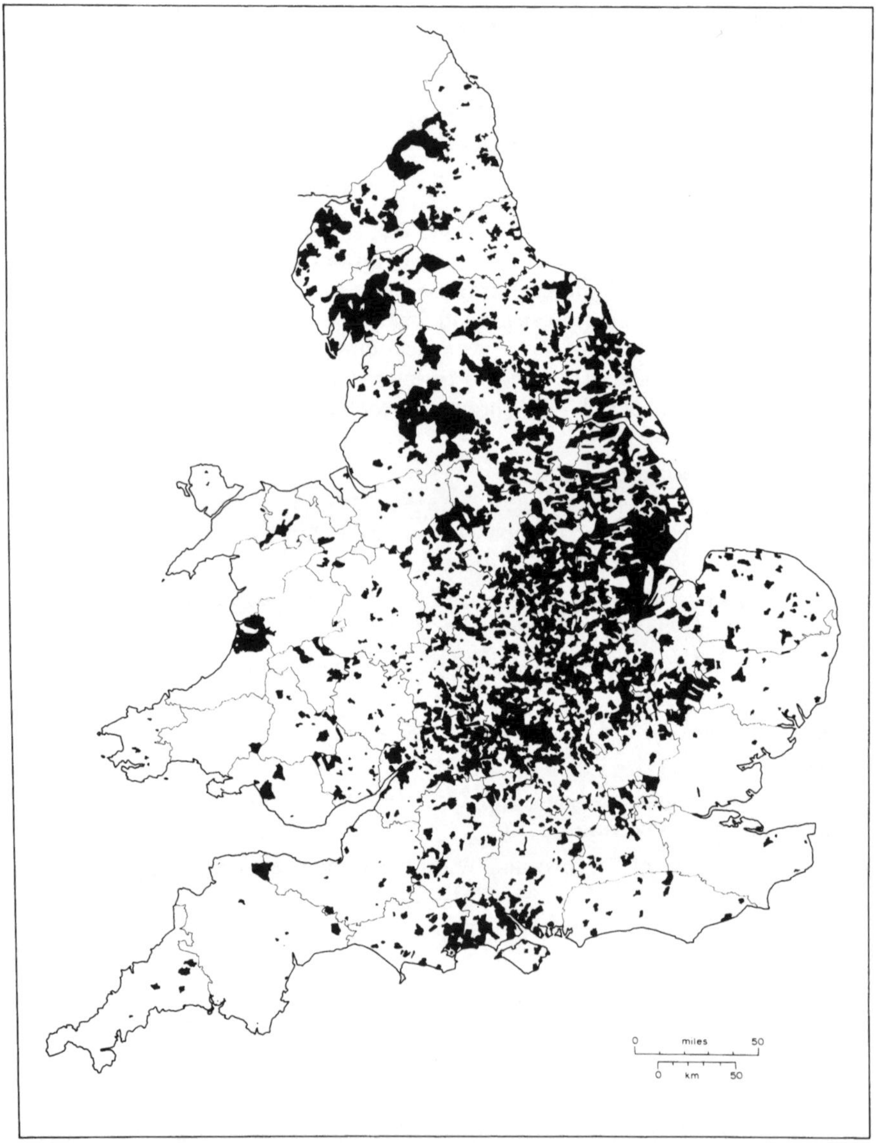

The coverage of England and Wales by tithe surveys. Compilation of this map is described on p. 112. Areas in black have no tithe surveys. White areas are covered by surveys.

THE TITHE SURVEYS OF ENGLAND AND WALES

ROGER J. P. KAIN

Senior Lecturer in Geography, University of Exeter

and

HUGH C. PRINCE

Reader in Geography, University College London

CAMBRIDGE UNIVERSITY PRESS

CAMBRIDGE

LONDON NEW YORK NEW ROCHELLE

MELBOURNE SYDNEY

CAMBRIDGE UNIVERSITY PRESS
Cambridge, New York, Melbourne, Madrid, Cape Town, Singapore, São Paulo

Cambridge University Press
The Edinburgh Building, Cambridge CB2 2RU, UK

Published in the United States of America by Cambridge University Press, New York

www.cambridge.org
Information on this title: www.cambridge.org/9780521246811

First published 1985
This digitally printed first paperback version 2006

A catalogue record for this publication is available from the British Library

Library of Congress Catalogue Card Number: 84–7100

ISBN-13 978-0-521-24681-1 hardback
ISBN-10 0-521-24681-4 hardback

ISBN-13 978-0-521-02431-0 paperback
ISBN-10 0-521-02431-5 paperback

Contents

Figures

Tables

Preface

Commutation of tithes from arbitrary and uncertain renders in kind to statutorily varying annual rent-charges, the appointment of a parliamentary commission to survey, value and apportion rent-charges among tens of thousands of separate parcels of titheable land in different states of cultivation, eventual redemption of tithes by capital repayments and, last but not least, the compilation of an atlas of agriculture from data laboriously collected by the commissioners, assistant commissioners, valuers and surveyors are all causes that would have appealed to the reforming disposition of Alexander Maconochie, first professor of geography at University College London. It is more than a happy coincidence that this book, written by two graduates with the help of numerous other alumni, should be completed in a year celebrating the 150th anniversary of Maconochie's appointment. The publication of the book also anticipates by two years the 150th anniversary of the passing of the Tithe Commutation Act in 1836 and the inauguration of the tithe surveys that form the subject of this study.

We are grateful to past and present members of the college for the inspiration, support and generous assistance they have given us. We owe special debts of gratitude to H. C. Darby who directed our early researches and has remained a constant source of help and encouragement, to fellow students of the tithe surveys, in particular, David Hartley, Michael Naish, Wynn Edwards, Malcolm Postgate, David Gramolt, Elizabeth Burrell, Elwyn Cox, Brian Dittmer, and John Chapman, who have provided many valuable reflections on their work and over many years have kept us informed about new publications and research in progress. During the past ten years, we have received helpful letters and much useful advice from Glanville Jones, Maurice Beresford, Tony Phillips, John Dodgson, Eric Evans, Michael Thompson, Ted Collins, Michael Turner, Harold Fox, Barrie Gleave, Colin Thomas, Alan Parton, Terry Slater, Clare Lukehurst, William Ravenhill, Robin Butlin, H. J. Dyos, Gordon Mingay, Harold Carter, Alan Harris, Frank Emery, Dennis Mills, Paul Laxton, Andrew

Charlesworth, Martin Daunton, Janet Hooke, Robert Perry and Jim Yelling. Many others have supplied information, replied to letters and answered questions. We deeply appreciate the kindness of Christie Willatts and the late H. C. K. Henderson who commented on and amplified accounts of their pioneering studies, and we thank Tony Cartwright for discussing the contribution of John Mosby.

We are grateful to *all* county archivists, who without exception answered questionnaires on the custody of tithe documents in 1973 and 1976 and revised the return (Table 3.4) in September 1982. We owe special thanks to F. G. Emmison, K. C. Newton, Felix Hull, and Hugh Hanley for help in directing us to relevant manuscripts. We remain greatly indebted to Charles Smith in the Inspection Room at the former Tithe Redemption Commission offices in Finsbury Square for his friendly guidance and amazingly detailed knowledge of the contents of the original maps, apportionments and files kept by the commission.

We wish to record our thanks to the editors of the *Agricultural History Review*, the *Cartographic Journal*, the *East Midland Geographer*, the *Geographical Journal* and the *North Staffordshire Journal of Field Studies* for permission to reproduce illustrations and passages from articles they have published and to thank M. Reed, editor of *Discovering past landscapes*, for permission to draw upon material from a chapter on the tithe files.

We gratefully acknowledge financial help given by University College London, the University of Exeter, the Leverhulme Trust and the Social Science Research Council towards bibliographic and cartographic work, and we thank our research assistants for their tireless efforts on behalf of this study. Roger Sinfield devoted several weeks to compiling a first draft of a tithe coverage map (frontispiece). Tom Dormer and Jill Jones sifted thousands of books and articles to supplement and update the bibliography. Tom Dormer, largely on his own initiative, composed and circulated the first two questionnaires to find out the types and numbers of tithe documents held by county record offices. Harriet Holt helped to collect material on the nature of tithes and on the making of tithe maps and apportionments by examining and abstracting data from all 14,829 tithe files. We thank John Bryant, Trevor Allen, Michael Young and Alick Newman at University College London and Rodney Fry and Terry Bacon at Exeter University, who have drawn the maps, and we thank Chris Cromarty and Andrew Teed for their care and skill in photographing cartoons and fading documents.

Brian Harley and Alan Baker have acted as guides, philosophers and friends to both of us for longer than we care to remember. We are grateful for their patience and understanding. Beyond all others, our wives have borne the brunt of trials and tribulations attending research and writing. Their gentle encouragement has sustained us.

Michaelmas Day 1983

Introduction

The first half of the nineteenth century was an age of statistical enquiries and cadastral surveys. Political and social problems were approached by select committees collecting facts and figures, parliament legislating reforms, commissions securing local agreements or confirming local awards, surveyors mapping and scheduling results. In response to threats of war and, after 1815, in seeking solutions to problems caused by agricultural depression, industrial reorganisation, migration of people to towns, crowding and disease, volumes of statistical information were collected and hundreds of parliamentary acts were passed. Surveyors and valuers were kept busy measuring and redrawing maps of villages that had been enclosed, surveying lines for proposed canals and railways, drawing plans for housing estates, laying out parks and gardens. In other countries, where smallholdings were exchanged and consolidated, where feudal properties were partitioned and where land passed from a public domain into private ownership, large-scale cadastral surveys were carried out: in Ireland, the Townland Survey; in France, the *ancien cadastre*; in the United States, the Original Land Survey.[1] In England and Wales, the largest and most detailed survey was that carried out under the Tithe Commutation Act of 1836.

Why in the eyes of the government did the tithe question loom so large and so menacingly in the 1830s that it called for draconian remedies by compulsory commutation requiring a large-scale nation-wide survey? In most parishes, tithes had been paid grudgingly but regularly for a very long time, and in a few places their payment may be traced back to the ninth century. During much of that time they had been regarded as continuing sources for grievance. Local disputes erupted from time to time when new incumbents or tithe owners demanded increased payments or when Quakers or other dissenters refused to pay customary charges. The nature of tithes and deep-seated causes of recurrent conflict are discussed in chapter 1.

Not until the nineteenth century did governments consider the tithe question as a serious or potentially serious threat to the maintenance of public order, but fears of widespread unrest were aroused by disturbances in 1830–2. To a prevailing dread of Jacobinism was added the spectre of chateau burning, peasant uprisings in many European countries and worsening agrarian troubles in Ireland that had sectarian as well as social and economic causes. Closer to home, Luddite violence and frame-breaking disturbed woollen manufacturing districts, crowds of angry demonstrators assembled on the outskirts of London, Manchester and Birmingham, and apprehension was growing that discontent was being fomented by secret people in remote spots deep in the countryside, plotting vast, shapeless, uncontrollable revolts that would spread like fire among ricks and barns in rural England. When flames lit night skies over Norfolk, Suffolk, Kent, Sussex, Hampshire, Wiltshire and Dorset in 1816–17 and again in 1830–2, the government was alarmed.[2] A new sense of urgency animated debates on tithes, and tithe owners felt impelled to find a quick solution to their problems.

The tithe question had deep economic causes. Tithes were a burden that fell most heavily upon land undergoing agricultural improvement. Tithe owners enjoyed unearned increments from higher yields obtained through investments made by tithe payers in enclosures, farm buildings, improved livestock, new crops, fertilisers and machinery. In the depression which followed the Napoleonic wars, prices of farm produce, particularly wheat – and wheat was subject to a great tithe – fell. Returns from capital in land and improvements also fell, farm rents were remitted, but tithe owners were still entitled to, and some collected in full, their tenth. Political economists considered the imposition of tithes a disincentive to investment and an obstacle to improvement.

Tithe payers felt discriminated against as countrymen, since they not only suffered agricultural distress but, through their tithes, bore a disproportionate share in the cost of maintaining an established church. Urban land paid little tithe but earned high rents and carried increasing numbers of people, including churchgoers. Farmers, especially enterprising capitalists, regarded the manner of collecting tithes in kind peculiarly archaic and humiliating. No other group of producers was required to set aside a proportion of their actual produce for a tithing man. In most parishes, the odium of rendering tithes in kind had been removed by commutation before the nineteenth century, but that highlighted the anomalous position of parishes where tithes remained uncommuted. Farmers reacted as a beleaguered minority group, oppressed by landlords, harassed by labourers and in conflict with urban masses demanding cheap food.

By 1830, most tithe payers and tithe owners were ready to surrender some benefits or claims to benefits for the sake of convenience, conformity and peace. Arguments for and against every possible measure of reform had already been rehearsed and it only remained for a reformed parliament to put together a bill that would render a fair money payment to tithe owners while freeing tithe payers from an encumbrance on their enterprise and removing a slight to their self-respect. Eric Evans discusses at length, and also in an abbreviated account, the political and ecclesiastical history of tithe commutation.[3] Here, in this book, chapter 2 traces the steps leading to the passing of the Tithe Commutation Act of 1836 and reviews details of its provisions. That after 1836 no essential changes were made in the mode of assessing or paying commuted rent-charges is an indication of the success of the settlement. The implementation of the act progressed swiftly and without much resistance. Between 1836 and 1845 the tithe commissioners completed 90 per cent of their work and almost all the rest was finished by 1855. Extensively enclosed midland counties are scantily covered by tithe surveys as are Westmorland, Lancashire and Gloucestershire, where large tracts of land were exempt from tithe payments.

For each tithe district, usually a parish in southern England or a township in northern counties, three documents were prepared: a map, an apportionment and a file. Methods of compiling these documents, their contents and their present whereabouts are described in chapter 3. Chapter 4 analyses and evaluates the comprehensiveness and accuracy of different classes of information provided by the surveys. In an important respect, much evidence has been tried and tested by contending parties: tithe owners jealously guarding their rights, tithe payers striving to rid themselves of burdensome imposts and assistant commissioners discharging their duty to adjudicate a fair and equitable rent-charge. The minutes of parish meetings testify to the zeal with which tithe owners pursued their claims whereas farmers and landowners sought to reduce their liabilities as far as possible. In all local enquiries, the most important evidence was that observed in the field. Acreages recorded in most surveys provide reasonably reliable guides to the extent of different categories of land use and crop yields. Acreages may be checked both internally and independently with other sources. When this is done, it is clear that some figures, especially for areas of low agricultural or titheable value, are rough estimates. Rounded figures for heathland, moorland and other marginal land are suspect, but checks do not point to a consistent direction of error. The great strength of the tithe surveys is their uniformity in compilation, permitting data from one tithe district to be compared with those from neighbouring districts in regional studies.

From the time of their deposition in the Tithe Commission archives the surveys have been consulted daily by lawyers searching for evidence of rights of way or property boundaries. Their value as historical records was recognised as early as 1856, when R. Dymond used tithe maps to trace lines of hedgerows in Devonshire parishes. Through the late nineteenth century historians with legal training exploited them as sources for reconstructing archaic field patterns and for uncovering relics of early tenurial arrangements. In the twentieth century, historians have continued to widen the search for origins of field systems, discovering remnants of open-field husbandry in western Britain and survivals of infield–outfield cultivation in lowland England. As fresh evidence has accumulated, ethnic and tenurial theories have been discarded and closer attention has been paid to the common sense of farming practice. Chapter 5 reviews studies of field systems which refer to or are based on evidence from the tithe surveys.

Geographers have examined how different types of soil and terrain have been used. Sir Dudley Stamp's Land Utilisation Survey was fortunate in having as its secretary E. C. Willatts who, almost at the same time as H. C. K. Henderson, learned the value of the tithe surveys as a source of land-use information. Willatts' method of studying all categories of land use in sample parishes differs from Henderson's method of abstracting data on the extent of arable land for large blocks of territory. The organiser of the Norfolk survey, J. E. G. Mosby, also recognised the importance of examining estate, farm and field boundaries and field-names as well as land use. These pioneer studies provided models for many detailed investigations illuminating the county reports of the Land Utilisation Survey. Work on the tithe records has been continued and expanded by students of H. C. Darby. At University College London three advances have been made: swifter methods of abstracting data developed by F. D. Hartley and E. A. Cox have enabled larger areas to be mapped; examination of the tithe files by E. A. Cox, B. R. Dittmer and their contemporaries has extended our knowledge of farming practices; sampling and computer mapping of the data make possible the analysis of a large number of relationships between land use, ownership, farm size and distance from markets. Studies of land use, including studies of uncultivated land, are discussed in chapter 6.

Chapter 7 deals with tithe data on crop and livestock farming. Two centuries of technical advances in agriculture, exemplified by the invention of new farm implements and machines, by the introduction of new methods of conserving and enhancing soil fertility, by rotating crops and applying new kinds of fertilisers, culminated in a period of High Farming at about the time the tithe surveys were completed. In most districts in England and Wales, scientific methods of farming had replaced traditional practices of bare fallowing, ridging and furrowing, communal grazing and periodic breaking of outfields. Arable husbandry had become increasingly specialised and localised, while underdraining with cheap tile drains had begun to improve the competitive position of clayland farms relative to those on light soils. Enclosure and reclamation of heaths, marshes and moors were reaching their furthest limits and farmers were beginning to take an interest in world markets and in advice offered to them by newly founded agricultural societies. Tithe files contain a wealth of information on local farming practices and throw fresh light on agricultural progress in every part of the country.

Chapter 8 critically examines studies of landownership and occupation that have drawn upon evidence from tithe surveys. Studies of landholdings are still in their infancy and, relative to those of field systems and land use, few attempts have been made to draw boundaries and reconstruct the pattern of farms and estates. Tithe apportionments are a rich archive of names of landowners and farmers and of the extent of properties, though, without some simple computer assistance, aggregating these data over more than small, local areas can prove very time-consuming. Also reviewed in this chapter are ways in which tithe survey data can be used in conjunction with parish land tax assessments in studies of landownership change through time. A very recent advance is the use of tithe maps and apportionments for house repopulation and in community reconstitution. In these exciting developments, tithe surveys provide a spatial dimension to the population censuses of 1841 and 1851.

A few problems concerning the reliability of the source remain unresolved, but what is daunting about the tithe material is its sheer bulk. Maps, apportionments and files for 11,800 tithe districts may be inspected. Within each there may be as many as 4,000 or as few as 2 parcels of land or tithe areas. In total, there may be possibly something of the order of 10^7 separate data units, and for each of these information on land use, owners, occupiers, acreage and tithe valuation may be available. A locational coordinate reference and also, to be wished for, some index of soil character should be added for purposes of identification and retrieval. A search may yield up to $10^7 \times 7$ items of information. To examine the interrelations between land use and farm size or between farm size and estate size, for example, many millions of computations are required. In addition, several topics may be examined at a parish scale from the contents of tithe files, from the census returns and from rate books. Some suggestions about how this work may be done are outlined in the last chapter.

This book attempts to provide an up-to-date guide and work of reference for users of the tithe surveys. It explains the history and usage of terms in the tithe documents that may serve as an aid to reading and interpreting the data. It refers to most published works that have been based on evidence from the tithe surveys. This provides an inventory and handlist of research already completed and suggests where further research might profitably be pursued. Finally, this volume serves as a general introduction to the detailed material that forms the basis of Roger Kain's *Atlas and index of the tithe files of mid-nineteenth century England and Wales*. It is hoped that these studies will lead to a broader understanding and deeper appreciation of the nation's agriculture in the mid-nineteenth century.

1

The nature of tithes

The burden of tithes

For almost a thousand years, to the passage of the Tithe Redemption Act in 1936, tithes were the heaviest direct tax on farming, and from their mode of collection the most repugnant. To be compelled against the dictates of conscience to contribute towards the maintenance of an established church was offensive to many dissenters and was resented by the poor whose condition was worsened while the clergy grew rich. But the strongest hostility was felt by farmers charged with the support of a sleeping partner who put nothing into their business but harassed them at lambing time, at haymaking and at harvest, at the very moment when the rewards of their efforts were being reaped[1] (Figs. 1.1 and 1.2). Before the introduction of graduated scales of income tax and the imposition of excess profits tax, tithes were not unjustly regarded as discriminating against those who wrested a living from the land, a burden not shared by tradesmen, manufacturers, wage-earners nor by foreign competitors. They were a tax on gross output, a form of share-cropping, increased by skilled management, diminished by incompetence, bearing most heavily on the additional gains obtained from extra investments of capital and effort. In short, they inflicted a penalty on enterprise and acted as a check upon improvements. Arthur Young condemned tithes as 'the greatest burthen that yet remains on the agriculture of this kingdom; and if it was universally taken in kind, would be sufficient to damp all ideas of improvement'.[2] It is, however, abundantly clear that during Young's lifetime agriculture made spectacular advances in spite of the continuing imposition of tithes. It is also true that payments in kind were abolished in many districts where improvements were carried out but commutation to a money rent-charge was not enforced by law throughout England and Wales until 1836, following a period of retrenchment and falling corn prices. The reform, when it came, was intended not so much to remove an impediment to further investment but to relieve agricultural

1.1 Rowlandson's 'Tithe Pig' – a political satire. Photograph reproduced by courtesy of the Trustees of the British Library.

distress. The depression of the 1830s proved that the incidence of tithes was at least as onerous when the profit margin in farming was reduced as it had been when expenditure on improvements was high. The problem that parliament then had to face in devising a monetary equivalent for the fruits of the earth was one of bewildering complexity and it is to the lasting credit of those who framed the Tithe Commutation Act of 1836 that a workable solution was found.

Predial, mixed and personal tithes

What exactly were tithes? Customarily they represented a tenth of the annual increase of the produce of the soil and were of three kinds: predial tithes, payable on the fruits of the earth, such as corn, hay, wood, fruit and other crops; mixed or agistment tithes, payable on animal products, such as lambs, colts, calves, wool, milk, eggs and honey; and personal tithes, payable on the clear gains of a man's labour and industry, generally levied

1.2 'John Bull and the locusts', a political satire of *c*. 1830. Photograph reproduced by courtesy of the Trustees of the British Library.

only on the profits of milling and fishing.[3] Attempts to impose tithes on servants' wages, on milled grains or on catches of fish rarely succeeded. Tithes on grain, hay and fruit were generally more valuable than those on other produce; the former frequently being worth as much as one-fifth of the annual rent of arable land, the latter amounting to about one-ninth of the rent of grassland. Liability might be reduced or avoided by fallowing arable land, by converting arable or meadow to grazing land, thereby substituting an agistment tithe for a predial tithe, by converting productive land to park or warren or allowing it to revert to waste, or by planting fields with trees. Commercial crops such as woad, hemp, flax, saffron, hops and tobacco were gradually subjected to tithes, but the introduction of fodder crops associated with new methods of convertible husbandry created special difficulties. In Suffolk in the seventeenth century turnips were tithed only when grown expressly for feeding beef cattle or for fattening mutton. When, as was more usual, they were fed to milking cows or to store sheep, tithe was taken not in roots but in dairy produce or in lambs.[4] Similar questions arose as the cultivation of sainfoin, clover, ley grasses, kale, carrots and potatoes became widespread. When cut for hay, clover and temporary grasses were included as predial tithes, but when they stood for seed a mixed tithe was paid. By common law, tithes were not payable on minerals or on anything that formed part of the freehold, although an ingenious Derbyshire parson argued that lead was subject to tithe, because it was believed that the veins increased annually.[5] Deer, rabbits, partridges, pheasants, fish and wild-fowl were titheable by special custom only, while the methods of tithing woodland produce differed widely from one locality to another.

The payment of personal tithes began to decline during the fourteenth century but the *Valor Ecclesiasticus* of 1535 shows that at this date they could still amount to between 5 and 20 per cent of a minister's income in rural areas and to even more in market towns.[6] The *Valor* records, for example, that the rectors of Farway and Northleigh in Devon received annual incomes of £10 and £3 10s from predial tithes and £5 and £1 16s 8d from personal tithes respectively. Both are small rural parishes, and the amount of personal tithe exceptionally large. The liability of day labourers to pay tithes was abolished by statute in 1549 but some customary payments in lieu of personal tithes survived into the eighteenth and nineteenth centuries. In general, however, payments levied on individuals became insignificant after 1549 leaving only two main categories of tithe: predial and mixed, each further sub-divided into great and small tithes.[7]

The following categories of land were customarily exempt from tithe payments:

(1) Lands naturally barren.
(2) Barren heath or waste improved or converted into arable or meadow for a period of seven years after improvement.
(3) Forest lands while in the occupation of the Crown or its lessee or tenant, but not if granted by the Crown in fee.
(4) Glebe lands in the occupation of the parson.
(5) Lands owned before 1215 by the Cistercians, Templars or Hospitallers.
(6) Lands which formerly belonged to one of the greater monasteries, and which had not paid tithes at the time of the dissolution.
(7) Lands which had paid no tithes from time immemorial.
(8) Lands in respect of which tithes were barred under the Tithe Act of 1832, which specified some lands which had not paid tithes for a very long time, the original cause of exemption being unknown.

Great and small tithes

In the first instance, tithes were paid to the rector of a parish, who might be a resident incumbent or an ecclesiastical appropriator such as a bishop, prior, prioress, monastery, nunnery or college. An absentee rector normally appointed a vicar to perform his parochial services and allotted to him a portion of the revenues of the benefice, usually the small tithes. The small, or vicarial, tithes included all the tithes except those of grain, hay and wood which constituted the great tithes, generally reserved for the rector. But the division between the great and small tithes was by no means fixed and unalterable. Ancient treatises classify hay as a great tithe, but in 23 of 34 parishes in Staffordshire studied by Evans, tithe hay, or its monetary composition in lieu, was collected as a small tithe.[8] Even corn tithe, usually guarded most jealously because of its value, was not always collected as a great tithe in eighteenth-century England.[9] In all matters concerned with tithing in England and Wales, not least the definition of what constituted great or small tithes, the ultimate arbiter was the 'custom of the parish'. The best source for unravelling the complexities of these local practices are the parish tithe files (PRO IR18). There is a file for each of the 14,829 tithe districts of England and Wales; their contents vary (see chapter 3) but those for some districts contain long and detailed accounts of the history of tithing practices which summarise assistant tithe commissioners' researches among glebe terriers and other parochial documents.[10] A number of modern historians have also consulted these latter documents and episcopal registers and have published descriptions of local tithing customs.[11]

Impropriation of tithes

At the time of the dissolution of the monasteries, rectories and tithes belonging to dissolved houses were vested in the Crown, and most were subsequently sold to laymen.[12] Instances of laymen appropriating tithes for their own are recorded as early as the twelfth century, but, after the sale of tithes forfeited to the Crown in the 1530s, about one-third of all great tithes was held by lay impropriators.[13] A bishop's estimate put the total number of impropriate livings at 3,849 in 1603, which is virtually identical to the figure of 3,845 out of a total of 9,284 livings given by Spelman in 1646. Impropriated livings were not evenly distributed over the country. In Kent, 140 out of 252 parishes were impropriate, while in Yorkshire the figure was as high as 63 per cent.[14] Figure 1.3 shows the distribution of lay and ecclesiastical tithe in Suffolk and Sussex at the time of commutation in 1836. It is clear that there were not only differences in the distribution of impropriate tithe from one part of the country to another but also marked differences at a local scale.

Once tithes had become private property they could be sold or leased at will. W. G. Hoskins describes a typical instance, at Wigston in Leicestershire, of the transference of tithes from a dissolved priory to a lay impropriator, and traces the frequent changes of ownership from one layman to another during the following century.[15] Lay impropriators still held nearly a quarter of the net annual value of all tithes at the time of commutation.

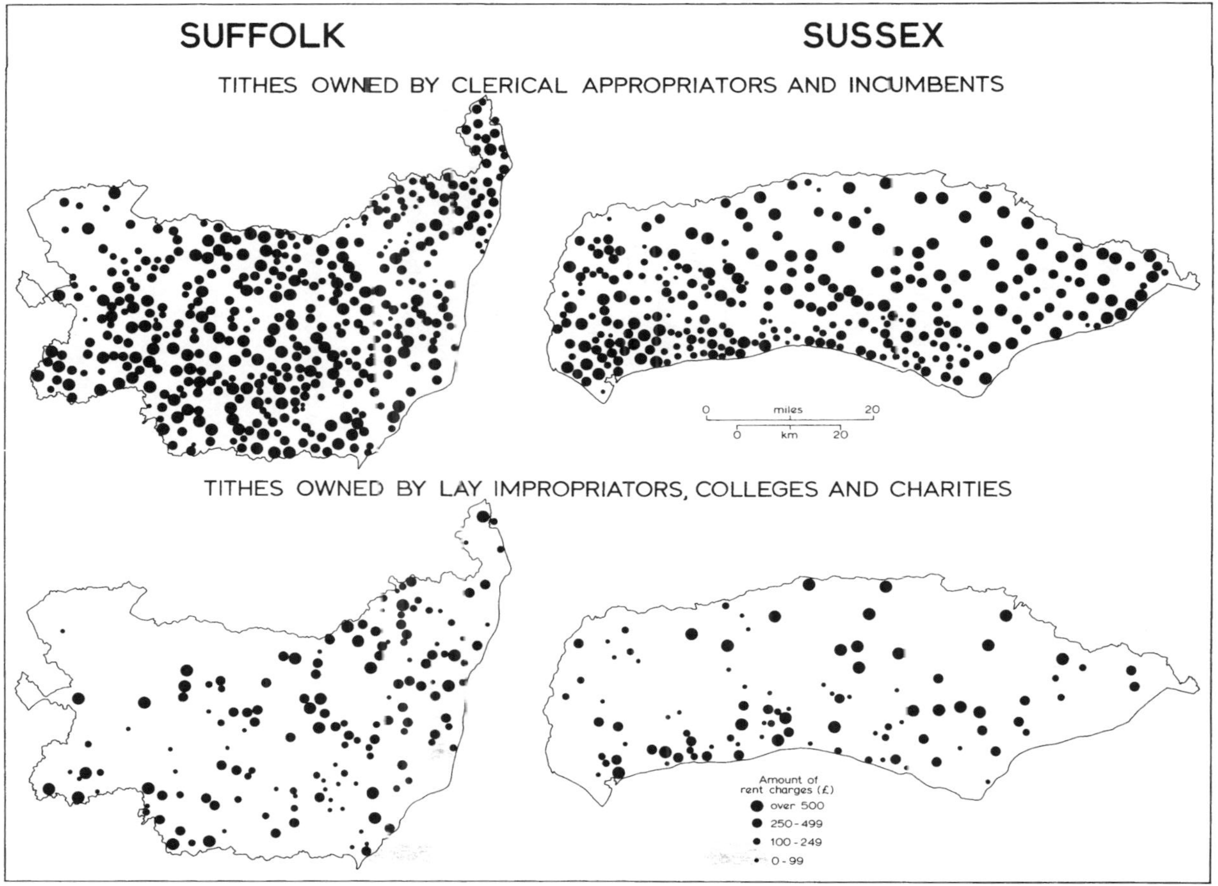

1.3 Clerical and lay tithe in Suffolk and Sussex. The upper pair of maps indicates amounts of tithe owned by clerical appropriators and incumbents; the lower pair amounts owned by lay impropriators, colleges and charities. Source: 'Return of tithes commuted and apportioned', 1887.

Tithe payment in kind

Until tithe was permanently commuted perhaps by an enclosure act or eventually by the Tithe Commutation Act of 1836, a tithe owner had the right to claim payment of tithe in kind (in actual produce from the fields at harvest, from the dairy, the sheep pens and pig styes) and he was also entitled to enter farms to exact his claim. Tithe barns were built to store the great tithes of corn (Fig. 1.4). Most great tithe was rendered in kind until the mid-seventeenth century from which time it was gradually supplanted by a variety of monetary payments, negotiated and arranged locally and which in time came to have the force of parish custom.[16] A variation on the straightforward monetary composition was the practice recorded in the tithe files of the counties of Cheshire, Shropshire, Somerset and Staffordshire where in some districts tithe was valued annually and then offered for sale to the occupiers. If they declined to purchase at the valuation, the tithe was taken in kind. In north Wales, particularly Anglesey and Denbigh, a valuation was avoided by offering the tithes at a public auction.

If somewhat eclipsed as the norm by the eighteenth century, tithing in kind did not disappear. In Eric Evans' opinion, R. E. Prothero (Lord Ernle) was wrong to state that 'at the close of the eighteenth century, comparatively little tithe was collected in kind'.[17] Prothero's view was based on the Board of Agriculture Reports, and passages from the reports referring to tithe in kind are abstracted in Appendix V of *English farming past and present*. The Board's reporters did, however, correctly identify the 'heartlands' of tithing in kind as the north-west and south-east of England. Tithe owners in both the metropolitan south-east and in the manufacturing districts of south Lancashire and north-east Cheshire were among those who clung most tenaciously to their ancient rights to tithe in kind. The three northern counties of Northumberland, Cumberland and Westmorland, the collegiate estates in Cambridgeshire and the south-eastern counties of Middlesex, Kent, Surrey, Sussex and Hampshire retained more than their share of tithes in kind, though the Board's reporters were wrong when they stated that collection in kind had ceased in the midland and western counties. Evans' analysis of evidence contemporary with the Board of Agriculture reports for 115 places recorded in F. M. Eden's *The state of the poor* (1797) and that produced by William Pitt's questionnaire on tithe reform in 1791–2 reveal that the collection of tithe in kind was by no means uncommon elsewhere[18] (Fig. 1.5). Evidence in the tithe files corroborates this view; tithing in kind is mentioned in 675 files. In the south-west, for example, payment of tithe in kind is recorded in 39 Devon and 24 Somerset parishes. In the midlands, the Board of Agriculture's reporters agreed with William Marshall who noted payment in kind in only one area – Bosworth Field in Leicestershire.[19]

1.4 Tithe barn, Abbotsbury, Dorset.

However, assistant tithe commissioners reported payment in kind *c.* 1840 in 9 Northamptonshire, 13 Nottinghamshire and 12 Oxfordshire parishes. In England and Wales respectively, Rutland and Merioneth are the only counties for which there are no references to tithe payment in kind in the tithe files.

The value of tithe collected in kind for the whole country has not been computed, though in the House of Commons in 1835 Sir Robert Peel declared that in the Property Tax Assessment of 1810 the value of tithe in kind was returned as £421,000 and various money payments in lieu of tithe in kind were valued at £1,932,000. In 1836, the total value of tithe remaining to be commuted under the Tithe Commutation Act was some £4 million, so that W. R. Ward is probably correct in stating that all the Property Tax Assessment lists tell us is that parsons were adept at evading their taxes 'and tithe in kind, being harder to conceal than cash, may have been better assessed and formed an even smaller proportion of the real receipts'.[20] We may estimate from the proportion of tithe districts with references to the payment of tithe in kind in the tithe files that probably only about 6 per cent by value, not the 18 per cent implied by the 1810 Assessment, was still rendered in kind by the early nineteenth century.

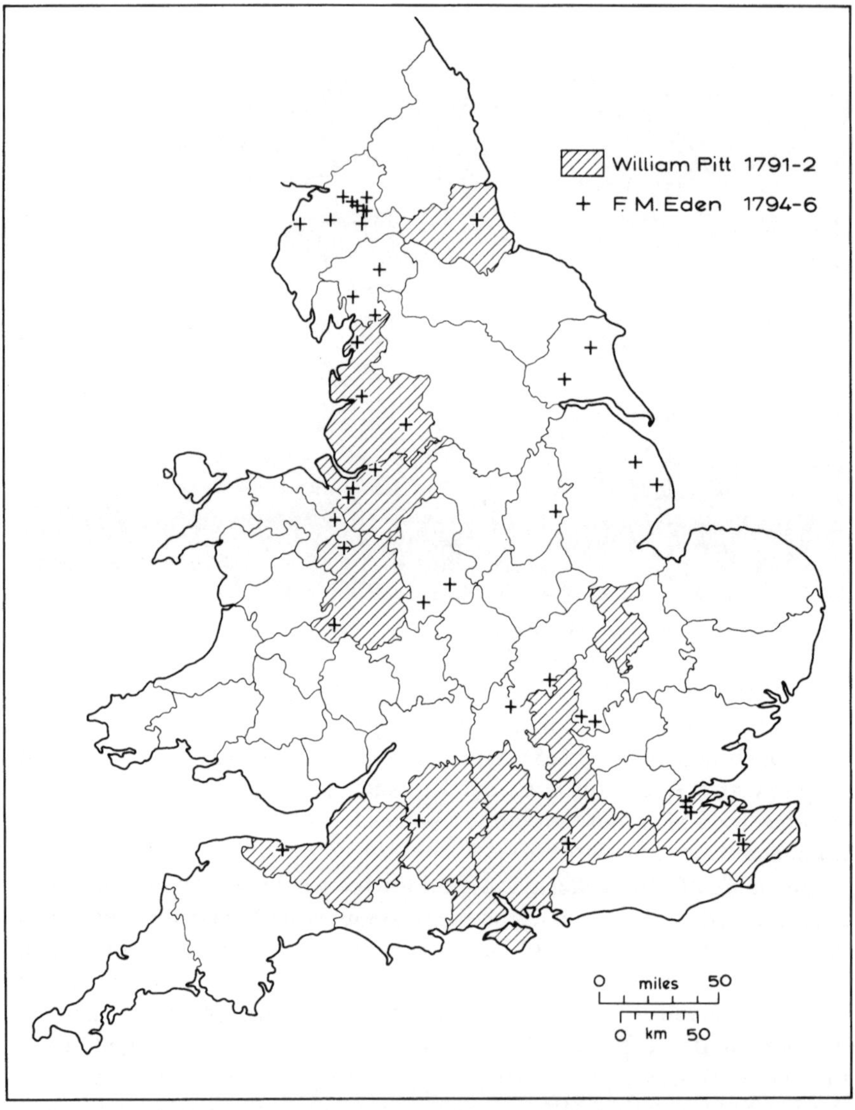

1.5 Tithe in kind in England and Wales *c.* 1800. Sources: F. M. Eden, *The state of the poor*; E. J. Evans, *The contentious tithe*, 1976, 22, cites results of questionnaire circulated by William Pitt, 1791–2, PRO 30/8/310.

Compositions and moduses in lieu of tithe in kind

Tithes were rendered in cash before 1836 by annual payments known as compositions, which might be adjusted from time to time or be terminated by either party, or alternatively by a modus which was a permanent charge on an article of titheable produce or on a piece of land.

Methods of assessing the level of compositions varied a good deal and contributed to the multiplicity of tithing customs which confronted parliament when framing permanent commutation legislation in the 1830s. The wide variation in the manner of assessment meant that some tithe owners got much closer to the 'tenth' than others. Those who could afford it might commission annual valuations of the growing crops as a basis for a cash composition each year, but this was expensive. A cheaper alternative was for the tithe owner to set a composition value per acre of each crop. But a fixed money payment was not strictly equivalent to a tithe which varied from year to year according to the amount and value of farm produce. For this reason, some composition agreements stipulated that a fixed sum be paid for an agreed number of years, some provided for the periodic revision of the payment, while others specified that the sum should fluctuate from year to year with the prices of some commodity, usually wheat, sometimes other cereals, in a few cases oats and barley jointly with wheat. The clergy were also reluctant to enter into arrangements that might bind their successors or that might permanently deprive them of the prospective benefits arising from improvements. Agreements to alter the methods of paying tithes were generally accompanied by full valuations of the amounts collected, together with schedules of the titheable lands and sometimes large-scale plans (see chapter 7).

Compositions could be raised to take account of increasing output and of course could be reduced where landowners were sufficiently strong. But usually compositions lagged well behind changes in output and the prevailing level of prices. Where a particular composition had become enshrined in the custom of the parish it might need litigation to alter it.

If payment of his tithes in kind was the most repugnant method for a farmer, then modus payments were the least satisfactory from a tithe owner's point of view. The existence of a modus in his parish was probably the greatest single obstacle to the full realisation of an incumbent's income. Moduses were small (certainly by the seventeenth century) payments made in lieu of the actual value of titheable produce. In the words of Lord Chief Justice Hardwicke in 1747, 'a modus is nothing more than an ancient composition between . . . the owners of land in a parish, and the rector, which gains strength by time'.[21] Some parochial moduses applied throughout a parish for a particular crop or animal. The tithe files reveal that in Somerset, twopence an acre was paid in many places in lieu of tithe hay, while in south-east England, moduses of a shilling an acre covered grass tithes in some marshland areas. Alternatively, farm moduses might exonerate all the lands of a particular farm for a sum of money fixed by the force of custom for all time. Not all moduses were rendered in cash, though this was the most usual.The modus in lieu of hay tithe from Tyddyn Mawr farm in Llanfihangel Esgeifiog parish in Anglesey consisted of a dinner every alternative Sunday for the officiating minister and a feed of corn for his horse. On the other Sundays they were both fed at Hendrefaig farm in Llanffinan parish where a similar modus applied![22]

The economic iniquity of a modus is clear enough. The modus was intended to be a rough equivalent of a tithe but as most moduses were fixed by the mid-sixteenth century at the latest, and generally earlier, the sums were clearly derisory some two or more centuries later. While some moduses were overturned by litigation, particularly in the course of the struggle by eighteenth-century clergy to increase their incomes, tithe files reveal that moduses still applied in at least 2,571 tithe districts *c.*1840. They were most numerous in the north and west of the country and most usually replaced tithe on hay and animals, particularly dairy cows and their milk. Some indication of the depressing effect on tithe revenue these moduses must have produced, at least on the product of small tithes, can be judged from the following list of counties and the number of places where assistant tithe commissioners considered that the operation of a modus required discussion in their reports, viz: Cheshire 191, West Riding of Yorkshire 178, Northumberland 168, Somerset 146, Shropshire 131, North Riding of Yorkshire 121, Cumberland 113. Furthermore, in some Cumberland and North Riding districts, for example, such corn tithe as was generated from old enclosures still paid only a nominal modus in 1836. Though collection in kind could be very expensive in upland England and Wales (up to 40 per cent was deducted from the gross produce of tithe when it was valued for commutation after 1836), a modus set aside could, as Eric Evans has shown, perhaps quadruple tithe income at a stroke.[23]

Tithe disputes

Payment of tithes in kind was a cause of endless disputes between farmers and tithe owners. It would, indeed, be an enormous task to compute the amount of time and effort diverted from the practice of husbandry and from pastoral care by these incessant quarrels over trifling matters and it would be even more difficult to discover how parsons and farmers obtained the money to pour into protracted legal battles, especially as the most persistent litigants struggled for the possession of nothing more than the value of the small tithes. Very costly proceedings were entered upon to determine which courts should hear such suits, who was liable to pay, how payments should be assessed and how or to whom they should be paid.[24] Frequent disputes arose concerning the nature of titheable produce. It was once decided that partridges were *ferae naturae* and therefore exempt from tithe, and a precedent was established for exempting domesticated turkeys. On another occasion, wild ducks were declared tithe-free, but eggs laid by tame ducks used to decoy them were held to be titheable. Not even the herbage on balks and headlands, nor the stubble left after a corn crop had been cut, nor wild cherries, nor fallen apples escaped the attention of some claimant, and the question of whether to tithe perry and cider was a cause for lengthy disputation.[25] But the most difficult cases of all were those involving the produce of woodland. In some areas such as North Wales and the Weald all woodlands were exempt, in others only certain trees (such as beeches in the Chilterns), in yet others the trunks and branches were exempt, but acorns, mast, foliage and even charcoal were titheable. In one such case timber trees of over twenty years' growth springing from the stools of older trees were adjudged to be subject to tithes.[26]

When tithes were allotted to more than one owner further litigation began, and tithes payable on Lammas lands and half-year commons had to be apportioned between different occupiers and then perhaps also assigned to different tithe owners. It was asked what constituted the vicar's tithe and how much belonged to the rector or lay impropriator. In the common fields at Cambridge different strips were tithed by different churches without regard to parish boundaries.[27] Were tithes to be collected by the owners and, if so, when? Must the farmer await the arrival of the tithe collector before carting his harvest, so risking a heavy loss in wet weather, or might he summon the collector on the pretext of gathering his harvest, then lift ten roots of turnips and send the man away with only one? Or should tithes be delivered to the owner, and if so to what place? Should milk be taken each day or every tenth day; should it be laid in the church porch or presented to the vicarage; and at what age should lambs be selected for tithing? At Castle Acre on Thomas Coke's estate, the vicar, Ambrose Pimlowe, complained that farm reorganisation and amalgamation carried out before 1716 had deprived him of his rightful dues by transferring titheable lands to the tithe-free Abbey Farm. In a written declaration he stated:

> Mr Smith, the Steward, has made a strange Alteration in late Doves Farm where Mr Stephn Blanch is present Tenant, and has taken from that farm this year most of the antient Titheable Sheep walk and laid it to the Abby Farm, and laid the antient Tithe free Abby Sheep walk to Doves now Blanch's Farm, wch I mentiond pticularly because Mr Blanch this year encreased his flock by an hundred ews more than he used to keep and I as Vicar demanded my tithe for the whole encrease . . . Mr Smith at first Resented it and we had the New Tavern some warm Words and he told me he would spend Mr Cokes Estate before I should have a farthing more than my usual Tithes out of that Farm. But when he saw I persisted in my demand, and that I determind to sue the Tenant, he proposed an expedient, which was to Represent it to Mr Coke and respit the Dispute till he came of Age (wch will be within 2 or 3 years) to which I consented for Quiet Sake.[28]

Both tithe payers and tithe owners were guilty of pettiness and sharp practices but Arthur Young considered the clergy the worse offenders. Even in France in the last year of the Ancien Régime, he observed that tithe 'was never exacted with that *horrid greediness* as is at present the disgrace of England'.[29]

There is certainly evidence that, at the time when Young was condemning tithe owners, the English clergy were engaged in a campaign to reassert their right to a full 'tenth' because they perceived that tithe revenue was static while agricultural productivity and output were increasing.[30] But, as Eric Evans asserts, 'tithe disputes were endemic in British society, and litigation was instituted by all manner of tithe owners'.[31] Some disputes concerned questions of what was or was not titheable, many were over disputed rights to increase compositions, and many were over what had become, from a tithe owner's point of view, that least satisfactory money payment, the prescriptive modus.[32]

Other disputes were occasioned by antipathy towards the established church. In the vanguard of early opposition on these grounds were the Quakers, though their carefully orchestrated propaganda may give a somewhat exaggerated picture of their grievances, at any rate by the eighteenth century.[33] But in the seventeenth century it was a real problem for this sect. A. B. Anderson who has analysed 1,234 separate incidents in which Lancashire Quakers suffered between 1650 and 1690 finds that seizure of goods for non-payment of tithes increases from about 2 incidents a year in the first half of this period to an average of 30 per annum in the 1670s and 1680s.[34] By the time of their great campaign against tithes in 1736, the number of prosecutions of Friends for non-payment of tithe had markedly declined by comparison with the second half of the seventeenth century. Tithe owners 'cooperated' by obtaining payment through distraints granted by the courts or sanctioned payment by Friends through third parties so avoiding them the embarrassment of paying directly to the established church.[35]

Tithe and agricultural improvement

It can be argued, however, that the moral dilemma which non-conformist groups faced when paying tithes was overshadowed in the eighteenth century by grievances arising from economic considerations. Tithes were a regressive tax which bore most heavily on lands whose yields were great but whose costs of production were also high. In areas where the profit to be gained was likely to be small, potential investors might have been deterred from venturing their capital because of the incidence of tithes. F. M. L. Thompson argues that the incidence of tithes would be taken into consideration when calculating an economic rent and it therefore added nothing to the charges paid by a tenant. But a tithe levied on profits made by a farmer's additional investments would fall on him alone and might be equivalent to a tax of 30 per cent. Assuming a return of 10 or 12 per cent on an investment, a farmer might expect to receive, after payment of tithes, between 7 and 8.5 per cent, which would still be a worthwhile reward.[36] An eighteenth-century land surveyor, John Tuke, presents a similar account in a somewhat different light. He supposes a farmer, possessing 10 acres of unimproved land in the North Riding of Yorkshire rented at 2s 6d an acre, rendering tithes in kind valued at 3d an acre, decides to plough it. The original rent, paid for a period of 5 years during which improvements are carried out, would add up to £6 5s 0d. Additional expenses incurred by the tenant for levelling, paring, burning, harrowing, liming, seeding and cultivation would amount to £115 1s 5½d. After paying tithes the farmer would gain £30 19s 3d, an average annual return on his outgoings of about 5.5 per cent, while the tithe owner who had risked nothing would make a clear profit of £15 7s 2½d.[37] It would be extremely difficult to ascertain how far investment was discouraged by a levy of this order, but clearly it should have militated most severely against undertaking such costly improvements as moorland reclamation, fen draining, marling and enclosing. The reports to the Board of Agriculture around 1800 found little specific evidence of schemes of this kind having been abandoned but were loud in complaints of a general character. In Somerset, Norfolk and other counties that had brought large areas of unproductive land into cultivation, tithes were not considered immoderate.[38] In Gloucestershire, where substantial improvements had been made, Thomas Rudge found that 'a solitary instance may possibly be produced, where a small quantity of land has been suffered to lie in a neglected state to defeat the demands of the tithe owner'.[39] On the other hand, John Boys claimed that in east Kent, 'there are immense quantities of poor land, which experience has proved might be made to produce good crops of turnips and clover'[40] but for the discouragement of paying tithes in kind. In Hertfordshire, it was observed that those parts subject to a reasonable annual money payment in lieu of tithes were generally farmed on improved methods, whereas lands liable to pay tithes in kind were often abandoned to almost total neglect.[41] But the evasions and subterfuges most frequently reported were unconnected with capital improvements. In Staffordshire, for example, William Pitt remarked:

> I have the most satisfactory proofs, from the evidence of several respectable cultivators, that the quantity of wheat sown is affected by the tithe system; they having assured me that they decline sowing wheat, and choose to manage their land in a grazing system, because they cannot bear the idea of paying the enormous rates that have been asked them by the titheman.[42]

It was the multiplicity of these minor grievances and imagined wrongs that clouded early nineteenth-century thinking on the subject.

As rates of compositions, values of moduses and practices of tithing in kind were prescribed by local customs, farmers in neighbouring parishes or townships were required to pay widely differing amounts of tithe. Many tithe files of the mid-nineteenth century record how farmers, out of frustration with the unreformed tithe system, practised evasive land-use management to minimise tithe payments. Yorkshire farmers seem to have been remarkably adept at farming in a mode that yielded the smallest amount of titheable produce. At Nidd in the West Riding, farmers took their ewes out of the parish immediately before lambing and again before shearing for the express purpose of depriving the vicar of his tithes of lambs and wool.[43] A farmer at Stutton also held land in Hazlewood, where a modus was payable in lieu of all small tithes. He milked and clipped his animals and had his mown meadows in Hazlewood so that he only paid agistment tithe in Stutton.[44] At Sherston Magna in Wiltshire the Tithe Commission's George Bolls found circumstances which were by no means unusual where parliamentary enclosure had extinguished tithes in part of a parish and replaced them with an allotment of land (see pp. 22–5). As the titheable and tithe-free lands in this parish were intermingled, occupiers could grow most of their corn crops in the tithe-free fields and feed their stock in those that were titheable.[45] Scottish teinds were abolished by act of parliament in 1633 so farmers such as those at Longridge in Durham with land in both England and Scotland summered their stock on the Scottish side of the Tweed to reduce tithe liability.[46]

The tithe files also contain evidence of the effect of tithe on agricultural improvement in the 1820s and 1830s as assistant tithe commissioners had to take account of any changes in the gross produce of a tithe district that might directly result from the general commutation of 1836. If they thought improvement or change affecting output would follow immediately, they could make an additional charge to protect the tithe owners' interests.

In February 1850, James Caird wrote a letter to *The Times* describing agriculture on Salisbury Plain. In it he said, 'the greater proportion of this extensive tract has been brought under tillage since the act for the commutation of tithes'.[47] In the 1830s and 1840s the possibility of converting pasture to arable after tithe commutation was a topic of local debate upon which assistant tithe commissioners were called to arbitrate at apportionment appeal meetings. The basis of dispute between tithe payers and tithe owners lay in the difference in value of arable and pasture tithes. Tithes were usually worth about one-fifth of the arable rent and about one-eighth or one-ninth of the grassland rent. The difference in value of grassland and arable tithes thus amounted to about a tenth of the rent. In marshland areas this difference was sometimes even greater, as traditionally extensive tracts were subject to a nominal modus of a few pence per acre regardless of quality or produce while they remained down to grass.

Where differences in the value of arable and pasture tithes were large, assistant tithe commissioners, assessing global rent charges, had to consider the probability of some grassland being ploughed up as a direct result of commutation. Tithe payers presented them with evidence to support the view that pasture would be little affected by tithe commutation while representatives of tithe owners forecasted phenomenal yields of grain from ploughed-up pastures once a commutation for tithe was effected. This topic is discussed at particular length in the tithe files of Cumberland, Northumberland, Yorkshire, Staffordshire, Oxfordshire and Lincolnshire, but nowhere in England was this question more fiercely debated than in the Romney Marsh district of Kent where there was a great difference between the nominal modus of one shilling per acre on grass and the tithe of highly productive arable.[48]

It is clear from the tithe files that both landowners and tithe owners were able to present evidence to support their opposing viewpoints. Opinions of the assistant tithe commissioners also differed widely and changed through time. Assistant commissioner Thomas Smith Woolley wrote in the Lydd tithe file in the winter of 1837 that the value of tithes would be vastly increased by ploughing up pastures, but he 'did not think this likely, the character is *essentially* grassland'.[49] By 16 December 1841 his opinion of the best and most likely use of marshland after commutation had changed. At Dymchurch he said,

> the whole of this very peculiar district would make splendid ploughland and I hope and believe that in a few years from the settlement of the tithe question it will be converted from a practically profitless sheep walk employing no labour and supporting no population to the most productive corn district in the three Kingdoms.[50]

His comments recorded in the files of Brookland, Dymchurch and Aldington testify clearly to his opinion that the tithe question had been holding back the ploughing of pasture.[51]

With the rising corn prices of the 1840s there can be little doubt of the extra profit to be obtained by breaking up some pasture. For reasons of prejudice and vested interest the desirability of this was not always acknowledged at commutation meetings. By about 1875 farmers had experienced a generation of high corn prices and the acreage of pasture in Kent had greatly decreased. The tithe apportionments show that *c.* 1840, 32 per cent of the county was down to grass. A sample of 55 Books of Reference to the first edition Ordnance Survey 1:2,500 plans shows that by *c.* 1875 only 24 per cent was under permanent grass.[52]

It can be suggested that in Kent, at least, Caird's prophecy of changes that might follow a Tithe Commutation Act had occurred. That a fair commutation for tithe facilitated the reduction of pasture there can be no doubt, though its precise role in accelerating this process and extending the arable acreage in England and Wales cannot be readily ascertained from parish tithe files. What is beyond doubt is that tithe payers and tithe owners were well aware of the possible effect of the removal of the tithe burden as evidenced by the time and money they spent marshalling and presenting their cases to assistant tithe commissioners at apportionment appeal meetings. Eric Evans has approached the factors affecting land owners' decisions to invest in improvements more directly by a search of estate papers. This led him to suggest that 'improvement was more readily put in train on land which was either tithe free or covered by small moduses, despite the fact that it was invariably subject to a higher rent. Tithe free land which came on to the market was advertised prominently as such, being considered a clear selling point.'[53]

The tithe commissioners in their annual reports to parliament also lost little opportunity to proclaim the beneficial effects of the Tithe Commutation Act whose provisions they administered. And, of course, there *was* much investment on drainage schemes, artificial manures and new farm buildings between 1836 and the onset of the great depression in the 1890s. But, as Eric Jones has demonstrated, there was at least as much investment in livestock fattening and mixed farming as in arable enterprises.[54] Grassland tithes were much lower than those of arable and in many places were reduced still further by the presence of a modus so that the case for tithe affecting the improvement of purely livestock farms is more difficult to sustain. But, as Evans concludes,

> It is important not to overlook the psychological effects of commutation, however. Tithe commutation created a climate of opinion favourable to reform, though there were other, better publicized, factors at work in the same direction. Despite the optimism of the tithe commissioners on the subject, it would be unwise to push the effect of commutation on improvement further than this. Agricultural England as viewed by Arthur Young in 1790 and James Caird in 1850 were very different places. Although Young and some of his followers overstated their case, it is clear that a national commutation in, say, 1800 would of itself have stimulated still more improvement on the less naturally fertile arable lands, particularly where tithe had been paid in kind. After 1836, the situation was more complex, the requirements more diverse. Far heavier injections of capital were required which made tithe calculations less crucial to the improvement equation in Caird's day than in Young's.[55]

Allotments of land in lieu of tithes

When tithes were dealt with under a parliamentary enclosure act, they were generally extinguished in exchange for allotments of land. Under the terms of many acts, tithe owners had the power to nominate a person to represent their interests as one of the commissioners appointed to administer the act, and in all cases where tithes were disposed of the agreement of the owners had to be sought and freely given. In every enclosure award which dealt with tithes, they secured compensation on a very generous scale, and under later enactments they obtained what can only be described as remarkable bargains.[56] There was no question of receiving allotments of as little as one-tenth of the titheable land. At the end of the eighteenth century one-fifth of the arable land and one-ninth of the pasture was normally ceded to them, practices which add weight to the argument that tithe was in fact a disincentive to improvement, and farmers and landowners were evidently keen to find a method of extinguishing tithes less costly than surrendering land.[57] During the Napoleonic wars the size of allotments increased and in 1792 in an exceptional parish, Shipton in Hampshire, the tithe owner acquired no less than three-tenths of the land and retained the right to collect vicarial tithes. In a study of the results of this procedure, based on an examination of 20 enclosure awards covering the period from 1793 to 1815, Vladimir Lavrovsky concluded that almost without exception, 'tithe commutation led to a diminution in the area owned by the peasantry'.[58] A further examination of awards relating to 60 parishes indicates that while the peasantry lost one-seventh of its land in tithe allotments, ecclesiastical estates were enlarged by 58.9 per cent.[59] These results correspond very closely with the outcome of an enclosure at Wigston Magna in Leicestershire, a typical midland village, described by W. G. Hoskins. There the tithe owner was awarded 380 acres or one-seventh of the land, and this allotment was provided with fences at the expense of the other proprietors.[60] On a broader scale, the findings of W. R. Ward suggest that 'the effect of commutation was to multiply the average glebe by a factor of 2 or 3'.[61] But, as E. C. K. Gonner has pointed out, there were marked regional as well as social differences in the manner of commuting tithes under parliamentary acts.[62] In some areas they were entirely extinguished; in others, moduses and compositions prevailed. Figure 1.6 is a map of the number of places where at least part of the tithes was commuted under the terms of enclosure acts between 1757 and 1835. As can be seen from the map, the redistribution of property associated with commutation was concentrated in particular areas. In the counties of early enclosure this was an unimportant process but in Yorkshire, for example, part at least of the tithes of 628 places was commuted, much being for land.[63] 'Thus, at the very time when churches within reach of revolutionary France were losing property wholesale, the Church of England was gaining it on a considerable scale throughout the midlands and the east.'[64] The course of commutation under the terms of enclosure acts which were printed as bills can be traced on Fig. 1.7.[65] About 2,230 such acts passed before 1835 provided for the abolition of the payment of tithes in kind.[66] In 1,510 of these, all tithes were extinguished by allotments of land made to the tithe owners; in 550, tithes were partly

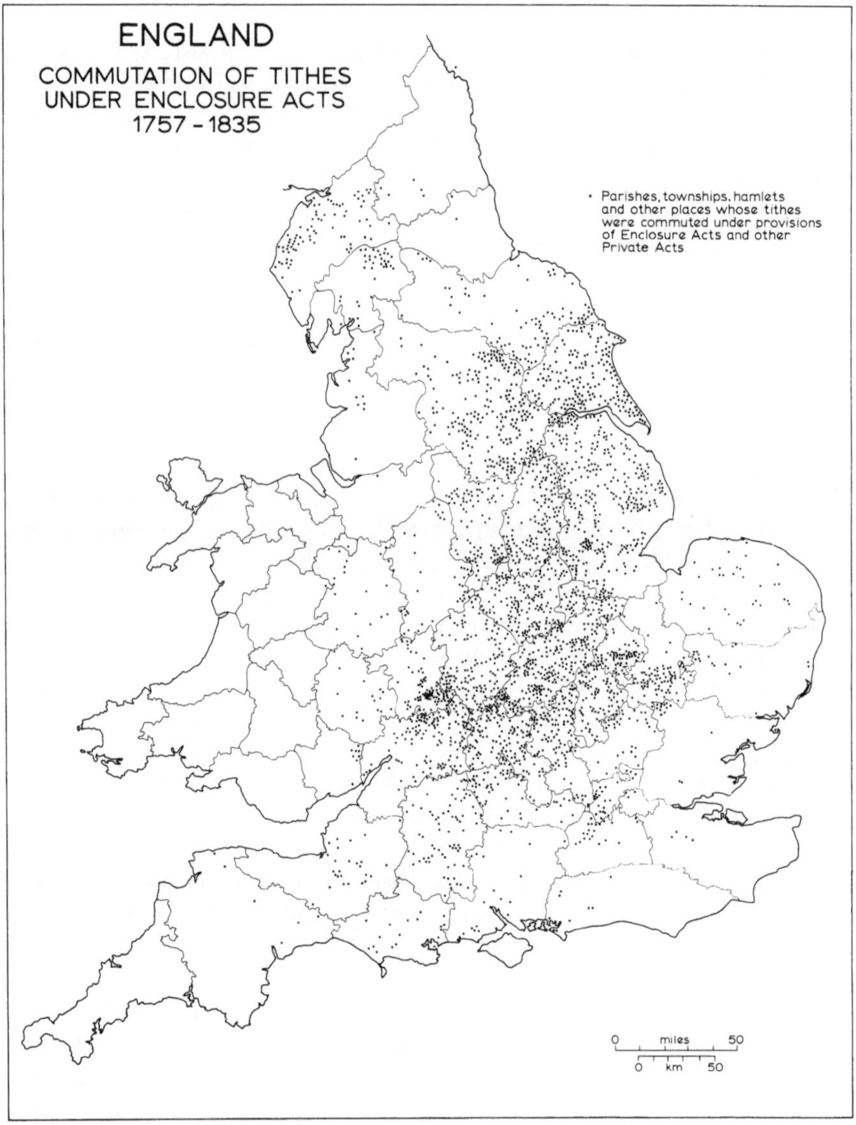

1.6 Commutation of tithes by enclosure acts in England, 1757–1835. Source: 'Return of tithes commuted. . .', 1836.

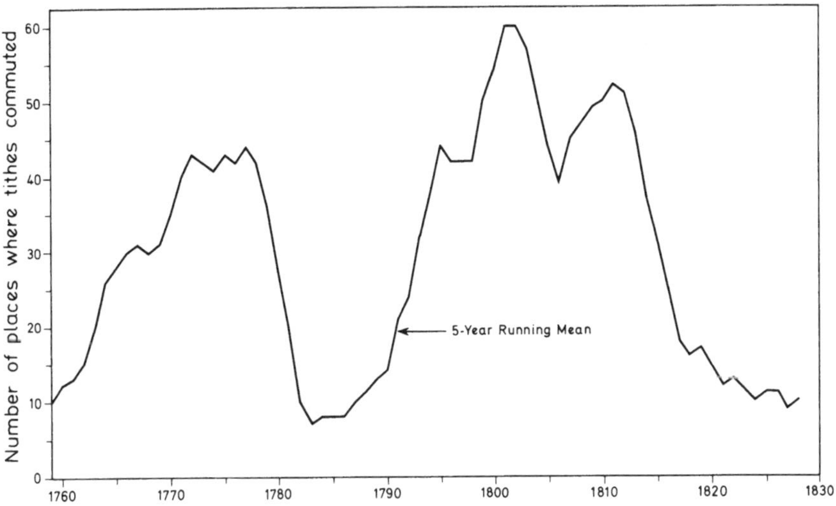

1.7 Progress of commutation enclosures in England, 1757–1829. Source: as Fig. 1.6.

extinguished by allotments of land and partly converted into annual money payments; in only 170 acts were tithes entirely converted into annual money payments.[67] That so high a proportion of the acts provided for the abolition of tithes and that compensation was fixed at levels that are, by any measure, very high, suggests that tithe payers were prepared to pay almost any price to be relieved of the burden, and it also indicates that the clergy held very powerful bargaining positions. In at least one parish, that of Weston Zoyland in Somerset, an application to enclose was flatly rejected by the Bishop of Bath and Wells on the grounds that the value of the proposed moduses might be reduced by the conversion of corn lands to grass.[68] By threatening to withhold their approval, tithe owners were able to dictate the terms on which enclosures might be proceeded with.

After the Napoleonic wars, crippling taxes, rates and tithes, uncertain corn prices, a succession of poor harvests, and a decline in domestic industry brought distress to many farmers and hunger to many labouring families. Hardship was greatest in south-east England where poor rates reached unprecedented levels where the exactions of tithe collectors were much harsher than elsewhere. Labourers begged for wages that would enable them to feed their families without having to apply for poor relief, while farmers clamoured for reduction in rents, for an easing of the burden of poor rates and, above all, for abolition of tithes in kind. William Cobbett, in speeches throughout the southern counties, repeatedly reminded farming audiences that privileges enjoyed by the clergy could not last much longer: 'there must be a *settlement of some sort*; and that settlement never can leave

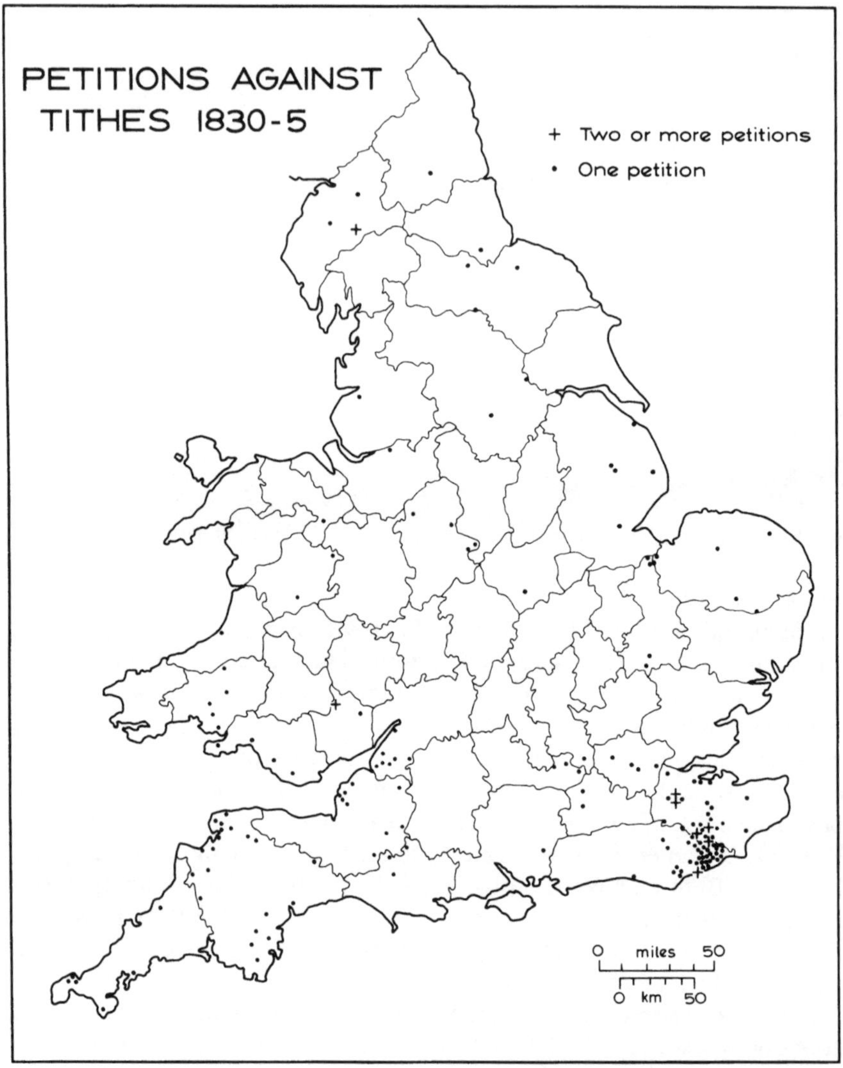

1.8 Petitions laid before the House of Commons against tithes from parishes in England and Wales, 1830–5.

that mass, that immense mass, of public property, called "church property", to be used as it now is'.[69] When violence erupted in Kent and in other southern counties in the autumn of 1830, it was directed not only against farmers' ricks and workhouses but in many parishes angry mobs attacked their parsons[70] (Figs. 1.8 and 1.9). In the uneasy peace that followed, the

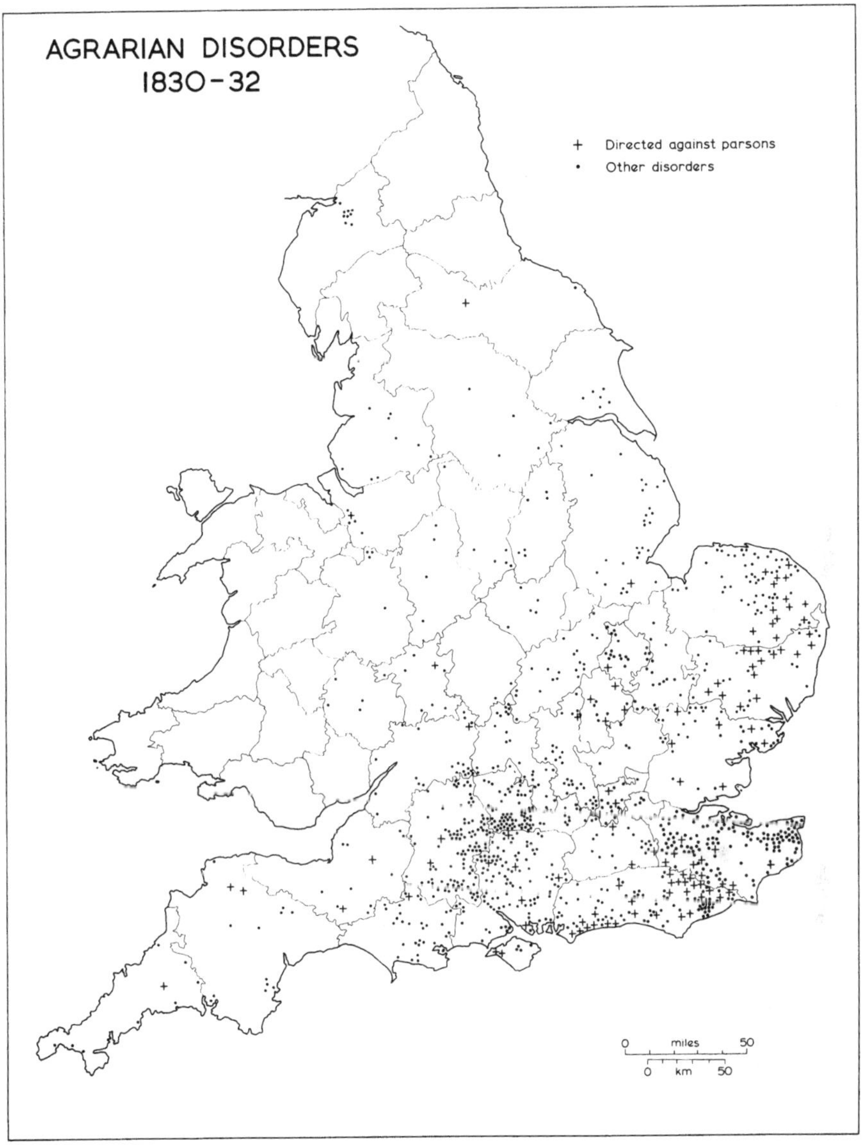

1.9 Agrarian disorders in England, 1830–2. Source: Hobsbawm and Rudé, *Captain Swing*.

clergy themselves began to deliberate on ways and means of bringing to an end abuses of the tithing system, and a measure presented to parliament finally became law in 1836.

2

The Tithe Commutation Act of 1836

For many centuries tithes had been paid grudgingly in most parishes and in a few this payment may be traced back over 900 years. During much of that time they had been a cause for grievances and had been regarded as a continuing source of irritation. From time to time additional demands by a new incumbent or by an assertive tithe owner had provoked outbursts of resistance, but for the most part it was possible to blame deviant groups of Quakers or more militant dissenters for stirring up trouble. Magistrates confidently dealt with such outbreaks as if they were fomented by a minority of activists who could be ostracised as religious cranks. On few occasions and in few localities were tithes seen as serious or potentially serious threats to the maintenance of public order, and not until the beginning of the nineteenth century did the government feel that the survival of the regime in any way depended upon a reform or abolition of the age-old practices of collecting them. The tithe question did not seem to be a rallying point for widespread popular uprisings and, indeed, it might well have been ignored even later had not other more pressing sources of discontent arisen.

Tithe in the post-Napoleonic depression

Teinds had been abolished in Scotland in 1633 and with the passage of the Irish Tithe Composition Act in 1823 their retention in England and Wales became an undesirable anachronism.[1] By this time the established church was no longer in a position to negotiate a tithe settlement on terms as favourable as those conceded under enclosure awards. In the recession following the Napoleonic wars, further territorial expansion of ecclesiastical estates by additional tithe allotments was unlikely to be countenanced either by parliament or by a large section of the tithe owners themselves. Another more generally acceptable solution had to be found without delay. The dilemma in which the church was placed by the effects of the agricultural depression in the post-Napoleonic period sprang from two causes. First, the collection of tithes in kind presented an all too obvious spectacle of clerical oppression when crops and livestock were taken from the fields of farmers on the verge of ruin, under the eyes of famished labourers. The incidence of the collection of tithe in kind fell heaviest in the southern counties and to a lesser extent in the north-west. It was a practice universally condemned by writers of the Board of Agriculture reports (see chapter 1). Secondly, more than half the cultivated land of England and Wales was subject to money payments, many of which had been fixed when corn prices were high and, on the recommendation of a Select Committee on Tithes in 1816, many such charges had been made binding upon the parties concerned and on their successors by leases entered into for periods of up to fourteen years.[2] When farm incomes fell these covenanted commitments became intolerable imposts, contributing to numerous insolvencies. These, in turn, increased difficulties experienced by landowners in finding tenants for vacant farms, even at greatly reduced rents. If it were possible, under these circumstances, to persuade landowners that no increase in rents was to be expected while tithes remained at their present levels, it would be much less difficult to persuade labourers that no increase in wages could be paid until tithes were either abolished or substantially reduced. The isolation of the church from the ruling landed classes as well as from the rural poor would then be complete. From the clergy's point of view, the most menacing aspect of the disturbances of 1830–2 was that farmers took little or no action to restrain the violence of the rioters, and at Benenden, Horsham, Mayfield, Brede, Selborne and other places in the Wealden districts of Kent, Surrey, Sussex and Hampshire they invited or offered encouragement to mobs to press demands for the abolition of tithes. The riots were quelled, 6 men and boys were hanged and 457 were transported to Van Diemen's Land and to New South Wales, but resentment remained as deep as before.

A final legislative solution to the tithe problem had to wait until parliament was itself reformed. John Christian Curwen, Whig MP for Carlisle and a practising farmer, was one of the principal agitators for reform in the immediate post-Napoleonic-war period. It was he who secured the appointment of a Select Committee in 1816 to consider the many petitions against tithes being placed before the House. The following year he won a debate on moduses and the claims and counter-claims arising from these customary payments.[3] The next important parliamentary debate on tithes did not take place until 1828 when Thomas Greene, MP for Lancaster, introduced what was effectively the first bill to procure a national commutation. Greene's solution was to authorise the establishment of corn rents in lieu of tithe. His bill was lost, largely as a result of arguments put forward by the tithe-owning interest in defence of their own claims to a share in the fruits of agricultural improvement.[4]

After being blamed in 1831 for the failure of the first parliamentary reform bill, the church found itself subjected to massive anti-clerical demonstrations. As Evans asserts, 'in the period 1831–4, it seems safe to say, the Church of England stood in more imminent danger of disestablishment than at any time before or since'.[5] The question facing the government was how to remove or greatly diminish the danger of continued strife and how to bring about a lasting settlement. It was clear that expropriations of land would only inflame a tense situation and that imposition of permanent charges unrelated to changing prices would be equally unacceptable. It was also evident that compositions based on the quantity and value of land, in effect surcharges on rents, provided no answer. What was required was a variable tax on farm output, regulated according to prevailing price levels. A corn rent, adjusted to current market prices of wheat or of other cereals, went some way towards achieving this objective, and from this simple device were derived the underlying basic principles of several proposed reforms. Between 1833 and 1836 no fewer than four attempts, three Whig and one Tory, were made to secure the passage of bills to commute tithes.

Whig attempts to secure national commutations in 1833 and 1834

On 18 April 1833 Lord Althorp introduced a bill for the commutation of tithes for a corn rent.[6] He suggested that tithe owners and landowners should be given a year to frame a voluntary agreement, after which either party would have the power to appoint valuers and to require the other party to appoint valuers. These agents would then value the tithes. Althorp himself realised that this would present difficulties and he subsequently proposed that the average of tithes over the past seven years should form the basis of composition. Later, in a committee of the whole House he decided to drop all compulsory clauses from his bill. In the opinion of the opposition this emasculated the measure, which they urged should be dropped in its entirety rather than be launched as a half-measure. A further objection was that the severity with which tithe was levied varied greatly from parish to parish. A very great difference between the rates of tithe paid by tithe payers in different places would have resulted from this proposal. Later in the session of 1833 the bill was lost and a deluge of petitions followed.[7]

On 15 April 1834 Lord Althorp introduced his second bill. This proposed to commute tithes for a money payment fixed in proportion to the rent payable on the land. Also, it was to give a power of redemption to landowners at 25 years' purchase once a money payment had been determined. Where redemption did not take place, the money payment could be converted into a rent-charge permanently settled on the land. The country was to be divided into districts and a valuer of tithes and a valuer of land were to be appointed in each district. The land valuer was to divide the land into two classes: first into arable land and secondly into that which was not arable, to be called 'pasture land' for the sake of simplicity. Althorp said that he, 'should not consider any land arable unless it had been broken up at some time within the preceding five years'.[8] The next stage was to value the tithes and apportion them to arable and 'pasture' land. These values would be submitted to courts of quarter-sessions and a mean tithe for each type of land calculated. This mean tithe rate would then apply to the whole of each sort of land in a district.

When introducing his measure for the commutation of tithes the following year, Sir Robert Peel conveniently summarised the objections to Lord Althorp's second tithe bill under three heads. First, there were those who objected to the way in which tithes were to be valued; secondly, there were objections to the use of average receipts over a period of years; and thirdly, there was much controversy over the correctness of establishing the principle of a fixed proportion between rents and tithes and its application universally over a large district without reference to land quality.[9]

The minority Tory government and tithe reform

When Sir Robert Peel rose on 24 March 1835 to introduce his measure for the commutation of tithes, he urged that the greatest possible encouragement should be given to voluntary commutation of tithes. He referred to a large number of parishes where tithes had been commuted under the terms of enclosure acts between 1757 and 1830 often at a cost of as much as £2,000. He proposed to put an end to the need for such expenditure in the following way: first, a commission should be set up to supervise the whole operation. Then, after due notice had been given, the tithe payers and tithe owners in every parish should meet to discuss ways and means of effecting an amicable settlement. The central commission would send out assistants to help frame agreements at no cost to the parishes. If at these meetings tithe payers responsible for two-thirds in point of value of the tithes could agree with the tithe owner, then their consent would bind other tithe payers. Agreements would state the total amount of money payment expressed as a corn rent, subject to periodic revision if desired by either party, and varying not with the price of wheat alone but with that of all grains. If all parties were agreeable, an allotment of land would be allowed instead of a corn rent.

In the course of the debate, Peel reaffirmed the Tory belief that a voluntary basis would be less inflammatory than any plan for compulsory commutation. In the light of experience gained from implementing this measure, future legislation could be framed to deal with those tithe districts which declined voluntary agreements.[10] But several voices were raised against the permissive nature of the bill. In the words of Lord John Russell, its 'voluntary nature offered but little prospect of success . . . nothing less than a generally compulsory regulation would lead to a general commutation and nothing less than that could be productive of any change sufficiently extensive to deserve being described as a great practical good'.[11] Peel had founded his faith on the number of voluntary commutations already made. But, as Mr Pryme pointed out in the debate, almost all these were included in enclosure acts under special circumstances.[12]

The Tithe Commutation Act of 1836

On 9 February 1836 Lord John Russell introduced his bill for the commutation of tithes in England and Wales. He reminded the House that various plans had been submitted to parliament, that none of them had been completed, yet none had really failed. He saw that tithe commutation had to be effected quickly, not only because of the abstract objections against tithes pointed out more than fifty years earlier but because 'tithe was now, as it was then, a discouragement to industry – a penalty on skill, a heavy mulct on those who expended the most capital and displayed the greatest skill in cultivating the land'.[13] In many respects Russell's bill resembled that put forward by Peel's short-lived government in the previous session with the important difference that if, after the passage of a period of time from the date of the bill becoming law, a voluntary agreement had not been obtained, then commutation would be imposed on the deadlocked parties. The machinery of operation was also based on Peel's proposal for a central commission and an army of assistants in the field, in fact, a formula that had been tried and tested with the Poor Law Amendment Act of 1834.

When the bill was debated in the House the middle ground of both Whig and Tory parties saw the prospect of at last getting a measure for tithe commutation on to the statute book. As Russell himself contended during the debate on the second reading of the bill, the fact that it was opposed by extremes on both sides of the House was proof that those like himself who steered a middle course had devised a measure which ultimately would satisfy all parties.[14] A repetition of the Irish tithe debacle could not be countenanced by either side.[15] Parliamentary debates on the tithe question in the 1830s usually divided along party lines: landowning Whigs favouring coercion, church-going Tories championing voluntaryism. Russell's bill allayed Tory concern about coercion by extending the period to reach a voluntary agreement from six months to over two years.[16]

The act passed on 13 August 1836 commuted all tithes in kind and substituted a fluctuating money payment known as a tithe rent-charge adjusted each year on the basis of the seven-year average price of wheat, barley and oats.[17] The amount of the tithe rent-charge was to be obtained by dividing £100 of tithe into three equal portions of £33 6s 8d, calculating how much wheat, barley and oats could be bought with each portion, and multiplying these quantities by the average price in succeeding years. In

1836 the septennial average price of wheat was 7s 0¼d per bushel, of barley, 3s 11½d per bushel, of oats, 2s 9d per bushel. At these prices £33 6s 8d bought 94.96 bushels of wheat, or 168.42 bushels of barley, or 242.42 bushels of oats. Each succeeding year the tithe rent-charge on £100 of tithe was to be the sum of the septennial average prices of these quantities of grain, and tables were to be published annually to enable the precise amount of any rent-charge to be calculated. In this way the relationship between the prices of the three cereals and the value of the money payment for which tithes were commuted was to be preserved.[18]

The Tithe Commission in London

Responsibility for tithe commutation was vested in a Tithe Commission set up on the model of the earlier Poor Law Commission.[19] Three commissioners – William Blamire, Capt T. Wentworth Buller and Rev Richard Jones – were appointed under the provisions of the 1836 act. William Blamire, the Commission's chairman, was a Cumberland farmer who represented his county in parliament as a Whig from 1831 to 1836 when he was required to resign by virtue of his tithe appointment. He was not a frequent speaker in the House and confined himself in the main to subjects concerning the Cumberland rural interest. In that part of the country tithe was very much a live issue during his years in parliament and, with experience he gained from Kendal and other tithe disputes, Blamire probably knew as much as anyone in the country about the practical difficulties associated with the unreformed tithe system.[20] From 1845 he combined the job of tithe commissioner with that of enclosure commissioner. His nineteenth-century biographer, Henry Lonsdale, speaks of his prodigious labours 'embodied in statutes and official reports'.[21] But, as Professor Spring observes, William Blamire's work was not only a paper contribution but also 'helped to re-make the face of rural England'.[22]

Rev Richard Jones was nominated to the Tithe Commission by the archbishop of Canterbury. He was an academic, had published two tracts setting out his views on commutation in 1833 and 1836 and continued to write on tithe matters after his appointment.[23] Though a church appointment, his work for the Tithe Commission showed 'no greater partiality to the interests of the church than Blamire's did to the farming interest'.[24] The third commissioner, Captain Buller, benefited from Lord John Russell's patronage. He was a landowner in Northamptonshire and Devon and was an active promoter of the Whig cause in the south-west.[25] The three tithe commissioners were based in London where they were supported by a secretary and assistant secretary and more than 30 clerks and 20 draughtsmen. Also working in the London office was the first assistant tithe commissioner to be sworn in, Lieutenant Robert Kearsley Dawson.

Dawson was seconded to the Tithe Commission from the Royal Engineers on 27 August 1836 and was given the task of organising and superintending the land surveys on which the permanent commutation was to be recorded. R. K. Dawson was the son of Robert Dawson (1776–1860), a celebrated topographical artist and surveyor. He was commissioned into the Royal Engineers in March 1816, from 1819 he worked as assistant to Thomas Colby on the triangulation of Scotland, and in 1825 accompanied Colby to Ireland. Here in 1829 he was put in charge of a staff of civil assistants engaged in sketching hills for the one-inch map. His men also collected material for county memoirs to the six-inch survey. Under his guidance and critical eye some notable talents emerged from the body of civil assistants and some excellent memoirs were produced.[26] In 1831 Dawson was called back to England and appointed a commissioner under the Reform Bill to settle and map the boundaries of parliamentary boroughs. Manuscripts of the maps which Dawson produced, mainly at the one-inch and two-inch scales, are bound in two volumes and preserved under his name in the British Library.[27]

Of all the varied survey activities with which Dawson was concerned before 1836, his association with the Irish Survey had the most profound influence on his approach to the organisation and specification of the tithe surveys. In particular he used the need for tithe maps as a reason for beginning a full cadastral survey of England and Wales on the Irish model (see chapter 3). His work with the tithe survey established him as an authority on cadastral mapping, and, at the same time as superintending the tithe survey, he was employed as surveying consultant to the Wakefield settlements in Australia and New Zealand; in 1840 he wrote a pamphlet entitled, 'Report on surveying considered with reference to New Zealand and applicable to the colonies generally'.[28]

Assistant tithe commissioners and local tithe agents

The Tithe Commutation Act required the tithe commissioners to confirm such voluntary agreements to commute tithes that were reached before 1 October 1838 and to impose awards in those districts where agreements could not be reached or where the commissioners considered the terms unfair to one or other party. In practice these powers were delegated to assistant commissioners and local agents whose recommendations were usually accepted in London. The duties of local agents were restricted to reporting on draft agreements and advising the tithe commissioners whether they should be confirmed; assistant tithe commissioners also conducted this business but in addition had the more responsible duty of framing awards.[29] In Eric Evans' words, these men 'became the "restless shuttles" of the commutation machinery, as they scurried from one parish to another, offering advice, settling disputes, confirming agreements and effecting compulsory commutation'.[30]

The volume of work that some local agents and assistant commissioners accomplished was quite prodigious. Henry Pilkington completed 422 reports on agreements in 16 counties between 1837 and 1846, writing 94 in 1839 alone.[31] From 1840 when he was appointed assistant commissioner he also attended many award appeal meetings. In some individual weeks in 1839 he visited and reported on 10 districts; on the single day of 17 June he wrote 4 reports and another 6 on 9–10 July. Even this workload pales in comparison with Thomas Hoskins' 538 reports written between 1838 and 1844 with no fewer than 203 completed in 1839 alone. With several townships to report on in a single day it is hardly surprising that the language of their accounts is sometimes terse and hastily penned.[32] When time was not pressing and if the man was somewhat romantically inclined, he could look about and describe the scenery. Of Challacombe on Exmoor, James Jerwood said in 1838:

> most of it is formed of that beautiful open sort of country where not a single tree hindrs the wind from blowing upon you – or solitary bush is wide enough to intercept the sunshine . . . there is plenty of room – you may ride for miles over the common – your road a sheep's track, and chance your only guide to find the right way out of it.[33]

By 1841 the impression had palled somewhat: 'I think the parish [Huntshaw] a poor one – its general appearance and quality are as rough as the most ardent admirer of moor, bog, and bramble land could wish to put his foot in.'[34]

Most local agents were practical men, well-versed in the farming and landscapes of one or two counties in which they undertook reports for the Tithe Commission. The more educated and able who from an early date were appointed full-time assistant commissioners, such as Thomas Smith Woolley of South Collingham near Newark in Nottinghamshire, conducted work over a large geographical area.[35] Inevitably this meant that they were less familiar with the agricultural systems of some areas in which they were reporting. They were all by dint of experience, if nothing else, practical valuers and required to be skilled negotiators. Without their careful handling of local disputes and the energy and diligence they brought to their work, the Tithe Commutation Act might have foundered. Applicants for these well-paid posts were most carefully vetted as the appointment to office of one, Joseph Townsend, demonstrates.

The appointment of an assistant commissioner

Exactly five weeks after the Tithe Commutation Act received the royal assent, a Buckinghamshire surveyor, Joseph Townsend, sought appointment as an assistant tithe commissioner. His background and qualifications throw light on the way in which executive staff were recruited and his career provides insights into how the act was implemented.

He was the eldest son of a small country landowner. Since the later seventeenth century, the Townsends had, by careful management, built up an estate of several hundred acres, adding farms and parcels of woodland around the family seat at Wood End in Medmenham. The principal properties lay on the borders of Buckinghamshire and Oxfordshire between Little Marlow, Hambleden and Lane End. The family also owned an outlying farm at Lewknor in Oxfordshire, title to which was a subject of relentless and costly litigation. When the dispute ended in 1834, Joseph Townsend's father held the property but was in debt to his lawyers and to his sons. The estate was kept intact by the exertions of the sons earning money in business. Both Joseph and his brother Richard, who had emigrated to New South Wales, were professional surveyors. Joseph had been apprenticed in 1813 to Stephen Godson, land surveyor of Hook Norton in Oxfordshire, and after qualifying had acted as land agent and surveyor to neighbouring large estates in the Chilterns. Having moved to Wood End with his wife in 1831 he set about putting the affairs of the estate in order and began to modernise the running of the farm, keeping full accounts and records of cropping and livestock. At the same time his practice as a surveyor appears to have been flourishing to give him an income of £500 to £600 a year and enable his wife to dress the household servants in new livery.[36]

In his own opinion, Townsend's principal qualification for employment by the tithe commissioners was that he had gained much experience in dealing with tithe problems during 21 years he had served as commissioner and surveyor under enclosure acts. On 17 September 1836, in submitting an application to the tithe commissioners, he wrote: 'I beg leave to add a list of the several Inclosures on which I have been engaged and the names of some of the important holders of landed property by whom I have had the honour to be employed.'[37] On 6 October he notes that other surveyors, land agents and former enclosure commissioners were being appointed as assistant tithe commissioners, among them Henry Dixon, an Oxfordshire gentleman with whom he jointly made the Harley allotment.[38] Evidently, the tithe commissioners were in no hurry to employ Townsend. They considered it advisable to examine closely his credentials and they called for testimonials concerning his work in Buckinghamshire from the Marquis of Chandos, concerning his Berkshire commissions from the Marquis of Downshire, concerning his Worcestershire commissions from Major Bund and E. W. Oldaker, and about his commissions in Warwickshire and Northamptonshire from Richard Scriven, agent to the Marquess of Northampton.[39] In answer to an enquiry, the Marquis of Downshire wrote to Townsend that it had given him much pleasure to state

> for the Information of the Tithe Commissioners of England and Wales that from my knowledge and experience of your abilities as a Land Surveyor and Valuator, having been employed on my business for some years under my Agent and Solicitor Mr Handley, I consider you qualified for the office of an assistant Tithe Comm^{r} for which I understand you have applied.[40]

For almost a year after receiving these testimonials the tithe commissioners continued to deliberate and make further enquiries. On 1 July 1837 one of the Commissioners, Rev Richard Jones, wrote to ask, 'if in the event of your being appointed an assistant commissioner, you could give up *all your time* to the service of the Commission and whether you could conveniently reside near London'.[41] That no decision had been reached at this date was made clear in Jones' reminder that he was 'but one of three, and not be disappointed if this application ends in little or nothing'.[42] Townsend replied by return of post that he would willingly devote all his time to the work of the Commission and he also agreed to take up residence near London, leaving the date of the move to be determined by the commissioners at their convenience. These assurances sufficed to secure his appointment. On learning the news, one of his sponsors, the Marquis of Downshire, wrote a cordial yet lordly letter congratulating him, trusting that his 'conduct in an official Situation will always be marked by Integrity & Ability in the Discharge of public Duties'.[43]

On becoming a full-time public servant, Townsend had to give up or subordinate many of his private business interests and also had to learn to exercise discretion in granting favours. In this respect the discipline of the office was firm and an assistant commissioner was given clear directions on how to conduct himself and on how far he might be permitted to exercise private initiative. On 7 August 1839 Townsend was cautioned in a letter dictated by Jones most strictly enjoining him 'not to act as referee in any case or under any circumstance so long as you are acting in the service of the Commission'.[44] In the delicate matter of settling appropriate rent-charges that might be seen to be justly arrived at by both tithe payers and tithe owners it was essential that the probity and impartiality of the commissioner's executive officers should be beyond reproach. In the performance of all his duties in the field the task of an assistant commissioner probably demanded more of his personal qualities as a fair-minded negotiator and trusted arbitrator than of his skill and competence as a surveyor and valuer.

Soon after his appointment Townsend was at work in Kent drafting awards in parishes bedevilled by the collection of tithes in kind. In 1838 and 1839 he acted in sixteen widely spaced tithe districts distributed with little regard for minimising his travelling (Fig. 2.1) and was called upon to travel as far afield as the East Riding of Yorkshire.[45] The voluminous minutes he took at some of the award meetings provide illuminating insights into the mechanisms of commutation. In all cases he succeeded in awarding rent-charges agreeable to all parties. It was probably in the Wealden parish of Hawkhurst that he was given his severest test. Here the problem centred on a tithe of hops. In 1818 the parishioners had entered into an agreement with the dean and chapter of Canterbury to pay 50s an acre for hops, 20s an acre for wheat and 12s 6d an acre for lent corn in lieu of tithes. Then came the agricultural depression with a fall in the price of hops from at times as high as £30 to at times as low as 50s a hundredweight. But, the lessee of the tithes continued to exact his full claim. Things came to such a pass that in April 1839 the tithe commissioners received from the parishioners a copy of a House of Commons petition against their tithes. Despite the evident acrimony the impartial Townsend was able to draft an acceptable award in 1840 and so ended over twenty years of strife between parish and clergy.[46]

The correspondence in the tithe file relating to Townsend's execution of the compulsory commutation of tithes in 29 townships in the extensive parish of Manchester in 1844 further exemplifies the role of an assistant commissioner in bringing together the interested parties, removing procedural obstacles, conducting negotiations in a fair manner, making sure that issues under discussion were fully and clearly understood by all concerned, securing agreement on the largest possible number of questions and bringing about a final settlement without acrimony or delay.[47] In all these respects, the conduct of the proceedings in Manchester was largely successful. As in many districts, a long and expensive tithe lawsuit settled twenty years earlier had made the parishioners reluctant 'to take upon themselves the risk of fresh disagreements', and through the dean of Manchester they appealed to the commissioners to make a compulsory award. The commissioners readily acceded and, somewhat too hurriedly, they called a meeting for which notices could neither be circulated nor published within the statutory time limit. The date of the meeting had to be deferred but from then onwards the business proceeded so smoothly that an award was drafted and concluded within one week. The dean and canons who had initiated the enquiry instructed their solicitors to write to the tithe commissioners expressing their satisfaction at the result. 'This important alteration', they wrote,

> has been effected in such a manner as to meet with almost universal approbation, and when any difference has been found to exist mutual explanations have never failed to produce the desired effect. We cannot omit this opportunity of expressing our respect for the Gentleman who has acted as the Assistant Commissioner – His manners have been most conciliatory and the intimate acquaintance he has

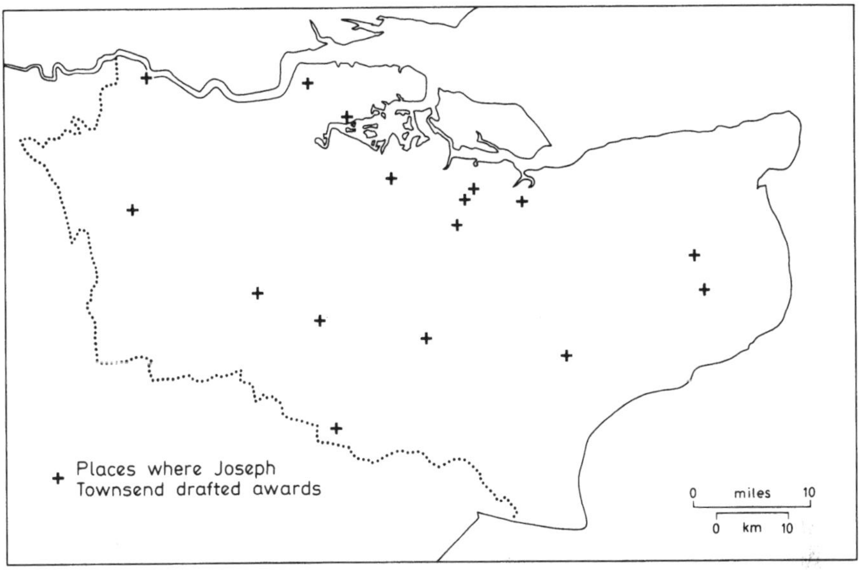

2.1 The work of assistant tithe commissioner Joseph Townsend in Kent. Source: tithe files.

manifested with the habits and feelings of the Inhabitants of this neighbourhood have peculiarly fitted him for the duties he has so ably performed.[48]

The desire of the parties to avoid at all costs a repetition of old quarrels and to maintain the strictest impartiality in complying with the terms of the award is evident in a letter from the solicitors acting for the dean of Manchester addressed to the tithe commissioners. Writing on behalf of the tithe owners in September 1847, it was observed that

the land owners have not appointed any person to make the Apportionment of the Rent Charge in the Townships of Manchester and Beswick. Unless particularly requested to assist the Commissioners we should avoid all connection with the land owners. We have at all times advised the tithe owners not to interfere but to leave the settlement to be worked out under the powers of the Commission and as the proceedings hitherto have been so satisfactory we should be sorry to be called upon to act in another capacity than as Solicitors to the tithe owners. If we retain our present independent position there cannot be discovered any ground for excitement or ill feeling and the advantages of the Commission will be apparent to every reasonable man.[49]

Again, the Commission was called upon to use its influence as an independent body to avert a clash between rival interests.

The claims of the service were not so exacting as entirely to prevent Townsend from leading a life befitting a country gentleman. On his estate at

Wood End in Buckinghamshire family funerals and marriages were solemnised, the parson was quarrelled with, a parochial dispute over payment of tithe and Easter offerings was confidently engaged upon and not easily resolved, the administration of a family bequest proved troublesome, rents were collected and repairs carried out, local charities were subscribed to and fêtes attended. It seemed appropriate that this respectable middle-aged squire should eventually be nominated as justice of the peace. But there was some coolness and hesitation among landowners in the county about the propriety of admitting one whose standing as a gentleman was compromised by his occupation as a surveyor and allegiance to the Conservative party.[50] His estate, though legally sufficient, was a rather small one; 'the quantity of landed estate requisite for acceptance into the landed gentry remained essentially a matter of social judgement'.[51] That he found it necessary in 1851 to write direct to Lord Carrington is evidence that there was nothing inevitable about his appointment. He had earlier tried an approach through Sir W. R. Clayton, the ex-Liberal MP for Marlow. In the borough election of 1849 he even went as far as to blunt his Conservative opinions and to vote for Sir W. R. Clayton and Mr Williams to improve his standing with neighbouring landowners.[52] Carrington apparently had no objection to Townsend on social grounds, but was worried about his supposed personal unpopularity in Marlow. The possible legal impropriety of appointing a servant of a public body was not discussed, though there was doubt about whether his duties would leave him sufficient time to be active on the bench.[53] These objections were removed by a recommendation from Lord Carrington, Townsend's neighbour and lord lieutenant of the county. On 19 February 1850 Townsend formally signified his intention to qualify for insertion in the commission of the peace. By this act his position in the ranks of the county gentry was secured.

Power and prestige in Buckinghamshire afforded him no protection in Somerset House. As early as 1849 Townsend remarked to Acton Tindal that he was dissatisfied with the small amount of work that had been given to him as an assistant tithe commissioner. Once again it appears that his politics were at fault. Townsend himself attributed his loss of favour to the fact that his political opinions differed from those of his superiors in office. In 1851 the Tithe Commission whose work was nearing completion was a ready prey for a government seeking reductions in public expenditure. Townsend was made redundant and all efforts failed to obtain his reinstatement in any other official employment. Both William Blamire, chairman of the Tithe Commission, and Lord Carrington, his neighbour, spoke on his behalf to the prime minister, Lord John Russell. Townsend himself wrote a personal letter to the prime minister pleading that,

> having passed 14 years in the Service of the Government in carrying into effect so important a measure as the Commutation of Tithes in all its stages, and having as

before mentioned sacrificed a professional income and commission in accepting the appointment of Assis[t] Tithe Com[r] I hope your Lordship will admit that I have some claim on the consideration of Her Majesty's Government and allow me now respectfully to make an offer of the continuance of my Services in some of the public Commissions now in progress or in such other way as may be eligible and may usefully occupy the time which the Tithe Com[n] has now left unemployed.[54]

The reply written ten days later by Arthur Russell from Downing Street was brusque and conclusive. It read:

I am desired by Lord John Russell to inform you in answer to your letter of the 27th ult. that he fears he sees no prospect that it will be in his power to comply with your request, in consequence of the number of long standing claims of other persons, already before him, and the great reductions that have been taking place in all public departments.[55]

Townsend must have been deeply discouraged by the curt manner of his dismissal. He pursued the matter no further, nor apparently did he resume his private practice. In February 1852 he signed his will and died ten years later. The Tithe Commission was a harsh master to the end.

Establishing tithe districts

The first task to be performed by the three commissioners appointed under the provisions of the act was to establish boundaries for every district in which tithes were paid separately. This was known as a tithe district to distinguish it from a parish or township. In the meaning of the act, districts included every place for which an overseer of the poor was appointed. The commissioners first sent written enquiries (Fig. 2.2) to all places listed as parishes and townships in the census returns but could and did, if necessary, form separate districts. This was sometimes necessary where tithe was paid separately in parts of parishes or townships. Occasionally, two or more townships or parishes were combined, a procedure which resulted in economies all round.[56] In all, 14,829 tithe districts were recognised and most were townships in northern England and parishes elsewhere. A minority were tithings, chapelries, manors, hamlets, extra-parochial places and such like, many of which districts enjoyed separate status solely for tithe commutation purposes. A tithe file was opened for each tithe district and into that file correspondence relating to the district was placed. For some 2,096 of these tithe districts the commissioners' labours involved no more than recording replies to their enquiries which confirmed that tithe was no longer payable in 1836. At this date exemption was usually by virtue of a complete enclosure commutation, or else tithe had been redeemed by direct merger in the land, most commonly where a tithe owner and tithe payer were one and the same person.

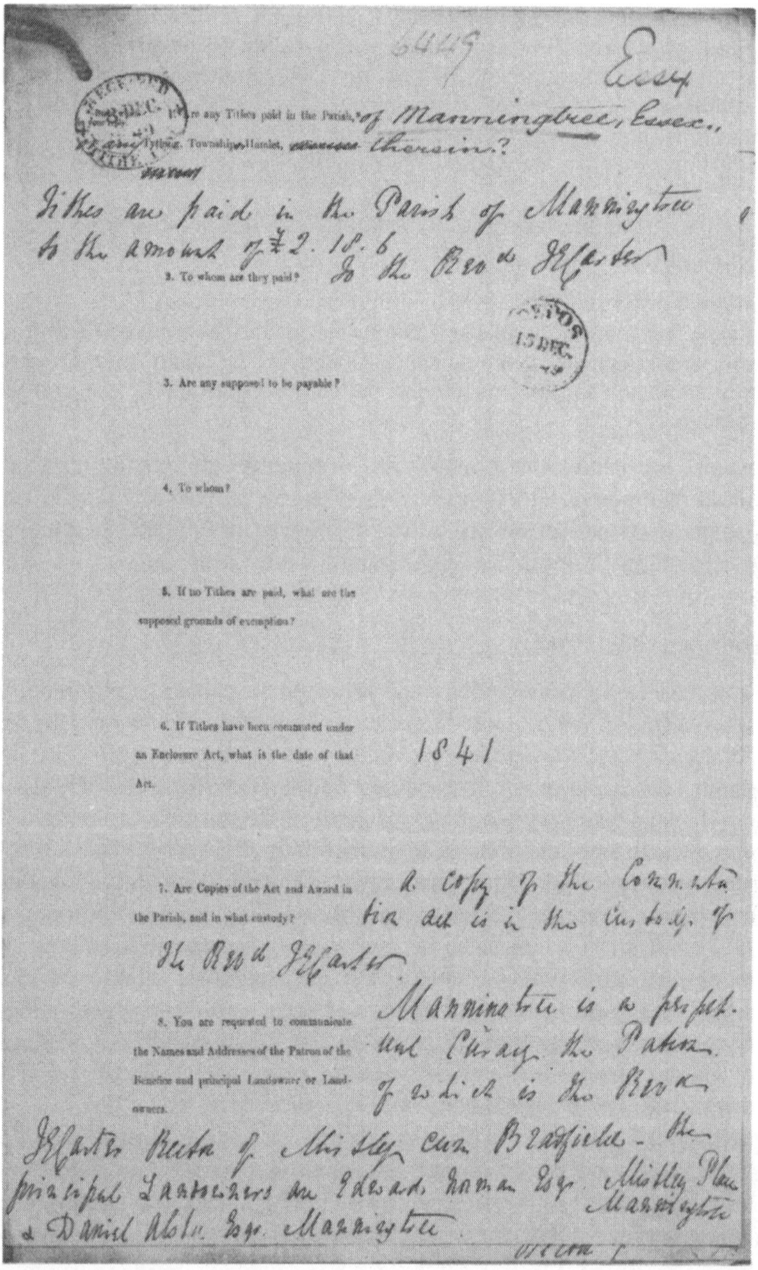
Essex

1. Are any Tithes paid in the Parish, of Manningtree, Essex., or any Tything, Township, Hamlet, therein?

Tithes are paid in the Parish of Manningtree to the amount of £2. 18. 6

2. To whom are they paid? To the Revd J.J. Carter

3. Are any supposed to be payable?

4. To whom?

5. If no Tithes are paid, what are the supposed grounds of exemption?

6. If Tithes have been commuted under an Enclosure Act, what is the date of that Act. 1841

7. Are Copies of the Act and Award in the Parish, and in what custody? A copy of the Commutation act is in the custody of the Revd J.J. Carter

8. You are requested to communicate the Names and Addresses of the Patron of the Benefice and principal Landowner or Landowners. Manningtree is a perpetual Curacy the Patron of which is the Revd J.J. Carter Rector of Mistley cum Bradfield – the principal Landowners are Edward Norman Esqr. Mistley Place & Daniel Able Esqr. Manningtree

2.2 Form sent by the tithe commissioners to each incumbent enquiring whether any tithes were payable in that district. Source: PRO IR 18/2421; photograph reproduced by permission of the Keeper, Public Record Office.

The existence of districts was usually not contested but what was frequently disputed was the exact configuration of boundaries. The demarcation of a boundary was particularly important for a person who was a tithe owner in one parish and a tithe payer elsewhere. Again, tithe payments themselves differed from parish to parish both in their nature and amount, so that a particular piece of land might carry a higher rent-charge if it were included in one parish than in another. Land subject to tithes on one side of a boundary might even be exempt on the other. Such was the case in those Kent parishes situated along the line of the Pilgrim's Way. Woods were subject to tithe in parishes to the north of the line but exempt by prescription to the south.

Where boundaries were uncertain, the owners of two-thirds (by value) of the land could require the tithe commissioners to enquire into and set out the boundaries of their district. This always preceded the commutation of tithes as the value of tithes would be affected by the extent of the district. Without the help of large-scale Ordnance Survey maps, the commissioners had to rely on the best available maps and documents and on local knowledge. The procedure was for landowners to submit a written description and a sketch plan of the claimed boundary line to the assistant commissioner appointed to decide the dispute. It was then necessary to support the claim with evidence of witnesses and documents. Representatives of landowners from the adjoining district also attended the hearing prepared with a counter description, sketch, documents and witnesses, after which the assistant commissioner decided the line on the preponderance of the evidence.[57]

Agreements for tithe rent-charge

Having discovered where tithes remained uncommuted and having set in train machinery to resolve disputed boundaries, the commissioners proceeded to their main tasks of, first, confirming rent-charges and, secondly, apportioning the global sum over various types of land in the district. The act enabled tithe owners and tithe payers to agree a value for the rent-charge at any time before 1 October 1838. Although the voluntary option was backed up by compulsory powers which could be invoked in deadlocked or dilatory districts after that date, it was the express policy of the tithe commissioners to encourage voluntary agreements. In following such a policy they were respecting the spirit of the act and the tenor of parliamentary debate.

To help landowners and tithe owners achieve a just and fair agreement, the Tithe Commission made available a mass of printed information sheets providing procedural guidance.[58] One of the most valuable of these was a *pro forma* indicating an acceptable form of words which could be used when drafting an agreement (Fig. 2.3). Parochial meetings to investigate the possibility of achieving an agreement could be called by owners of not less than a quarter of the land *or* tithes and if the owners of two-thirds (by value) of the land *and* of the tithes could agree a rent-charge in lieu of tithes, this would be binding on the remainder. 'Thus, as at enclosure, a few substantial property holders could dictate terms to the many whose collective stake was smaller.'[59] Once a draft agreement was prepared it was sent to the tithe commissioners who instructed an assistant commissioner or a local tithe agent to visit the district and charged him with writing a report advising whether the agreement was fair to all parties and suitable for confirmation prior to apportionment. To help the Tithe Commission's local representatives judge these agreements and to organise and standardise their reports, they were issued from November 1837 with forms on which a number of questions were printed with spaces provided for answers. These answers provide much information on local landscape, farming practices and the output of agriculture and for historians are perhaps the most important source documents remaining in the tithe files (see chapter 3). Two basic types of printed form were used and in any one county only one type of form was in general use. Exceptions to this rule are so rare as to be explained by an agent or assistant commissioner not having any of the correct forms to hand and suggest, in the absence of the letter books and papers of the tithe commissioners, that commutation was probably organised on a county-by-county basis.[60]

During the first year of commutation the small number of agreements made did not require the employment of assistant commissioners and local agents on anything approaching a full-time basis. During this early period officials were sent to far-flung areas of the country. J. D. Merest, for example, reported on a number of agreements reached in 1837 in districts in Staffordshire, Shropshire and Lincolnshire but thereafter he worked only in East Anglia. In any one county, one agent reported on a clear majority of districts (Table 2.1). Over 80 per cent of reports on agreements for Somerset districts were completed by Robert Page; John Farncombe officiated at 158 of the 188 Sussex agreement enquiries. Charles Howard of Melbourne, Yorkshire, worked mainly in northern England; Henry Gunning of Whittlesford, Cambridgeshire, in East Anglia; James Jerwood of Teignmouth, Devon, in south-west England. John Fenton and Aneurin Owen were entrusted with most of north Wales and Thomas Hoskins and John Johnes with south Wales.[61] Agricultural practices, land values and tithing customs varied from one part of the country to another so that there was clearly some advantage in employing men with specialist regional experience who would be quick to spot attempted transgressions by one

2.3 Specimen 'Articles of Agreement' as supplied by the Tithe Commission. Source: PRO IR 18/5138; photograph reproduced by permission of the Keeper, Public Record Office.

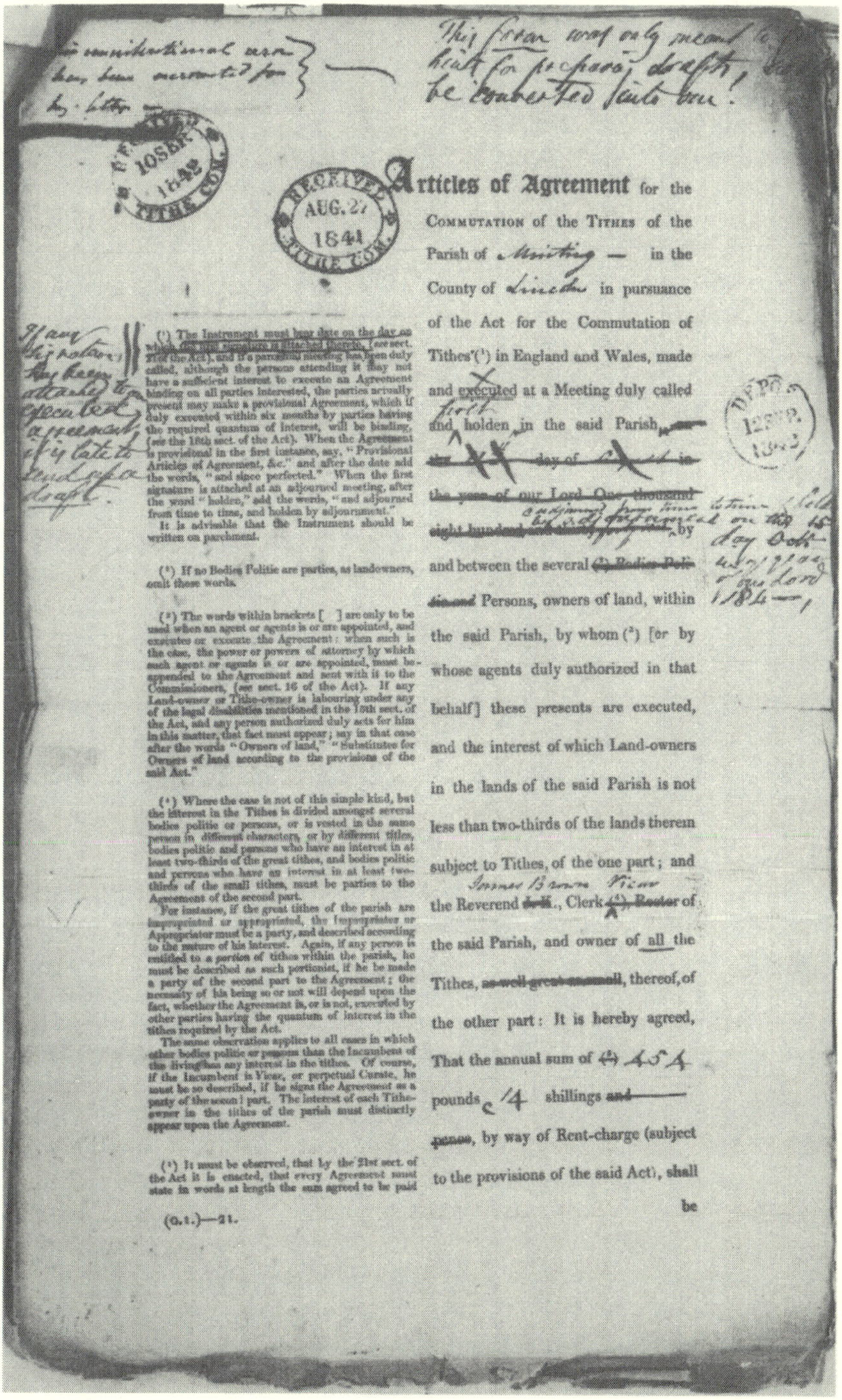

Articles of Agreement for the COMMUTATION of the TITHES of the Parish of ______ in the County of ______ in pursuance of the Act for the Commutation of Tithes(¹) in England and Wales, made and executed at a Meeting duly called and holden in the said Parish, ~~on the ___ day of ___ in the year of our Lord One thousand eight hundred and ___~~, by and between the several ~~(²) Bodies Politic and~~ Persons, owners of land, within the said Parish, by whom (³) [or by whose agents duly authorized in that behalf] these presents are executed, and the interest of which Land-owners in the lands of the said Parish is not less than two-thirds of the lands therein subject to Tithes, of the one part; and the Reverend ~~[illegible]~~, Clerk ~~(⁴), Rector~~ of the said Parish, and owner of the Tithes, ~~as well great as small~~, thereof, of the other part: It is hereby agreed, That the annual sum of (⁵) ______ pounds ______ shillings ~~and ______ pence~~, by way of Rent-charge (subject to the provisions of the said Act), shall be

(¹) The Instrument must bear date on the day on which the last signature is attached thereto, (see sect. 17 of the Act), and if a parochial meeting has been duly called, although the persons attending it may not have a sufficient interest to execute an Agreement binding on all parties interested, the parties actually present may make a provisional Agreement, which if duly executed within six months by parties having the required quantum of interest, will be binding, (see the 18th sect. of the Act). When the Agreement is provisional in the first instance, say, "Provisional Articles of Agreement, &c." and after the date add the words, "and since perfected." When the first signature is attached at an adjourned meeting, after the word "holden," add the words, "and adjourned from time to time, and holden by adjournment."

It is advisable that the Instrument should be written on parchment.

(²) If no Bodies Politic are parties, as landowners, omit those words.

(³) The words within brackets [ ] are only to be used when an agent or agents is or are appointed, and executes or execute the Agreement: when such is the case, the power or powers of attorney by which such agent or agents is or are appointed, must be appended to the Agreement and sent with it to the Commissioners, (see sect. 16 of the Act). If any Land-owner or Tithe-owner is labouring under any of the legal disabilities mentioned in the 19th sect. of the Act, and any person authorized duly acts for him in this matter, that fact must appear; say in that case after the words "Owners of land," "Substitutes for Owners of land according to the provisions of the said Act."

(⁴) Where the case is not of this simple kind, but the interest in the Tithes is divided amongst several bodies politic or persons, or is vested in the same person in different characters, or by different titles, bodies politic and persons who have an interest in at least two-thirds of the great tithes, and bodies politic and persons who have an interest in at least two-thirds of the small tithes, must be parties to the Agreement of the second part.

For instance, if the great tithes of the parish are impropriated or appropriated, the Impropriator or Appropriator must be a party, and described according to the nature of his interest. Again, if any person is entitled to a *portion* of tithes within the parish, he must be described as such portionist, if he be made a party of the second part to the Agreement; the necessity of his being so or not will depend upon the fact, whether the Agreement is, or is not, executed by other parties having the quantum of interest in the tithes required by the Act.

The same observation applies to all cases in which other bodies politic or persons than the Incumbent of the living has any interest in the tithes. Of course, if the Incumbent is Vicar, or perpetual Curate, he must be so described, if he signs the Agreement as a party of the second part. The interest of each Tithe-owner in the tithes of the parish must distinctly appear upon the Agreement.

(⁵) It must be observed, that by the 21st sect. of the Act it is enacted, that every Agreement must state in words at length the sum agreed to be paid

(G.1.)—21.

Table 2.1 *Assistant commissioners, local tithe agents and reports on rent-charge agreements*

County	No. of tithe districts	No. of districts exempt from tithe	No. of reports on agreements	Principal local agent/asst. commissioner & no. of reports compiled		Second ranking local agent/asst. commissioner & no. of reports compiled		No. of other local agents/asst. commissioners
England								
Bedfordshire	128	67	23	J. Pickering	5	F. Browne Browne	4	5
Berkshire	188	31	101	T. C. Parr	35	J. Townsend	10	8
Buckinghamshire	214	70	59	F. Browne Browne	19	J. Townsend	13	7
Cambridgeshire	177	83	67	H. B. Gunning	16	W. Heard	11	10
Cheshire	477	10	278	J. Holder	132	T. Sudworth	54	8
Cornwall	212	–	116	J. Jerwood	70	W. Glasson	44	4
Cumberland	247	45	51	J. J. Rawlinson	24	H. Pilkington	13	6
Derbyshire	316	47	95	R. B. Phillipson	21	F. Martin	20	9
Devonshire	478	10	222	J. Jerwood	122	F. Leigh	73	5
Dorset	283	16	176	G. Bolls	116	J. Jerwood	22	5
Durham	313	16	202	H. Pilkington	101	C. Howard	41	7
Essex	418	17	296	R. Kynaston	63	W. Heard	51	12
Gloucestershire	349	109	122	G. Bolls	37	C. Pym	31	3
Hampshire	354	38	189	A. O. Baker	46	R. Kynaston	23	12
Herefordshire	252	10	154	T. Hoskins	103	C. Pym	27	3
Hertfordshire	138	19	79	W. Heard	37	J. Townsend	11	8
Huntingdonshire	112	48	31	J. West	9	T. S. Woolley	5	5
Kent	417	11	196	T. S. Woolley	46	T. P. Hilder	38	14
Lancashire	469	18	200	F. Martin	82	H. Pilkington	31	6
Leicestershire	353	130	43	J. Pickering	17	T. S. Woolley	13	6
Lincolnshire	757	266	187	J. Pickering	63	T. S. Woolley	47	14
Middlesex	102	16	17	J. M. Mathew	4	F. Browne Browne	3	7
Monmouthshire	144	5	71	T. Hoskins	56	J. Johnes	12	1
Norfolk	732	53	483	J. D. Merest	161	H. B. Gunning	109	11
Northamptonshire	340	162	40	J. West	16	T. S. Woolley	9	4

Northumberland	548	29	274	H. Pilkington	173	J. Donaldson	51	4
Nottinghamshire	278	120	50	J. Pickering	17	T. S. Woolley	11	8
Oxfordshire	267	94	80	T. C. Parr	28	H. Jemmett	13	9
Rutland	59	20	15	E. Greathed	6	J. Pickering	4	3
Shropshire	454	18	208	G. Ashdown	42	G. C. Symons	34	14
Somerset	501	11	333	R. Page	284	C. Pym	37	5
Staffordshire	332	18	137	R. B. Phillipson	26	G. Ashdown	19	15
Suffolk	522	25	355	H. B. Gunning	86	J. D. Merest	64	13
Surrey	150	10	72	J. Pickering	29	H. Meteyard	12	9
Sussex	323	8	188	J. Farncombe	158	T. S. Woolley	11	8
Warwickshire	248	57	70	T. S. Woolley	26	T. S. Woolley Jr.	9	8
Westmorland	98	9	42	J. J. Rawlinson	19	H. Pilkington	11	5
Wiltshire	336	38	182	G. Bolls	144	A. Owen	17	5
Worcestershire	208	49	84	T. Hoskins	43	C. Pym	17	4
York City	36	6	7	C. Howard	7	—	–	–
Yorkshire, E. Riding	352	109	74	C. Howard	43	R. B. Phillipson	8	8
Yorkshire, N. Riding	520	62	203	C. Howard	76	R. B. Phillipson	40	7
Yorkshire, W. Riding	642	96	201	C. Howard	71	R. B. Phillipson	53	9
Wales								
Anglesey	76	2	55	J. Fenton	42	A. Owen	13	–
Brecon	84	3	60	T. Hoskins	52	J. Johnes	8	–
Caernarvon	73	2	57	J. Fenton	50	A. Owen	7	–
Cardigan	74	–	54	T. Hoskins	42	J. Johnes	11	1
Carmarthen	83	–	56	T. Hoskins	29	J. Johnes	26	1
Denbigh	107	–	94	A. Owen	47	J. Fenton	43	2
Flint	42	1	31	A. Owen	18	J. Fenton	8	2
Glamorgan	137	6	52	T. Hoskins	38	J. Johnes	14	–
Merioneth	34	–	24	A. Owen	16	J. Fenton	8	–
Montgomery	75	1	59	J. Fenton	40	A. Owen	17	1
Pembroke	147	5	94	T. Hoskins	55	J. Johnes	37	2
Radnor	53	–	31	T. Hoskins	20	J. Johnes	10	1

Sources: The tithe files of England and Wales (PRO IR 18/1–14829).

party and who with their local understanding would perhaps better gain the respect and confidence of tithe owners and landowners than would a stranger. It is likely also that economy of time and money was of some concern to the Tithe Commission. Assistant commissioners were paid three pounds a day plus accommodation and travel expenses and local agents a fee inclusive of expenses of five guineas per report. Assistant commissioners' time and expenses could be saved by minimising the geographical range over which they worked while local agents on piece rates could press ahead and keep up a good rate of reports if excessive time was not spent travelling. Exceptions to this general pattern of activity were 'senior' assistant tithe commissioners, such as T. S. Woolley who worked in no fewer than 24 counties and was often sent to write a second report where a first agent had delivered a less than adequate piece of work.

Some 6,740 reports on draft agreements by assistant commissioners and local agents are preserved in the tithe files. An overwhelming majority of these agreements were confirmed by the tithe commissioners even in cases where the man on the spot had some reservation about the level of rent-charge agreed. It was also rare for a local agent to challenge an agreement even if his own valuation of the tithes departed quite considerably from the agreed rent-charge, providing he was confident that each 'side' was aware of how their situation related to neighbouring districts. As Eric Evans notes, the Tithe Commission took an agreement voluntarily entered into as *prima facie* evidence of reasonableness.[62]

The deadline established in the act for arriving at an agreement was 1 October 1838. In the event, pressure of work during 1838 was such that the Tithe Commission accepted a number of agreements for confirmation between 1839 and 1841.[63] In the autumn of 1838 the process of compulsory commutation began in districts where attempts to come to an agreement had failed. Moduses, a common cause of lawsuits in the pre-1836 period, were also a frequent cause of tithe owners and tithe payers failing to achieve a voluntary agreement for commutation after 1836.

Compulsory awards of tithe rent-charge

If agreement could not be reached, an assistant tithe commissioner representing the tithe commissioners was empowered to hold a local enquiry, to frame a draft award, hear objections, make amendments where necessary, and finally recommend confirmation of an award which then became binding on the tithe owners and tithe payers. Though there was a sense of inevitability about this process once the commissioners had been invited to proceed to an award (before 1840) or had decided that events required them to intervene and impose an award (after 1840), every opportunity was provided for the various parties to put their case fairly to an assistant commissioner. The Tithe Commission informed the incumbent by letter of its decision to proceed to an award and notified the date on which an assistant commissioner would hold an award meeting in the tithe district. This meeting had to be advertised 21 days in advance by a notice affixed in a prominent place, usually by the minister on the church door. A copy of this notice had to be sent to the Tithe Commission as confirmation that due notice had been given (Fig. 2.4). Tithe owners and tithe payers were also sent an outline of the order of proceedings the assistant commissioner would follow on his visit (Fig. 2.5).[64] In particular, this indicated to tithe owners and landowners what facts the assistant commissioner would require and at what point in the proceedings they would be able to present their cases.

Assistant commissioners based their award on the average value of tithes over the seven years from Christmas 1829 to Christmas 1835 (Clause 37). If a monetary composition had been in effect and good records had been kept, this initial task was straightforward. Problems and strife usually arose where moduses were claimed by farmers or where tithe had been collected in kind. In the latter case, deductions could be made to allow for costs of collection. These were usually 20–25 per cent but might rise to 40 per cent in hilly districts with poor roads, remote from a tithe barn. In many parishes not only were tithes paid to several different tithe owners but payments were made in several different ways, and it was not always certain what constituted a tithe payment. Excluded from the provisions of the act, except in special circumstances to be decided by the commissioners, were Easter offerings, mortuaries or surplice fees, tithes of fish or fishing, personal tithes other than those of milling, mineral tithes, payments in lieu of tithes in the City of London, fixed annual rent-charges in cities or towns and lands whose tithes had previously been commuted or extinguished by acts of parliament. By far the largest number of exemptions were those covered by enclosure awards.

The essential principle enshrined in the awards was that commutation was based on the *actual value* of tithes paid in immediately previous years, not on what an assistant commissioner thought their value ought to have been, though they were able to make some concession where they considered that the actual produce of the land had been affected by extraordinarily high or low farming. A draft award might be challenged by tithe payers or tithe owners on grounds of error or dissatisfaction. An appeal meeting would then be held and a supplementary award drafted if the assistant commissioner upheld the appeal (Fig. 2.6). Once the awarded rent-charge was confirmed by the tithe commissioners it was binding on all parties.

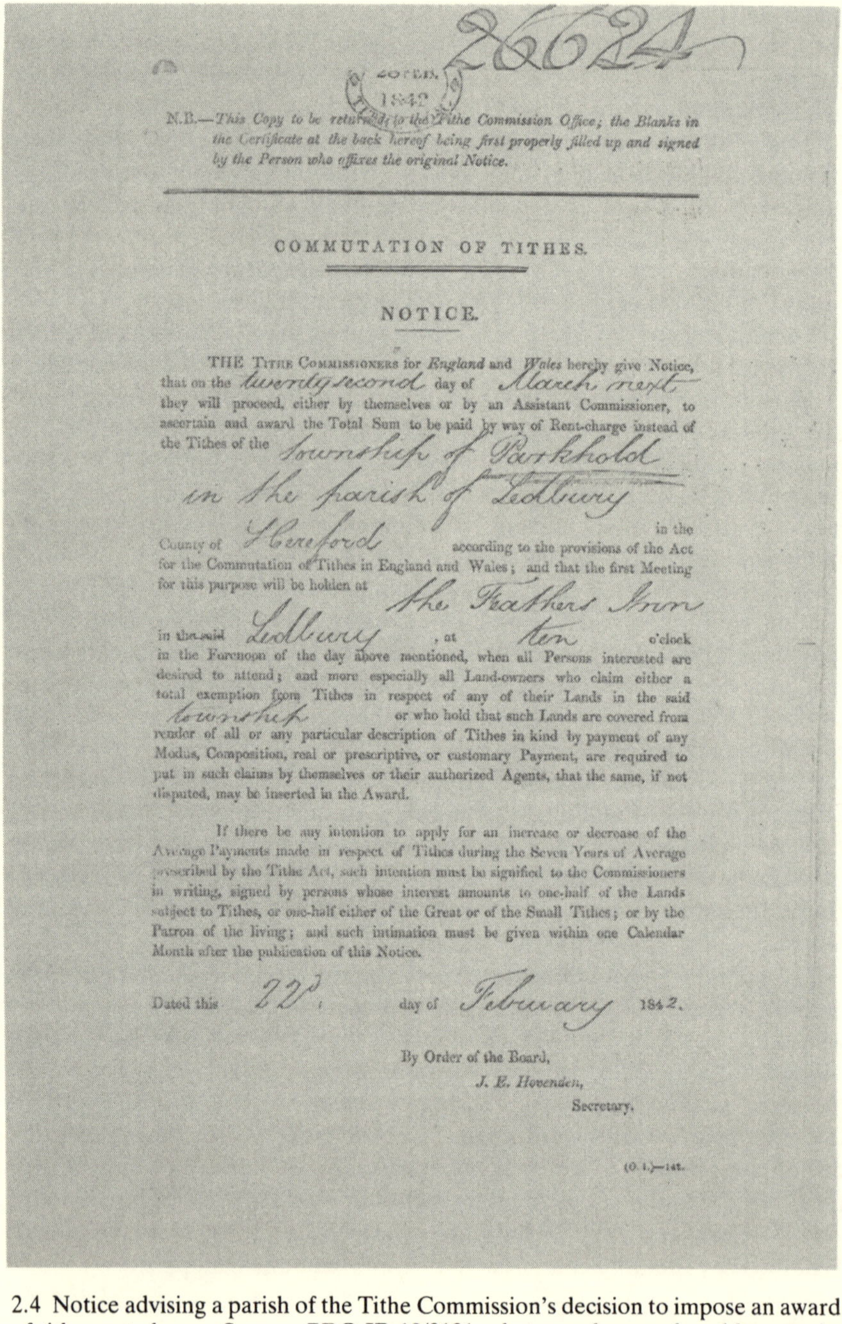

26624

COPIED. 1842

N.B.—*This Copy to be returned to the Tithe Commission Office; the Blanks in the Certificate at the back hereof being first properly filled up and signed by the Person who affixes the original Notice.*

COMMUTATION OF TITHES.

NOTICE.

THE TITHE COMMISSIONERS for *England* and *Wales* hereby give Notice, that on the twenty second day of March next they will proceed, either by themselves or by an Assistant Commissioner, to ascertain and award the Total Sum to be paid by way of Rent-charge instead of the Tithes of the Township of Parkhold in the parish of Ledbury in the County of Hereford according to the provisions of the Act for the Commutation of Tithes in England and Wales; and that the first Meeting for this purpose will be holden at The Feathers Inn in the said Ledbury, at ten o'clock in the Forenoon of the day above mentioned, when all Persons interested are desired to attend; and more especially all Land-owners who claim either a total exemption from Tithes in respect of any of their Lands in the said township or who hold that such Lands are covered from render of all or any particular description of Tithes in kind by payment of any Modus, Composition, real or prescriptive, or customary Payment, are required to put in such claims by themselves or their authorized Agents, that the same, if not disputed, may be inserted in the Award.

If there be any intention to apply for an increase or decrease of the Average Payments made in respect of Tithes during the Seven Years of Average prescribed by the Tithe Act, such intention must be signified to the Commissioners in writing, signed by persons whose interest amounts to one-half of the Lands subject to Tithes, or one-half either of the Great or of the Small Tithes; or by the Patron of the living; and such intimation must be given within one Calendar Month after the publication of this Notice.

Dated this 22d. day of February 1842.

By Order of the Board,
J. E. Hovenden,
Secretary.

(O. 1.)—1st.

2.4 Notice advising a parish of the Tithe Commission's decision to impose an award of tithe rent-charge. Source: PRO IR 18/3131; photograph reproduced by permission of the Keeper, Public Record Office.

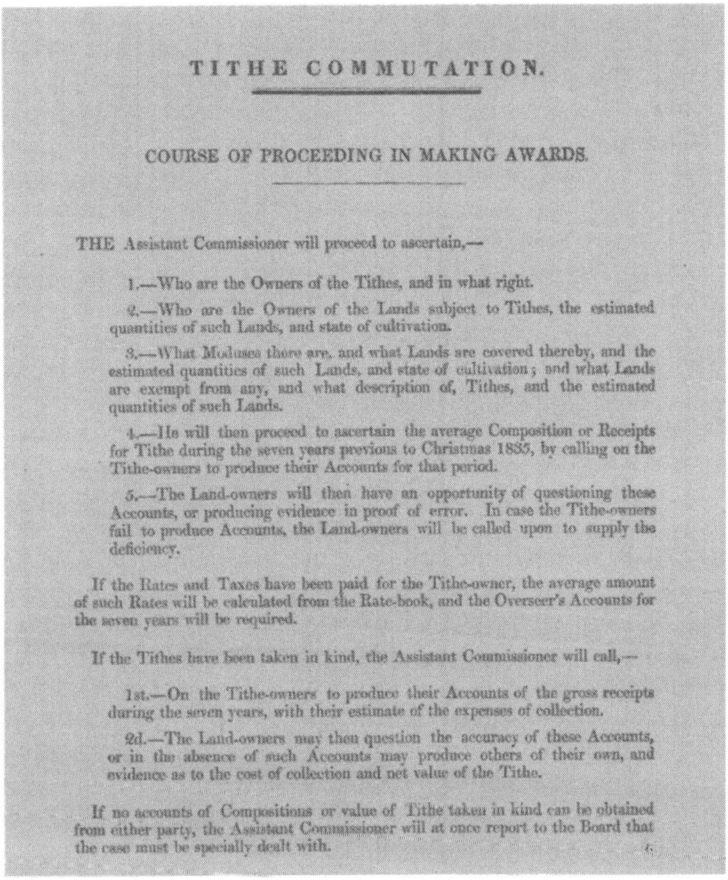

TITHE COMMUTATION.

COURSE OF PROCEEDING IN MAKING AWARDS.

THE Assistant Commissioner will proceed to ascertain,—

1.—Who are the Owners of the Tithes, and in what right.

2.—Who are the Owners of the Lands subject to Tithes, the estimated quantities of such Lands, and state of cultivation.

3.—What Moduses there are, and what Lands are covered thereby, and the estimated quantities of such Lands, and state of cultivation; and what Lands are exempt from any, and what description of, Tithes, and the estimated quantities of such Lands.

4.—He will then proceed to ascertain the average Composition or Receipts for Tithe during the seven years previous to Christmas 1835, by calling on the Tithe-owners to produce their Accounts for that period.

5.—The Land-owners will then have an opportunity of questioning these Accounts, or producing evidence in proof of error. In case the Tithe-owners fail to produce Accounts, the Land-owners will be called upon to supply the deficiency.

If the Rates and Taxes have been paid for the Tithe-owner, the average amount of such Rates will be calculated from the Rate-book, and the Overseer's Accounts for the seven years will be required.

If the Tithes have been taken in kind, the Assistant Commissioner will call,—

1st.—On the Tithe-owners to produce their Accounts of the gross receipts during the seven years, with their estimate of the expenses of collection.

2d.—The Land-owners may then question the accuracy of these Accounts, or in the absence of such Accounts may produce others of their own, and evidence as to the cost of collection and net value of the Tithe.

If no accounts of Compositions or value of Tithe taken in kind can be obtained from either party, the Assistant Commissioner will at once report to the Board that the case must be specially dealt with.

2.5 Order of proceedings followed by an assistant tithe commissioner when framing an award. Source: Shropshire Record Office 3651/T/I; photograph reproduced by courtesy of Shropshire Record Office.

The apportionment of tithe rent-charge

Once an agreement or an award was confirmed by the commissioners, the rent-charge could be apportioned over the parish lands. Landowners had a right to agree upon the principles of apportionment but, if none were agreed upon, rent-charge was apportioned according to the average titheable produce and the productive quality of the land (Clause 33). This clause gave landowners a right to apportion rent-charge property-by-property or field-by-field. Landowners could also choose between one gross sum for their whole estate or could assign rent-charge in portions to each farm or occupation. Thus the rent-charge for the parish of Wye in Kent was apportioned among farms, and parcels of woodland, formerly exempt, came to be charged jointly with titheable lands belonging to farms of which they formed parts.[65] Without instructions to the contrary, a valuer carrying out an apportionment would be inclined to adopt the simplest method, namely apportioning in gross upon estates. However, advice given in contemporary guides and legal manuals usually favoured a field-by-field apportionment which, if a little more expensive in the short-term, would be beneficial to landowners in the long-term when land was sold. For example, G. H. Whalley stated in his commentary on the Tithe Act, 'there are, of course, cases in which the first and simplest mode may be preferable, and hence the latitude of discretion accorded, but these are exceptions, and every landowner should satisfy himself that his case is such an exception, before he permits the apportionment to be so completed'.[66] Whichever method was used, and a wide variety or combination of practices might be adopted, an apportionment was recorded on a map and in a written schedule. These maps and schedules of apportionment together constitute what is usually termed by historians 'the parish tithe survey'.

It was inevitably difficult to apportion the rent-charge equitably among lands of differing quality and differing utilisation, not because the actual use of the land was difficult to determine, but because its titheable produce was likely to change from time to time. In practice, there was no way of assessing the probability of lands being converted to other uses, and the only alternative to rating all lands alike at the same value was to differentiate them on the basis of their observed state of cultivation.

The specifications of tithe maps and the detailed nature of apportionment documents are discussed in chapter 3, but the essential purpose of a survey was to provide an accurate measurement of the acreage of each parcel of land, or tithe area, and to record its observed state of cultivation. For the purpose of valuation, the state of cultivation was entered as 'arable', 'grass', 'meadow', 'pasture', 'common', 'wood', 'coppice', 'plantation', 'orchard', 'hop ground' or 'market garden'. There were, of course, different interpretations of these categories and additional categories inserted in some localities. In general, the most important distinction was between arable land, regularly ploughed and cropped, whose tithes amounted to about one-fifth of the value of the rent, and permanent grassland, whose tithes represented less than one-eighth of the rent. In the west of England and in Wales, 'arable' appears also to have included all ley grasses. In many parishes no distinction was made between meadow that was mown for hay once a year or more, and pasture that was normally used exclusively for grazing, yet the assessment of an acre of meadowland might be as much as eight times that of

---

2.6 Supplementary award made after an award appeal. Source: PRO IR 18/107; photograph reproduced by permission of the Keeper, Public Record Office.

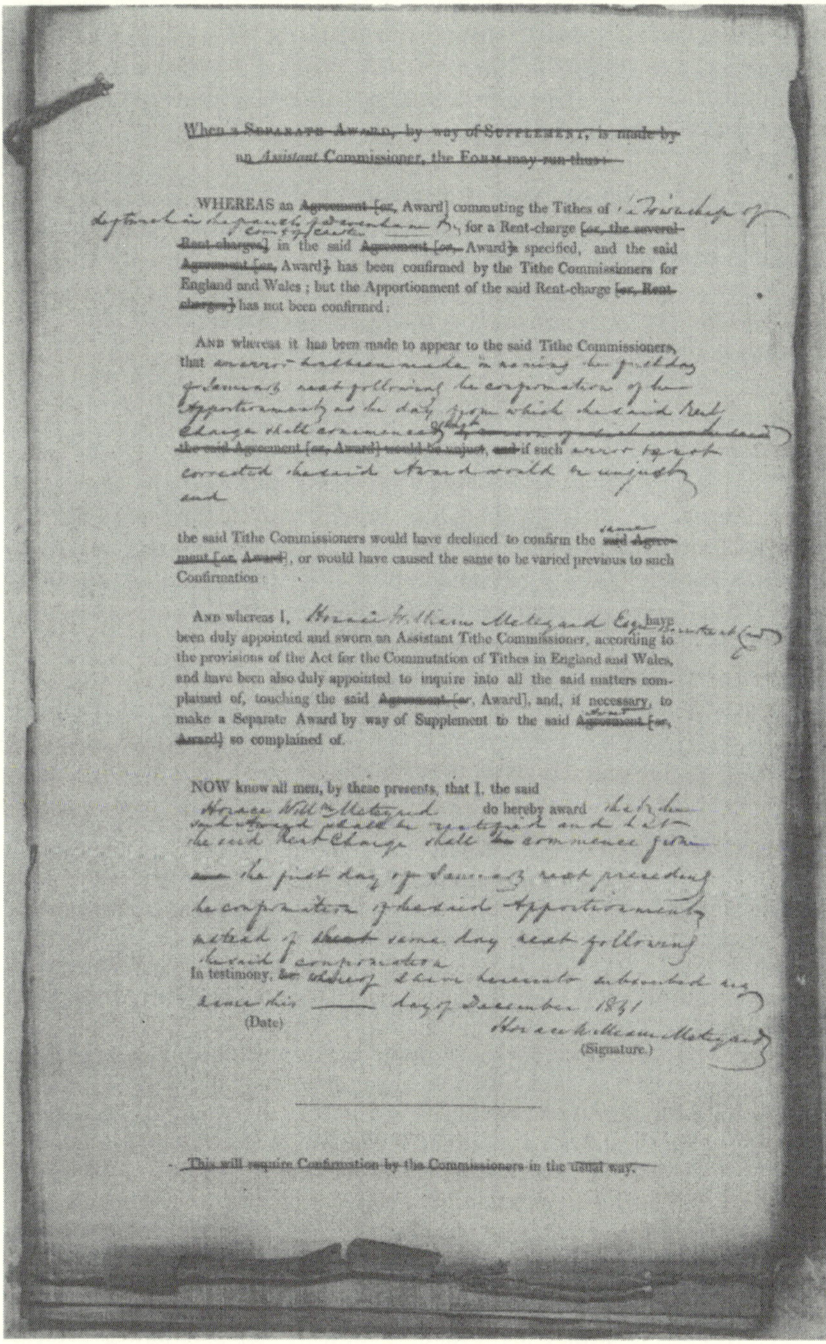

When a SEPARATE AWARD, by way of SUPPLEMENT, is made by an *Assistant* Commissioner, the FORM may run thus:

WHEREAS an Agreement [or, Award] commuting the Tithes of ... for a Rent-charge [or, the several Rent-charges] in the said Agreement [or, Award] specified, and the said Agreement [or, Award] has been confirmed by the Tithe Commissioners for England and Wales; but the Apportionment of the said Rent-charge [or, Rent-charges] has not been confirmed:

AND whereas it has been made to appear to the said Tithe Commissioners, that ... the said Agreement [or, Award] would be unjust, and if such error be not corrected the said Award would be unjust and

the said Tithe Commissioners would have declined to confirm the same said Agreement [or, Award], or would have caused the same to be varied previous to such Confirmation:

AND whereas I, Horace William Meteyard Esq. have been duly appointed and sworn an Assistant Tithe Commissioner, according to the provisions of the Act for the Commutation of Tithes in England and Wales, and have been also duly appointed to inquire into all the said matters complained of, touching the said Agreement [or, Award], and, if necessary, to make a Separate Award by way of Supplement to the said Agreement [or, Award] so complained of.

NOW know all men, by these presents, that I, the said Horace Will.m Meteyard do hereby award ... the said Rent Charge shall commence from the first day of January next preceding ...

In testimony whereof I have hereunto subscribed my name this ... day of December 1831

(Date)

Horace William Meteyard

(Signature.)

This will require Confirmation by the Commissioners in the usual way.

pasture. Woods, coppices and plantations were not always separately distinguished and were omitted in many parishes where they were tithe-free. Lands devoted to orchards, hop grounds or market gardens were usually classified according to their actual state of cultivation, but they might be rated as arable or grass and charged with a supplementary or extraordinary rent-charge.

A special problem confronted the commissioners in apportioning the rent-charge of Lammas lands and commons. These were owned in severalty for only a part of a year; from Lammas to Candlemas they lay open to common grazing. At High Wycombe in Buckinghamshire the rent-charge was apportioned among two or more owners of the same plot of land in such circumstances. Similar considerations affected apportionments on gated or stinted pastures.

In districts with large acreages of unimproved land, such as moorland, which generated little titheable produce, or extensive tracts of modus land, landowners could save some expense of surveying and valuing by apportioning the rent-charge due to these lands on other land owned by them, usually improved farm land around their farm house, provided that the total rent-charge on that land did not exceed one-third of its annual rent. The residue (but perhaps the greater area) of their holding was deemed nominally tithe-free and did not need to be mapped.[67]

Apportionment was not always a straightforward task of obtaining acreages of estates and assigning relative proportions of a global rent-charge to them, as, at its simplest and in theory, was all that the act required. Joseph Bennett of Tutbury noted some of the problems that he and fellow tithe apportioners faced:

> The difficulties of effecting agreements between the tithe owners and tithe payers, are as nothing in comparison with the difficulties of fairly and equitably apportioning the gross sum among the landowners, to the satisfaction of all. The landowners are mostly of one mind while they have the tithe owner to contend with; but when that question is disposed of, they begin to think of their individual interests and are opposed to each other as to the principle upon which the rent charge should be divided.
>
> The man who has been occupying the estate in a manner to produce the greatest value of tithe, contends that he has too large a proportion of tillage to form the proper basis of adjustment for ever; and on the other hand the man who has been in the contrary extreme and has occupied his estate so as to yield the tithe owner very little, or perhaps nothing, contends that the apportionment should be made on the basis of the existing mode of occupation, and that because he has paid little or nothing for seven years, or for twenty years, or more, he cannot be charged with what he has not paid.[68]

Completed apportionments were made available for inspection by landowners (Fig. 2.7) who had a right of appeal. Apportionment appeal

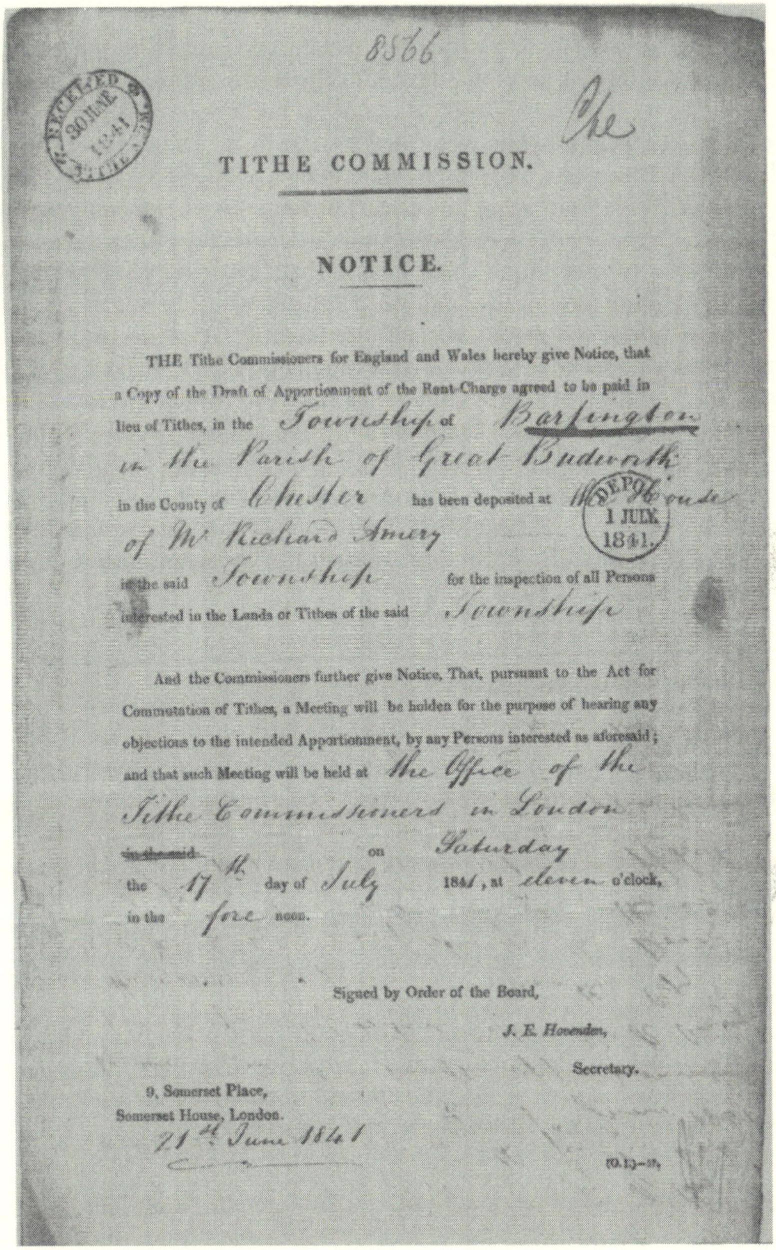

8566

The

TITHE COMMISSION.

NOTICE.

THE Tithe Commissioners for England and Wales hereby give Notice, that a Copy of the Draft of Apportionment of the Rent-Charge agreed to be paid in lieu of Tithes, in the Township of Bartington in the Parish of Great Budworth in the County of Chester has been deposited at the House of Mr Richard Amery in the said Township for the inspection of all Persons interested in the Lands or Tithes of the said Township

DEPOT 1 JULY 1841

And the Commissioners further give Notice, That, pursuant to the Act for Commutation of Tithes, a Meeting will be holden for the purpose of hearing any objections to the intended Apportionment, by any Persons interested as aforesaid; and that such Meeting will be held at the Office of the Tithe Commissioners in London ~~in the said~~ on Saturday the 17th day of July 1841, at eleven o'clock, in the fore noon.

Signed by Order of the Board,

J. E. Hovenden,

Secretary.

9, Somerset Place,
Somerset House, London.
21st June 1841

(O.1.)—18.

2.7 Notice declaring that a completed apportionment was available for landowners' inspection. Source: PRO IR 18/13721; photograph reproduced by permission of the Keeper, Public Record Office.

meetings were held in the parish in the presence of an assistant commissioner and minutes of these meetings are usually preserved in the parish tithe file. 'Apportionment appeal meetings could be stormy affairs, as it was there that landowners were able to appreciate for the first time only when the draft apportionment was complete what their precise burden would be.'[69] To set aside an apportionment, assistant commissioners needed concrete evidence that an apportioner had acted unfairly or incompetently. The only appeals that had much chance of success were those where it could be demonstrated to an assistant commissioner's satisfaction that there was an inequality of charge on lands of similar use and those appeals where it was alleged that there were boundary errors or land-use errors.[70] It is an unfortunate reflection on valuers and surveyors who were employed to make apportionments, that such errors were sometimes detected, either by an assistant commissioner at an appeal meeting or by Lieutenant Dawson's staff in London prior to confirmation of apportionment and map. The compilation of a 'parish tithe survey' was entrusted to private valuers and civilian surveyors appointed and paid for by landowners. The Tithe Commission's role in this final process was one of supervising, checking, arbitrating and confirming.

Tithe valuers and land surveyors

An apportionment of agreed or awarded tithe rent-charge involved surveyors at two levels: first, as valuers to assess the quality and use of land and apportion proportions of the global rent-charge in accordance with principles established by landowners and, secondly, as land surveyors to construct a map and book of reference of a district to serve as a permanent record of the apportionment. Where adequate maps of a district existed (see chapter 3), only valuation was required and landowners could dispense with professional help entirely. More usually a new map had to be made or some older survey brought up-to-date.

> It is a common practice with landowners to appoint a surveyor to make the map, at the same time that they appoint the valuer to apportion. It should be borne in mind that the map, being part of the business of the apportionment, is left to the valuer to prepare by the very terms of his employment (Clause 34), and whether he will adopt the map so made by the surveyor is a matter entirely in his own discretion.[71]

In practice, the normal procedure was for landowners to appoint the same individual or firm for the survey, map and apportionment and the Tithe Commission provided *pro formas* of contractual agreements which landowners and surveyors might use. These agreements specified the principles of apportionment to be employed, levels of remuneration, timetable of work and such indemnities as seemed appropriate (Fig. 2.8).

Lieutenant R. K. Dawson, the assistant commissioner seconded from the Royal Engineers to organise and superintend the tithe surveys, was confident that the mapping as well as the valuation could be carried out by civilian surveyors. He thought that there were sufficient country surveyors immediately available in 1836 to initiate the work and that these could train further recruits as the work proceeded.[72] Dawson's recommendations for civilian control of the tithe surveys flew in the face of a victory for military control of the Survey of Ireland. Colonel Thomas Colby, director of the Ordnance Survey, was not satisfied with the quality of work produced by civilian surveyors while Dawson, on the other hand, remained impressed with the standards of his own civil assistants on the Irish Survey.[73] But he was also aware of some common failings of country surveyors. His key to successful employment of civilians was a strict system of supervision from London, the issue of sheets of detailed instructions and advice, and careful checking of completed work against field notes (see chapter 3). Testing the accuracy of survey work associated with apportionment of rent-charge was a fundamental component of the procedure devised by the tithe commissioners for implementing the Tithe Commutation Act.

Apportioners and surveyors were appointed by landowners usually after placing advertisements in the local press (see Fig. 2.9).[74] For example, the tithes of the parish of Drewsteignton in Devon were commuted by agreement in 1838 and advertisements for an apportioner and valuer of the Poor Rate and for a surveyor were placed in the *Trewman's Exeter Flying Post* at the end of the year. A valuer was appointed to apportion the tithes in January and he agreed to complete his work within three months of receiving a map of the parish from the surveyor. The landowners' solicitor received at least four offers to map Drewsteignton, one from a London address, but they appointed a local man, William Jole of Plymouth, at the end of January 1839.[75]

The employment of a local surveyor as at Drewsteignton was the usual practice. All but one of the Kent tithe maps which bear the name of their surveyor were produced by men living in London or the county itself. The sole exception is the map of the Wealden parish of Woodchurch, the work of J. McLachlan of Stowmarket in Suffolk. On Kent maps, 67 surveyors are named but the overwhelming majority produced only one or two plans of parishes near their homes. Notable, however, are 5 surveyors who between them made a considerable contribution to the tithe survey of Kent. The districts in which they worked are indicated on Fig. 2.10. Of the 5 firms, one in particular stands out. Thomas Thurston of Ashford produced at least 58 maps and worked in all parts of the county. Not all his maps were entirely new surveys, however, as most of the Romney and Walland Marsh maps were revised either from surveys made by Thomas Hogben in 1760–5 or from N. and F. Giles' surveys of 1812–13. Lieutenant Dawson examined

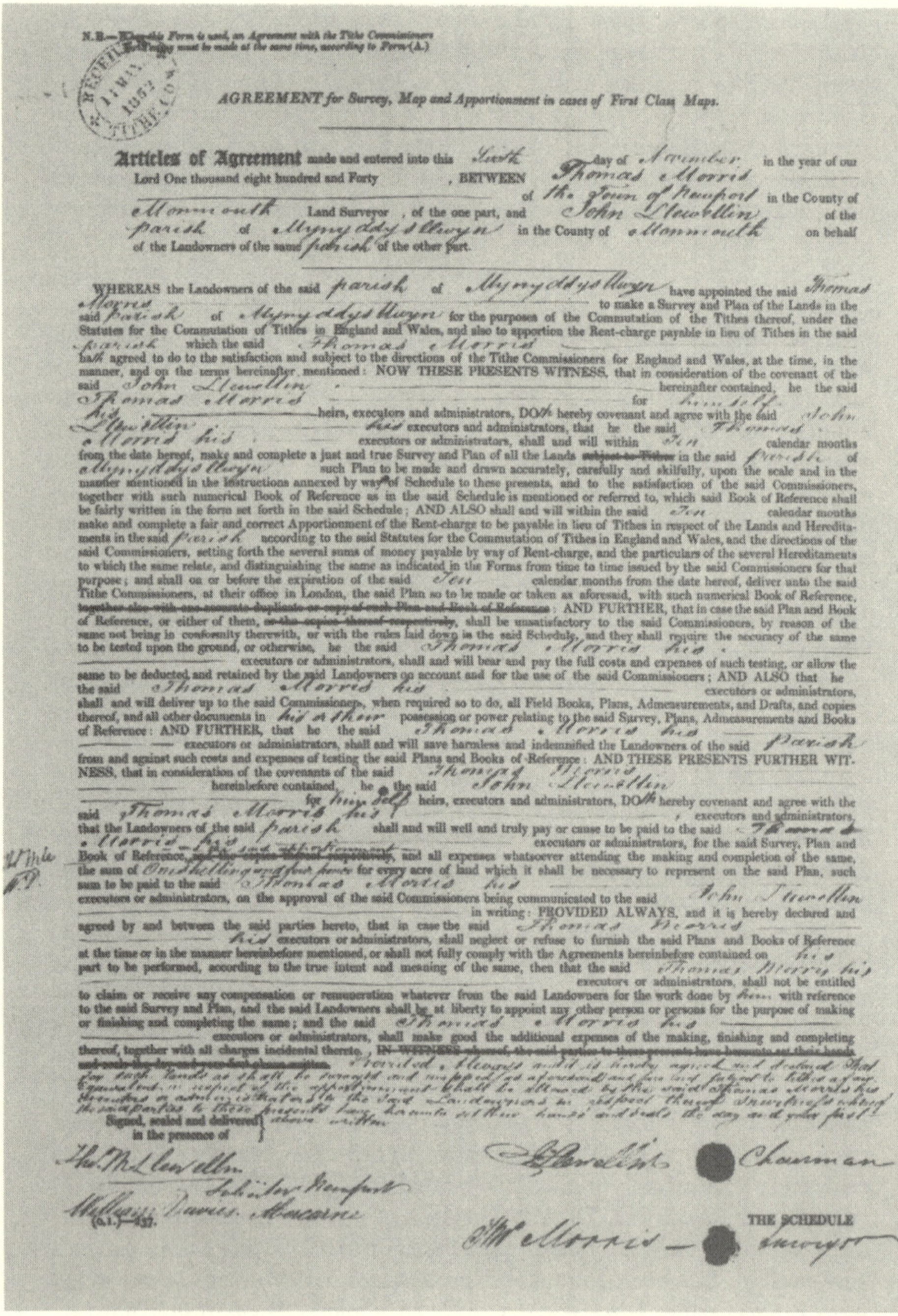

N.B.—When this Form is used, an Agreement with the Tithe Commissioners must be made at the same time, according to Form (A.)

AGREEMENT *for Survey, Map and Apportionment in cases of First Class Maps.*

Articles of Agreement made and entered into this Sixth day of November in the year of our Lord One thousand eight hundred and Forty , BETWEEN Thomas Morris of the Town of Newport in the County of Monmouth Land Surveyor , of the one part, and John Llewellin of the parish of Mynyddyslwyn in the County of Monmouth on behalf of the Landowners of the same parish of the other part.

WHEREAS the Landowners of the said parish of Mynyddyslwyn have appointed the said Thomas Morris to make a Survey and Plan of the Lands in the said Parish of Mynyddyslwyn for the purposes of the Commutation of the Tithes thereof, under the Statutes for the Commutation of Tithes in England and Wales, and also to apportion the Rent-charge payable in lieu of Tithes in the said parish which the said Thomas Morris hath agreed to do to the satisfaction and subject to the directions of the Tithe Commissioners for England and Wales, at the time, in the manner, and on the terms hereinafter mentioned: NOW THESE PRESENTS WITNESS, that in consideration of the covenant of the said John Llewellin hereinafter contained, he the said Thomas Morris for himself his heirs, executors and administrators, DOth hereby covenant and agree with the said John Llewellin his executors and administrators, that he the said Thomas Morris his executors or administrators, shall and will within Ten calendar months from the date hereof, make and complete a just and true Survey and Plan of all the Lands ~~subject to Tithes~~ in the said Parish of Mynyddyslwyn such Plan to be made and drawn accurately, carefully and skilfully, upon the scale and in the manner mentioned in the Instructions annexed by way of Schedule to these presents, and to the satisfaction of the said Commissioners, together with such numerical Book of Reference as in the said Schedule is mentioned or referred to, which said Book of Reference shall be fairly written in the form set forth in the said Schedule; AND ALSO shall and will within the said Ten calendar months make and complete a fair and correct Apportionment of the Rent-charge to be payable in lieu of Tithes in respect of the Lands and Hereditaments in the said parish according to the said Statutes for the Commutation of Tithes in England and Wales, and the directions of the said Commissioners, setting forth the several sums of money payable by way of Rent-charge, and the particulars of the several Hereditaments to which the same relate, and distinguishing the same as indicated in the Forms from time to time issued by the said Commissioners for that purpose; and shall on or before the expiration of the said Ten calendar months from the date hereof, deliver unto the said Tithe Commissioners, at their office in London, the said Plan so to be made or taken as aforesaid, with such numerical Book of Reference, ~~together also with one accurate duplicate or copy of such Plan and Book of Reference~~: AND FURTHER, that in case the said Plan and Book of Reference, or either of them, ~~or the copies thereof respectively~~, shall be unsatisfactory to the said Commissioners, by reason of the same not being in conformity therewith, or with the rules laid down in the said Schedule, and they shall require the accuracy of the same to be tested upon the ground, or otherwise, he the said Thomas Morris his executors or administrators, shall and will bear and pay the full costs and expenses of such testing, or allow the same to be deducted and retained by the said Landowners on account and for the use of the said Commissioners; AND ALSO that he the said Thomas Morris his executors or administrators, shall and will deliver up to the said Commissioners, when required so to do, all Field Books, Plans, Admeasurements, and Drafts, and copies thereof, and all other documents in his or their possession or power relating to the said Survey, Plans, Admeasurements and Books of Reference: AND FURTHER, that he the said Thomas Morris his executors or administrators, shall and will save harmless and indemnified the Landowners of the said Parish from and against such costs and expenses of testing the said Plans and Books of Reference: AND THESE PRESENTS FURTHER WITNESS, that in consideration of the covenants of the said Thomas Morris hereinbefore contained, he the said John Llewellin for himself his heirs, executors and administrators, DOth hereby covenant and agree with the said Thomas Morris his executors and administrators, that the Landowners of the said parish shall and will well and truly pay or cause to be paid to the said Thomas Morris his executors or administrators, for the said Survey, Plan and Book of Reference, ~~and the copies thereof respectively~~ and Apportionment, and all expenses whatsoever attending the making and completion of the same, the sum of One shilling and four pence for every acre of land which it shall be necessary to represent on the said Plan, such sum to be paid to the said Thomas Morris his executors or administrators, on the approval of the said Commissioners being communicated to the said John Llewellin in writing: PROVIDED ALWAYS, and it is hereby declared and agreed by and between the said parties hereto, that in case the said Thomas Morris his executors or administrators, shall neglect or refuse to furnish the said Plans and Books of Reference at the time or in the manner hereinbefore mentioned, or shall not fully comply with the Agreements hereinbefore contained on his part to be performed, according to the true intent and meaning of the same, then that the said Thomas Morris his executors or administrators, shall not be entitled to claim or receive any compensation or remuneration whatever from the said Landowners for the work done by him with reference to the said Survey and Plan, and the said Landowners shall be at liberty to appoint any other person or persons for the purpose of making or finishing and completing the same; and the said Thomas Morris his executors or administrators, shall make good the additional expenses of the making, finishing and completing thereof, together with all charges incidental thereto. ~~IN WITNESS whereof, the said parties to these presents have hereunto set their hands and seals the day and year first above written.~~ Provided Always and it is hereby agreed and declared that ... the said parties to these presents have hereunto set their hands and seals the day and year first above written

Signed, sealed and delivered in the presence of

Thos. M. Llewellin, Solicitor Newport

William Davies, Abercarne

J. Llewellin, Chairman

Thos. Morris — Surveyor

THE SCHEDULE

(O.I.)—137.

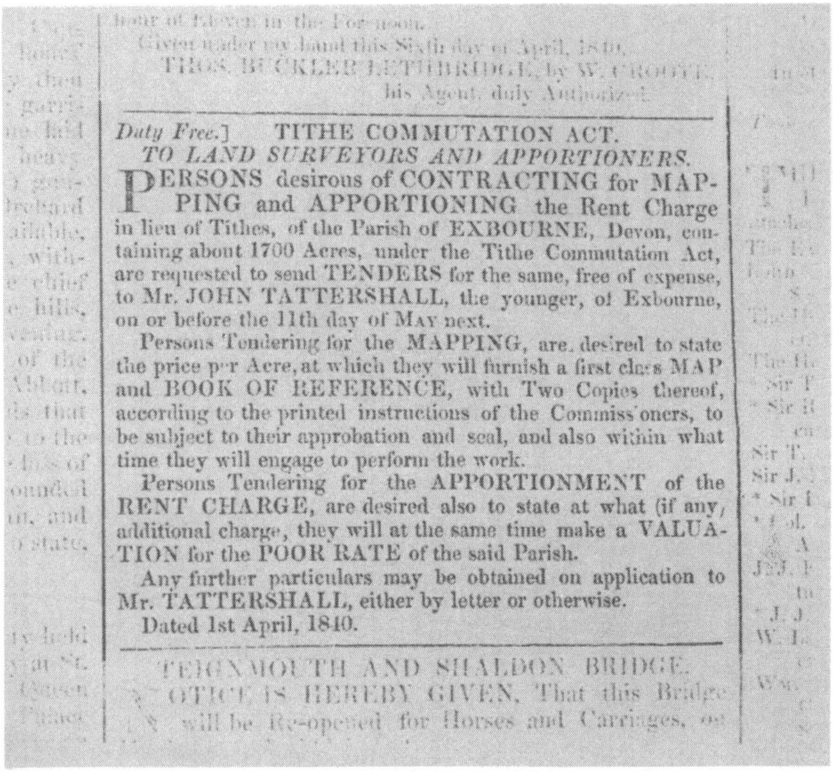

Duty Free.] TITHE COMMUTATION ACT.
TO LAND SURVEYORS AND APPORTIONERS.

PERSONS desirous of CONTRACTING for MAPPING and APPORTIONING the Rent Charge in lieu of Tithes, of the Parish of EXBOURNE, Devon, containing about 1700 Acres, under the Tithe Commutation Act, are requested to send TENDERS for the same, free of expense, to Mr. JOHN TATTERSHALL, the younger, of Exbourne, on or before the 11th day of MAY next.

Persons Tendering for the MAPPING, are desired to state the price per Acre, at which they will furnish a first class MAP and BOOK OF REFERENCE, with Two Copies thereof, according to the printed instructions of the Commissioners, to be subject to their approbation and seal, and also within what time they will engage to perform the work.

Persons Tendering for the APPORTIONMENT of the RENT CHARGE, are desired also to state at what (if any,) additional charge, they will at the same time make a VALUATION for the POOR RATE of the said Parish.

Any further particulars may be obtained on application to Mr. TATTERSHALL, either by letter or otherwise.

Dated 1st April, 1840.

TEIGNMOUTH AND SHALDON BRIDGE.
NOTICE IS HEREBY GIVEN, That this Bridge will be Re-opened for Horses and Carriages, on

2.9 Advertisement placed in *Trewman's Exeter Flying Post*, 16 April 1840, for a surveyor and apportioner at Exbourne, Devon. Photograph reproduced by courtesy of Devon and Exeter Institution.

these maps and acceded to the landowners' request that they form the basis of commutation surveys. Thurston made tracings of them at a scale of six chains to an inch (13.3 inches to a mile) and brought them up to date.[76] The works of the four other surveyors named on Fig. 2.10 show a much more restricted distribution. Frederick and Henry Drayson did most of their tithe-commutation work in the Faversham area of east Kent but were also employed by some Wealden and north-west Kent landowners. Alexander Doull's contracts were principally in north Kent while the tithe mapping of

2.8 Agreement for survey, map and apportionment in cases of first class maps. Source: PRO IR 18/14586; photograph reproduced by permission of the Keeper, Public Record Office.

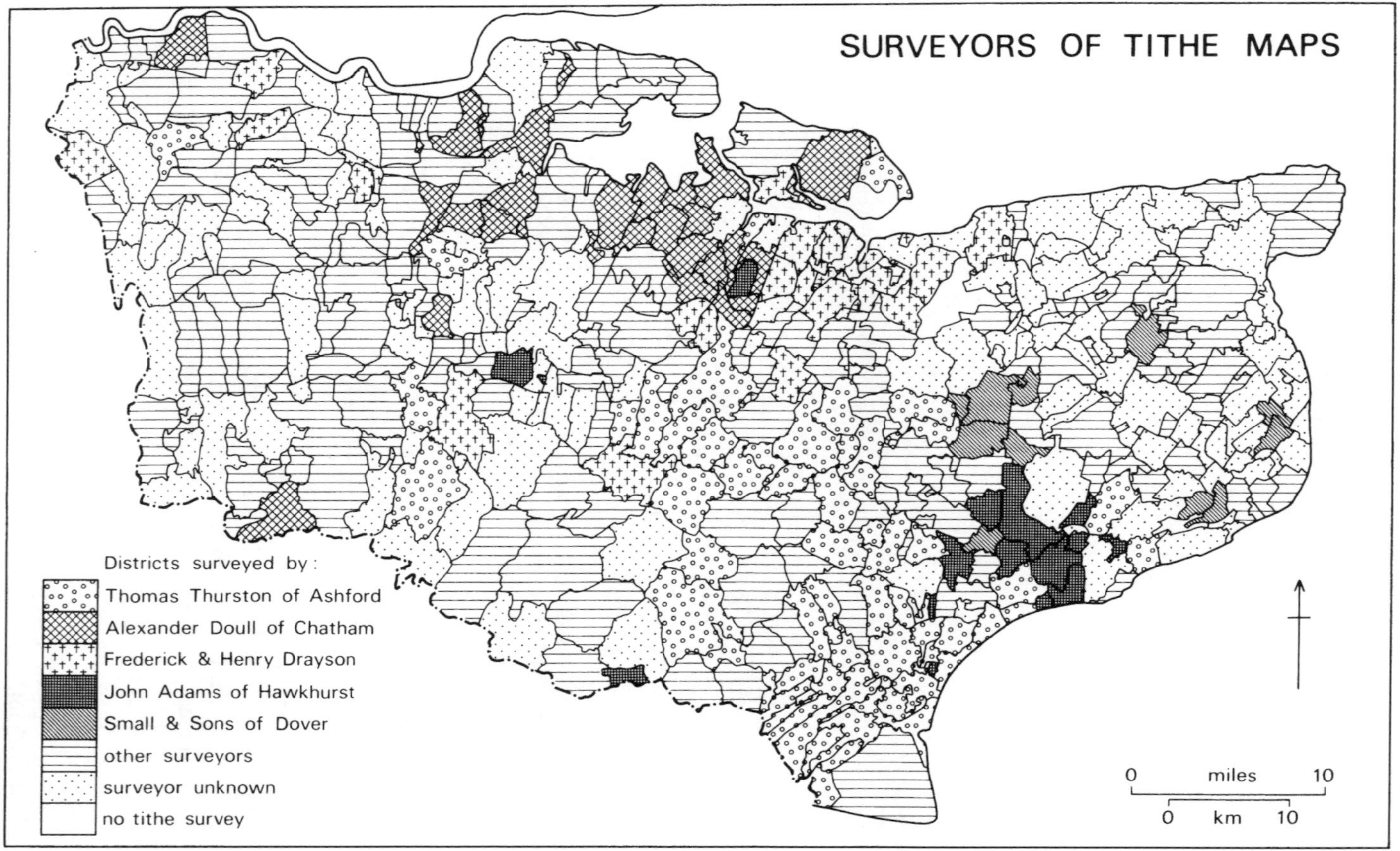

2.10 The surveyors of Kent tithe maps. Source: tithe maps.

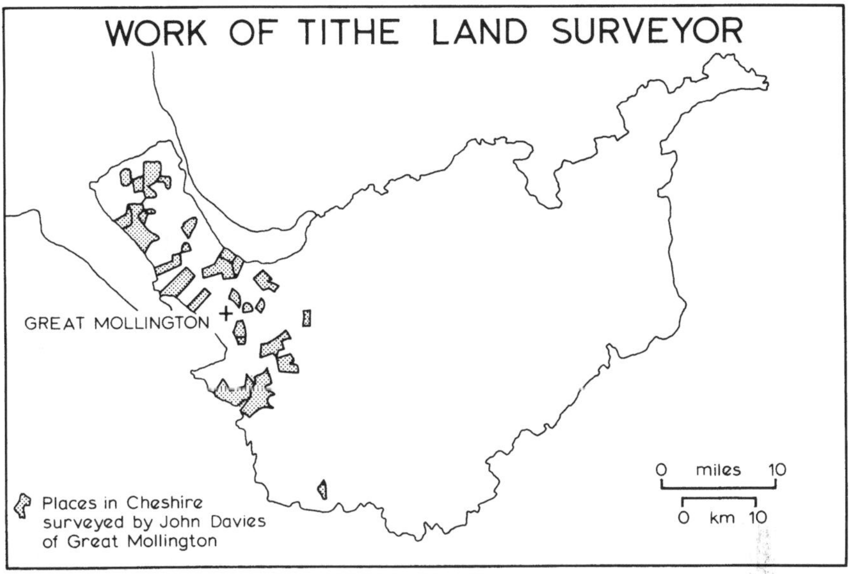

2.11 Places in Cheshire surveyed by John Davies of Great Mollington. Data provided by Mr P. Laxton, University of Liverpool.

Small and Sons and John Adams was confined mainly to the east of the county.[77]

This picture of landowners employing local men with local knowledge to apportion their tithe rent-charge and map their lands is repeated across the country. John Davies of Great Mollington who prepared at least 30 tithe maps in Cheshire conducted most of his commissions around his home parish in the Wirral (Fig. 2.11).[78] Most Essex tithe maps were made by local surveyors such as Robert Baker of Writtle, Gilbert and Tayspill of Colchester and J. King and Son of Saffron Walden.[79] Similarly, Brian Dittmer found that of 93 maps covering north-west Wiltshire whose surveyor was named, 38 were drawn by Chippenham men and 19 by Cirencester surveyors.[80]

Valuers, as distinct from surveyors, who acted as both apportioners and map-makers, also practised locally.[81] Many were men of wide experience and deep knowledge of local farming. John Farncombe, who considered himself 'extensively engaged in the apportionment of the rent-charges' in Sussex was also 'employed by the tithe commissioners as their usual local agent for the county, in reporting on agreements for the Commutation of tithes'. He had also farmed 'a great many soils and systems applicable thereto' and had been a valuer for twenty-five years when he wrote the Royal Agricultural Society of England's Prize Essay 'On the farming of Sussex' in 1850.[82]

The progress of tithe commutation

Almost all the 11,800 tithe apportionments and maps for England and Wales were confirmed within twenty years of the Tithe Act while a majority had been completed as early as the end of 1844. The report of the tithe commissioners to the House of Commons for 1856 records only seven apportionments still in progress.[83] The essential data from the 'Abstract of Tithe Proceedings' which accompanied their report for that year are reproduced in Table 2.2. The progress of the commissioners' work can be judged from Figs. 2.12, 2.13 and 2.14, compiled from six-monthly and later annual returns of tithes commuted in each county published in the House of Commons sessional papers.

The first parochial meeting for commutation of tithes was held on 29 September 1836 and the first agreement was received on 27 October. By the end of February 1837, the tithe commissioners had received 38 voluntary agreements but had been unable to approve any of the maps which recorded the details of apportionment.[84] At this date the Tithe Act was very much a dead letter, although efforts were made to conceal this fact from the public. On 16 February 1837, Sir Edward Knatchbull questioned Lord John Russell

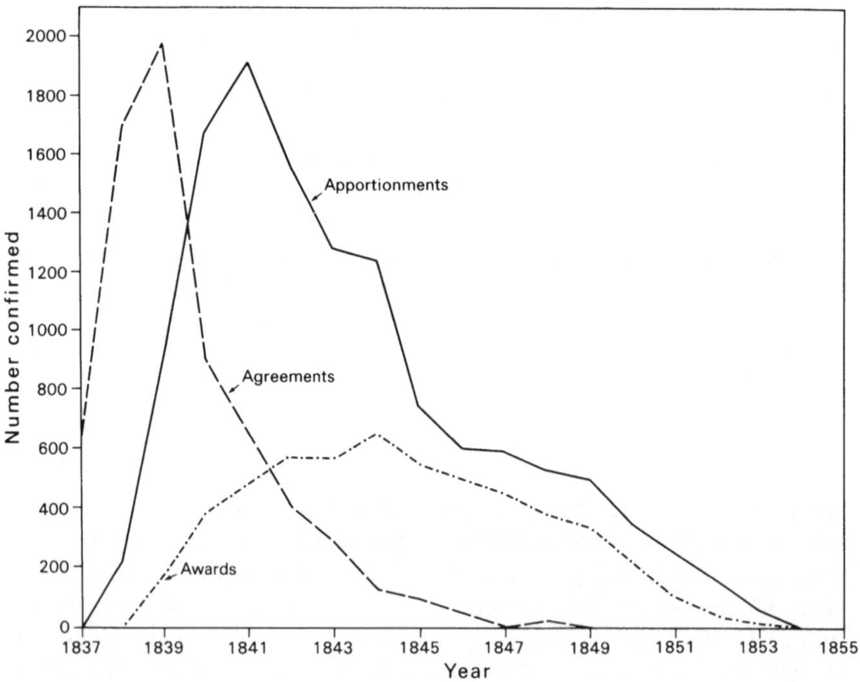

2.12 Graph of the number of agreements, awards and apportionments in England and Wales, 1837–55. Source: 'Returns of tithes commuted . . .'.

Table 2.2 *'Abstract of tithe proceedings' (31 December 1856)*

Number of agreements received			7,070
Do.	confirmed	6,778	
Do.	superseded by awards	290	
			7,068
Leaving actually in progress			2
Number of awards received			5,626
Do.	confirmed	5,421	
Do.	superseded by agreements	164	
			5,585
Leaving actually in progress			41
Total number of agreements and awards confirmed			12,199
Tithe districts in which the rent-charges have been disposed of by merger or redemption		397	
			12,164
Number of apportionments received			11,767
Number of tithe districts in which the rent-charges remain to be disposed of			35
Number of applications for the redemption of rent-charge received			201
Number of redemptions confirmed			191
Do.	in progress		10
Number of apportionments received			11,767
Do.	confirmed		11,760
Do.	in progress		7
Number of altered apportionments received			1,624
Do.	confirmed	1,428	
Do.	withdrawn	91	
			1,519
Do.	actually in progress		105
Number of applications for the exchange of glebe lands received			678
Number of exchanges confirmed		625	
Do.	withdrawn	26	
			651
Do.	actually in progress		27
Number of mergers of tithe or rent-charge received			14,070
Do.	confirmed		14,070
Do.	in progress		0

in the House about a rumour he had heard that tithe commutation was at a virtual standstill. In his reply, Russell acknowledged the existence of such a rumour but denied that it had any foundation in truth. The tithe commissioners, he said, were quite happy with the act.[85] But under oath later in the

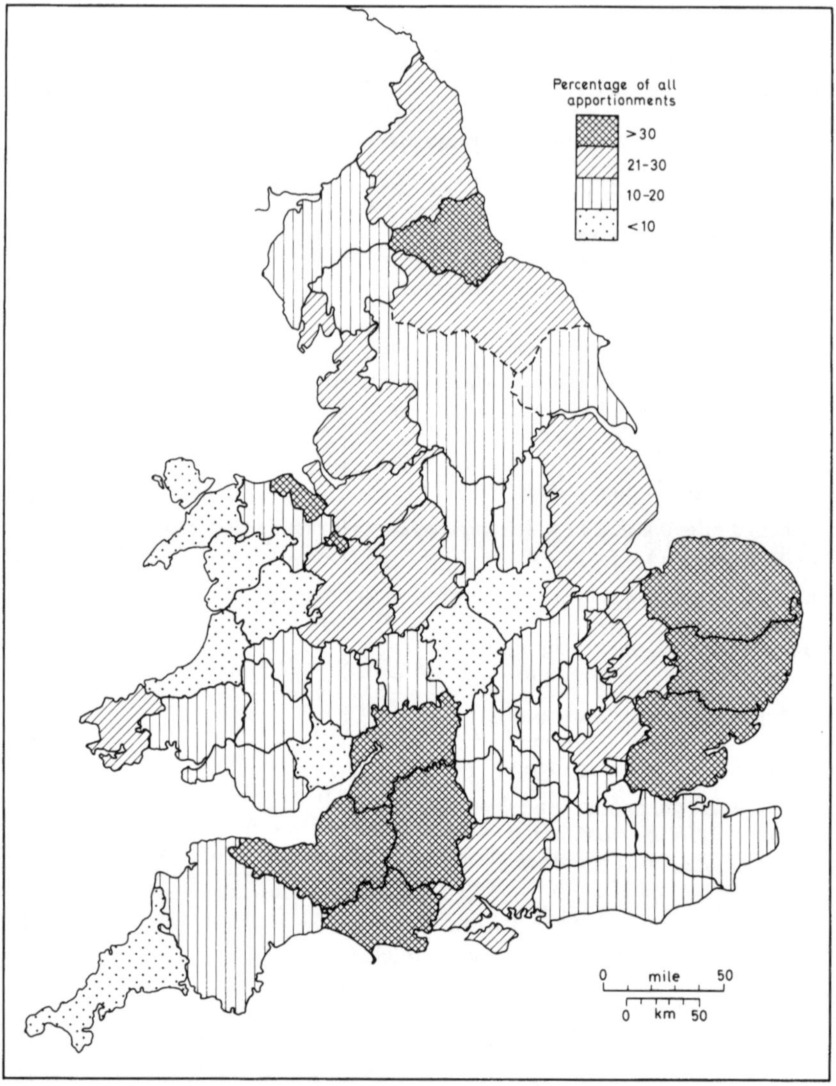

2.13 Map of the percentage of apportionments confirmed in England and Wales by December 1840, by counties. Source: as Fig. 2.12.

year, William Blamire, chairman of the Tithe Commission, recalled discussing the nature of tithe maps with Lord John Russell who referred him to Mr Spring Rice, chancellor of the exchequer.[86] Spring Rice received a letter from the commissioners putting the problems that they were encountering over tithe maps to him just two days after Russell's denial in the House.[87] The problems centred on the commissioners' uncertainty as to the precise

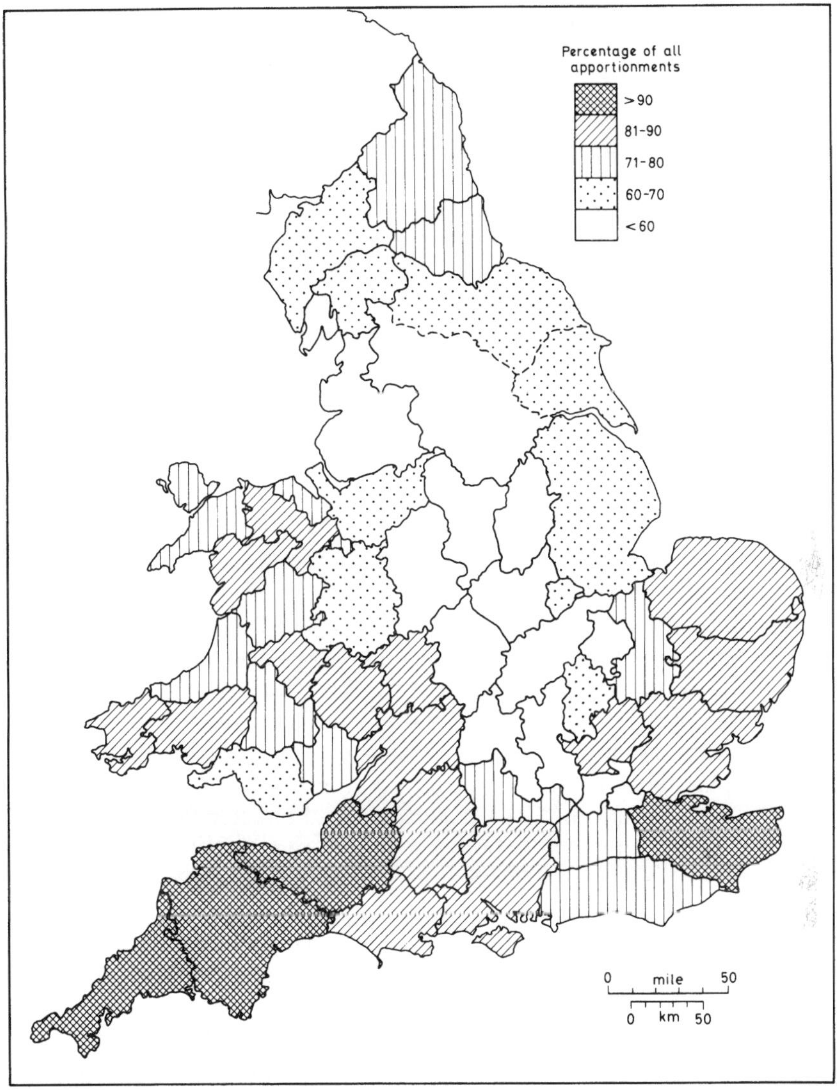

2.14 Map of the percentage of apportionments confirmed in England and Wales by December 1845. Source: as Fig. 2.12.

character and especially the accuracy of maps which they could approve for commutation purposes. They felt, on the advice of Lieutenant Dawson, that the maps they had received were insufficiently accurate or drawn at scales too small to permit their acceptance as an official record of tithe commutation, even though they had been accepted as suitable by the landowners concerned. A select committee was appointed to investigate this question and a wide-ranging debate ensued about the nature of maps required for commutation and whether they could be combined to produce a general cadastral survey of the kingdom (see chapter 3). In the event, the Tithe Commutation Act was amended in July 1837 to relieve the tithe commissioners of the duty to sanction map accuracy and to enable landowners to present maps at scales and to specifications different from those contained in Dawson's printed instructions to tithe valuers and surveyors.

Uncertainty over the nature of tithe maps put an early brake on the apportionment of tithe rent-charge. This problem affected the whole country but there were marked regional variations in the speed of commutation and apportionment. In 1839, the tithe commissioners reported that 'districts in which tithes have generally been taken in kind or let on annual valuations, contain elements of struggle and litigation, from which the rest of the country is free'.[88] On the other hand, as can be seen from Fig. 2.13, a rapid start was made in East Anglia and the West Country. In Norfolk, for example, 497 out of 660 tithe surveys were made before 1841; in Essex, 272 out of 389. In the opinion of the tithe commissioners the area of slowest progress was south Wales where tithe and tithe commutations were among the grievances which fuelled the Rebecca Riots.[89] That proceedings were tardy in south Wales can be seen from Figs. 2.13 and 2.14. Yet more striking is the backward nature of midland England. Fewer than 60 per cent of tithe surveys in these counties had been confirmed by 1845. Though the absolute number of parishes requiring commutation of tithes under the act was small in this area, the situation was very complicated where only portions of tithe in a parish had been commuted under the terms of enclosure awards. For instance, the township of Great Claybrook in Leicestershire consisted of 1,071 acres and contained 98 houses. All that remained to be commuted were a tithe of pigs worth 20s and a tithe of a mill worth 5s. The tithe commissioners were reluctant to award a rent-charge of 25s and then to proceed by map and apportionment to finish the commutation because of the inordinate expense relative to the value of the tithes.[90] Many similar, if less extreme cases, must have slowed the final stages of midland commutation.

While voluntary commutation was proceeding rapidly, the tithe commissioners limited the imposition of awards. The apportionment of agreed rent-charges provided at least as much if not more work, 'than can be proceeded with at once by such Mappers and Apportioners as have the confidence of the country'.[91] They would contemplate the imposition of awards at this early date only in districts where litigation was in progress or where tithe had been taken in kind. The commissioners thought that most tithe would be commuted by agreement, and the final figure of some 7,000 agreements proves them to have been right.

The work of commutation built up to a peak in the early 1840s and in general was conducted in an orderly and peaceful manner: 'angry appeals are the very rare exception; contented acquiescence is the general rule', the commissioners noted in 1840.[92] There were some quiet grumblings about the lag of time between commutation and apportionment, which, as Fig. 2.12 indicates, was considerably more than the six months that the legislature had envisaged. Despite this, the tithe commissioners adhered strictly to their policy of upholding the privilege of tithe payers to have rent-charges apportioned by agents of their own selection.[93] By 1848, with the bulk of their work completed or well under way, the commissioners turned their attention in earnest to problem cases. These were mostly districts where rent-charges were expected to be small, where delay was occasioned by the uncertain state of the law under Lord Tenterden's act – where moduses had been only partially commuted by enclosure acts – and, finally, the tithes of extra-parochial places to which the Crown had a *prima facie* right. The commissioners spelt out in no uncertain terms the unnecessary expense that inaction might incur, especially as in many instances the matter could be ended by a simple instrument of merger where the tithe owner and landowner was one and the same person.[94]

By July 1849 the end of the tithe surveys was clearly in sight. The commissioners stated, with no inconsiderable pride, that they hoped to complete all the commutations by 1857. But they were less confident that they would achieve an early completion of apportionment.

> The conducting of this operation constitutes the greater part of our Office work at present, and will continue to press upon us until our labours close. Deaths among the persons appointed to apportion, and other causes of delay, may prolong a few of these cases. Still we see ground for expecting that we shall get through this work by August, 1851.[95]

With but few exceptions they gained their objective. The last survey was completed in 1866.

The achievements of the settlement of 1836

The achievements of the settlement of 1836 are remarkable if for no other reason than their durability. The provisions of the act withstood the test of time. Writing in 1854, the clerk to the copyhold and tithe commissioners stated that there was not a single instance on record of an objection to an apportionment ever having been made by a reversioner.[96] With some important modifications, tithe rent-charges continued to be paid on the original basis for one hundred years. Tithe owners chafed under their liability to pay rates on moneys they received but their responsibility was reaffirmed 60 years after the act was passed. Farmers were dissatisfied with the method of calculating the rent-charges but the only remedy applied was a limit on the maximum payment. The proportions of wheat, barley and oats fixed in 1836 gave undue weight to fluctuations in the price of oats which rarely entered the market, while that of wheat, whose price was sensitive to worldwide changes and fell steeply after 1879, was under-represented. Moreover, prices quoted in the *London Gazette* were those of high-quality grains sold to dealers, not values of crops at the farm gate before transport charges were added. Another cause of dissatisfaction, that of extraordinary rent-charges on hop grounds and market gardens, was removed in 1886 by the redemption of the capital value of the charges at a rate of 4 per cent per annum.[97] In 1891 an upper limit was placed on the level of rent-charges to prevent them exceeding the value of rents.[98] They were restricted to no more than two-thirds of the gross annual value of the land. By the same act responsibility for paying rent-charges was laid squarely on the landowner. In 1918, rent-charges were fixed for the following eight years at their current level, which then stood at £109 3s 11d of their 1836 par value.[99] In 1925 new levels were fixed and provision was made for voluntary redemption of rent-charges by means of annual repayments over a period of 60 years.[100] By the Tithe Act of 1936 the capital values of all remaining rent-charges had to be redeemed.[101] A new form of payment, known as a redemption annuity, was to be paid into the funds of Queen Anne's Bounty over a period extending from October 1936 to October 1996.[102] Allowances were made for costs of chancel repairs, hitherto borne by some owners of rectorial tithes, and all other outstanding charges and payments were redeemed.

3

Tithe maps, apportionments and files

The tithe commissioners succeeded in resolving many of the complex problems that had previously embittered relations between tithe payers and tithe owners. In a majority of parishes they were able to secure an agreement within the statutory period of two years; in the remainder they imposed an award. Throughout the country they carried out their task with speed and thoroughness, setting down details of the survey for most parishes in three documents: a map, an apportionment and a file. In spite of the additional work involved in valuation and apportionment, most of the survey was completed in about one-tenth of the time taken by the Ordnance Survey to complete its large-scale plans. Yet speed was obtained without undue loss of accuracy. The reports submitted to the commissioners, surviving minutes of local enquiries, and correspondence in the tithe files testify to the vigilance of tithe payers and tithe owners, each jealously guarding their rights or pretended rights against infringement by the other party.

Tithe commutation and a general survey of England and Wales

Immediately after his secondment to the Tithe Commission from the Royal Engineers on 27 August 1836, Lieutenant R. K. Dawson began working out details of the technical specification for maps the Tithe Commutation Act required as a record of commutation in each district. From the outset Dawson saw the need for tithe maps of three-quarters of the parishes of England and Wales as an opportunity for obtaining a full cadastral survey of the country. He wrote to the tithe commissioners about this on 8 September 1836, setting out the advantages to be obtained from combining the tithe survey with a general cadastral survey.[1]

Dawson was clearly aware that the first half of the nineteenth century was something of an age of cadastral surveys throughout the whole of Europe. As well as telling the tithe commissioners about the Townland Survey of Ireland under the direction of his 'friend Colonel Colby', he drew their attention to the cadastral survey of France and to the Swedish system of land registration based on cadastral plans. He noted that similar surveys were in progress in Austria, Bavaria, Savoy and Piedmont, and suggested that, 'in many of the States of Continental Europe, Cadastral Surveys have long been in progress, at an annual expense commensurate with the importance attached to the possession of such documents'.[2]

In the same letter he set out an impressive list of advantages to be derived from a similar survey of England and Wales. These included the resolution of boundary disputes, easier transfer of real property, and identification of the best lines for new roads, railways and canals. The government would also obtain an accurate statement of the 'real capabilities of the country' and be able to decide where investment in improvements might be most beneficial. He concluded this review by saying that, 'the necessity which now exists, for Surveys of nearly the whole country, for a specific purpose presents means for forming a General Survey or Cadastre, at such a cheap rate, that the opportunity cannot be lost without exposing those who ought to represent its importance, to the certainty of future censure, if they fail to perform that imperative duty'.[3] Dawson considered that the survey could be carried out by civilian surveyors under strict supervision and with rigorous checking.

In his scheme the overall organisation of the survey would be made the responsibility of a controller assisted by three district commissioners each assigned to a third of the country. They in turn would allocate two counties to each of 26 superintending commissioners recruited from 'the better class of surveyors'. Their job would be to test the accuracy of plans submitted by field surveyors. If there were about 740 of these, and if they each surveyed about 10,000 acres a year, Dawson thought the whole operation could be completed in the five years before appointments made under the Tithe Act were due to lapse.[4] Dawson's schedule of the cost of this work is set out in Table 3.1. His figures are based on estimates of average rates charged by surveyors and valuers. For example, he reckoned 9d per acre for the land-survey element as an average of the actual cost of such work which varied from 2d to 1s 6d per acre.[5] In the event Dawson's ability to estimate costs proved less than adequate as the commutation surveys alone cost over two million pounds.

R. K. Dawson's specifications for tithe maps

Before the tithe commissioners would lend their support to Dawson's proposal, they requested a detailed report from him on the precise nature, scale and construction of plans required by the Tithe Act. They received this on 29 November 1836 and in it Dawson elaborated further on his idea for combining tithe commutation with a full cadastral survey and specified the

Table 3.1 *Lieutenant R. K. Dawson's estimate of the cost of a 'general survey' in conjunction with the tithe survey*

Survey and valuation for the purposes of the Tithe Commutation Act:	
Cost of surveying 33,408,000 acres at 9d per acre for tithe commutation after deducting one-third to account for use of existing maps.	£ 835,200
For valuing same at 3d per acre.	417,600
Total	1,252,800
Additional expense for a complete content survey of England and Wales:	
Cost of surveying the 3,712,000 acres of 1,080 parishes where tithes were already commuted after deducting one-third to account for use of existing maps.	124,000
Cost of levelling watercourses and watersheds at 10s per mile.	72,300
Cost of extra trigonometrical points required to combine the parish plans into general maps.	58,700
Total extra expense	255,000

Source: British Parliamentary Papers (House of Commons), 1837, XLI, 'Copy of papers respecting the proposed survey of lands under the Tithe Act', p. 6.

type of map he considered the Tithe Act required.[6] He thought that tithe maps should portray both tithe district and tithe area boundaries with absolute accuracy. There was no real case for disputing the first of these points. It was important to know the exact area of a district to enable a fair and just apportionment of rent-charge. However, the accurate representation of field boundaries was not at all necessary for the immediate purposes of commutation though, of course, a vital element in any large-scale, cadastral survey. Dawson put forward two arguments in favour of the exact positioning of field boundaries on tithe maps. First, he stated that the Commutation Act was designed to provide a once and for all settlement of the tithe question. In order to avoid future litigation it was important that fences be accurately portrayed so that particular tithe areas could always be identified. Second, he drew attention to the need for testing the accuracy of other maps which landowners might choose to use to reduce the expense of commutation. He concluded that 'it so happens, fortunately for the facility and economy of the whole operation, that the means necessary to effect the first of these objects are means which will ensure the attainment of the second'.[7] The means he had in mind was to specify maps at a scale of three chains to an inch (26.7 inches to a mile), constructed by a strict system of triangulation.

Dawson thought maps on a three-chain scale the smallest from which it was possible to measure quantities directly. He also considered this the usual scale for estate maps and thought that conformity would facilitate incorporation of these into the tithe survey.[8] An analysis of Kentish maps produced between 1800 and 1836 supports Dawson's view. More than three times as many maps were produced at this scale compared with smaller four- or six-chain scales (20 inches and 13.3 inches to the mile respectively).[9]

Having decided upon a scale, Dawson then described a system of triangulation for parish surveys. The following extract concerns his method for the internal triangulation of a parish:

> 1st. To measure two straight lines through the entire length and breadth of the parish.
> 2dly. To connect the ends of these lines by means of other measured lines; and
> 3dly. From these connecting lines (by measured triangles and offsets) to determine the entire Parish Boundary.[10]

To complete the interior detail of parishes, other lines were required. Dawson suggested that some might connect particular features like churches, windmills and obelisks; others might be measured from one object within a parish to similar objects in adjacent parishes; together with, 'such other lines to be measured among the preceding lines, and connecting them with one another, as may be requisite for determining the position of fences and other objects not previously obtained'.[11] Similar lines might also be set out and used to check the accuracy of existing surveys. In all cases, construction lines were to be left on the final drawings in red ink to provide a check on map accuracy.

Some examples of the diagrams Dawson produced to illustrate these points are reproduced in Fig. 3.1, and Fig. 3.2 illustrates some of the conventional signs that he recommended. In 3.1(i), he demonstrates the procedure to be followed in setting out the boundary of a parish and calculating its area. The two main lines measured through it are AB and CD, with AC, BC, BD, and AD as the connecting lines. Triangles (T) are constructed on the connecting lines and offsets (a) are set out from the measured lines to the parish boundary. Remoter parts of the boundary are determined by constructing further triangles with sides EF, GH, IK etc. In conducting these operations, 'the expedients in use among practised Surveyors will of course be resorted to for overcoming any difficulties which may attend the measurement of these main lines, and the theodolite offers a never-failing resource in all cases where a departure from the direct line is inevitable'.[12] Dawson used 3.1(ii) to show how his main lines could be employed to test the accuracy of existing surveys. Points (b) are those at which the main lines are crossed by fences. Accurate measurement of these, 'together with the line of the external boundary, and calculated contents as before obtained, will in general afford a sufficient test of the accuracy of old

Table 3.2 *Lieut.-Colonel R. K. Dawson's estimate of the cost of surveys to 1856 for which a general survey in the 1830s would have been applicable*

	£
Tithe Commutation (England and Wales): 11,764 plans of parishes and tithe districts, representing, by estimation, 29,410,000 acres; and two copies of each plan etc.	1,715,583
Inclosure (England and Wales): 697 plans representing 450,779 acres; and two copies of each plan, including the cost of plans annexed to deeds of exchange etc.	45,077
Parochial Assessment (England and Wales): 512 plans of parishes, representing, by estimation, 1,280,000 acres, including the cost of official examination.	64,000
Total estimated cost of the surveys and plans which passed through the hands of the tithe and inclosure commissioners.	1,824,660
Railways (England, Wales and Scotland): The surveys and plans made for deposit with Parliament and purchase of land for 12,227 miles of authorised lines and 24,454 miles of projected lines at a moderate estimate of the prices paid during the last 30 years.	1,630,250
Health of Towns (England and Wales): Survey and block plan of London with levels and further detailed surveys extending over 20 square miles, 66 plans of other towns made for the general board of health, exclusive of Liverpool, Hull, and Edinburgh.	74,920
	£3,529,830
To the aforesaid might be added a considerable sum in respect of surveys for roads, canals, water supply, and the sale and transfer of property, which I have no means of estimating.	
Copyhold, Inclosure, and Tithe Commission, 21 April 1856	

Source: British Parliamentary Papers, 1856, XIV, *Report from Select Committee on Ordnance Survey of Scotland*, Appendix V, 125.

surveys, which is one of the most important objects aimed at in these directions'.[13] On 3.1(iii) he showed how, by retaining construction lines on finished plans, it would be possible to identify tithe areas when fences were removed. Numbers 1–4 are four tithe areas within the external boundary ACBD. The lines and offsets required to determine the position of the internal fences are shown as the dotted lines EF, GH, GI and EK. Provided that the main lines AB and CD can be set out with accuracy, then by leaving construction lines EF, GH etc. on the plan and by measurement on the ground, the boundaries of the original tithe areas can always be identified.

In all these matters, Dawson's military survey training is quite evident and

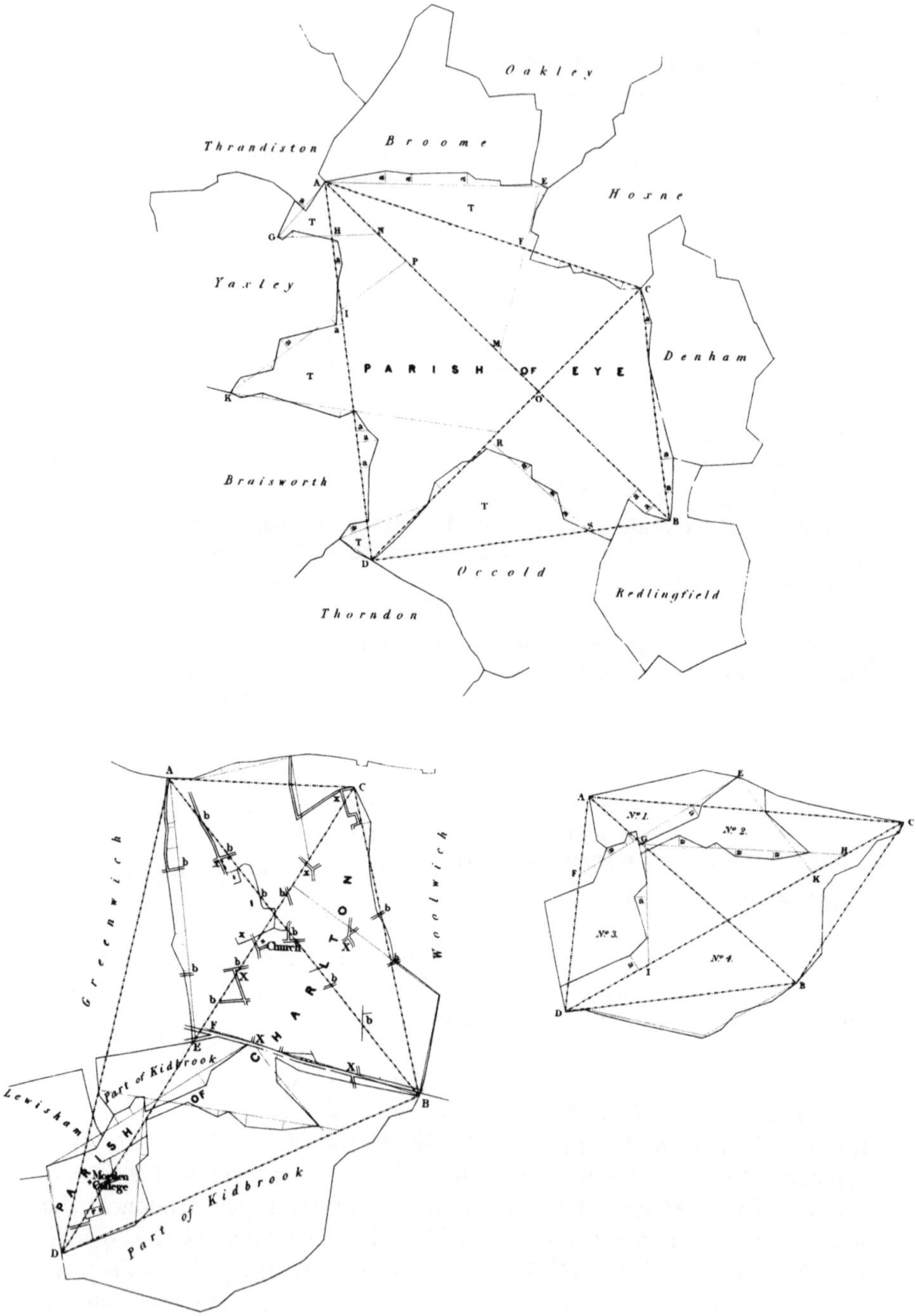

3.1 Three diagrams which accompany R. K. Dawson's report on the specification for tithe maps. Source: 'Copy of papers respecting the proposed survey of lands under the Tithe Act . . .'.

his recommendations follow very closely those of contemporary military survey manuals. For example, Colby in his 1825 *Instructions for the interior survey of Ireland* required that 'the bearings and distances . . . are to be laid down on the plots and penned in with light blue lines, that they may shew the relative accuracy of the work . . .'[14] The only difference was the colour of ink.

The Tithe Commission's views on tithe maps

The tithe commissioners were very pleased with Dawson's report. On 4 January 1837, their secretary wrote to him saying that

Considering the permanent nature of the record which it is meant that the instrument of apportionment, with the Plan which is to be annexed to it, should constitute, it appears to the Commissioners to be their duty to require such Plans as will ensure a possibility, and, as far as may be, a facility for ascertaining precisely the extent and position of lands to be declared subject to or free from the rent-charges to be created under the Tithe Act, when the present boundaries of those lands have been altered or displaced. The Commissioners are of the opinion that the Scale recommended in your Report, and the lines of construction proposed to be left marked on the Plans, are essential for this purpose, and they authorize you to communicate this opinion to all parties with whom you are, or may hereafter be in correspondence or communication on the subject.

The commissioners were quite clear about the type of map necessary for tithe commutation. Tithe maps were to be first class, accurate plans at a scale of 26.7 inches to a mile constructed according to a system of internal triangulation. Such maps would be ideally suited to form a basis for a full cadastral survey of the nation.

The Tithe Act itself contained contradictory clauses on the nature of maps it required.[15] The 35th clause stated that

the Valuer or Valuers or Umpire may, if they think fit, use for the Purposes of this Act any Admeasurement, Plan or Valuation previously made of the Lands or Tithes in question of the Accuracy of which they shall be satisfied; and that it be lawful for the Meeting at which such Valuer or Valuers shall be chosen to agree upon the Adoption for the Purpose aforesaid of any such Admeasurement, Plan or Valuation, and such Agreement shall be binding upon the Valuer or Valuers; provided always, that Three Fourths of the Land Owners in Number and Value shall concur therein.

But the 63rd and 64th sections of the act required the tithe commissioners to sanction the accuracy of every map by affixing their official seal as a final duty when confirming the commutation of tithes in a district.

. . . if the Commissioners shall approve the Apportionment they confirm the Instrument of Apportionment under their Hands and Seal, . . . and every Recital or Statement in or Map or Plan annexed to such Confirmed Apportionment or Agreement for giving Land, or any sealed Copy thereof, shall be deemed satisfactory Evidence of the Matters therein recited or stated, or of the Accuracy of such Plan.

Clearly there were some grounds for ambiguity here. On the one hand, the act entitled landowners to adopt any plan of their choice, whilst on the other, the tithe commissioners were required to certify the accuracy of every map before confirming an apportionment.

By the end of February 1837, the tithe commissioners had received 38 voluntary agreements for tithe commutation but they were unable to approve any of the accompanying maps.[16] One of the first examples of a grossly inaccurate map being adopted by landowners as a basis for commutation came from the north-Kent parish of Tonge. It was drawn at the recommended scale of 26.7 inches to a mile, was accepted by three-quarters of the landowners, and was sent up to Lieutenant Dawson's office for approval in February 1837. Here the sizes of fields were computed from the map and compared with acreages in the book of reference. Errors of up to 100 per cent were found. For example, Dawson found two fields, one stated to be three-and-a-half acres and the other only three-quarters of an acre. On the plan they were represented as nearly the same size, one being two acres and the other two-and-a-half acres. Further enquiries at Tonge revealed that the map had been enlarged from a small-scale plan more than thirty years old. Dawson maintained that it would be impossible from this map to identify parcels charged with tithe if field boundaries were altered, although in the short term landowners would have saved themselves the expense of a new survey.[17] Richard Jones, the church representative on the Tithe Commission, thought it very likely that similar problems would occur where existing surveys were adopted for tithe purposes. At this date the Tithe Act was, as noted in chapter 2 above, very much a dead-letter.

A Select Committee appointed

The tithe commissioners remained convinced that accurate maps were necessary for an effective and lasting commutation for tithes. But by pressing for accuracy they were increasing an already considerable cost of commutation for some landowners. In a letter to the chancellor of the exchequer, Mr Spring Rice, the commissioners reiterated Dawson's arguments for combining tithe surveys with a general survey of the whole country in the hope that some of the cost of cadastral accuracy might be defrayed from the public purse.[18] They also outlined other tax collection advantages that would accrue from a full cadastral survey. In particular they referred to maps required for assessing Poor Rates under the New Poor Law. The Poor Law commissioners strongly supported both the idea of a general survey and the method of producing parish maps described by Dawson. Edwin Chad-

3.2 Some of the conventional signs which Dawson prepared for tithe surveyors. Source: as Fig. 3.1.

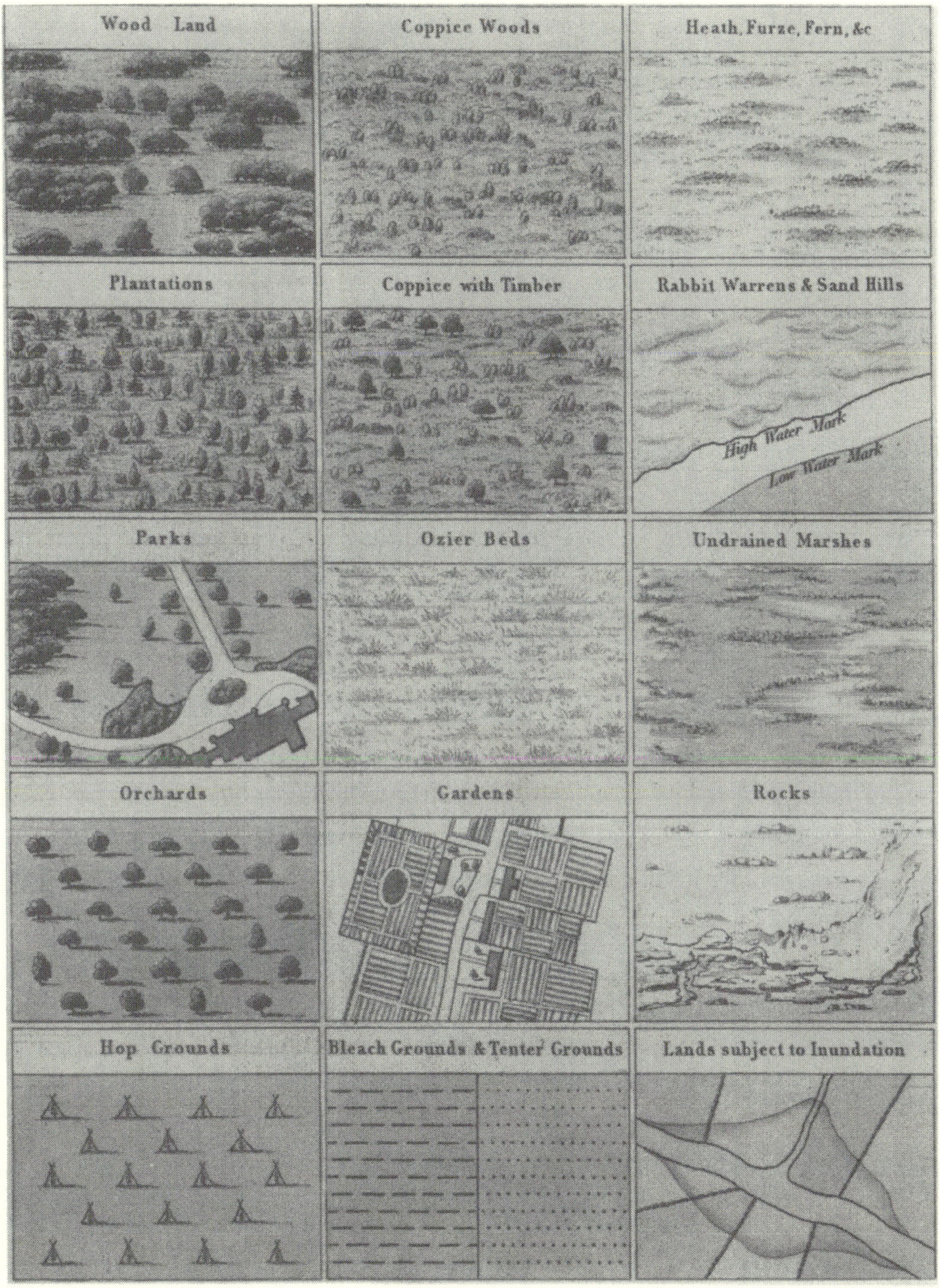
Wood Land
Coppice Woods
Heath, Furze, Fern, &c
Plantations
Coppice with Timber
Rabbit Warrens & Sand Hills
High Water Mark
Low Water Mark
Parks
Ozier Beds
Undrained Marshes
Orchards
Gardens
Rocks
Hop Grounds
Bleach Grounds & Tenter Grounds
Lands subject to Inundation

wick, their secretary, wrote the following note to the tithe commissioners on 5 January 1837:

The Poor Law Commissioners are sensible of the great advantage which will result, both to owners and occupiers of land and other real property, and to the public in general, from the adoption of the uniform and well-considered system which is suggested in the Report, and which has received your sanction; and they desire to assure you, that they shall have much satisfaction in furthering, by every means in their power, so judicial and useful a measure . . .[19]

The tithe commissioners concluded their appeal to Spring Rice by asking whether:

such maps shall be attained at enormous expense at some future period, or whether the large sums of money which must now be expended on the maps, good or bad, supplied for the purposes of the Tithe Act, instead of being wasted for all other public purposes, shall be so expended as to be the means, as far as it goes, of supplying all the wants of the Nation as connected with surveys.[20]

These arguments persuaded the chancellor of the exchequer to appoint a House of Commons select committee on 16 March 1837 under the chairmanship of Mr Shaw Lefevre: 'to consider the best mode of effecting the Surveys of Parishes for the purpose of carrying into effect the Act for the Commutation of Tithes in England and Wales'.[21] In April 1837, the committee heard evidence from the three tithe commissioners, from Lieutenant Dawson and from John Matson, a Cumberland farmer who acted as commissioner when the tithes of all the Kendal townships were commuted by special act of parliament.

The committee had to decide whether accurate maps were needed for tithe commutation; maps which might be combined into a general survey, and then be reduced, engraved, and published on the six-inch scale in conformity with the Ordnance Survey of Ireland. The committee soon realised that for the immediate purposes of commutation and apportionment it was not necessary to have a map at all. Even the chairman of the tithe commissioners, William Blamire, stated that an accurate schedule would suffice.[22] But it was the future confusion that might result from the adoption of such a system that the tithe commissioners stressed in their evidence. The act of 1836 put the onus of providing proof of tithe liability or exemption firmly in the court of the landowner, so it was not so much in the church's interest as in the landowners' that titheable plots could be identified for all time. But Richard Jones, speaking on behalf of the church, thought that tithe owners could take little comfort from this. In his evidence he remarked:

a clergyman goes to drive off a sheep from a particular portion of land; the landowner says, 'that is exempt from tithes'; the clergyman says, 'it is upon you to prove that';

and they go to law. It will be a poor satisfaction to the church or the public during such litigation to be able to say that the onus lies with the landowner.[23]

There were three main situations in which landowners might be unwilling to produce new, large-scale maps. These occurred first in areas where large tracts of land were tithe-free, second, where parochial or township maps had been recently produced for other purposes, and, third, where maps of individual estates were available for combination into a parish map. In all these circumstances, the production of new maps specifically for tithe commutation would have involved landowners in extra cost. William Blamire thought a large number of landowners would say, 'we are entitled to give you a map on any scale we think fit, and you have no right to call into question the accuracy of that map'.[24] During April 1837, while the select committee was hearing evidence, groups of landowners petitioned the House of Commons requesting that the tithe commissioners' proposals for large-scale maps be defeated or that the proposed surveys be made at public expense.[25]

After weighing the evidence, the select committee reported in May 1837 their recommendation that precise, accurate maps were not required for successful tithe commutation. Its conclusion was influenced by matters of cost to landowners and by the spirit of the 1836 act which was to encourage voluntary commutations wherever possible. The committee recommended some relaxation of the 63rd and 64th clauses of the Tithe Act to relieve the commissioners of the duty of sanctioning map accuracy. Shaw Lefevre accepted that this might lead to litigation in the future but he thought that, 'the anticipated difficulties, as far as they affect the Land Owners, will naturally occur to those individuals who compose the meeting where the valuers are chosen, and will doubtless receive from them due consideration. . .'[26]

The Tithe Commutation Act amended in 1837

In June 1837, a bill to amend the Tithe Commutation Act was introduced to the House of Commons. It was given a speedy passage through both Houses and became law on 15 July.[27] An opportunity for a cadastral survey of the full kingdom was lost.[28] The maps accepted by the tithe commissioners are on a variety of scales and made at a variety of dates. As a body the tithe maps were quite unsuitable to form the basis for a national cadastral survey. The country, 'lost its last chance of a cadastral system on the continental pattern, with all that means in terms of cheap and simple property transfers'.[29]

The debate over registration of land was to recur time and again. Unnecessary expense and duplication of surveys did occur as Dawson predicted. In 1856, while giving evidence before the select committee on the

Ordnance Survey of Scotland, Dawson estimated the cost of surveys which would not have been needed if a national government survey had been carried out in the 1830s. His estimates are set out in Table 3.2.

Robert Kearsley Dawson, the engineering officer seconded to organise the tithe survey, who initiated the idea that it could be combined with a general survey of the nation, found himself caught up in what had begun as a technical debate over specifications of tithe maps but had ended as a highly political issue which threatened to reopen a breach between landowning and tithe-owning interests. Dawson himself was piled with scorn, not least by his friend and former superior officer, Colonel Colby, who in a letter to his wife on 26 May 1837 wrote, 'my having been in London is most fortunate, for poor Dawson's complete failure in the tithe commutation business would have cast a sad damp on all our work if I had not been there to avert the evil'.[30] It is not entirely clear what it was that Colby meant by this statement. Tithe commutation itself had hardly begun; it was only in his attempt to launch a full cadastral survey that Dawson was unsuccessful. It is possible that Colby was expressing anger at Dawson's insistence through the whole length of the debate that a general survey could be carried out by civilians, without help, let alone direction, from the military to whom Colby was so firmly committed in survey matters.[31] Nor was Dawson himself to blame for rejection of the scheme. Responsibility for that rests with the 1837 select committee. Dawson was to look back on its decision later in life with some bitterness. Writing to the registrar general in 1852 he said:

> And had the requirements of that Act (the Tithe Act) been carried out, the deposited Records in the Tithe Office should now have afforded accurate returns of the acreage of about five-sixths of the Parishes in England and Wales, and might have been made the basis, as was indeed at one time contemplated by the Government, of a perfect system of Agricultural Statistics.[32]

Even the Ordnance Survey was in the end to turn its back on a full survey of England and Wales recording ownership and occupation of land as well as the acreage and land use of individual parcels. But, to the lasting credit of Dawson is the fact that within the space of only a few years his method of surveying parishes on trigonometrical principles was in common usage by a growing corps of country surveyors. In the words of Butler Williams, professor of geodesy at the College of Civil Engineers, Putney, in 1844,

> The mode of conducting the operations for parish surveys by great lines, embracing the whole of the district to be surveyed, described in Captain Dawson's 'Instructions to Tithe Surveyors', is now universally adopted, and no acknowledged surveyor would now proceed with isolated surveys of separate fields, to be afterwards combined into a general map.[33]

First- and second-class tithe maps

The first section of the amended Tithe Act relieved the commissioners of the need to certify the accuracy of every map accompanying apportionments and permitted them to establish two classes of tithe map. 'First-class maps' are those which the commissioners considered sufficiently accurate to serve as legal evidence of boundaries and areas and can be identified by the certificate of accuracy signed by two tithe commissioners which they bear and also by the presence of the Commission's official seal (Fig. 3.3). All first-class maps and accompanying field books were carefully checked by Lieutenant Dawson's staff in London (see chapter 4). The technical specification that Dawson prepared before the 1836 act was amended still applied to first-class maps, with the exception that the commissioners no longer considered it essential for a system of conventional signs to be used.

> The maps which will be most acceptable to the tithe commissioners are the plain working plans, with the lines of construction, names and reference figures shown upon them, and with no other ornament or colour whatever; and the most ready way of obtaining the seal of the commission will be to send up the actual working plan.[34]

Dawson's instructions were printed by the Commission and made available to landowners' solicitors so that they could be incorporated into contracts

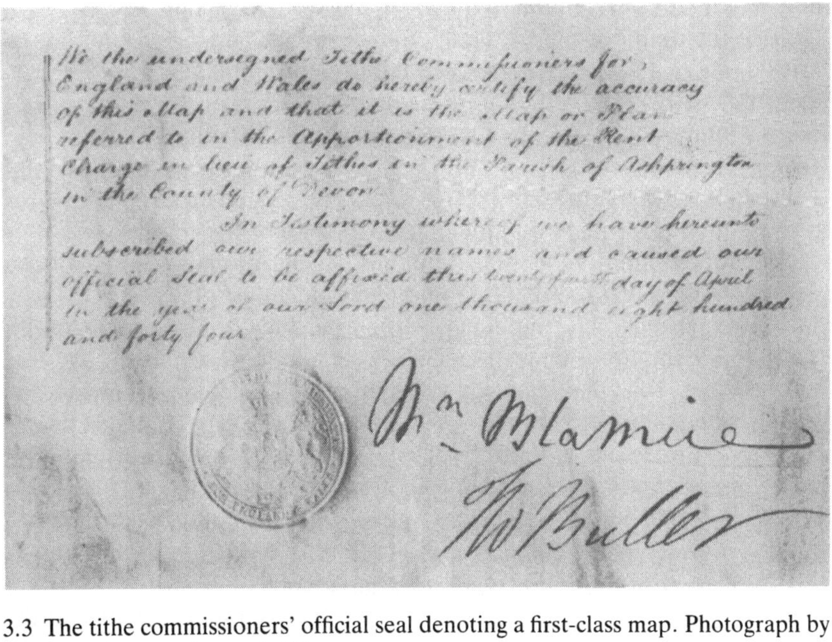

We the undersigned Tithe Commissioners for England and Wales do hereby certify the accuracy of this Map and that it is the Map or Plan referred to in the Apportionment of the Rent Charge in lieu of Tithes in the Parish of Ashprington in the County of Devon

In Testimony whereof we have hereunto subscribed our respective names and caused our official Seal to be affixed this twenty fourth day of April in the year of our Lord one thousand eight hundred and forty four

Wm Blamire
TW Buller

3.3 The tithe commissioners' official seal denoting a first-class map. Photograph by courtesy of Devon Record Office.

drawn up between landowners and surveyors when the former commissioned a first-class map of their tithe district.[35] Extracts from these instructions are set out in Table 3.3.

The category of second-class maps includes those which were intended to be first-class but which failed Dawson's tests and were not subsequently corrected to the Commission's satisfaction. One such map is that of the parish of Drewsteignton in Devon, the compilation of which indicates some potential and actual pitfalls for landowners and surveyors.[36] In 1838 landowners and tithe owners of this parish entered into a voluntary agreement for tithe rent-charge which was subsequently confirmed by the tithe commissioners.[37] Later in the year the landowners advertised in *Trewman's Flying Post*, a Devon county newspaper, for tenders from surveyors who would construct them a first-class map of Drewsteignton. During December 1838 and January 1839 their solicitor received four tenders, and on 29 January they offered a contract to a Plymouth man, William Jole. His was the lowest tender, calculated at a flat rate of 9d per acre for an estimated 5,000 acres, and he agreed to 'furnish one first-class map and book of reference to the published instructions of the Tithe Commissioners'.[38] Construction of the map was long delayed and was not ready for the landowners to inspect until August 1840. Both the Tithe Commission and the landowners had pressed for its completion; Jole in reply pleaded the inclement nature of the weather throughout 1839 and the fact that the parish was much hillier than he had anticipated. He considered also that he had been 'completely deceived with regard to the outlay required – had I known at the commencement that the Parish contained so much more than was stated I should not have undertaken the work'.[39] But the landowners also had reason to feel deceived because Jole's map failed the Tithe Commission's tests for first-class maps because 'it is not constructed on principles to entitle it to be received as such'.[40] In his explanation to the landowners Jole argued that this failure was 'in consequence of the very hilly and rough state of the country generally which rendered it not only difficult but in some parts almost inaccessible to measure in the way prescribed'.[41] In his letter of tender Jole cited as his only previous experience his mapping of urban parishes of St Andrew and St Charles in Plymouth. Other surveyors who tendered were able to state that their previous work had been approved by the Tithe Commission and one asked what were to prove to be very pertinent questions about the nature of the terrain, the extent of the parish, the size of enclosures, the number of houses and so on.[42] After a long wait, Drewsteignton's landowners got a second-class map but they got it very cheaply. They ignored Jole's repeated requests for advances of money and settled for a reduction of the acreage rate to 7½d in return for agreeing to accept a second-class map.[43]

The Drewsteignton tithe map is, however, far from representative of the body of second-class maps. Some were indeed relegated to this category

Table 3.3 *Extracts from R. K. Dawson's instructions for 'the Preparation of Plans for the purpose of the Tithe Commutation Act'*

Description of Plan required

1. The Plan is to be made on good drawing paper previously mounted on linen, and is required to represent, in their true relative positions, the several objects which now occupy the surface of the ground, such as railways, roads, rivers, lakes, ponds, canals, streams, drains, parks, woods, fences, houses and other buildings, bridges, etc., also the boundaries of counties and their various subdivisions, such as ridings, lathes, wapentakes, rapes, hundreds, parishes, townships, etc., and all the details usually given in estate surveys.
2. The boundaries or limits of all lands and parcels of land which are to be treated separately under the provisions of the Tithe Commutation Acts, are to be marked on the Plan, whether they be defined by fences or not; and where no boundary fences exist, the exact limits are to be shown on the Plan with a dotted line.
3. Each separate parcel of land should be numbered upon the Plan, the numbers following in succession from No. 1 to the highest number required. These numbers are to correspond with those given in the Reference Book in which will be specified the name and description of each field or inclosure, with its true quantity or contents in statute measure, the names and description of the owners and occupiers thereof, the state of cultivation of the several lands, whether as arable, meadow, pasture, wood, coppice or common land, garden, orchard, hop ground, or howsoever otherwise.
4. The Plan is to be drawn to the scale of Three chains to One Inch in rural parishes, and Two chains or One chain to an inch in towns.
5. The ordinary usage in other respects is to be observed of placing the North towards the top of the Plan, writing the name of the parish and county as a title, the name and address of the surveyor, the date of performance, the scale, and the total contents.
6. The lines of construction or chained lines, wherever practicable, are to be disposed in the form of triangles, each triangle having a proper proof line measured within it.
7. All lines measured over steep slopes are to be reduced to the horizontal plane.
8. The chained lines are all to be drawn upon the Plan in red ink, and marked with a reference to the number of the line in the field-books, or to the page of the book in which the notes of the measurement are entered.
9. The entries in the field-books are to be made with ink in the field, and the chained lines are to be numbered consecutively throughout the books.
10. The quantities are not to be written upon the Map, but in the Reference Book only.
11. It is essential that the Plan, when completed, should be such as that the admeasurement on the Plan of the inclosures therein represented should correspond with the quantities assigned to them in the book of reference, and such also as to bear the test of the comparison of any lines which the Tithe Commissioners may desire to have measured upon the ground with similar lines drawn upon the Plan.
12. The working Plan, prepared as above, together with the original field-books and Reference Book, must be sent to the office of the Tithe Commission for examination, otherwise the accuracy of the work can only be proved by measuring testing lines upon the ground.

Table 3.3 cont.

13. The Tithe Commissioners will not pledge themselves to seal a Map to which any of the following objections apply, without testing its accuracy upon the ground:–
    1. Where the means afforded are insufficient to prove the accuracy of the work in all its details.
    2. Where the Map does not agree with the field-books.
    3. Where the field-books have been kept in pencil.
    4. Where alterations have been made in the field-books without a satisfactory explanation being afforded.
    5. Where the offsets exceed a chain in length.

after failing to match the first-class specification, but by far the larger number are those maps 'which three-fourths of the landowners are desirous to use, but which the parties do not mean to submit to the test of the commission'.[44] These are not all necessarily inferior to first-class maps; some were not eligible for first-class status simply because of their small scale without regard to their internal accuracy because 'maps on a smaller scale than four chains to an inch do not admit of being accurately tested as to quantities; and no map on a smaller scale can therefore receive the seal of the Commission'.[45] While the Commission still retained its full powers to refuse to confirm an apportionment accompanied by a map which Lieutenant Dawson's office deemed wholly unsatisfactory, maps were rejected in only very exceptional circumstances.[46] The published specification for second-class maps contains nothing to ensure planimetric or topographic accuracy but is concerned mainly with the way information on the maps was to be set out and linked to that in the apportionments. Most refusals to confirm on first submission were for reasons of clerical or procedural errors as at Nantwich in Cheshire in 1846 (Fig. 3.4).

Second-class tithe maps were usually based, at least in part, on existing parish or estate maps. Field boundaries and locations of buildings would be brought up-to-date, unsurveyed areas filled in and the whole redrawn to the tithe commissioners' requirements as regards district and tithe area boundaries and reference numbers (Fig. 3.4). For example, in 1844 surveyor John Thorpe of Stenton traced a copy of an 1818 survey of Hinckley in Leicestershire for tithe commutation and resurveyed the town of Hinckley itself. The old and new maps were tied together to constitute a second-class map of the district.[47] Substantial savings in cost to landowners could be

3.4 Examination paper provided for the guidance of landowners and valuers and used by the Tithe Commission to record remarks on the draft apportionment and map. Source: PRO IR 18/153; photograph reproduced by permission of the Keeper, Public Record Office.

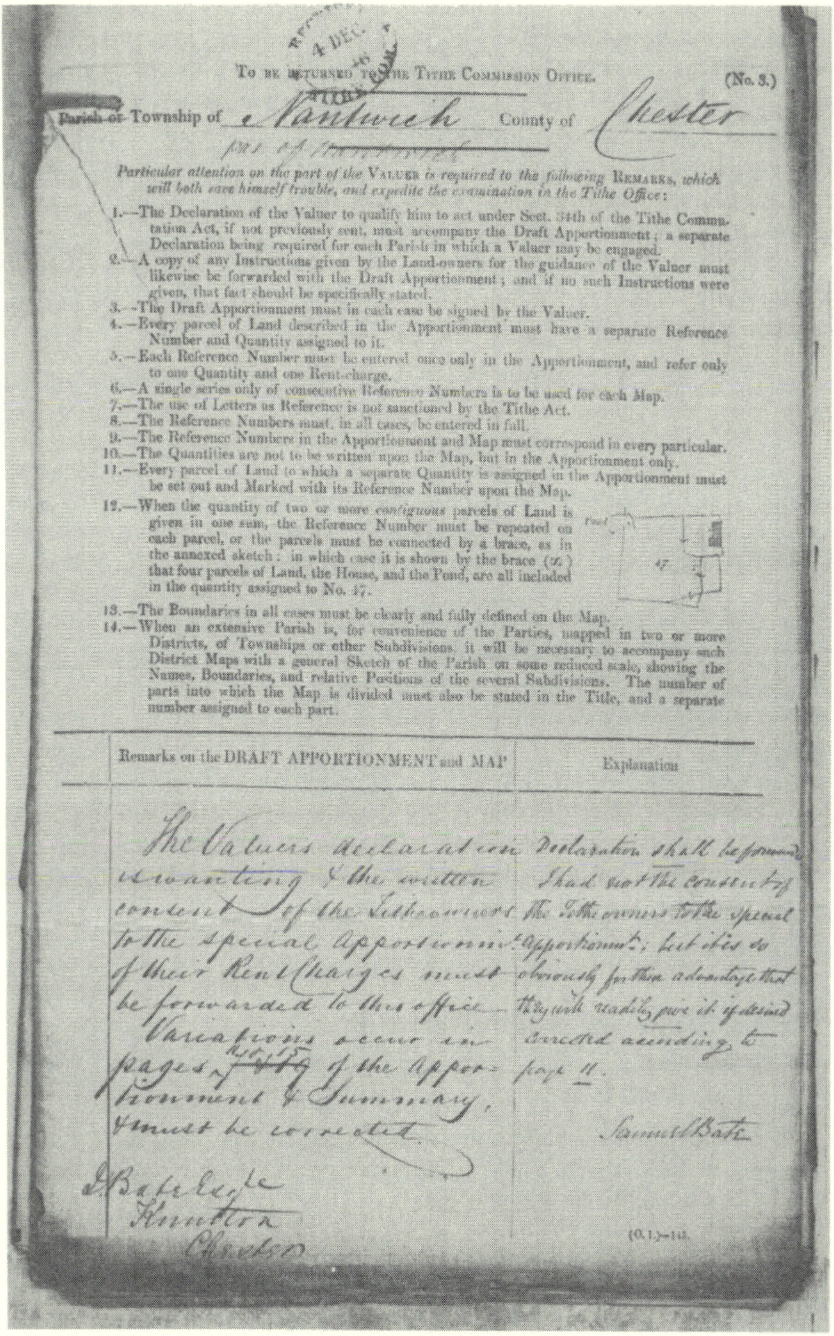

TO BE RETURNED TO THE TITHE COMMISSION OFFICE. (No. 3.)

~~Parish of~~ Township of Nantwich County of Chester

part of Nantwich

Particular attention on the part of the VALUER *is required to the following* REMARKS, *which will both save himself trouble, and expedite the examination in the Tithe Office:*

1.—The Declaration of the Valuer to qualify him to act under Sect. 34th of the Tithe Commutation Act, if not previously sent, must accompany the Draft Apportionment; a separate Declaration being required for each Parish in which a Valuer may be engaged.
2.—A copy of any Instructions given by the Land-owners for the guidance of the Valuer must likewise be forwarded with the Draft Apportionment; and if no such Instructions were given, that fact should be specifically stated.
3.—The Draft Apportionment must in each case be signed by the Valuer.
4.—Every parcel of Land described in the Apportionment must have a separate Reference Number and Quantity assigned to it.
5.—Each Reference Number must be entered once only in the Apportionment, and refer only to one Quantity and one Rent-charge.
6.—A single series only of consecutive Reference Numbers is to be used for each Map.
7.—The use of Letters as Reference is not sanctioned by the Tithe Act.
8.—The Reference Numbers must, in all cases, be entered in full.
9.—The Reference Numbers in the Apportionment and Map must correspond in every particular.
10.—The Quantities are not to be written upon the Map, but in the Apportionment only.
11.—Every parcel of Land to which a separate Quantity is assigned in the Apportionment must be set out and Marked with its Reference Number upon the Map.
12.—When the quantity of two or more *contiguous* parcels of Land is given in one sum, the Reference Number must be repeated on each parcel, or the parcels must be connected by a brace, as in the annexed sketch: in which case it is shown by the brace (x) that four parcels of Land, the House, and the Pond, are all included in the quantity assigned to No. 47.
13.—The Boundaries in all cases must be clearly and fully defined on the Map.
14.—When an extensive Parish is, for convenience of the Parties, mapped in two or more Districts, of Townships or other Subdivisions, it will be necessary to accompany such District Maps with a general Sketch of the Parish on some reduced scale, showing the Names, Boundaries, and relative Positions of the several Subdivisions. The number of parts into which the Map is divided must also be stated in the Title, and a separate number assigned to each part.

Remarks on the DRAFT APPORTIONMENT and MAP	Explanation
The Valuers declaration wanting & the written consent of the Tithe owners to the special Apportionment of their Rent Charges must be forwarded to this office. Variations occur in pages [illegible] of the Apportionment & Summary, & must be corrected	Declaration shall be forwarded. I had not the consent of the Tithe owners to the special Apportionment; but it is so obviously for their advantage that they will readily give it if desired. Corrected according to page 11. Samuel Bate

J. Bate Esq[re] Knutton Chester

(O. 1.)—145.

made by these methods. For instance, the second-class map of Bilstone parish, also in Leicestershire, was reduced from a working plan at the three-chain scale 'corrected and partly resurveyed by Samuel Morris and William Thorpe' in May 1850.[48] For compiling this map, 256 acres derived from the earlier survey were billed to the landowners at a copying charge of 2d an acre plus 2 guineas for 'examining and correcting old map'. A new survey required for the remaining 436 acres was charged at Dawson's recommended rate of 9d an acre.[49]

Authors of contemporary textbooks on tithe commutation procedure exhorted landowners to commit the extra expense that a first-class survey entailed. G. H. Whalley argued, for example, that:

> It is often a matter of grave deliberation and doubt amongst the landowners of a parish, whether they will put up with any old map they may chance to possess, or will at once construct for the apportionment an efficient map, which, by receiving the tithe seal, will be evidence in all time to come of quantities and estates. There can be no doubt that a parish which can boast such a map will be better off, in many respects, than its neighbour without one; and a map, with such legal qualifications, can never be procured, unless now as part of the apportionment.[50]

The cost of a first-class map could vary considerably around Dawson's average figure of 9d an acre depending on local topography. Moreover, total cost in relation to the rent-charge varied considerably depending on land value and factors such as the intermixture of titheable and tithe-free land. It could also be prohibitively expensive to survey at three chains to an inch districts with large extents of moorland. The tithe commissioners calculated that 2,333 of the 11,800 tithe maps were assigned to the first-class category.[51] As might be expected from the above comments, first-class maps are rarer in northern, upland counties and also in the midlands where often only part of a district remained titheable. On the other hand, in Kent, more than half the tithe maps are first-class (Fig. 3.5).

The characteristics and content of tithe maps

At three chains to an inch, tithe maps representing large parishes with detached portions, such as Dagenham or North Benfleet in Essex, may cover as much as 10 square metres. James Walker, a civil engineer, estimated in 1854, that a map of England alone at this scale would cover nearly 6½ acres and take 46,950 sheets of paper of the same size as the published sheets of the Ordnance Survey of Ireland.[52] Although not all tithe surveys are on the three-chain scale and they do not cover the whole of England, they are extant for most of Wales so an estimate of the surface area of the whole body of tithe maps would not be far short of Walker's figure. For large parishes and townships in upland areas, smaller scales were the

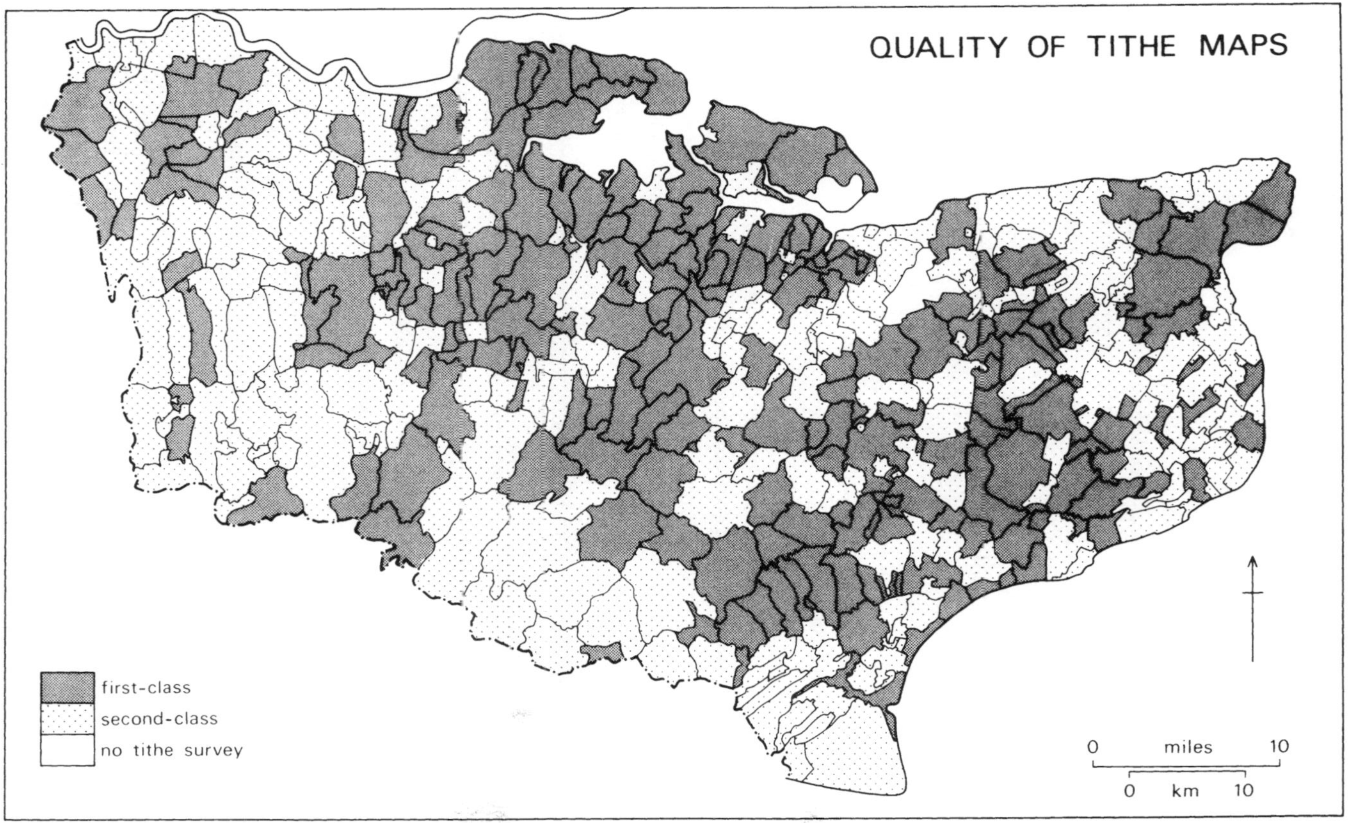

3.5 First- and second-class tithe maps in Kent. Source: tithe maps.

only practicable choice. Often, villages and towns are drawn at a larger scale of one or two chains to an inch and appended to the main tithe map.

All tithe maps, whatever their origin, show the boundaries of the tithe district. The natural unit for tithe commutation was the parish but where these were very large, as in the northern counties, townships were used instead. Also in southern England some villages, hamlets and extra-parochial places were designated as separate districts. This practice was quite common where there was more than one nucleation of settlement in a parish or where detached portions were separated by some distance.

Tithe maps also show the boundaries of the tithe areas within a parish. Tithe areas usually corresponded with fields, but in some instances, as at Rhosbeirio in Anglesey, they constituted whole farms or more rarely, as at Marske-by-Sea in Yorkshire where there was only one landowner, a whole township. In early surveys, where the sum to be apportioned was agreed, it could be considered unnecessary to assign a separate rent-charge to each parcel of land, but re-apportionment when fields changed hands proved so inconvenient that the practice was abandoned in 1840. After that field-by-field surveys were required.

On most maps the boundaries of enclosed fields are represented by continuous lines and those of unenclosed fields by dotted lines. Occasionally, hedges, fences and gates are also portrayed. The amount of other detail shown on tithe maps varies considerably. Most maps mark the courses of streams, canals, ditches, drains, the outline of lakes and ponds and lines of roads and paths. Some, such as the second-class map of Gittisham, Devon (Fig. 3.6), use conventional symbols recommended by Dawson in the first edition of his 'Instructions' to identify different types of land. Some maps differentiate between commons, heaths, rabbit warrens, ozier beds and undrained marshes. On many maps, coniferous- and deciduous-tree symbols of different sizes depict mature woodlands, plantations, parks and sometimes coppice and coppice-with-standards. Characteristically, inhabited buildings are tinted red, while barns and other structures are shaded in grey. Brickworks are shown on the map of Frindsbury in Kent while maps of industrial areas, like that of Wolverhampton (Fig. 3.7), distinguish a greater variety of buildings. On this map chapels are marked and named as are the principal places of manufacture such as the Shrubbery iron works. A few maps are rendered in full colour, to distinguish tithe-free land or various properties or farms or to show different categories of land use. Of 120 tithe maps in north-west Wiltshire inspected by B. R. Dittmer, 32 are coloured in such a way as to show the land use of each parcel of land. The colours used are mainly brown for arable, light-green for meadow and pasture and dark-green for woodland.[53] This is an exceptionally high proportion, the work of a group of surveyors from Cirencester; of more than 300 tithe maps of the Chilterns inspected by F. D. Hartley, only one in every 30 or 40 are coloured

3.6 Part of the second-class tithe map of Gittisham parish, Devon. Photograph reproduced by courtesy of Devon Record Office.

3.7 Part of the tithe map of Wolverhampton. Photograph reproduced by permission of the Keeper, Public Record Office.

in this way.[54] Hop grounds, orchards and gardens are much more frequently indicated by symbols on tithe maps according to Dawson's convention.

A few working copies of tithe maps have survived among surveyors' papers deposited in county record offices and occasionally tracings are found in the tithe files. The tithe file of North Ormsby in Lincolnshire contains a tracing of a working plan used by the valuer when making his apportionment of rent-charge and this shows the crops grown in each field and other details (Fig. 3.8). First-class tithe maps are often plainer in appearance than second-class, reflecting the Commission's advice noted above that a plain working plan with construction lines was the kind most likely to be certified first-class (Fig. 3.9).

Fig. 3.10 is an extract of the 1844 tithe map of Winterborne Kingston in Dorset. It shows part of the village and some of West Field. Dotted lines indicate boundaries of tithe areas or strips in the open field while continuous lines bound closes around the village. In 1848 Winterborne Kingston was enclosed and its pattern of fields and landownership totally transformed. Such was the extent of alteration that a complete re-apportionment of the rent-charge over the parish was required. Part of this altered apportionment map is reproduced as Fig. 3.11. Now all tithe areas are bounded by solid lines indicating their enclosed state. Typically, altered apportionment maps cover only a small part of a parish; events causing such sweeping changes in parish cadasters were rare after about 1850.

As well as topographical detail, most maps provide at least some biographical information to help unravel their provenance. Quite often they bear the name of the person who surveyed them and a date which may be the date of the survey or of redrawing and amalgamation of some earlier surveys. Also an indication of the scale is usually shown in the form of a measured scale bar. First-class tithe maps are identified by the presence of the tithe commissioners' seal.

Tithe apportionments

The apportionment is a roll of parchment sheets, $21\frac{1}{3}$ inches by $18\frac{3}{4}$ inches. Blank *pro formas* with headings and ruled columns were printed by Shaw and Sons of Fetter Lane, London, and put on sale to valuers. The same forms were used regardless of whether rent-charge was apportioned by properties or by individual fields, and whether by valuation or by equal acreable charge. As a result the body of tithe apportionments is more uniform than the set of maps. Originally all apportionments were fixed to the maps but most have since been detached and are stored separately. The longest apportionment contains 399 pages, those of 100–200 pages being not uncommon, but the average is 23 pages. In total, the apportionments run to some 271,000 sheets of parchment.[55]

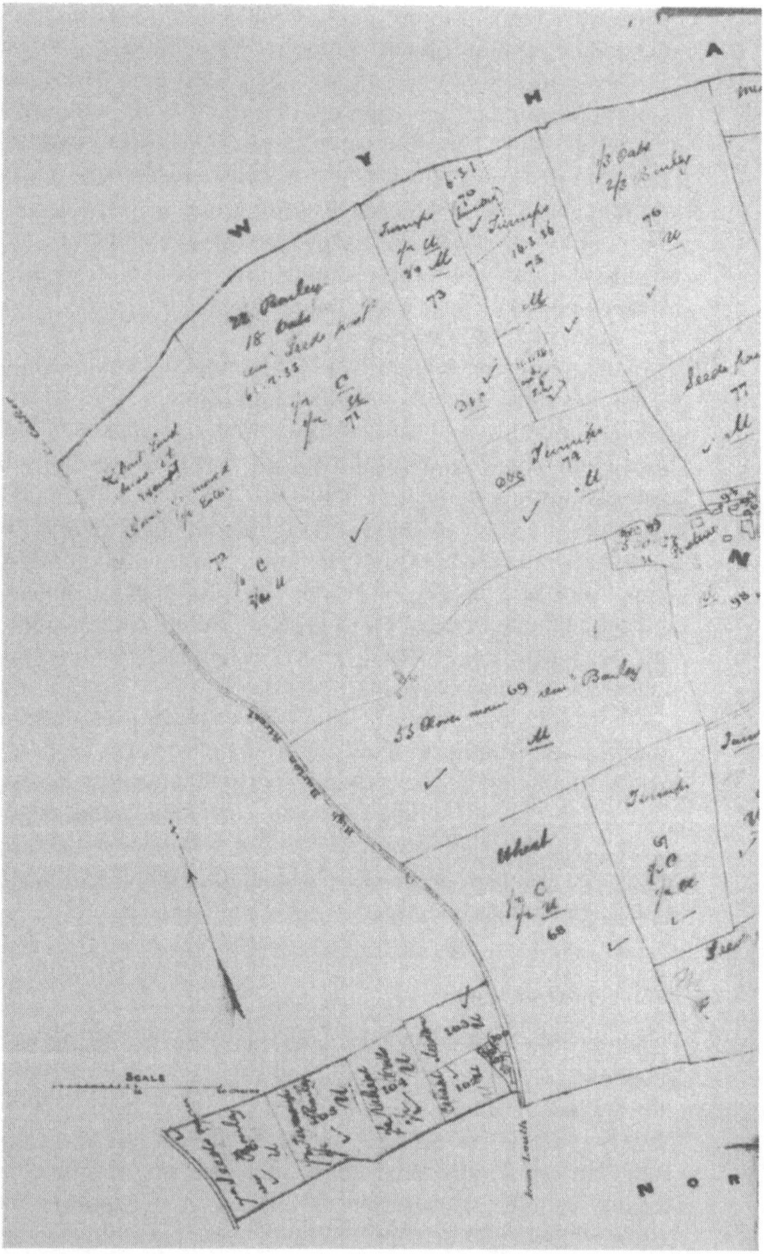

3.8 The valuer's working plan of North Ormsby in Lincolnshire preserved in the tithe file. Source: PRO IR 18/5166; photograph reproduced by permission of the Keeper, Public Record Office.

ELKINGTON

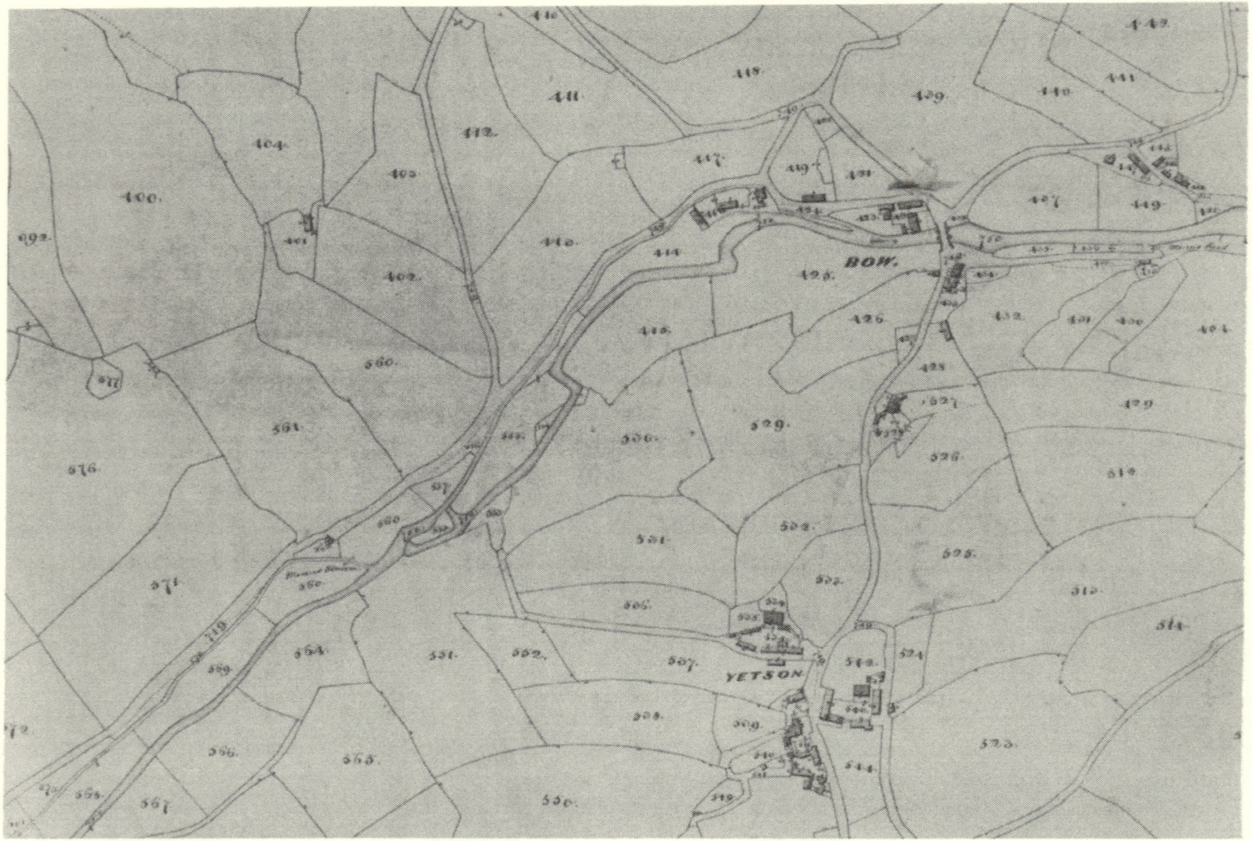

3.9 An extract from the first-class map of Ashprington, Devon, drawn at three chains to an inch in 1843. Photograph reproduced by courtesy of Devon Record Office.

The first section of an apportionment contains a statement of the articles of agreement for commutation or a recital of the award, giving the names of the commissioners, assistant commissioner, surveyor or valuer and the owners of tithe. It also states the date of confirmation of the apportionment, the area of the tithe district, the area subject to tithes and an estimate of the area of arable, grass and other kinds of land subject to tithes. Comments on the nature of lands exempt from tithes specify whether tithe had already been commuted, whether they were ancient monastic lands or whatever. Often, a list of tithe payers is attached. For ease of use of the main part of the apportionment, a reference index to the page numbers of the schedule of apportionment on which each tithe area is to be found is generally appended.

The second and most important part of the apportionment roll is the schedule of apportionment in which each tithe area, numbered on the accompanying plan, is listed under the name of its owner and occupier (Fig. 3.12). In a parish which still lay in open fields, as many as three thousand separate tithe areas may be enumerated; in a majority there are several hundred. In some districts the rent-charge is apportioned by farms, occasionally without a survey being made of each field; in a very few, no apportionment is made so that the whole titheable area of a district constitutes a single tithe area. Where, as in the majority of schedules, a tithe area is a field, the field name is recorded; where it is not a field it is described, for example, as a 'house and garden', a 'piece of water', a 'chalk pit', or an 'ice house'. Its state of cultivation is entered for purposes of valuation according to local practice, almost all schedules distinguishing arable and pasture and woodland and noting orchards, market gardens and hop grounds which might carry an extraordinary rent-charge. There are some instances of actual crops being noted, as at Erbistock in Denbighshire, Narford in Norfolk and South Warnborough in Hampshire (Fig. 3.13). As more tithe apportionments are inspected for various purposes this practice, once thought to have been quite unusual, is being more frequently encountered. A. D. M. Phillips, for example, has found that for 12 of the 239 tithe apportionments in Staffordshire, valuers recorded crops rather than land use under 'state of cultivation'.[56]

In some areas the amount of detail in the state of cultivation column differs from district to district. In the Vale of Clwyd, for example, the state of cultivation columns for some districts were left blank probably because rent-charge was apportioned on an acreable basis (Fig. 3.14). In some Wealden parishes such as Penshurst, combinations of use, as for example meadow and arable, wood and pasture, are recorded. On the whole, such variants are quite rare; in a large majority of districts the basic distinction between arable and pasture is clearly made. Following the state of cultivation column, the statute acreage of each tithe area in acres, roods and

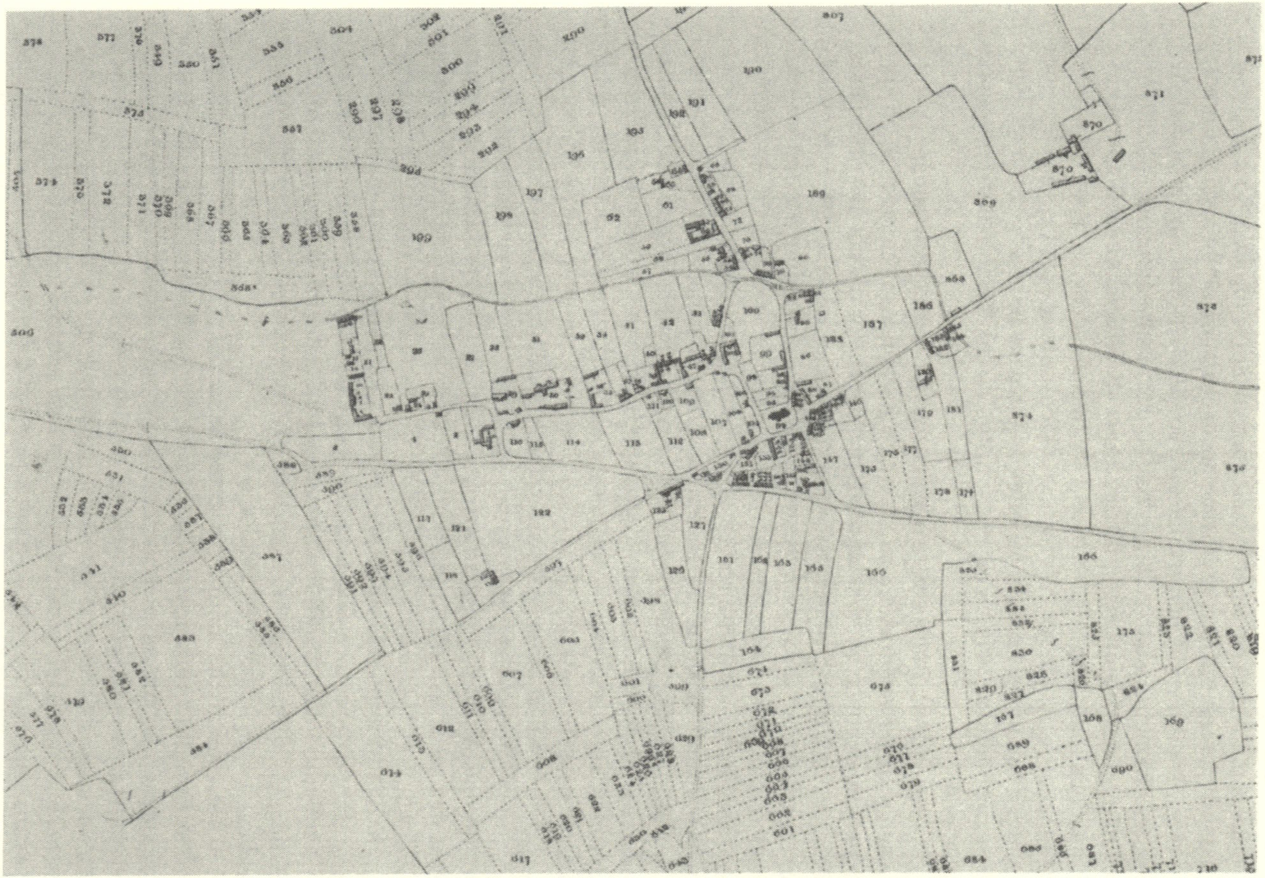

3.10 Part of the tithe map of Winterborne Kingston, Dorset, in 1844 showing the presence of open fields at this date. Photograph reproduced by permission of the Keeper, Public Record Office.

3.11 An extract from the altered apportionment map of the same part of Winterborne Kingston made in 1848 after enclosure. Photograph reproduced by permission of the Keeper, Public Record Office.

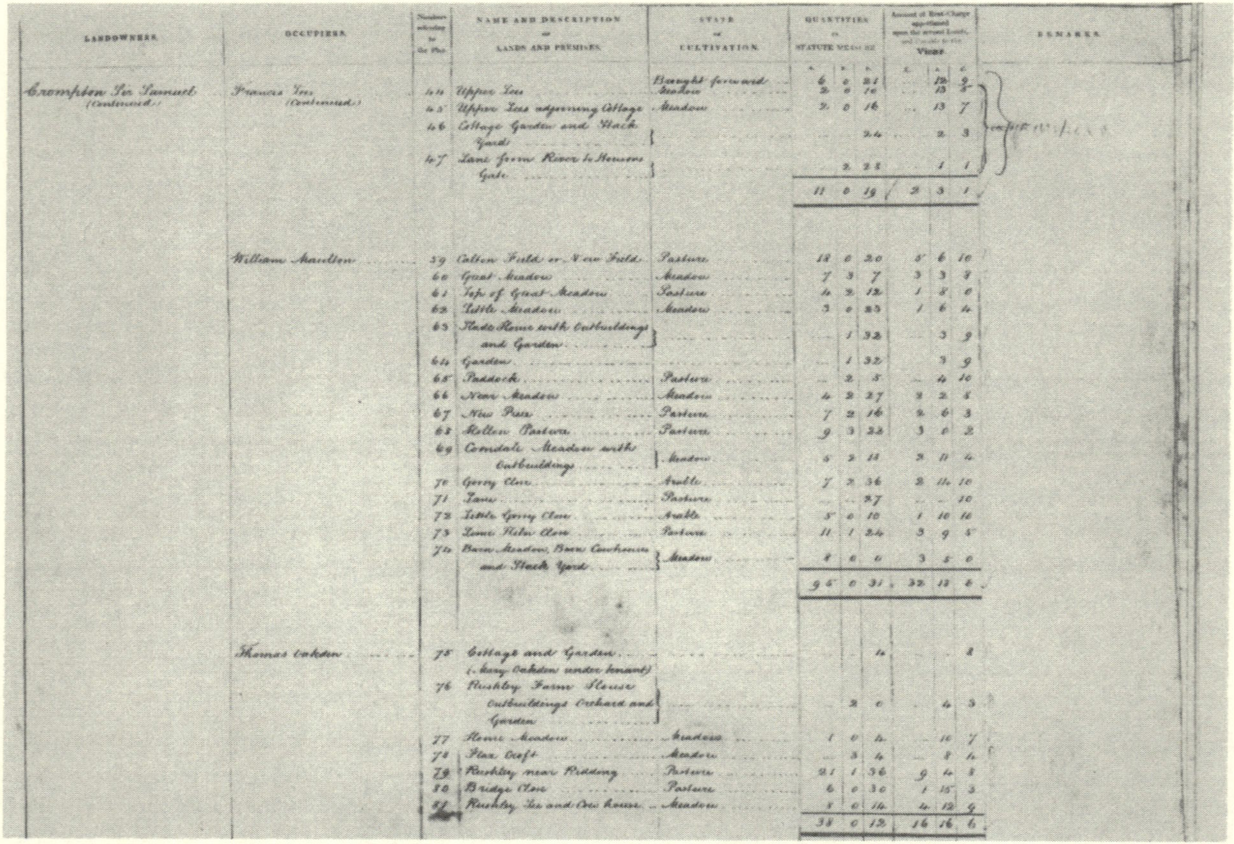

LANDOWNERS	OCCUPIERS	Numbers referring to the Plan	NAME AND DESCRIPTION of LANDS AND PREMISES	STATE of CULTIVATION	QUANTITIES in STATUTE MEASURE A.	R.	P.	Amount of Rent-Charge apportioned upon the several Lands, and Payable to the Vicar £.	s.	d.	REMARKS
Crompton Sir Samuel (Continued)	Francis Lees (Continued)			Brought forward	6	0	21		12	9	
		44	Upper Lees	Meadow	2	0	10		13	5	
		45	Upper Lees adjoining Cottage	Meadow	2	0	16		13	7	
		46	Cottage Garden and Stack Yard				24		2	3	
		47	Lane from River to Stevens Gate			2	28		1	1	
					11	0	19	2	3	1	
	William Maulton	59	Calton Field or New Field	Pasture	18	0	20	5	6	10	
		60	Great Meadow	Meadow	7	3	7	3	3	8	
		61	Top of Great Meadow	Pasture	4	2	12	1	8	0	
		62	Little Meadow	Meadow	3	0	25	1	6	4	
		63	Slade House with Outbuildings and Garden			1	32		3	9	
		64	Garden			1	32		3	9	
		65	Paddock	Pasture		2	5		4	10	
		66	New Meadow	Meadow	4	2	27	2	2	5	
		67	New Piece	Pasture	7	2	16	2	6	3	
		68	Mollow Pasture	Pasture	9	3	22	3	0	2	
		69	Comdale Meadow with Outbuildings	Meadow	5	2	11	2	11	4	
		70	Gorsy Close	Arable	7	2	36	2	14	10	
		71	Lane	Pasture			27			10	
		72	Little Gorsy Close	Arable	5	0	10	1	10	16	
		73	Lime Kiln Close	Pasture	11	1	24	3	9	5	
		74	Barn Meadow, Barn Cowhouse and Stack Yard	Meadow	8	0	0	3	5	0	
					95	0	31	32	13	8	
	Thomas Oakden	75	Cottage and Garden (Mary Oakden under tenant)				4			2	
		76	Rushley Farm House Outbuildings Orchard and Garden			2	0		4	3	
		77	Home Meadow	Meadow	1	0	4		10	7	
		78	Flax Croft	Meadow		3	4		8	4	
		79	Rushley near Ridding	Pasture	21	1	36	9	4	8	
		80	Bridge Close	Pasture	6	0	30	1	15	3	
		81	Rushley Lee and Cow house	Meadow	8	0	14	4	12	9	
					38	0	12	16	16	6	

3.12 A page from the schedule of apportionment of rent-charge in Ilam, Staffordshire, where field-by-field apportionment was employed. Photograph reproduced by permission of the Keeper, Public Record Office.

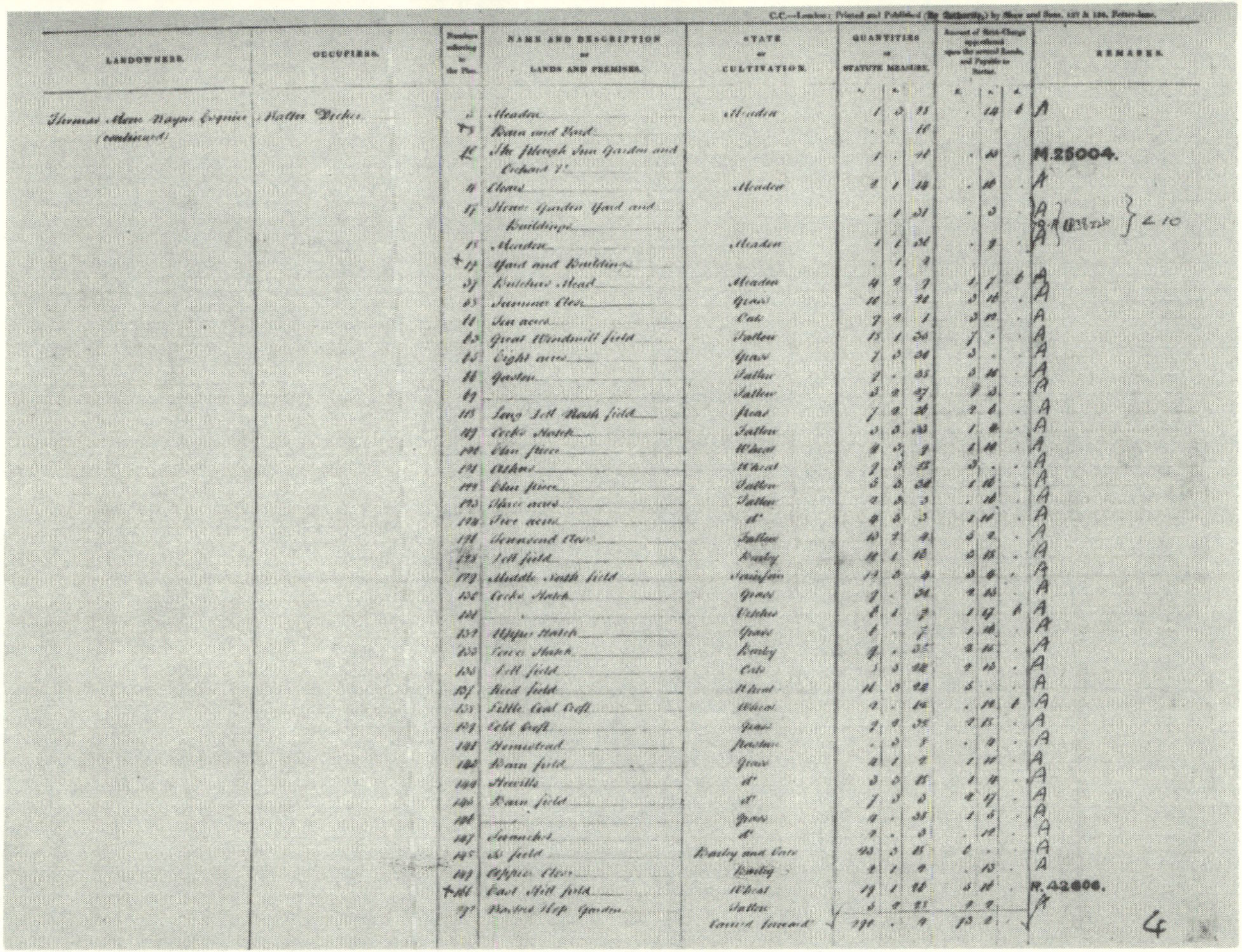

3.13 A page from the schedule of apportionment of South Warnborough, Hampshire, in which the crops grown in each field are listed in the 'state of cultivation' column. Photograph reproduced by permission of the Keeper, Public Record Office.

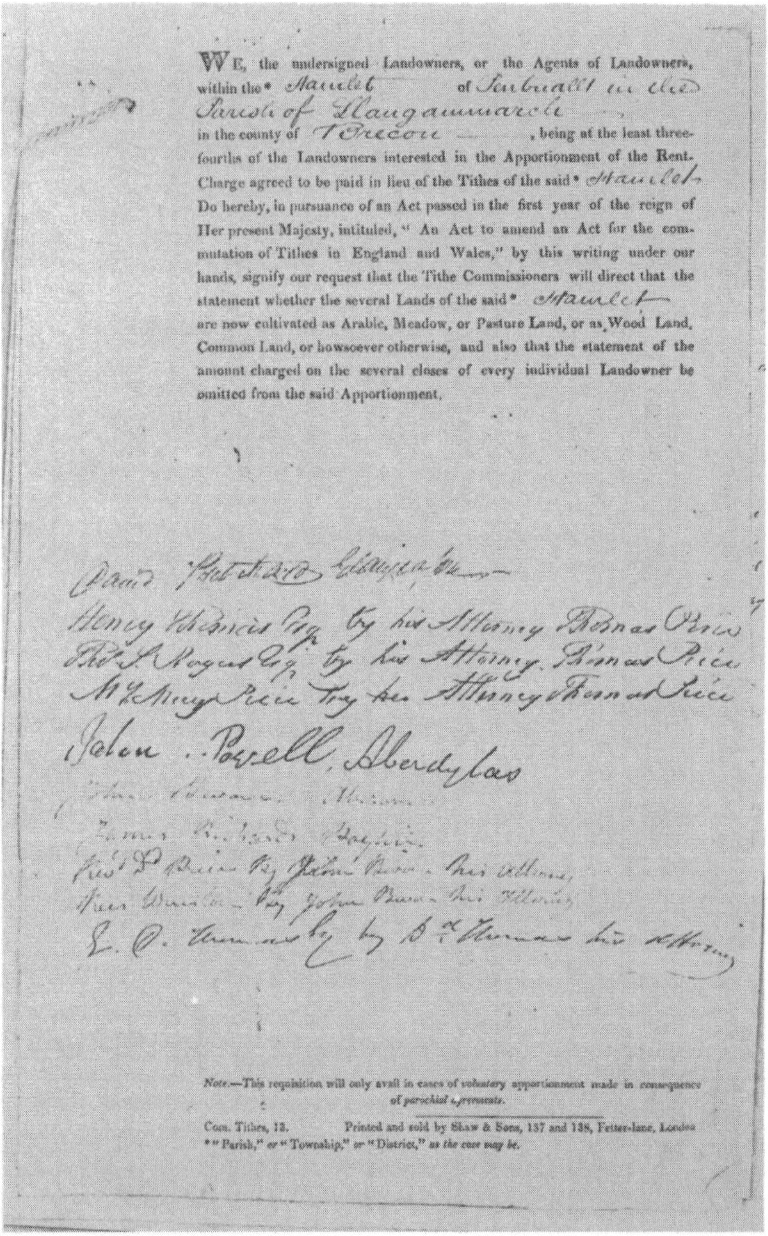

WE, the undersigned Landowners, or the Agents of Landowners, within the* Hamlet of Penbuallt in the Parish of Llangammarch in the county of Brecon, being at the least three-fourths of the Landowners interested in the Apportionment of the Rent-Charge agreed to be paid in lieu of the Tithes of the said* Hamlet Do hereby, in pursuance of an Act passed in the first year of the reign of Her present Majesty, intituled, "An Act to amend an Act for the commutation of Tithes in England and Wales," by this writing under our hands, signify our request that the Tithe Commissioners will direct that the statement whether the several Lands of the said* Hamlet are now cultivated as Arable, Meadow, or Pasture Land, or as Wood Land, Common Land, or howsoever otherwise, and also that the statement of the amount charged on the several closes of every individual Landowner be omitted from the said Apportionment.

John Powell, Aberdylas

Note.—This requisition will only avail in cases of *voluntary* apportionment made in consequence of *parochial agreements.*

Com. Tithes, 13. Printed and sold by Shaw & Sons, 137 and 138, Fetter-lane, London

* "Parish," or "Township," or "District," *as the case may be.*

3.14 Agreement to apportion rent-charge by properties in the hamlet of Penbuallt, Brecon. Source: PRO IR 18/13963; photograph reproduced by permission of the Keeper, Public Record Office.

perches is given together with the value of the rent-charge apportioned to it (in the usual form of entry where apportionment is parcel-by-parcel). A final column in the schedule of apportionment is left for 'remarks', which sometimes explain special valuations, such as those attached to mills or intakes from the waste. Most schedules are completed in manuscript, a very few, like that of Deal in Kent (a part of a page of which is reproduced in Fig. 3.15), were printed.

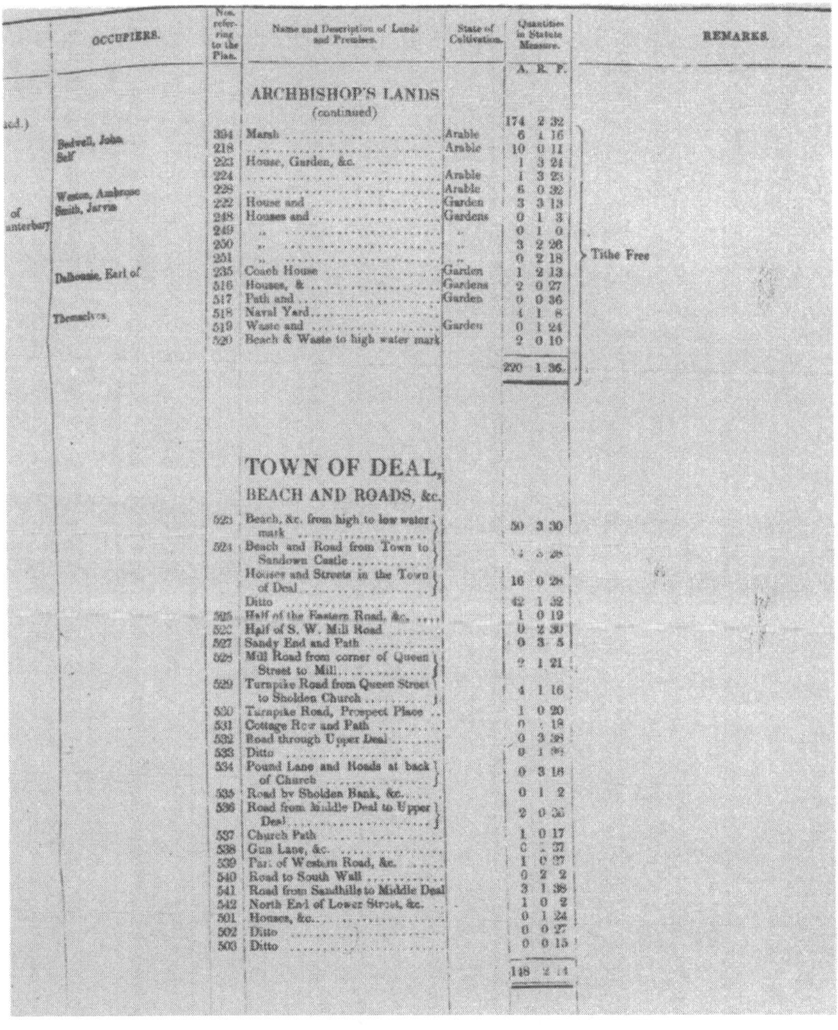

	OCCUPIERS.	Nos. referring to the Plan.	Name and Description of Lands and Premises.	State of Cultivation.	Quantities in Statute Measure. A. R. P.	REMARKS.
			ARCHBISHOP'S LANDS (continued)			
...ued.)					174 2 32	
	Bedwell, John	394	Marsh	Arable	6 1 16	
	Self	218		Arable	10 0 11	
		223	House, Garden, &c.		1 3 24	
		224		Arable	1 3 25	
	Weston, Ambrose	228		Arable	6 0 32	
of	Smith, Jarvis	222	House and	Garden	3 3 13	
...anterbury		248	Houses and	Gardens	0 1 3	
		249	"	"	0 1 0	
		250	"	"	3 2 28	
		251	"	"	0 2 18	Tithe Free
	Dalhousie, Earl of	235	Coach House	Garden	1 2 13	
		516	Houses, &	Gardens	2 0 27	
		517	Path and	Garden	0 0 36	
	Themselves	518	Naval Yard		4 1 8	
		519	Waste and	Garden	0 1 24	
		520	Beach & Waste to high water mark		2 0 10	
					220 1 36	
			TOWN OF DEAL, BEACH AND ROADS, &c.			
		523	Beach, &c. from high to low water mark		50 3 30	
		524	Beach and Road from Town to Sandown Castle		[illegible]	
			Houses and Streets in the Town of Deal		16 0 28	
			Ditto		42 1 32	
		525	Half of the Eastern Road, &c.		1 0 19	
		526	Half of S. W. Mill Road		0 2 30	
		527	Sandy End and Path		0 3 5	
		528	Mill Road from corner of Queen Street to Mill		2 1 21	
		529	Turnpike Road from Queen Street to Sholden Church		4 1 16	
		530	Turnpike Road, Prospect Place		1 0 20	
		531	Cottage Row and Path		0 [illegible] 19	
		532	Road through Upper Deal		0 3 38	
		533	Ditto		0 1 [illegible]	
		534	Pound Lane and Roads at back of Church		0 3 18	
		535	Road by Sholden Bank, &c.		0 1 2	
		536	Road from Middle Deal to Upper Deal		2 0 [illegible]	
		537	Church Path		1 0 17	
		538	Gun Lane, &c.		0 [illegible] 37	
		539	Part of Western Road, &c.		1 0 37	
		540	Road to South Wall		0 2 2	
		541	Road from Sandhills to Middle Deal		3 1 38	
		542	North End of Lower Street, &c.		1 0 2	
		501	Houses, &c.		0 1 24	
		502	Ditto		0 0 27	
		503	Ditto		0 0 15	
					148 2 [illegible]	

3.15 An extract from the printed schedule of apportionment of the parish of Deal in Kent. Photograph reproduced by permission of the Keeper, Public Record Office.

The third section of the apportionment roll is a summary of the schedule of apportionment (Fig. 3.16). Here all landowners in the tithe district are listed alphabetically with names of the occupiers of their various holdings. The acreage of the holding and the total amount of rent-charge apportioned upon it are stated. At the end of the summary list these figures are totalled so

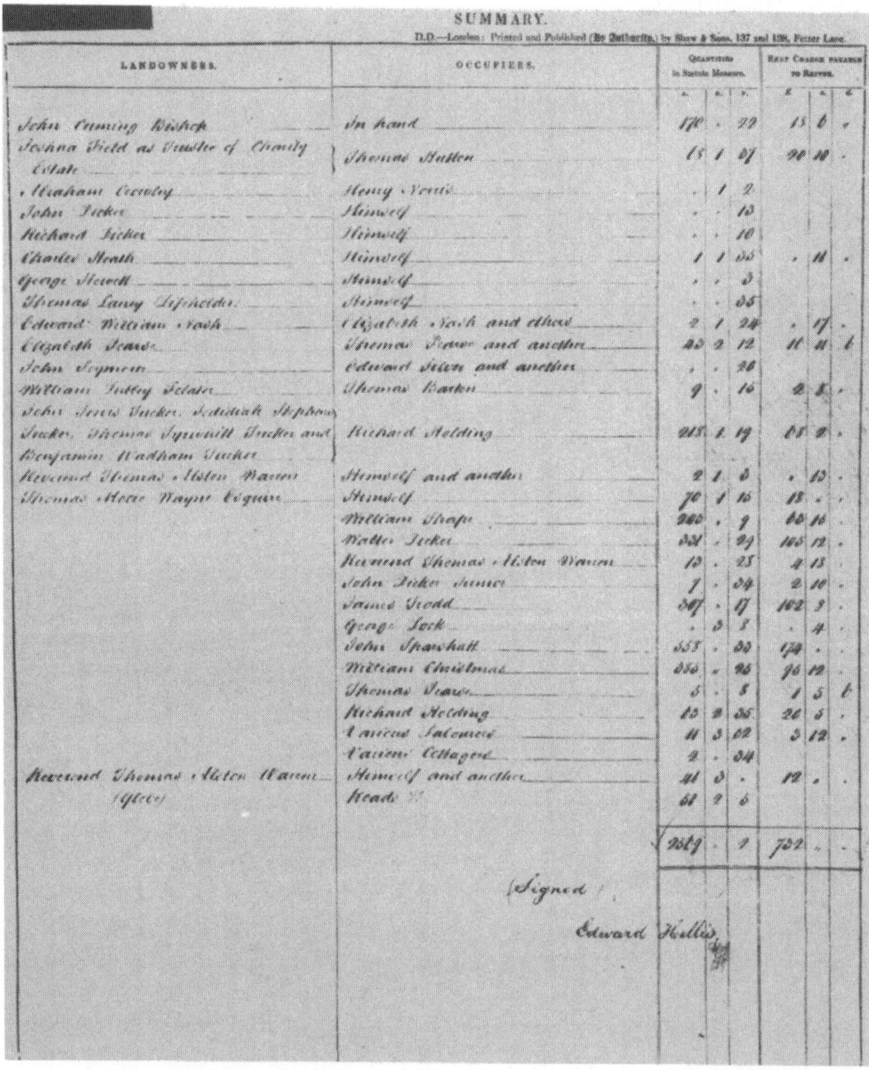

SUMMARY.

D.D.—London: Printed and Published (By Authority,) by Shaw & Sons, 137 and 138, Fetter Lane.

LANDOWNERS.	OCCUPIERS.	Quantities in Statute Measure. a.	r.	p.	Rent Charge payable to Parson. £	s.	d.
John Cuming Bishop	In hand	170	.	29	15	6	.
Joshua Field as Trustee of Charity Estate	Thomas Hutton	18	1	07	90	10	.
Abraham Crowley	Henry Norris	.	1	2			
John Tucker	Himself	.	.	13			
Richard Tucker	Himself	.	.	10			
Charles Heath	Himself	1	1	35	.	11	.
George Hewett	Himself	.	.	3			
Thomas Lacey Lifeholder	Himself	.	.	35			
Edward William Nash	Elizabeth Nash and others	2	1	24	.	17	.
Elizabeth Pearse	Thomas Pearse and another	45	2	12	11	11	6
John Seymour	Edward Allen and another	.	.	20			
William Sutley Sclater	Thomas Barton	9	.	16	2	5	.
John Lewis Tucker, Jedediah Stephens Tucker, Thomas Sygrovill Tucker and Benjamin Wadham Tucker	Richard Holding	215	1	19	65	9	.
Reverend Thomas Alston Warren	Himself and another	2	1	3	.	13	.
Thomas Moore Wayne Esquire	Himself	70	1	16	18	.	.
	William Sharpe	240	.	9	65	16	.
	Walter Tucker	331	.	27	105	12	.
	Reverend Thomas Alston Warren	13	.	25	4	13	.
	John Tucker Junior	7	.	34	2	10	.
	James Trodd	307	.	17	102	3	.
	George Lock	.	3	8	.	4	.
	John Sparshatt	558	.	30	174	.	.
	William Christmas	350	.	25	96	19	.
	Thomas Pearse	5	.	8	1	5	6
	Richard Holding	15	2	35	26	5	.
	Various Labourers	11	3	02	3	12	.
	Various Cottagers	2	.	34			
Reverend Thomas Alston Warren (Glebe)	Himself and another	41	3	.	12	.	.
	Roads &c	61	2	6			
		2569	.	7	722	.	.

(Signed)

Edward Hollis

3.16 The last page of the summary of the schedule of apportionment of South Warnborough parish in Hampshire. Photograph reproduced by permission of the Keeper, Public Record Office.

that a global figure of the rent-charge for which tithes have been commuted in the district is stated. The acreage of roads, waste and other land exempt from tithe is usually added to the acreage subject to tithe, and finally the total amount of rent-charge agreed or awarded is stated.

The fourth and final section of the apportionment roll contains altered apportionments made after the original apportionment was confirmed. In a few parishes, parcels of land have passed undivided from generation to generation, but such places are exceptional. Over much of the country changes in ownership have been frequent, estates have been broken up and land has been put to new uses. In 1854 William Blamire stated that there were already 976 altered apportionments in the custody of the tithe office.[57] Altered apportionments record major changes in the shape, size and status of the original tithe areas resulting from severance or subdivision. The building of railways, construction of new roads, re-allocation of land under an enclosure award, and other public works all necessitated altered apportionments. When changes affected a large part of a parish a separate new apportionment might be made. Reference has already been made to an instance of this type at Winterborne Kingston in Dorset. New reference numbers given to altered tithe areas may be differentiated from the original numbers by the addition of a letter or sign, thus an original area 134 may be designated 134A, 134a, A134 or even A134aa.

Tithe files

A separate tithe file, kept for each tithe district, contains some additional information, not only on procedures adopted in commutation, but on farming practices in the locality. The tithe files were briefly described in an article written by the secretary of the Tithe Redemption Commission in 1957 but their modern use as a source of historical data dates from the years around 1960 when they were 'discovered' by a group of research students from the Geography Department, University College London. Two of these, Elwyn Cox and Brian Dittmer, have drawn attention to the value of tithe-file documents for agrarian historians in an important article in *Agricultural History Review*.[58] Although the files were heavily weeded before the First World War, surviving correspondence and miscellaneous notes throw light on the demeanour of the clergy, on the interests of parishioners, on property disputes, on leases, on the upkeep of roads, and on the operation of local markets. In addition to these details are statements amplifying the terms of the agreement or award. The transfer of glebe lands, sale of tithe barns, conditions attached to compositions, arrangements for mergers and redemptions, reasons for exemptions and enquiries into the validity of settlements made at the time of enclosure may be recorded.

There are 14,829 tithe files in all and these can be classified into three broad groups on the basis of their contents. First, about 2,200 files relate to districts where tithe was no longer payable in 1836 or had been redeemed by merger in the land. Most of these contain little more than a brief statement by a representative of the Tithe Commission to confirm that all tithes had been extinguished.

A second group consists of some 6,000 files of districts where commutation was effected by compulsory award. Files for these places usually contain a draft award and minutes of meetings held in the presence of an assistant commissioner who called witnesses on behalf of various parties, cross-questioned them under oath, and recorded their statements either verbatim or as notes. It is difficult to generalise about what information might be recorded in these 'minutes'. Reasons for failing to reach an agreement varied considerably, but the more complex the problems the more likely it is that extensive records were generated. Another variable is the attitude of the different assistant commissioners; their interpretation of what they were expected to do did vary. And the weeding operation was carried out haphazardly, leaving some files almost empty whilst others have scarcely been touched.

A third group of files pertains to some 6,740 districts where tithe was commuted by agreement and where, therefore, an assistant tithe commissioner or local tithe agent was required to submit a written report on the agreement (see above chapter 2). To help the Tithe Commission's local representatives judge agreements and to organise and standardise their reports, they were issued from November 1837 with forms on which a number of questions were printed with spaces for answers. These provide much information on local landscapes, farming practices and output of agriculture. Report forms were not usually weeded out except where an agreement was replaced by a compulsory award, and in some files a report is the only document which has survived.

Two basic types of printed report form were used (with minor changes in format over the years) and these have been described with the aid of specimen answers from an Essex and a north-west Wiltshire parish by Cox and Dittmer.[59] In any one county only one type of form was in general use. In mainly arable-farming counties of the country it was expected that agreed rent-charges would be checked by calculating a tenth of the gross produce of the crops, usually by multiplying estimated crop acreages by average yield. Grassland in these areas was valued according to the yield of hay and the agistment value of the pasture. In mainly pastoral livestock-rearing counties of the west, an alternative much shorter form was used eliciting the value of grassland products, and calling for an estimate of the number of various sorts of stock kept. Figure 3.17 indicates that the 'arable' type of form was used in the east and south of the country and the 'pastoral' type in the west and in Wales. Some counties are in somewhat anomalous positions. Shropshire

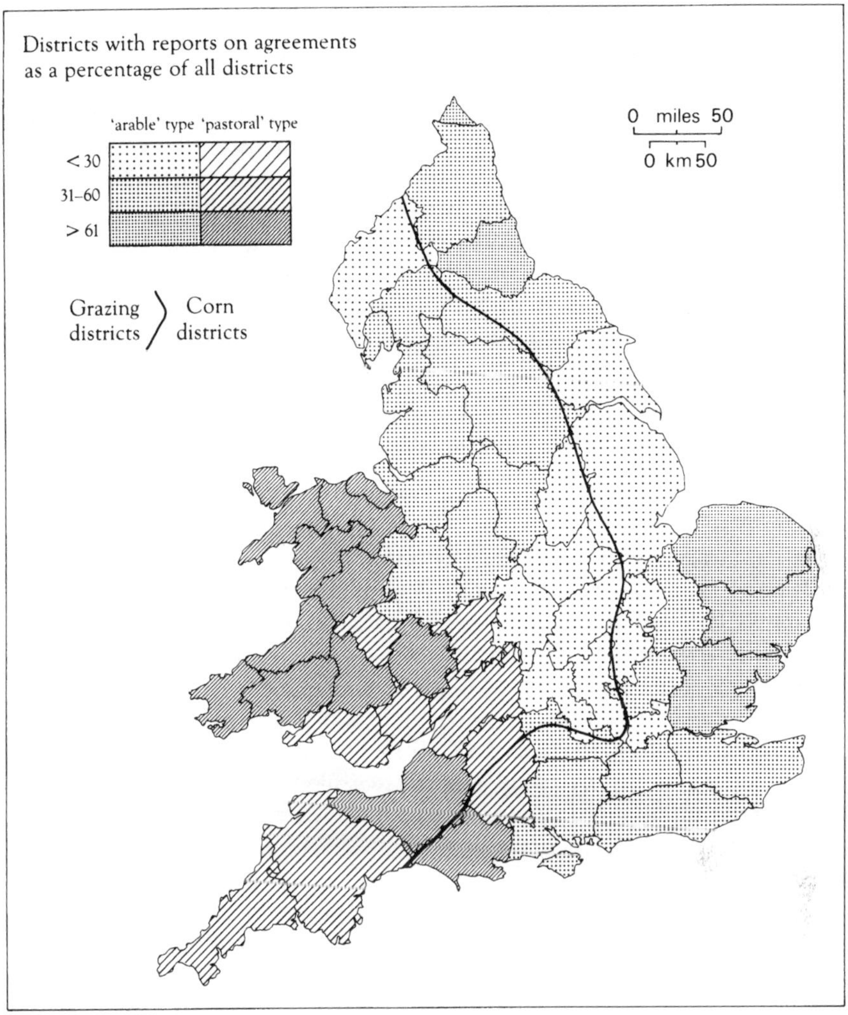

3.17 Coverage of 'arable' and 'pastoral' types of report on tithe agreements in England and Wales. Source: tithe files; line dividing grazing from corn districts from J. Caird, *English agriculture in 1850–51*, frontispiece.

reports are of the 'arable' type, although in counties to the south and west, 'pastoral' forms were used. In view of the long tradition of dairy farming in Cheshire it might be expected that the 'pastoral' type of report would have been used there, but, for reasons that are not known, the 'arable' type was used throughout this county.

Both types of report contain a record of certain preliminaries: the dates and places of meetings, numbers of landowners and their interest, the quantity of glebe, amount of the rates, the value of tithes collected in kind or compounded during the years of average (1829–35), the relationship of this sum to that of neighbouring districts, whether it included amounts for personal, mineral or fish tithes, and whether the agreement reached was fair and could be confirmed. On 'arable' reports questions on these topics are printed and answered on the forms; with 'pastoral' reports this information is found in a supplementary hand-written report which the agent usually attached to his completed questionnaire. The critical questions were 'Is the agreement fair?' and 'Should the agreement be confirmed?' To help answer these, agents were asked to furnish some quantitative data on land use, crops and yields and add descriptive information on matters related to assessing a fair rent-charge.

Quantitative data on farming in tithe file reports on agreements

The 'arable' reports required local agents to provide either 'a rough valuation of the tithes of the parish' (1838 forms), or (from later 1838 onwards) 'a description and rough estimate of the amount of the titheable produce'. Under this heading a great deal of material useful to historians is provided. The valuations generally set out the titheable acreage of the district and the amounts of meadow and pasture, woodland, common and specialist land uses such as orchards, gardens and hops which, because of the high value per acre of their produce, were sometimes required to bear an extraordinary rent-charge (Fig. 3.18). But of these land uses, only the arable and meadow and pasture categories are recorded over the whole country. Woodland is often not recorded because it was exempt from tithe, as in the Chilterns or in the Weald, and common and unfarmed land were difficult to assess and, because of low titheable value, often did not merit careful measurement. 'Gardens' were sometimes narrowly defined as market gardens but more usually included cottage gardens where these were titheable. Hop acreages in those areas where extraordinary charges did not apply were commonly subsumed in the arable acreage as were gardens when these were not separately identified. Orchards were either enumerated separately or included with pasture. In a separate table after the land-use data, the local agent or assistant commissioner set out acreages of crops grown on the arable, their yields and the prices which he used to calculate the gross produce of the arable.

On the 'pastoral' type of report form local agents were asked to estimate the acreage of arable defined as 'land actually ploughed in the present or last season, whether sown with corn, planted with roots or fallow, but excluding seeds'. They were also asked to state the number of acres of pasture including seeds. In the tithe apportionments on the other hand and also in 'arable' reports, the term 'arable' usually included land that had been

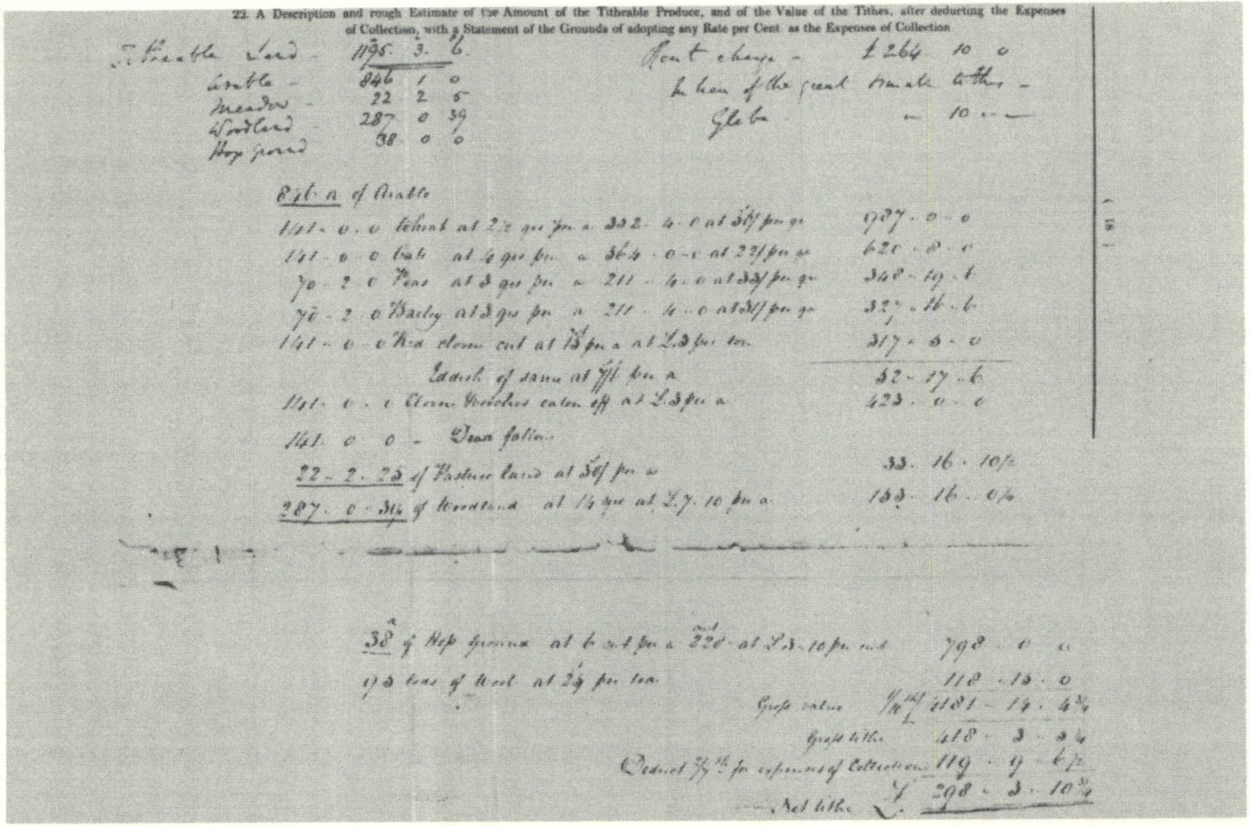
22. A Description and rough Estimate of the Amount of the Titheable Produce, and of the Value of the Tithes, after deducting the Expenses of Collection, with a Statement of the Grounds of adopting any Rate per Cent as the Expenses of Collection

3.18 'Description and rough estimate of the titheable produce' at Newington, Kent. Source: PRO IR 18/3728; photograph reproduced by permission of the Keeper, Public Record Office.

ploughed within the years of average. For western counties, however, the 'pastoral' reports definition is a realistic interpretation of arable because seeds were usually pastured for at least three years and quite often for ten or more years before being ploughed up again. Further comments on land-use definitions are made in chapter 4 below.

In 'pastoral' reports, the acreage of crops was not asked for but rather question 2 said 'What is the course of crops?' (Fig. 3.19). It is possible to derive estimates of the acreage of individual crops by dividing the acreage of arable by the number of courses (excluding the seeds courses) in the rotation. In fact, this is exactly the method by which most tithe agents produced their 'rough estimate of the amount of titheable produce' in eastern counties. However, for a number of reasons it is not possible to derive the acreages of all crops in all districts in this way. Firstly, more than one rotation might be stated without an indication of the proportion of the district to which each applied. Secondly, rotations were sometimes less than fully described; at Marham Church in Cornwall, William Glasson recorded a rotation of 'wheat, barley or oats – part potatoes and a small quantity of turnips'.[60] From such an imprecise description of the rotation it is not possible to derive crop acreages. Yield figures are not usually entered on the printed 'pastoral' forms but are to be found in manuscript reports which accompany them.

Local agents were not required to state the acreage of woodland on printed 'pastoral' forms; usually only coppice and underwood were titheable. Sometimes woodland amounts were written in at the end of a form or included in a covering manuscript report. This practice varied from agent to agent and from assistant commissioner to assistant commissioner as well as from county to county; woodland acreages were infrequently stated in Gloucestershire and Herefordshire, for example. Nor were acreages of market gardens or hops required for 'pastoral' forms which means that consistent data on hop cultivation in counties such as Worcestershire are not available.

In short, data on land use and crops in 'pastoral' reports are not as comprehensive or as consistently recorded as in 'arable' reports. On the credit side, assistant tithe commissioners and local agents were required to enter the number of cows, bullocks, horses and sheep kept in a tithe district in answer to question 12 of the 'pastoral' questionnaire. On 'arable' reports the produce of grassland was assessed by the agistment value of pasture and the yield of hay. Stock numbers were presented infrequently and incidentally in 'arable' reports or put, as in Lancashire, not in the form of numbers but rather as a density of stock which the pasture could support.

Descriptions of parish farming in tithe file reports on agreements

In 'arable' reports assistant commissioners were asked to 'Describe the parish and the quality of the lands, the system of farming, and whether the quality of the produce has been affected by any extraordinary instances of high or low farming.' On the relatively small number of report forms used in 1838, the same request was made but phrased as two separate questions. The 'pastoral' reports required 'Remarks, stating the peculiar circumstances of the parish which may affect the value of the tithe.' The difference in breadth of the questions is reflected in the value of the answers, though the predilections of a particular assistant commissioner could greatly influence what was written. Some made do with cryptic one- or two-sentence answers on 'arable' forms and others filled all available space on 'pastoral' reports and greatly exceeded their limited brief.

In any one county, one agent reported on a clear majority of districts (Table 2.1 in chapter 2). Therefore, the value of the descriptive material (as with the quantitative data) can vary from one part of the country to another in line with the different approaches of particular commissioners. Over 80 per cent of the reports on agreements for Somerset districts were completed by R. Page who wrote much fuller answers than usual on 'pastoral' forms. On the other hand, John Farncombe who reported on 158 of the 188 agreements in Sussex wrote very brief, rather stereotyped accounts which depresses the value of the tithe files as a source in this county despite a good (58 per cent) coverage of reports on agreements. Some of the fullest descriptions were compiled by Henry Gunning who worked extensively in Norfolk, Suffolk and Cambridgeshire. His accounts usually occupy two full sides of closely written foolscap and discuss markets, the quality of different types of land, rotations, summer fallowing and the cultivation of root crops, meadows and pastures, types of stock, and the nature and extent of woodland and waste.[61] He was knowledgeable about high farming, frequently commenting on the types of manures and fertilisers employed, turnip culture, artificial feedstuffs and underdrainage. He frequently spiced his factual accounts with anecdotes: at one parish he mentions the idleness and drinking habits of the population, at another he speaks of paupers having been recently shipped to North America. In several Denbighshire reports, John Fenton similarly found space to discuss local folklore. For instance, at Llanelian yn Rhos he wrote about the powers of the water well. By inscribing the name of a person on a stone and throwing it in the well, 'diverse disorders would fall upon them'. The malediction could only be removed by paying the keeper of the well to remove the stone. She reportedly enjoyed a thriving trade.[62]

Although most descriptive material in the tithe files relates to agriculture and local tithe practices, the files can throw light on many other topics such

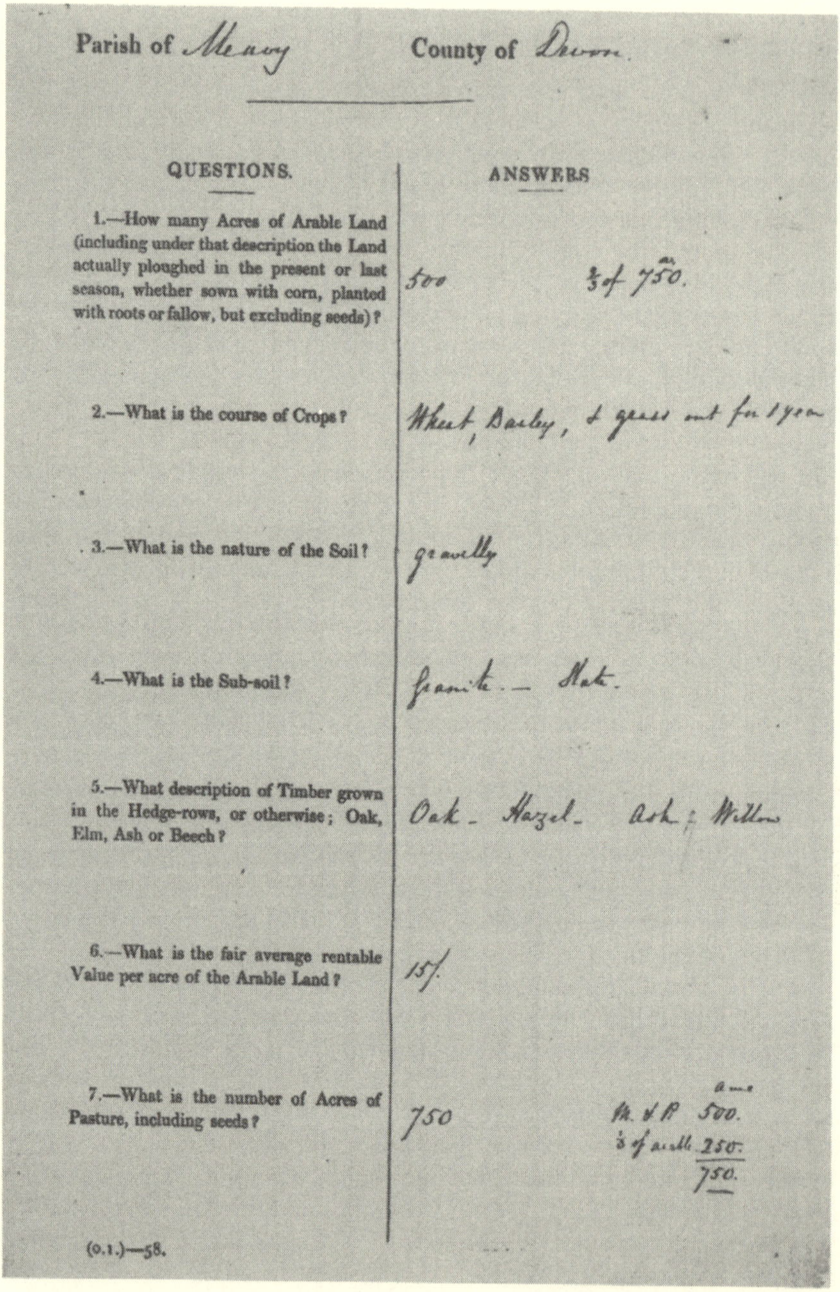

Parish of Meavy County of Devon.

QUESTIONS.	ANSWERS
1.—How many Acres of Arable Land (including under that description the Land actually ploughed in the present or last season, whether sown with corn, planted with roots or fallow, but excluding seeds)?	500 ⅔ of 750.
2.—What is the course of Crops?	Wheat, Barley, & grass out for 1 year
3.—What is the nature of the Soil?	gravelly
4.—What is the Sub-soil?	Granite — Slate.
5.—What description of Timber grown in the Hedge-rows, or otherwise; Oak, Elm, Ash or Beech?	Oak – Hazel – Ash & Willow
6.—What is the fair average rentable Value per acre of the Arable Land?	15/.
7.—What is the number of Acres of Pasture, including seeds?	750 M. & P. 500. ⅓ of arable 250. 750.

(O.1.)—58.

3.19 An extract from the report on the tithe agreement at Meavy, Devon (continued on facing page). Source: PRO IR 18/1396; photograph reproduced by permission of the Keeper, Public Record Office.

(2)

QUESTIONS.	ANSWERS.
8.—What is the nature of the Soil?	
9.—What is the Sub-soil?	
10.—What description of Timber?	
11.—What is the number of Acres of Common?	746.
12.—Stock:	
Number of Cows?	100.
Ditto - Bullocks?	70.
Ditto - Horses?	80
Ditto - Sheep?	1500.
13.—What is the fair average rentable Value of the Pasture?	20/.
14.—Ditto, of the Common?	1/.
	£. s. d.
15.—Average Composition on the seven years previous to Christmas 1835 -	214.
Add average amount of Rates, if paid by the Occupiers or Landowners for the Tithe-owner - - - -	

as church incomes and the condition of the clergy, attitudes of parishioners, relationships between labourers and farmers, and the general structure of the community and the way it organised and administered itself. This information is of great value to historians and historical geographers working on the nineteenth century. Much of it is unequalled in its wealth of detail at any other period. The problem is that information on a particular topic is probably to be found scattered through many dozens or even hundreds of files so that most researchers have been unable to devote the time necessary to search through them. To facilitate such searches all the files have now been subject-indexed to enable material to be more easily retrieved.[63]

The coverage of the country by tithe surveys

Many counties were almost entirely covered by the work of the tithe commissioners. The major exceptions, as Gilbert Slater demonstrated, were places which dealt with their tithes at the time of parliamentary enclosure. The results of Slater's calculations indicate that Cornwall, Kent and Devon had respectively 98.6, 97.8 and 97.4 per cent of their areas covered by tithe surveys. In Northamptonshire, where 51.8 per cent of land was subjected to parliamentary enclosure, tithe surveys cover only 23.5 per cent of the county.[64] Using R. K. Dawson's estimate of the average size of a tithe district as 2,500 acres, then the whole body of tithe surveys covers some 29,500,000 acres, about three-quarters of England and Wales.[65]

The frontispiece map shows those tithe districts in England and Wales for which there is a tithe map and apportionment. It has been compiled by comparing the Public Record Office list of tithe districts with the names of parishes and townships listed in the keys to the county index sheets of the first edition Ordnance Survey six-inch maps published around the year 1880. A number of discrepancies arise from the alteration of county boundaries and from the amalgamation of parishes, townships, hamlets, chapelries and tithings, and a few from changes in name. Some anomalies have been resolved by reference to later editions of Ordnance Survey maps for verification of township boundaries. The first edition six-inch key sheets are not ideal for this purpose but they are the best available small-scale maps portraying parish boundaries. They largely preceded the parish amalgamations which followed the Local Government Act of 1888, although many include changes brought about by various Divided Parishes Acts in the 1870s. Changes were most in evidence on the fringes of urban areas. The Tithe Index edition of the old series Ordnance Survey one-inch maps delineates boundaries of tithe districts plotted from the tithe maps themselves but its large scale precludes its practical use for the production of a small-scale coverage map of England and Wales, the purpose of which is not to provide a map of the extent of titheable land but simply to indicate those places for which there is a map and apportionment.

Very broadly, the distribution of unsurveyed areas resembles that of parliamentary enclosure, tithe coverage being sparse in the extensively enclosed midland counties and much more complete in western districts and Wales. On the other hand, Westmorland, Lancashire and Gloucestershire are relatively scantily covered, while both Norfolk and the northern half of Yorkshire are rather more fully surveyed than might be expected from a map of enclosures. In detail, however, many parishes enclosed by act of parliament had not abolished their tithes. In Bedfordshire, Buckinghamshire, Northamptonshire, Leicestershire and Warwickshire, in particular, the incidence of enclosure and tithe surveys shows most imperfect correspondence. In the parish of Paulerspury in Northamptonshire, for example, 2,500 of a total of 3,030 acres were enclosed by act in 1819 yet the entire parish was surveyed at tithe commutation. Also, several parts of the country characterised by old enclosures were not subject to tithes. This fact is of significance in Sussex where surveys were carried out in almost all parishes but covered only the small remnants of titheable lands.

Figure 3.17 indicates the coverage of England and Wales by the two types of printed reports on tithe agreements. There are marked variations in the availability of reports, county by county, reflecting both the general level of tithe commutation and the ratio of commutation by agreement and award. Highest percentages occur in Wales where much tithe remained and was commuted by agreement; Denbigh heads the list with 88 per cent and seven other Welsh counties exceed 70 per cent coverage. The files of East Anglian counties are also particularly rich (Essex 71 per cent, Suffolk 68 per cent, Norfolk 66 per cent) as are those of a number of western counties (Somerset 66 per cent, Dorset 62 per cent, Hereford 61 per cent). The smallest numbers are to be found in midland counties where many districts had been exonerated from tithe payment at enclosure or where only small amounts remained payable and awaited compulsory award (Leicestershire 12 per cent, Middlesex 17 per cent, Bedfordshire, Northamptonshire and Nottinghamshire 18 per cent).

Custody of tithe survey documents

All the original tithe apportionments and maps and subsequent altered apportionments and maps are now in the custody of the Public Record Office at Ruskin Avenue, Kew, Surrey. Typescript catalogues of the documents are available in the search rooms at Kew and they have also been published in two volumes by the List and Index Society.[66] The catalogues have been prepared from the manuscript Tithe Redemption Office handlist and list in alphabetical order, county by county, those tithe districts with both a tithe map and apportionment. The name of the parish where this was different from the tithe district is also recorded with the status of the tithe district as a parish, township, lordship or hamlet etc.

The Public Record Office has microfilm copies of all tithe apportionments, and maps and positive copies of these, or photographic prints from them, can be purchased. The Tithe Redemption Office, Barrington Road, Durrington-on-Sea, Sussex, also has a set of microfilms and an inspection room where they can be studied by prior appointment. It is fairly easy to use microfilm copies of tithe apportionments as the page size fits film format quite well. But most tithe maps are photographed on several frames of film which makes finding individual tithe areas a tiresome business.

Only one tithe file was kept for each district and that is now deposited with the Public Record Office. These are catalogued county-by-county with tithe districts arranged by alphabetical order of parishes within counties. This means that where tithe districts are coterminous with townships, for example, it is necessary to know both township and parish names to find the press mark of a tithe district. A list and index of all files is in the press.[67]

Two statutory copies of the tithe map and apportionment were produced at the time of commutation. One was deposited with the incumbent and churchwardens to be kept in the parish chest and another was deposited in the diocesan registry. These copies have sometimes been lost, damaged or transferred to a county record office. Table 3.4 indicates the number of tithe surveys held by county record offices in England and Wales. It has been compiled from answers given by county archivists to questionnaires circulated in 1973, 1976 and 1982.

A continuous process of change in administrative areas has superimposed a new order of county boundaries on the pattern of counties which existed at tithe commutation. Some tithe districts have 'moved' to adjoining counties occasionally to 'return' at a later date. By and large, county record offices have established collections of tithe surveys which reflect the county distribution of tithe districts at the time of original survey. In England these collections have largely survived sweeping changes brought about by local government reorganisation in the 1970s. In Norfolk, for example, two depositories of east and west Norfolk have been amalgamated into a single county establishment, but this still maintains two separate collections of tithe documents. Herefordshire and Worcestershire are now administered by one county council but separate repositories of historical documents are retained. In Sussex, however, a few tithe surveys have changed hands. Here several parishes formerly in the eastern division have been transferred to west Sussex and a similar transfer of tithe surveys between the two record offices has occurred.

In Wales the organisation of county repositories has been drastically affected by changes in local government boundaries. Denbigh and Flint,

Table 3.4 *Tithe surveys in English and Welsh record offices*

Name of Record Office	Number of tithe maps	Number of tithe apportionments	Diocesan or parish copies
England			
Bedfordshire	60	60	Both
Berkshire	144	140	Both
Buckinghamshire	128	127	Both
Cambridge & Ely	35	31	Both
Cheshire	599	599	Both
Cornwall	216	216	Both
Cumbria – Cumberland	208	207	Both
" – Westmorland etc. (at Kendal)	95	89	Both
Derbyshire	244	216	Both
Devon	519+	519+	Both
Dorset	268	268	Both
Durham	80	80	Parish
Essex	395	395	Both
Gloucestershire	331	286	Both
Hants & I. of Wight	327	335	Both
Hereford & Worcester – Herefd	562	562	Both
" " – Worc.	148	149	Both
Hertfordshire	164	165	Both
Humberside	52	58	Parish
Huntingdon	64	64	Diocesan
Kent	347	328	Both
Lancashire	351	351+	Both
Leicestershire	256	256	Both
" – Rutland	12	12	Both
Lincolnshire	528	559	Both
Norfolk	700+	700+	Both
Northants	176	176	Both
Northumberland	524	524	Both
Nottinghamshire	131	131	Both
Oxfordshire	218	218	Both
Shropshire	287	115	Parish
Somerset	480	480	Both
Staffordshire	140	120	Parish
" Lichfield	500+	500+	Diocesan
" Wm Salt Library	51	51	Parish
Suffolk East	300+	300+	Both
" West	181	177	Both
Surrey	150	150	Both
Sussex East	123	123	Both
" West	184	184	Both
Warwickshire	340+	340+	Both
Wiltshire	290	290	Both
Yorkshire North	210+	210+	Parish

Table 3.4 cont.

Name of Record Office	Number of tithe maps	Number of tithe apportionments	Diocesan or parish copies
Yorkshire South	1	2	—
" West	19	25	—
Wales			
National Library of Wales	960	964	Diocesan
Clwyd	101	103	Both
Dyfed – Carmarthen, Cardigan, Pembroke	70	67	Parish
Glamorgan	120	119	Parish
Gwent	71	74	Parish
Gwynedd – Caernarvon	69	69	Both
" – Merioneth	34	34	Both
" – Anglesey	65	65	Both

together with the Edeyrnion district of Merioneth are linked to form the Clwyd Record Office. The record offices of Pembroke, Cardigan and Carmarthen now form the Dyfed Archives and Caernarvon, Dolgellau, Llangefni and Anglesey now make up Gwynedd Archive Service. Fortunately, students seeking a tithe survey of a particular Welsh parish will find all Welsh diocesan copies in the National Library of Wales.

The number of tithe surveys held by county record offices is increasing all the time by receipt of new depositions, usually from parish collections or documents which had strayed into private hands at some time in the past, and by acquisition of photocopies to fill gaps in collections. About 10,000 tithe surveys are held and available for local inspection. The actual number of tithe districts for which a map and apportionment are available in county record offices is somewhat less than this because of some overlap between parish and diocesan copies. In Cheshire Record Office, for example, 599 tithe maps include 445 diocesan and 154 parish copies. Cheshire also possesses a complete set of microfilm copies of 452 original tithe maps. In Hertfordshire, the 158 tithe maps noted in Table 3.4 represent, in fact, only 116 tithe districts. In some cases duplication of documents was taken into account when county archivists completed our questionnaires. Thus Cornwall Record Office points out that its totals do not include duplicate maps and apportionments.

The complex ecclesiastical geography of counties such as Kent also has a bearing on the deposition of tithe surveys in county archives offices. A former Kent archivist, Dr Felix Hull, pointed out that the Kent Archives Office holds diocesan records for Rochester, some parish copies for the middle third of the county, i.e. the Archdeaconry of Maidstone, and a number of unofficial copies and original drawings for parishes in the east of the county. East Kent is included in the diocese of Canterbury and the diocesan copies are held in the Cathedral Library, an independent repository run jointly with the City of Canterbury. The three Staffordshire repositories also admit to a degree of duplication in their holdings. Lichfield Joint Record Office has tithe apportionments and maps not only for the Archdeaconry of Stafford but also for the Archdeaconry of Shropshire, including Oswestry Rural Deanery, and for half the parishes in the former Archdeaconry of Derby, the remaining tithe surveys for which are kept in Derby Borough Library. Thus it is not only to county record offices that a student should turn for a locally held copy of a tithe survey, but to all ecclesiastical, municipal and university archives. For example, surveys of the diocese of Oxford are held in the Bodleian Library, those for the diocese of Ripon are in Leeds City Archives, for Gloucester in Gloucester City Library, for Cambridge in Cambridge University Library, while the Borthwick Institute of Historical Research holds some surveys of the diocese of York. A full list of diocesan repositories, together with addresses of county record offices, is to be found in the current edition of the HMSO publication, *Record repositories in Great Britain*.

The figures in Tables 3.4 should be used only as a guide to the likelihood of finding a tithe map and apportionment for a particular parish in a local repository. In fact, the chances of being able to do this are quite good; the overall probability is about three to one. A definitive answer to the presence of a particular tithe survey in a local collection is to be found in the index or catalogue of tithe surveys compiled by each record office. Some of these have been published and are listed in Table 3.5. Other offices have either a

Table 3.5 *Published guides/lists of collections of tithe apportionments and maps in local archive offices*

England	
Bedfordshire	*Catalogue of the maps in the Bedfordshire County Muniments* (1930); *Catalogue of the Enclosure Awards, Supplementary catalogue of maps, and list of awards upon tithe in the Bedfordshire County Muniments* (1939); *Guide to the Bedfordshire Record Office* (Bedfordshire County Council, 1957) and *Supplement* (1962)
Berkshire	*Guide to the Berkshire Record Office* (1952)
Buckinghamshire	*Catalogue of maps*, Bucks. Record Office Occasional Pubs. 3, 1961; *Annual report and list of accessions for 1981* (1982)
Cambridgeshire	Dorothy M. Owen, *Ely records, a handlist of the records of the Bishop and Archdeacon of Ely* (1971)
Cumberland	*Cumberland tithe awards* (1978)

Table 3.5 cont.

Devon	*Devon Record Office brief guide: Part 1 – official and ecclesiastical*
Essex	F. G. Emmison (ed.), *Catalogue of maps in the Essex Record Office* (1947) and *Supplement* (1952); *Guide to the Essex Record Office* (1969)
Gloucestershire	I. Gray and E. Ralph (eds.), *Guide to the parish records of the City of Bristol and the County of Gloucester* (1965); Isabel Kirby, *Diocese of Gloucester: a catalogue of the records of the Bishop and Archdeacons* (1968)
Hertfordshire	*Catalogue of manuscript maps in the Hertfordshire Record Office* (1969)
Kent	F. Hull, *Guide to Kent County Archives* (1958); *Guide to Kent County Archives Office, first supplement* (1971)
Lancashire	R. Sharpe France, *Guide to the Lancashire Record Office* (1962)
Northamptonshire	*Northamptonshire History News*, 24 (1975), 5–6
Nottinghamshire	P. A. Kennedy (ed.), *Guide to the Nottinghamshire Record Office*, (1960)
Northumberland	H. A. Taylor, *Northumberland history: a brief guide to records and aids in Newcastle upon Tyne* (1963)
Oxfordshire	*Summary catalogue of the privately-deposited records in the Oxfordshire Record Office* (1966)
Staffordshire	Lichfield Joint Record Office, *Cumulative handlist, Part 1: Diocesan, probate and church commissioners' records in Lichfield Joint Record Office* (1970)
East & West Sussex	F. W. Steer (ed.), *A catalogue of Sussex estate and tithe award maps*, Sussex Record Society, Vol. 61 (1962), 175–208; M. J. Burchall, *Index of East Sussex parish records, 1275–1870* (1975); F. W. Steer and I. M. Kirby (eds.), *Diocese of Chichester, a catalogue of the records of the Bishop, Archdeacons, and former exempt jurisdictions* (1966); F. W. Steer and I. M. Kirby (eds.), *Diocese of Chichester, a catalogue of the records of the Dean and Chapter, Vicars Choral, St Mary's Hospital, colleges and schools* (1967)
Wiltshire	R. E. Sandell, *Abstracts of Wiltshire tithe apportionments*, Wiltshire Record Society, Vol. 30 (1975)
East Yorkshire	M. W. Barley, 'Parochial documents of the East Riding', *Yorkshire Archaeological Society Record Series*, 99 (1939)
West Yorkshire	Margaret L. Faull and S. A. Moorhouse (eds.), *West Yorkshire: an archaeological survey to A.D. 1500. Vol. 1: Sources, environment and the county to A.D. 1066* (1981)

Table 3.5 cont.

Wales	
Caernarvonshire	B. R. Parry, 'The Caernarvonshire Record Office', *Local Historian* 3 (1967), 113–23
Carmarthenshire	Susan Beckley, *The Carmarthenshire Record Office: Survey of archive holdings* (1980)
Flint	A. G. Veysey, *Guide to the Flintshire Record Office* (FRO, 1974)
Gwent	Gwent County Record Office, *Guide to research No. 4 – history of houses*

typescript catalogue or a card index of tithe surveys. Many of these provide more information about each tithe survey than the 'official' Tithe Redemption Office handlist used as the basis of the Public Record Office catalogue. Information recorded may include the date of agreement or award and of the survey and apportionment, names of land surveyors and an indication of which maps have been sealed as first-class plans.

4

The accuracy of the tithe surveys

No one in the least familiar with the bitter struggles between tithe payers and tithe owners that endured without respite for centuries can have the slightest doubt that the parties brought together after 1836 to commute and apportion those precious objects of their strife would study every section of the tithe acts with minute attention, would haggle over their rights to take, or not to forgo, the smallest item of payment to which a claim might be made, and would follow closely behind the assistant commissioner or local tithe agent and the surveyor and valuer as they inspected the fields and drew their cadastral plan. So far as the interests of the parishioners were concerned, no survey, with the possible exception of an enclosure survey, was ever carried out under such close scrutiny. But are the records of the inquest truthful and how may their accuracy be tested?

An evaluation of accuracy is an essential step in the use of any historical data source but the level of accuracy which is acceptable should not be measured against some external absolute; the accuracy required will vary according to the questions being asked of the documents.[1] For the purposes of most historians and historical geographers, it is important to know to what extent a tithe district corresponded to a parish or township, to what extent a tithe area corresponded to a field, to what extent the state of cultivation corresponded with the actual land use at the time of the survey and to what extent estimates of crop acreages and yields reflected the actual produce of the land. To all these questions reasonably satisfactory answers can be given by examining the internal evidence of the documents themselves and subjecting them to comparison with independent sources. It would be incautious to disregard the strictures of the professional witnesses reviewed below, although their testimony may have been tainted with prejudice and was directed mainly towards planimetric inaccuracies in the tithe maps. In the final analysis, the surveys must be judged by their internal consistency and by their faithfulness to contemporary descriptions. As sources for reconstructing the salient features of mid-nineteenth century landscapes they pass all but the most stringent tests with considerable credit, if not flying colours.

The legal status of tithe surveys

Only tithe maps and apportionments have the status of legal documents. The tithe files contain, in addition to general correspondence, either a record of the way in which an agreement for commutation was reached or information which an assistant tithe commissioner used to impose a just award. None of this material has any legal status. On the other hand, the 1836 act expressly directed the tithe commissioners to furnish maps that might be admitted as evidence in courts of law in deciding questions of title to land, general and public rights in a township, and the existence of common rights in an unenclosed parish. These requirements were relaxed by the Tithe Act amendment acts of 1837 and 1839 which released the commissioners from the duty of sealing maps that, in their opinion, did not warrant certification as true representations of exact quantities and boundaries.

The result of these government decisions, in the words of John Meadows White, solicitor to the Poor Law and tithe and enclosure commissioners was that:

> Five-sixths of the tithe maps are not only on too small a scale for ordinary practical purposes, but are perfectly useless for many of the public requirements, of the present day [1853]. Indeed, any professional man will bear testimony to the fact that if one of these secondary maps be produced to verify the parcels or boundaries of an estate, as part of the title, the fact of its not being a sealed map is at once notice that it is inaccurate and not to be relied on for legal testimony.[2]

Only first-class maps were suitable for enclosure purposes under the 1845 General Enclosure Act. R. K. Dawson, appointed assistant commissioner under that act as well as the tithe acts, commented in evidence before the Select Committee on the Ordnance Survey of Scotland in 1856 that:

> no second-class map has been used for the purposes of inclosure; they must be first-class maps, because the Inclosure Commissioners are forced to certify that they have actually examined the maps and found them correct . . . The second-class tithe maps are used only to a limited extent for the purpose of the Inclosure Act, when the landowners agree to accept them as the basis for settling their claims; but for the purpose of setting out the allotments, an accurate and perfect survey is invariably required.[3]

Courts of law have not always been consistent in their acceptance of tithe surveys as evidence, as P. W. Millard demonstrates in his review of tithe law. In the cases of Wilberforce v. Hearfield (1877) and Frost v. Richardson (1910) it was held that even a sealed map is not admissible as evidence of boundaries between two adjoining properties. But in Gifford v. Williams (1869) a tithe map was received in evidence on a question of title in a partition action. In Smith v. Lister (1895) a sealed tithe map was admitted in evidence on an issue of public right in part of a township while even a second-class tithe map was received in evidence of the non-existence of a public road in Attorney General v. Antrobus in 1905. In Stoney v. Eastbourne Rural District Council and the Duke of Devonshire (1927) an opposite judgement was made when it 'was held that a tithe map could not be accepted as evidence of the non-existence of a public right of way which might have been, but was not inserted in it and was not relevant to the purpose for which the map was made'.[4]

All tithe maps and apportionments are, however, still conclusive as evidence in disputes between tithe owners and tithe payers. They are good enough to have prevented frivolous litigation that might have resulted from the transfer of land with its attendant rent-charges as well as from changes in the state of cultivation, in the direction of roads, and in the removal of fences. Moreover, the maps have been considered sufficiently accurate to serve as the bases for other official enquiries. They were consulted, for example, by the Ordnance Survey (and sometimes found wanting) when drawing parish boundaries on the first 1:2,500 plans.[5]

Examination and testing of maps by the Tithe Commission

The linchpin of R. K. Dawson's scheme for obtaining accurate maps from unsupervised private surveyors which the tithe commissioners would be able to certify accurate, was the application of a system of rigorous checks to the completed work. This fundamental principle governed the detailed specification of the maps discussed above in chapter 3 (Table 3.3), and was backed by the sanction of the commissioners who could refuse to accept a map unless it was corrected. They also had powers to require testing lines to be set out on the ground in residual cases of uncertainty or dispute (Table 4.1). Professional land surveyors who, through their Land Surveyors' Club, had been vehemently opposed to the financial terms on which the then Tithe Bill had proposed to employ its members for tithe mapping, were also reluctant to submit their work to an official examination.[6] Many were particularly sensitive about their professional status and expertise and were quick to take offence when the accuracy of their maps was called into question. Surveyors did not, according to William Blamire, willingly submit maps for testing. Many an old country surveyor is reputed to have said, 'Neither our maps, nor our fathers', nor our grandfathers' were ever called into question *qua* accuracy, and we do not know why the Tithe Commissioners should now assume the power to test our maps, and we shall advise all parties who have confidence in us to refuse to permit our maps to be tested.'[7] The main

Table 4.1 *Extracts from R. K. Dawson's instructions for the 'Preparation of plans for the purpose of the Tithe Commutation Act' which relate to the testing of finished maps*

1. The Lines which the Tithe Commissioners will require to have measured on the ground, for testing the accuracy of the Map of . . . . . . in the county of . . . . . . are Three lines in the form of a well-shaped triangle, with a proof line from one of the angles to the opposite   miles in length, or more than
2. In measuring these lines, all intersections of fences are to be noted, and offsets taken within the ordinary limit of a chain's length.
3. All junction points of fences are to be noted which fall within Two chains of the measured lines; and when their distance exceeds One chain, an offset triangle is to be measured instead of the single offset.
4. The fields in which the angular points of the triangle occur are to be wholly surveyed, or enough of their boundaries ascertained to determine precisely the position of those points on the Map.
5. The entries in the field-books are to be made with ink in the field, and any alterations which require to be made in them are to be attested by the initials of the Surveyor; and an explanation of the cause of the alteration is also to be entered.
6. A protraction of the testing lines on the scale of . . . chains to an inch is to be sent with the field notes to the office of the Tithe Commissioners.
7. N.B. – The lines should not be less than Six Miles in length, where the parish or district to be tested will admit of it; and not generally more than Eight miles for any parish of 4,000 acres. For a parish of greater extent, another mile may be added for every thousand acres additional.

object of the testing was to ensure that 'the system of triangulation adopted is perfect and complete *per se*, and next that the filling up of the triangles is accurate, and that the acreage given is fairly represented by the maps'.[8] Lieutenant Dawson, who was in charge of the department responsible for conducting the tests, explained the *method* used as follows:

> It is the duty of the examiner to see that the lines of construction, or measured lines, are systematically and properly disposed; and that the measurements recorded in the field-books are properly indicated on the map. Any discrepancy between the map and field notes leads to the rejection of the map; and when doubts arise as to the originality of the field notes, or from circumstances of a suspicious nature, such as apparent alteration in the field notes, or an unsystematic arrangement of lines of construction, recourse is had to testing upon the ground. The ground test consists of straight lines, measured by an independent surveyor, in the form of a triangle, with one or more interior proof-lines. The intersections of fences, and other detail determined by these lines, when laid down in position and compared with similar lines drawn upon the original plans constitute one of the severest tests that can be applied.[9]

The effectiveness of this method was widely recognised and approved by other bodies for testing maps. For example, the 1850 report of the land registration and conveyancing commission recommended that Dawson's system of checking should also be applied to the maps of real property which it proposed.[10]

When landowners desired a first-class map and had contracted for such with a surveyor, the completed map, preferably the plain, working plan, had to be sent with the field book to the Tithe Commission who returned its comments on specially printed forms with space for parish replies in explanation of examiners' remarks. At Frome Vauchurch in Dorset, to which Fig. 4.1 refers, the landowners and the Tithe Commission were clearly at cross purposes. Dawson had written to the landowners saying that they must send up the field books if they wished their map to be examined for accuracy. But it is clear from the landowners' explanation that they did not wish their map, compiled in part from an old survey and in part from some new work, to be sealed.[11]

The work of testing maps must have been a prodigious effort. By 21 March 1844, the London office had tested 2,017 maps, the work of 405 surveyors, and had approved 1,399, had rejected 521 and were still considering 97.[12] To expedite this operation, and presumably also to ensure consistency between examiners, these last were provided with printed examination papers which provided a 'check-list' of potential faults and a convenient schedule for organising their comments. Study of these examination papers is important as it reveals the range of tests which were applied and the particular aspects of accuracy with which the Tithe Commission was and was not concerned. A typical example of one of these forms which are found occasionally in the tithe files is that for Madehurst, Sussex, completed by examiner William Jackson on 23 September 1839 (Fig. 4.2). All the checks which it lists are concerned with establishing the planimetric accuracy of the map and are not concerned at all with topographic content as regards buildings, types of roads, nature of boundaries, representation of land use by symbol, and other features often portrayed on a tithe map. The presentation of the latter information was incidental to commutation purposes and clearly the Tithe Commission was not concerned to verify it all, though landowners did have an opportunity to check such matters for themselves when the draft apportionment was lodged for their approval. The Madehurst tithe map appears to have been something of a disaster for its surveyor: Jackson's final comments with which Dawson agreed were that the 'whole of this work is traversed, and is not checked throughout, many lines of construction are required and as the field book appears to be a copy I consider no dependence can be placed in the accuracy of the work'.[13] Jones, the surveyor, was advised to get to work with his theodolite to increase the number of proof lines.

Lieutenant Dawson's office was certainly able to detect involuntary mistakes in maps. In one such map some 400 errors were pointed out and

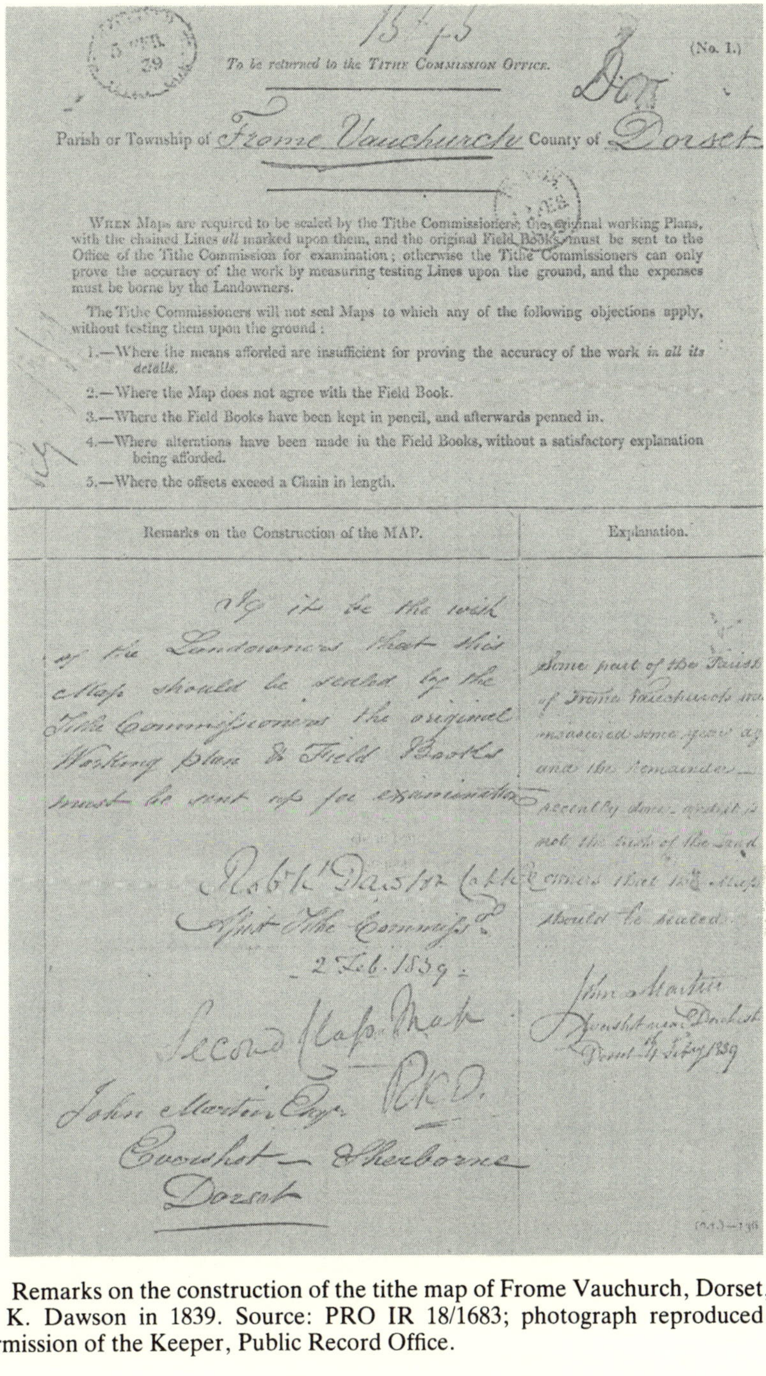

1843

(No. 1.)

To be returned to the Tithe Commission Office.

Dor

Parish or Township of Frome Vauchurch County of Dorset

When Maps are required to be sealed by the Tithe Commissioners, the original working Plans, with the chained Lines *all* marked upon them, and the original Field Books must be sent to the Office of the Tithe Commission for examination; otherwise the Tithe Commissioners can only prove the accuracy of the work by measuring testing Lines upon the ground, and the expenses must be borne by the Landowners.

The Tithe Commissioners will not seal Maps to which any of the following objections apply, without testing them upon the ground:

1.—Where the means afforded are insufficient for proving the accuracy of the work *in all its details.*

2.—Where the Map does not agree with the Field Book.

3.—Where the Field Books have been kept in pencil, and afterwards penned in.

4.—Where alterations have been made in the Field Books, without a satisfactory explanation being afforded.

5.—Where the offsets exceed a Chain in length.

Remarks on the Construction of the MAP.	Explanation.
If it be the wish of the Landowners that this Map should be sealed by the Tithe Commissioners the original Working plan & Field Books must be sent up for examination Robt. K. Dawson Capt. Asst. Tithe Commissr. 2 Feb. 1839. Second Class Map R.K.D. John Martin Esqr. Evershot — Sherborne Dorset	Some part of the Parish of Frome Vauchurch was measured some years ago and the remainder recently done and it is not the wish of the Land owners that this Map should be sealed. John Martin Evershot near Dorchester Dorset 4 Feby 1839

4.1 Remarks on the construction of the tithe map of Frome Vauchurch, Dorset, by R. K. Dawson in 1839. Source: PRO IR 18/1683; photograph reproduced by permission of the Keeper, Public Record Office.

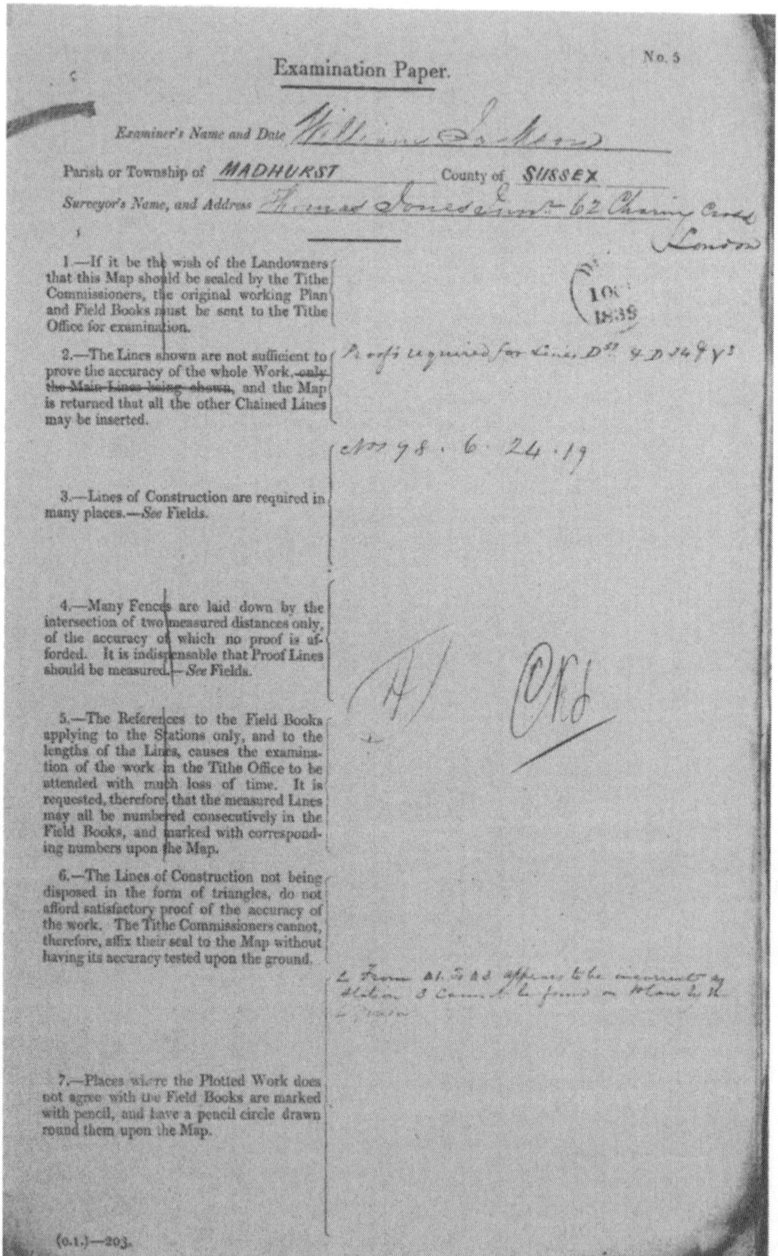

No. 5

Examination Paper.

Examiner's Name and Date William Jackson

Parish or Township of MADHURST County of SUSSEX

Surveyor's Name, and Address Thomas Jones Junr 62 Charing Cross London

10 Oct 1839

1.—If it be the wish of the Landowners that this Map should be sealed by the Tithe Commissioners, the original working Plan and Field Books must be sent to the Tithe Office for examination.

2.—The Lines shown are not sufficient to prove the accuracy of the whole Work, ~~only the Main Lines being shown~~, and the Map is returned that all the other Chained Lines may be inserted. — Proofs required for Lines D[illegible] 4 D 24 & 13

Nos 78. 6. 24. 19

3.—Lines of Construction are required in many places.—*See* Fields.

4.—Many Fences are laid down by the intersection of two measured distances only, of the accuracy of which no proof is afforded. It is indispensable that Proof Lines should be measured.—*See* Fields.

(A) OKd

5.—The References to the Field Books applying to the Stations only, and to the lengths of the Lines, causes the examination of the work in the Tithe Office to be attended with much loss of time. It is requested, therefore, that the measured Lines may all be numbered consecutively in the Field Books, and marked with corresponding numbers upon the Map.

6.—The Lines of Construction not being disposed in the form of triangles, do not afford satisfactory proof of the accuracy of the work. The Tithe Commissioners cannot, therefore, affix their seal to the Map without having its accuracy tested upon the ground.

2 From A1 to A2 appears to be incorrect by station 3 [illegible]

7.—Places where the Plotted Work does not agree with the Field Books are marked with pencil, and have a pencil circle drawn round them upon the Map.

(o.1.)—203.

4.2 Examination paper completed by William Jackson in 1839 after testing the Madehurst, Sussex, tithe map surveyed by Thomas Jones Jr of Charing Cross. Source: PRO IR 18/10406; photograph reproduced by permission of the Keeper, Public Record Office.

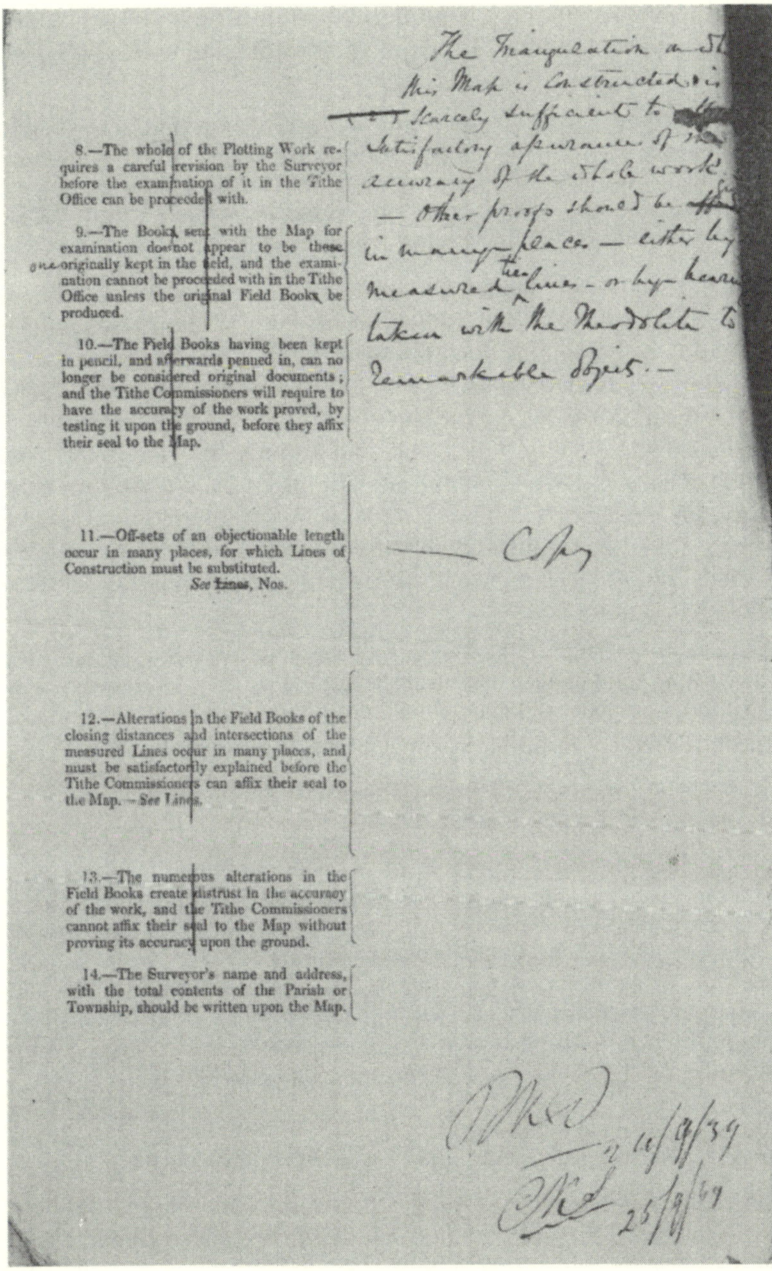

8.—The whole of the Plotting Work requires a careful revision by the Surveyor before the examination of it in the Tithe Office can be proceeded with.

9.—The Books sent with the Map for examination do not appear to be these one originally kept in the field, and the examination cannot be proceeded with in the Tithe Office unless the original Field Books be produced.

10.—The Field Books having been kept in pencil, and afterwards penned in, can no longer be considered original documents; and the Tithe Commissioners will require to have the accuracy of the work proved, by testing it upon the ground, before they affix their seal to the Map.

11.—Off-sets of an objectionable length occur in many places, for which Lines of Construction must be substituted.
See ~~Lines~~, Nos.

12.—Alterations in the Field Books of the closing distances and intersections of the measured Lines occur in many places, and must be satisfactorily explained before the Tithe Commissioners can affix their seal to the Map.—*See Lines.*

13.—The numerous alterations in the Field Books create distrust in the accuracy of the work, and the Tithe Commissioners cannot affix their seal to the Map without proving its accuracy upon the ground.

14.—The Surveyor's name and address, with the total contents of the Parish or Township, should be written upon the Map.

The triangulation on which this Map is constructed is scarcely sufficient to give satisfactory assurance of the accuracy of the whole work. — Other proofs should be afforded in many places — either by measured tie lines — or by bearings taken with the theodolite to remarkable objects. —

— Copy

[illegible] 11/9/39

[illegible] 25/9/39

admitted and in that of Tonge in north Kent errors of up to 100 per cent were found (see above, chapter 3).[14] By 1841 the tithe commissioners felt it necessary to warn that:

maps are sometimes sent here containing errors of which the mappers are conscious, and the existence of which they attempt to conceal, by tampering with and making compensating errors in the field books, or original records of admeasurement which they are required to send with the maps. No examination in this office can enable us to detect here wilful and fraudulent errors of this description.[15]

Landowners who were vigilant and exercised their rights could bring such frauds to light. A map was deposited in a parish for twenty-one days prior to confirmation of the apportionment. At the end of this period an assistant commissioner could be required to attend a meeting at which errors might be pointed out and it was his duty to see that the final map was corrected. But the tithe commissioners feared that landowners did not inspect maps carefully. The accuracy of a map could also be checked by setting out test lines on the ground and having them carefully measured (Fig. 4.3). However, the Tithe Commission had no authority to defray the expense of such trials and no clear power to levy charges on responsible parties. It concluded in 1841:

Unquestionably we believe, that the maps to which we have attached our seal are very much more accurate than they would have been had they not gone through the ordeal of this office; but we think it prudent that the landowners should know what description of errors we can detect here, and what may escape detection.[16]

R. K. Dawson, architect of the tithe survey, also had some reservations about the first-class maps considering that they:

would have been better maps, certainly, if they had been founded upon a scientific basis of triangulation, as the maps of the Ordnance Survey are, and if they had been made under proper superintendence, supervision and control; but those maps were only first seen by the Tithe Commissioners when sent to them for the purpose of examination, being then complete. The maps were made according to the instructions which the Commissioners had issued, but the Commissioners had no personal supervision of them during their construction, and therefore those maps, I dare say, will be less perfect than the finished maps of the Ordnance Survey.[17]

Nineteenth-century map users' opinions of tithe map accuracy

In making any assessment of nineteenth-century map users' opinions of tithe map accuracy it is important to distinguish between comments relating to the first and second classes of maps. Second-class maps received almost universal condemnation as planimetrically untrustworthy. Most witnesses who appeared before the various select committees on the Ordnance Survey and into matters such as town improvement, enclosure, and registration of

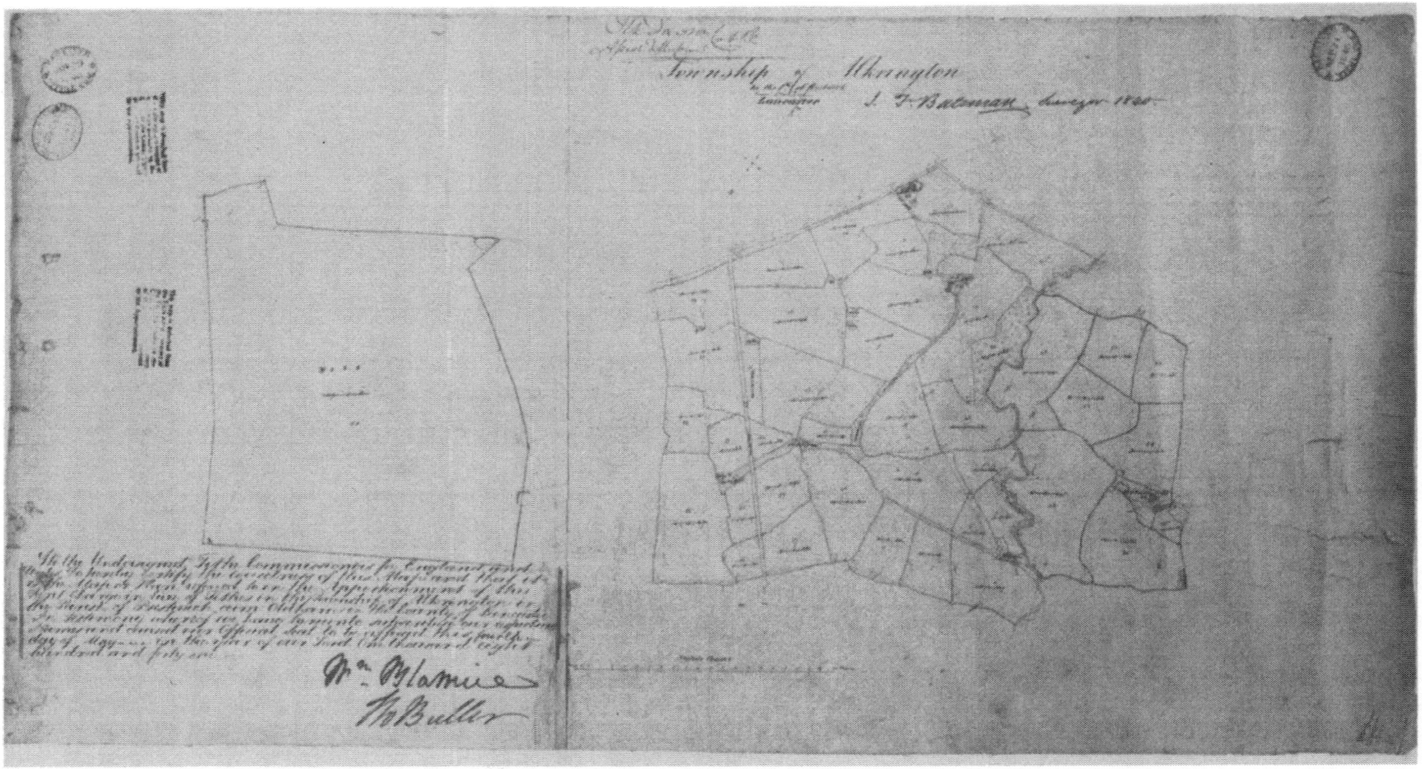

4.3 First-class tithe map of Alkrington township, Lancashire, 1840. Photograph reproduced by permission of the Keeper, Public Record Office.

title to land in the 1840s and 1850s would probably have agreed with Francis Marston of Hopesay near Ludlow, who was a practising farmer, a land agent with enclosure experience, and was employed as a tithe commutation surveyor and valuer. He dismissed second-class maps as 'not worth a straw'.[18] Indeed rather than use them he would prefer to 'go by my own eye; I could guess better than the measure stated in many second-class maps'.[19] Such opinions were probably formed without any 'scientific' sampling of this class of map and were doubtless coloured by the commentators' experiences or hearsay of one or two infamously inaccurate maps. Modern cartometric tests of tithe maps reviewed in the following section suggest that Marston and others were unfair in embracing all second-class maps with that judgement.

With first-class maps opinion was more varied; they had their detractors, particularly within the Ordnance Survey, and their champions, amongst whom can be counted land agents and country solicitors who used tithe maps in day-to-day matters of rural land management. The sale and transfer of land from the mid-nineteenth century was much facilitated by the availability of tithe surveys as William Blamire, copyhold and tithe commissioner, explained in evidence before a parliamentary commission in 1854:

> Numbers of people come to the office daily to examine maps, and to get particulars of certain properties, and tracings of those properties which they attach to conveyances in place of or in elucidation of the old and original designation of the property . . . and I observe in country papers when property is to be sold there are references to tithe maps. 'Number so-and-so on the tithe map?' – Exactly.[20]

One such land agent was Mr S. Vessey of Spilsby in Lincolnshire who wrote a letter to the Treasury in 1853 about the proposed scale for Ordnance Survey maps:

> I am concerned in the management of property in many parishes where the tithes have been commuted and where first-class plans (tested by the Tithe Commissioners) have been adopted. I have no trouble in those parishes. It facilitates the conveyance of real property, and combines *certainty, simplicity*, and *economy*, and will be a document that may be relied on for ages to come.[21]

Some support for the value of first-class tithe maps (and yet more castigation of the second class) came from other more unexpected quarters. The year1845 has been described as 'the great railway year' which generated an increased demand for maps for plotting railway routes.[22] The published one-inch scale maps of the Ordnance Survey were not really suitable for this detailed work and engineers turned to the larger scale maps of the Tithe Commission. In April 1856 Lieutenant-Colonel Dawson said, 'Numberless applications were made to the Tithe Commissioners for copies of their maps for setting out railways. Then was found the great inconvenience of the second-class maps. The first-class maps were found to be highly satisfactory;

but the second-class maps to a very great extent were worthless.'[23] Yet engineer T. Hawksley had found some quite good second-class maps:

> their inaccuracy, such as it is, is mostly a minute thing, or it consists in many cases of a simple twist in the lines . . . we find when we come to put two or three triangles together, that they do not exactly meet at the points where they should meet, or they a little overlap or underlap each other, and then the surveyor compresses it or extends it a little to allow for that, and that results in a very small inaccuracy.[24]

On the other hand, Thomas Bauch, a railway engineer for more than twenty-five years who himself had prepared 'one or two' first-class tithe maps, also had 'occasion to use them in the preparation of railway plans where the Ordnance plans were not published, but I certainly have quite given them up'.[25] However, it appeared that it had been his practice to inspect hand copies rather than the original maps and that most of the errors he referred to arose in the copying operation. This should perhaps be taken as a warning by present-day students working with diocesan or parish copies of the tithe surveys.

Perhaps the most telling nineteenth-century assessment of the planimetric accuracy of the tithe surveys came not from the Tithe Commission, nor from land agents, engineers or solicitors familiar only with surveys of some local area, but from officers of the Ordnance Survey during discussion of a national cadastral survey in the 1850s. For a second time in the nineteenth century the government had to decide whether some if not all tithe maps could be incorporated into a cadastral survey of the kingdom. Lieutenant-Colonel Tucker of the Ordnance Survey boundary department, an officer 'of twenty-nine years of varied experience on the duties of the Ordnance Survey in England, Ireland and Scotland, [whose] opinion deserves at least equal consideration to that of Lieutenant-Colonel Dawson', was directed by Lieutenant-Colonel Hall to examine the tithe maps.[26] His recommendation was that the second-class plans be rejected *in toto*. Certainly one unnamed tithe map which he consulted contained an inaccurate parish boundary but later in his report he had to admit that, 'a few may be tolerable, or prepared from recent survey made for the purpose'. He thought that the first-class plans were no doubt much better but it would have been difficult to piece together parish tithe surveys based only on internal triangulation.[27] Similar conclusions were reached by another officer, Captain R. E. Gossett who:

> carefully examined, and in many ways tested, a number of the picked best first-class tithe commission maps made by private surveyors; the result of my examination is the discovery that they are utterly worthless for incorporation into a general map of the United Kingdom. As to the second-class maps, the officials of the Tithe Office did not deem it worth my while to examine them, so inferior did they consider them.[28]

But as Henry Warburton, a member of the select committee which enquired in 1837 into the nature of maps required by the Tithe Commutation Act, told the Treasury in a letter dated 23 March 1854 setting out his views on the proper scale for the Ordnance Survey, neither the tithe commissioners nor R. K. Dawson were chargeable with the defects of tithe maps since:

> they gave full warning that the maps, prepared under the direction and at the expense of the parishes, were and would be very inaccurate. The country is reminded of the penalty it incurred by not placing, at that time, the direction of the requisite parochial surveys in the hands of the Ordnance.[29]

Accuracy was sacrificed for administrative expediency and the principle of voluntaryism on which the 1836 Act was founded.

A test of the planimetric accuracy of a sample of tithe maps

On balance, nineteenth-century opinion on the planimetric accuracy of tithe maps, particularly of the second-class maps, was unfavourable. Much of this comment was, however, impressionistic; few commentators attempted to quantify the amount of error they encountered. The one or two much-publicised cases such as the Tonge experience were eagerly seized upon by the anti-tithe survey lobby and used as ammunition for their condemnation of the whole body of tithe maps.

A recent study of the planimetric accuracy of tithe maps carried out by J. M. Hooke and R. A. Perry suggests that maps like that submitted from Tonge were probably quite exceptional and that as a body second-class tithe maps are tolerably accurate.[30] They selected a sample of twenty-two second-class maps and one first-class map of south-east Devon parishes and calculated percentage errors incorporated at a number of stages in the maps' lives. The major and minor triangulation nets and the lengths of chainage control lines and offsets were re-examined (Fig. 4.4). Consideration was given to the accuracy of draughtsmanship and the degree of paper deformation resulting from storage. In summary, their tests produced error values for areal measurements averaging 3.94 per cent and, for linear measurements, 2.71 per cent. Both figures include about a 1.0 per cent error as a result of parchment distortion (Table 4.2). For the most part, the errors in question are of the displacement of a field boundary by a few yards, the elongation or compression of a parish boundary by a similar amount, perhaps the marking of a field boundary where at the time of commutation there should have been none. Further cartometric analyses of some Leicestershire tithe maps indicate that levels of planimetric accuracy are not consistent across an individual map; this is particularly true of maps such as those of Carlton and Hinckley parishes which are a combination of old and new surveys.[31]

To the *cartographic historian* concerned with evaluating the work of country surveyors, perhaps in comparison with that of the Ordnance Survey,

4.4 Part of the tithe map of Honiton parish, Devon, showing construction lines and chainage distances. Photograph reproduced by courtesy of Devon Record Office.

Table 4.2 *Results of accuracy measurements on some Devonshire tithe maps*

(A) *Percentage error in scale bar length*

Scale (in chains)	Map	Error	Scale (in chains)	Map	Error
6	Axminster	−1.00	4	Silverton	−1.24
	Broad Clyst	0.00		Stoke Canon	−2.56
	Colyton	+0.97	3	Colaton Raleigh	+0.50
	Gittisham	−3.05		Harpford	−1.60
	Kilmington	−0.72		Honiton	−0.55
	Rewe	−1.70		Luppitt	+0.75
	Salcombe Regis	−2.48		Monkton	−0.48
	Shute	+0.34		Northleigh	+1.60
	Stockland	−0.44		Ashprington	−1.36

(B) *Group means and means of standard deviations of percentage error in areas*

Scale (in chains)	No. of maps	Test1a				Test 1b				Test 1c			
		$\lvert\bar{X}\rvert$	$\lvert\bar{s}\rvert$	$\bar{X}$	$\bar{s}$	$\lvert\bar{X}\rvert$	$\lvert\bar{s}\rvert$	$\bar{X}$	$\bar{s}$	$\lvert\bar{X}\rvert$	$\lvert\bar{s}\rvert$	$\bar{X}$	$\bar{s}$
6	6	2.49	2.57	−1.78	3.08	2.73	2.87	−1.33	3.63	3.55	3.52	−2.43	4.15
4	3	2.26	2.22	+0.50	2.88	3.16	1.97	−0.90	3.88	3.88	2.33	−1.38	4.15
3	5	3.74	2.80	−0.84	4.54	3.06	3.27	−0.52	4.64	4.69	3.29	−1.26	5.26
All	14	2.99	2.62	−0.94	3.88	2.95	2.80	−1.07	4.14	3.94	3.05	−1.90	4.70

(C) *Group means and means of standard deviations of percentage error in length*

Scale of group (in chains)	No. of maps	$\lvert\bar{X}\rvert$	$\lvert\bar{s}\rvert$	$\bar{X}$	$\bar{s}$
6	9	2.22	2.12	−0.20	2.87
4	3	4.06	3.33	−3.87	3.54
3	7	3.01	1.86	−1.31	3.42

such lapses are evidence for a damning criticism of the tithe surveys. But, what is important in the assessment of tithe maps as *sources of information for present-day historical studies* is to set the assessment of accuracy into a context of questions being asked of the maps. What questions are historians asking that require the level of accuracy demanded by the Ordnance Survey for a cadastral survey? The studies reviewed in the following chapters reveal few such questions. Rather the accurate transfer of elements of the mid-nineteenth century landscape from the tithe maps to modern base maps which is one fundamental use of tithe surveys, will depend for success as much, if not more, on the amount of landscape change since tithe times as on the accuracy with which lines were drawn on the original tithe maps.

Checking tithe maps before extracting data

There are a number of simple checks which all users of tithe maps might consider before extracting data. For example, it is important to know what units the lines on a particular map are separating. Most, but not all, tithe maps mark the boundaries of unenclosed parcels of land by dotted lines and enclosed fields by solid lines. Dotted lines may represent property divisions, separating holdings in an open arable field or common meadow, or they may represent either permanent or temporary divisions between lands of different utilisation in a field belonging to a single farmer.[32] It is generally possible to confirm this distinction by referring to the apportionment but contemporary private estate maps may be of some help in reaching a decision. Private estate maps of this period are, however, of only limited value for general testing of tithe surveys, because most of them were either consulted by the tithe surveyors or are themselves copied from tithe maps. Some were drawn by the same surveyor. Estate maps and sales catalogues may be of most use in checking or amplifying data on the state of cultivation.

A few errors and omissions are revealed by checking the original documents against surviving diocesan and parish copies, but, as these are certified true copies, any discrepancies indicate nothing more than the extent of variations in mid-nineteenth century clerical exactitude. On the other hand, differences between information shown on a map and that recorded in an apportionment are worth investigating. In many tithe districts map and apportionment were compiled at different dates, so that what appear to be inconsistencies are attributable to changes having taken place in the intervening period. Where apportioning was long delayed after approval of the map, perhaps because of disputes, land represented by woodland symbols on the map might have been cleared for grass or arable by the time it was described in the apportionment; similarly, tracts mapped as heath or marsh might be returned as improved land. In a few parishes changes were actually taking place at the time of the survey and these are occasionally noted in the 'remarks' column of the apportionment. References might be made here to felling and grubbing up of tree stumps, to enclosure of commons, or to tree planting. Where farm or estate boundaries are marked on a map, similar discrepancies may be noted. Again, they can often be ascribed to the use of an outdated map, but there is a further consideration that many holdings extend beyond parish boundaries and only small parts may be represented on one map.

In all studies using tithe surveys it is essential to proceed from a close study of the map to the apportionment and if this is done conscientiously there is very little room for doubt about the overall reliability of the record. But if planimetric data are needed then objective tests such as those devised by

Hooke and Perry might be appropriate. For this purpose, their paper presents a clear statement of a method that can be followed.

The reliability of summaries of tithe district land use in apportionments and files

The preamble to the tithe agreement or award usually states whether an entire parish is included in the survey or what portions are excluded, and these statements can be verified by reference to contemporary assessments for parish rates or for poor rates. The preamble is followed by a summary of the area of land (often only that which was titheable) given over to each of the states of cultivation recognised for commutation. Similar sets of data are often to be found in the tithe files. These summary statistics have been used in several studies as sources for land-use information but there is considerable doubt about their accuracy.[33]

In very many parishes these figures are derived from estimates, and inaccuracy can occur through misestimation. Some assistant tithe commissioners such as Charles Pym stated that they specifically viewed parishes to make their estimates, but others, including William Glasson who compiled a large proportion of Cornwall reports, accepted without question land-use data supplied by local landowners. Further, the summaries often refer to a time earlier than the date of agreement (though they are usually contemporary with that of an award). Although the date of confirmation of an agreement or award for commutation is inscribed upon the first page of the tithe apportionment, the date to which land-use summaries refer is rarely recorded in the apportionment. Occasionally it is stated in the tithe file. For example, the summary for Folkestone was taken from a survey made in 1830, while at Midley in Kent it was computed from the tithe map.[34] More commonly, the summaries are prefaced by statements such as, 'by recent survey', 'by actual survey', 'by new survey', or 'by admeasurement'.[35] Other statements suggest that some summaries are of much earlier date. At Bicknor near Sittingbourne in north Kent the summary was obtained 'from an old survey', while at Maidstone it had been computed 'from an old map'.[36]

Tithe-free land, or land whose tithes had already been commuted, are not always described and included in the summaries. Major gaps in the tithe survey appear where parishes had commuted their tithes at the time of parliamentary enclosure. Where enclosure awards dealt with all the land in a parish there is no problem: usually there is no tithe survey. William Eagle in his guide to tithe commutation legislation points out that only rarely did commutations under enclosure acts extend over a whole parish, and for the most part they were confined to open-field lands which were allotted and enclosed.[37] The tithe documents for these partly commuted parishes rarely yield information on the enclosed lands, but only on those parts held in severalty before the enclosure act together with those parts still unenclosed at the time of the tithe survey. The danger of generalising from these possibly atypical areas need not be overemphasised. The tithe surveys of Cumberland are particularly deficient in this respect. Only 2 of the 51 Cumberland tithe file estimates cover the whole of a tithe district; the remainder have either data for only part of a district or none at all.

Comments on the accuracy of the summary schedules have been made by a number of researchers who have used them. Elwyn Cox in his thesis on Essex agriculture says, 'the totals were more generally estimates, not calculated from the summation of the areas of each individual plot, and, therefore, their accuracy is suspect'.[38] Speaking more particularly of the Essex summaries he says, 'however, it seems likely that the proportions between the various categories of land were reasonably accurate, and that what errors there were cancelled each other out – there is certainly no evidence to suggest that the area of any one type of land was consistently over or under-estimated at the expense of others'.[39] In the Chilterns, F. D. Hartley found that some of the summary totals added up exactly to the total acreage of a parish, but others showed slight discrepancies:

> One cause may be that glebe land is included in the arable and grass totals, and then given again under a category 'glebe'. The result obtained then exceeds the total acreage of the parish. In other schedules the roads may not be included in the total parish acreage. Sometimes the acreages of the houses and gardens have been added to one of the other totals or divided between the totals of arable and grass. Before using these acreage totals, then, it is necessary to account for all the categories as completely as possible, in order to reduce the degree of error if it is desired to express them as percentages.[40]

In his study of the Breckland, Malcolm Postgate carried out a random check on the accuracy of the summaries by totalling the individual tithe areas under each land-use category. His conclusion is that the estimates are accurate enough to validate their use in an overall survey.[41] In Montgomeryshire, J. M. Powell found that 'discrepancies are never great and the tithe surveyors' estimates may be taken as valid'.[42] Of the 129 parishes in John Chapman's Monmouthshire study area, summaries of 42 are expressed in great detail down to the nearest perch, for 66 they are rounded to the nearest acre, and for 21 parishes they are presented in more generalised forms, in at least one instance rounded to the nearest thousand acres. But he finds that parishes whose estimates are loosely approximated are evenly intermixed with those whose estimates are expressed in precise quantities. No geographical concentrations of unreliable data are apparent and no single total is so grossly inaccurate that it distorts the overall picture.[43]

It is possible, also, to make some assessment of the accuracy of the summaries by comparing them with land-use data recorded in the schedules of apportionment, although allowance must be made for the fact that these may be some years apart in date, about two years on average, infrequently less than one year and rarely more than five. Schedules of apportionment describe the state of cultivation and list measured acreages of all parcels of land. By adding these up it is possible to obtain an accurate summary of the total acreage of various types of land in a parish. Such a comparison has been made for a sample of 41 Kent parishes containing 93,570 acres, or 9.4 per cent of the county area. A null hypothesis was set up to the effect that there is no difference between the tithe apportionment estimates and the summated totals from the schedules of apportionment. A non-parametric Wilcoxon matched-pairs signed-ranks test was employed and for each class of land use the null hypothesis was accepted.[44] This confirms Cox's belief, for example, that there is no systematic bias towards over- or under-estimation of acreages of particular categories of land use. It is a view which receives further support from Phillips' comparison of twelve Staffordshire tithe apportionments which recorded crops in the state of cultivation column with the land-use summaries of those places: 'in no case was there a variation of more than ten per cent in the area of the main categories of land-use between the two sources'.[45] Further corroboration arises from Mrs R. E. Porter's investigations in Cheshire: 'a number of estimates were tested against their respective schedules and the results suggested discrepancies of only a few per cent'.[46]

While for most tithe districts the two sets of data show a close correspondence, some differences could lead to an incorrect classification in very detailed choropleth mapping. With blocks of parishes, inaccuracies cancel each other out; for individual parishes errors may be very real. It would also be unwise to use the estimates to obtain a picture of land use unless the nature and extent of land exempt from tithe is known. Discrepancies are likely to be greatest in those parts of the country with large tracts of waste land, moorland, heath, and other types of land of low value which generated little titheable produce and were not carefully estimated or measured. Errors can frequently be found in stated quantities of other types of land such as timber woodland as usually only underwood was titheable. In Cumberland, many old enclosures were covered by moduses and only recently enclosed commons paid any tithe in kind. Local agents often remarked on the scale of error involved with acreages of common in schedules to tithe agreements in northern counties. Boundaries were uncertain: at Bootle in Cumberland, for example, surveyors included parts of a fell which in fact lay outside the township.[47] Also, where land was poor, the difference between arable and pasture rental was not necessarily very marked so that even this land-use division is less trustworthy than in areas of southern England where land-use estimates were first tested and used by historians. Again at Bootle, large acreages of common which were just occasionally ploughed are returned as arable in the schedule.[48] At Newton in Cumberland, J. J. Rawlinson considered that a large amount of land had been returned as arable in the tithe agreement which was in fact permanent pasture, so he adjusted his own figure accordingly. Thomas Martin was also aware of this problem in Cumberland, as he was in Lancashire and other counties, and noted that land which might be ploughed as well as land that was ploughed had been included in the schedules of Ribton, Seaton and Thursby.[49]

Commons were usually exempt from tithe in north and west Yorkshire and moorland boundaries were also uncertain, sometimes only known for a parish as a whole and not for individual townships. There was potential here for some double counting and omission. The tithe files of the several townships of Masham parish in the North Riding, for example, note the existence of tracts of moorland in written commentaries but do not enumerate their acreage.[50] Reference to the tithe apportionments reveals that there were 6,464 acres of common in the whole parish over which all townships had rights of use.

The foregoing comments suggest that little reliance can be placed on acreages of those categories of land which, for reasons of local circumstances, generated little titheable produce or were covered by trifling moduses. Assistant commissioner Charles Howard's practice in several West Riding townships can perhaps serve as a final caution. In his reports he often comments that the schedules are accurate as far as they relate to enclosed lands but that there is doubt as to the exact boundaries of extensive, unenclosed moors. However, he says that, as he had no intention of apportioning any rent-charge on the moors, the fact that common acreages were inaccurate was of no material concern![51]

Entries in the 'state of cultivation' column of apportionments

Perhaps the most equivocal of all information contained in schedules of apportionment is that describing the state of cultivation of tithe areas. The exact criteria used for land-use classification are not immediately obvious. However, it is clear beyond doubt that the system of recording and mapping land use proposed by R. K. Dawson in 1836 was not widely followed once the Tithe Act was amended. This means that corroboration of the 'state of cultivation' is rarely found in the form of conventional symbols on the tithe map. Woods, gardens, hops and the like could be unequivocally identified in the field and are frequently shown by symbols on the maps. But the distinction between permanent grassland and rotation grasses was not always clear-cut. It is important to know how the tithe surveyors tackled this problem and so to be aware of how they classified land as 'arable' or 'pasture'.

Initially, the commissioners' interpretation of the Tithe Commutation Act itself serves as a guide. Land which was judged to have been ploughed within the previous three years for crops, rotation grasses, or fallow was to be regarded as arable. Lands 'which have not been under the plough within three years preceding Christmas 1836' were to be recorded as grass.[52] Even if these instructions were strictly followed, problems of interpretation remained in counties where convertible husbandry was widely practised in the mid-nineteenth century.[53] Also different practices were adopted in compiling land-use data for schedules to agreements and for reports on agreements. In 'pastoral' reports on agreements, assistant tithe commissioners and local agents were asked to enter as arable 'land actually ploughed in the present or last season, whether sown with corn, planted with roots or fallow, but excluding seeds'. In 'arable' reports and all articles of agreements, on the other hand, arable land was usually any land ploughed in the previous three years (as defined by the act) or perhaps in the previous seven years, the period over which the act required tithe receipts to be averaged.[54] Although what tithe valuers recorded as arable may not have been what modern surveyors would record as arable, we may be fairly sure that it was what *local contemporaries* would have understood by the term. A field survey was needed in order to apportion the tithe rent-charge equitably over various classes of land in a parish unless special arrangements for apportionment were agreed. Accuracy was essential. The value of tithes was frequently assessed at about one-fifth of the arable rent and at about one-eighth or one-ninth of the grassland rent. A difference in classification could cost tithe payers considerable sums of money, which in itself helped to ensure that unreasonable definitions would be challenged. As F. D. Hartley has neatly put it,

> On the one hand the parson and lay impropriator would claim their due; on the other hand the farmers and landowners would attempt to reduce the claim as much as possible. These two forces pulling against each other would surely produce a truthful record . . . always the most important piece of evidence was that observed in the field.[55]

In many tithe apportionments grassland is described simply as 'grass', but often a finer classification into pasture, downland, moorland, meadow, marsh and saltings is employed. Meadow is usually, but not always, defined as mown grassland, its produce being expressed in hundredweights per acre in the tithe files. 'Pasture' is land that was grazed and valued in shillings per acre or by the number of stock it supported. Marshland and moorland categories are probably the least satisfactory and accurate; often marshes were included in the pasture category. In some counties these inconsistencies may be partly explained by the fact that marsh and moor grassland was not liable to tithe on produce but was subject to a nominal modus. Therefore, it was unnecessary to distinguish between various types of grassland as the modus applied irrespective of quality, type, and gross produce. Where saltings, downland and moorland pastures were distinguished separately it was because they were liable for a lower charge. In the north-Kent parish of Swanscombe, for example, four types of grassland were recognised in 1843. Most valuable was the 120 acres of meadow yielding 21 hundredweights of hay which at 3s a hundredweight was worth 63s an acre. Pasture, occupying 66 acres, was valued at 35s an acre, whilst the pasturage of 80 acres of saltings was valued at only 20s an acre and that of downland at only 22s an acre.[56]

In short, when any comparison is being made on the basis of land-use data from tithe surveys it is imperative to ensure that like is being compared with like. Arable land, as has been shown, meant different things to tithe agents in the west and east of England and even to compilers of the tithe apportionment and the tithe file of the same district in western counties.

Crop and livestock data in the tithe files

Few of the crop acreages, yields and livestock numbers in reports on agreements in justification of an assistant commissioner's or local agent's assessment of a fair rent-charge have been taken from an actual survey. Frequently the arable acreage, itself often an estimate, was divided by the number of courses in the generally followed rotation. Nor were yields always those that had actually been obtained in the previous harvest. For the purposes of tithe commutation, a fair *par rent-charge* over the years of average, 1829–35, was required and to assess this, average acreages and average yields could be more appropriate and fairer than those relating to one particular season. It is important to remember that this generalising filter was applied by local agents at a stage when they were compiling data. For example, in districts of varied soils, farmers might practise two or three rotations but yields quoted would be a parish average for each crop. T. S. Woolley noted the implications of this mode of assessment when reporting on tithe districts in different parts of Kent. Of the calculations he made at Bromley he said, 'it is not to be supposed that the course of cropping on which I have founded my calculations is universally or even generally adopted in the Parish. Almost every occupier farms his land as circumstances may seem to require, without very rigid adherence to a particular rotation of crops.'[57] At Sutton Valence he noted that agents of the Dean and Chapter of Canterbury, 'had formed their estimate on their opinion of the proper course to be pursued though they did not consider it had been generally adopted nor indeed any regular system'.[58]

Finally in Shoreham parish, 'scarcely two farmers can be found who follow the same course of husbandry'.[59] On other occasions, assistant commissioners were further frustrated in their quest for accuracy. Woolley thought three crops to a fallow a fair assessment in Beckenham but could not get more accurate details as all the farmers had gone to a ploughing match at Chislehurst and at Shipborne he could make no valuation on his visit on 10 February 1845 as the land was covered with snow.[60] Sometimes local agents consciously depressed yields where they were convinced that unusually high farming with above-average investment was being practised. In 1837 at West Stow in Suffolk, T. S. Woolley wrote: 'in making my calculations I have taken an average of crops on the arable land, not taking the actual produce as now cultivated – but such as I think could be relied on with ordinary farms. The present produce would probably be much greater.'[61] In Warwickshire, on the other hand, the reverse happened where local agents found that yields were not as high as they ought to have been because of the local practice of close-cropping. The yields recorded in the valuations appear much higher than might be expected from local agents' frequent descriptions of low farming in their reports. Woodland yields quoted in the files are of little value as usually only underwood or coppice was titheable. For example, at Bilsthorpe, Grove and Thorney in Nottinghamshire, John Pickering quoted annual values of 9s to 11s an acre; his 33s at Normanton-on-the-Wolds and 40s at Ramskill are closer to the full value of woodland in this part of the country.[62] Similarly at Cranford in Middlesex, Horace Meteyard valued wood and plantation at 40s but at Isleworth the recorded 12s represented only the produce of underwood cut once in ten years.[63]

Because the data often relate only to the titheable portion of produce and because they were estimates of what might be produced on an average rather than what actually was, it is to be expected that tithe file figures will differ from those recorded by other, independent valuations made on a particular date. For example, Cox and Dittmer have published an extract from the Rayleigh, Essex, tithe file which contains measured acreages as well as two estimates. Estimates of the acreage of wheat differ from the measured acreage by 165 and 181 acres, an error of about 25 per cent.[64] A. D. M. Phillips has compared tithe file crop data for two Staffordshire parishes with acreages of crops recorded in the state of cultivation columns of the apportionments. Both sets of data for Milwich parish date from 1838 and show some similarity for wheat, oats and fallow but little correspondence in acreages of seeds and clover. In Worston, where the report on agreement was made in 1838 but the apportionment was not confirmed until 1845, there is virtually no similarity. Phillips accepts that evidence from these two places is inconclusive but cautions: 'it is clear that variations existed between these crop estimates and those crop acreages recorded in the tithe schedules. At best, the crop estimates in the questionnaires should note broadly the main crops grown within a parish.'[65] A similar comparison with Nottinghamshire data has yielded more positive results. Here Phillips discovered three districts whose reports on agreements and schedules of apportionment listing crops were compiled in the same years. He concludes, 'although there is a high level of correlation between the tithe file and the tithe schedule crop data, the crop areas in the tithe files appear generalised, with crops occupying but a small acreage tending to be omitted'.[66]

Estimates of crop yields in the reports on agreements were just as subjective as the estimates of acreage but were much less easily checked by the assistant commissioners. To a large extent the Commission's representatives were in the hands of the farmers but, of course, the tithe owner was present in the background poised to protest at any flagrant understatement of gross produce.

The cautionary comments discussed so far relate to counties where an 'arable' type of agreement report form was used. They must be applied with even greater force to that smaller number of counties where 'pastoral' type forms were employed. As noted in chapter 3, actual acreages of crops are rarely stated in 'pastoral' reports; generally, the acreage of arable excluding seeds and then the usual crop rotation are given. From these data it is possible to derive estimates of the acreages of individual crops – dividing the arable acreage by the number of courses minus the number of seeds courses in the rotation. Where, as all too often occurs, more than one rotation is given, where the courses in a rotation are not numbered, or where two crops were grown in one course this method cannot be used. For example, at Marham Church in Cornwall, William Glasson recorded a rotation of 'wheat, barley or oats – part potatoes and a small quantity of turnips'.[67] With such an imprecise description of the rotation it is clearly not possible to derive crop acreages. Further problems arise where, as in many counties in the west of England and in Wales, leys were of considerable and variable length. Table 4.3 indicates a variety of ways in which one assistant commissioner described leys in the one county of Pembrokeshire.

For a number of reasons, great caution must be applied to the use of tithe file livestock data. First, and in common with some of the land-use and crop data, stock numbers are very often generalised and rounded to the nearest 10 or 100. Sheep numbers in Devon appear to be rounded to the nearest 1,000! Some generalisation is understandable and to be expected in districts with extensive tracts of high, open moorland; comments on the difficulties of estimating sheep numbers in such areas are frequent in North Riding files. But, some commissioners in some places, Cornwall for example, took pains to count exact numbers. Secondly, the time of year when observations were made clearly influenced the number of animals available for counting, particularly in the case of sheep. If tithe data relate to the middle of winter, lambs and some first-year ewes might appear in the enumerations of lowland

Table 4.3 *Terms used by assistant tithe commissioner William Hoskins to describe long leys in Pembrokeshire*

PRO IR 18 reference no.	Tithe district	Description of ley
14624	Crunwear	seeds and laid up in grass 6 or 7 years
14607	Bletherstone	seeds and lay 6 or 7 years
14623	Crinow	clover and lay 7 or 8 years
14605	Bayvil	the land is laid down several years
14611	St Brides	5 or 6 years in grass
14619	Clarbeston	clover and grass ley 7 or 8 years
14648	Hodgeston	clover 3 to 5 years
14649	Hubberston	laid down in pasture 5 or 6 years
14620	Clydey	clover 5 or 6 years lay
14657	Lampeter Velfrey	lay 6 to 10 years
14664	Llandilo	clover in grass 5 or 6 years
14684	Llysyfrane	clover and rye grass and lay 10 years
14687	Maenclochog	lay up for natural grass – 5 or 6 years
14697	Monachlogddu	clover and then left to lay in pasture 4 or 5 years
14796	Whitechurch in Kemes	seeds and grass 3 to 6 years
14710	Pembroke St Mary	clover and then left to lay in pasture 4 or 5 years

parishes, while if taken in June, as were the later, official Agricultural Statistics, this would be the time of maximum sheep numbers in upland parishes. In some places, particularly in Gloucestershire where it was the practice to buy in sheep according to the season, Charles Pym considered that numbers varied so much that he could not attempt to put a figure to them. In Monmouthshire, assistant commissioner John Johnes decided to circumvent this by producing estimates of the numbers of stock he considered ought to be kept in a parish rather than taking the number he found at the time of his visit. Thirdly, a valuation of stock in a breeding parish was more difficult than in a grazing parish where simple counting of heads might suffice. As Frederick Leigh remarked at South Molton in Devon, to produce a realistic valuation of stock in a breeding parish, 'a knowledge of the business of rearing cattle, with its attendant casualties, varieties of seasons, and other risks of local character and fluctuations in prices, acquired by much observation and practice, is requisite'.[68] Fourthly, while references by assistant tithe commissioners and local agents to attempts consciously to deceive them about land use and crops are rare, they frequently felt that they were being intentionally misled by landowners about the number of stock kept on their farms. Some farmers in Pembrokeshire refused to cooperate with assistant commissioner John Johnes by barring their folds and dairies so he had to base his estimates on what he saw in neighbouring parishes. It was not only Welsh farmers who were reluctant to disclose livestock numbers. At Kings Caple, George Bolls said, 'but with regard to the quantity of stock, I will not vouch for its correctness as I find it almost impossible to ascertain the exact numbers of stock in Hereford'.[69] As with crop statistics, there was an element of recording what ought to have been, of what might have been expected on an average, rather than what actually was.

As far as the use of the cropping and livestock data from tithe files as a source for agricultural historians and historical geographers is concerned, recent studies have confirmed the main guidelines and underlined the valuable cautions offered by Cox and Dittmer in their pioneering paper.[70] In particular the inexactitude of the statistics must be borne in mind when analysing them and it is unwise to place too much reliance on the precision of data for any one place. The contents of a single tithe file may yield only a small amount of information and that not always to be relied on, but all tithe data gain in strength when those for one parish are ranged alongside those of its neighbours and those for one region against those of another.

The owners and occupiers of land

When the commissioners enquiring into the registration of land reported in 1850, the bulk of the tithe survey was complete and the possibility was raised of using tithe apportionments and maps as the basis of a system of land registration. Conveyancing land at that time was a very expensive business as a result of the need of 'manifold, intricate, chargeable, tedious and uncertain' enquiries into the title of land.[71] A general register would have diminished such burdens and the commissioners recommended that it might be based on maps tested according to Dawson's procedure for examining tithe maps and that tithe apportionments should be the model for a land index.[72] In evidence before the commissioners in 1857, William Blamire was of the opinion that for every parish for which there was a tithe survey there would not be the slightest difficulty in preparing an accurate statement of the owners of land and a map showing their respective lands for the purposes of land registration. It would also have been quite cheap. The tithe commissioners could have prepared a statement of the names of owners directly from the apportionments.[73]

For the purposes of the Tithe Act, an owner of land meant every person in actual possession or in receipt of rents and profits from a parcel of land. The owner of property so defined was the person who paid the incidental legal expenses of commutation and, although he may not in every case have been the legal owner, in most cases he certainly was. Some mortgagees and tenants for life were, however, assumed as owners for tithe commutation, as

R. E. Sandell has found in some Wiltshire parishes for which the pattern of landownership is known from other, independent sources.[74] In reply to a question about whether the Tithe Commission investigated the legal basis of an 'owner's' interest, William Blamire replied, perfunctorily, 'Oh dear, no.'[75]

An independent check on the names of occupiers of land listed in the schedule can be made by using parish rate books. A further check is provided by the census enumerators' books compiled for the censuses of 1841 and 1851. They record, house-by-house, the names of everyone living in a parish or enumeration district at the time of the census and in 1851 also record the acreages of farms. These names appear as occupiers in the tithe apportionments and the houses should be marked on the accompanying map. A number of studies reconstructing the demographic structure of parishes in the mid-nineteenth century have combined tithe and census data and have commented on the accuracy with which the tithe apportionments record the names of land occupiers (see chapter 8). For example, June Sheppard in one of the first of these studies, compared enumerators' returns and tithe apportionments for some east Yorkshire parishes and found only very small discrepancies. Most of these could be explained by differences in date between the two documents.[76] Where discrepancies are large, as in the south Cardiganshire area studied by Colin Thomas, it seems that it is the acreage figures of the census which are at fault and that the tithe apportionments are a truthful record.[77] Spencer Thomas in his study of the parish of Llansantffraid also found that the tithe apportionments contained a more reliable record of land occupiers than did the census. He found that census enumerators did not employ consistent criteria for classifying individuals as farmers. By referring to the names recorded in the tithe apportionments it is apparent that people occupying only a very few acres styled themselves 'farmers' in the census.[78] On the other hand, there is evidence that in some tithe districts the word 'occupier' was restricted to leasehold tenants. In Bookham, Surrey, several landowners are named as occupiers of all the cottages and houses on their estates, the actual residents doubtless being their servants and farm labourers. Nor can a number of people known from other sources to have resided in the parish be traced in the tithe survey; they were probably sub-tenants of the persons named as occupiers for commutation purposes.[79]

Altered tithe apportionments

A few late altered apportionments may be compared directly with the first edition Ordnance Survey 1:2,500 plans to test their accuracy. In a few exceptional instances, the land-use information in the Books of Reference compiled in connection with the 1:2,500 plans published before 1880 and also the acreages of arable, grass and orchards in the Agricultural Statistics collected annually after 1866 may be compared with the tithe surveys. But no valid conclusions as to the accuracy of the original tithe surveys may be drawn from such comparisons because new apportionments for whole parishes were only required when field arrangements and land use were completely transformed by incidents such as enclosure. Moreover, some data recorded in the Ordnance Survey Books of Reference and in the Agricultural Statistics which appear to be equivalent are not strictly comparable with those in the tithe surveys. Following its enclosure, the rent-charges for Edlesborough in Buckinghamshire were re-apportioned in 1875. The acreage of arable amounted to 2,980, that recorded as grass, 1,231, that of orchards, 43½, compared respectively with 3,806, 1,040, and 63 acres given in the Agricultural Statistics of the same year. Edlesborough, however, was an elongated parish with eight detached portions in which farms making agricultural returns occupied land in several adjoining parishes. Moreover, 114 acres of Hudnall Common, scheduled as grass in the tithe survey, were not included in the Agricultural Statistics, while some orchards carrying an extraordinary rent-charge were entered as grass in the tithe apportionments.[80] At this scale, the methods employed in collecting data are too unlike to allow a just assessment of their reliability to be made. In a different context, tithe survey information compares favourably with that derived from the Books of Reference. In transcribing land-use data from these 'area books', a major discontinuity appears along the county boundary between Middlesex and Hertfordshire. This line is evident neither on maps drawn from the tithe survey data nor on land-utilisation survey maps of the 1930s.[81] Such comparisons, while not conclusive, suggest at least that the tithe material is not inferior to that obtained from other sources.

5

Evidence of field systems

When Frederick Seebohm used a tithe map of 1816 to illustrate his account of the open fields of Hitchin, he hinted at the potentialities of the 'tithing maps of many parishes besides Hitchin' as sources for the study of field systems, but he was curiously silent on the subject of the later and more abundant tithe commutation records.[1] Even before the tithe survey of the whole country was complete, tithe apportionments had been used as a source of data on the size of fields.[2] The most enduring contribution that Seebohm and Meitzen made to agrarian studies was to establish beyond question the value of both contemporary and recent maps in differentiating field systems in neighbouring regions.[3] They followed a retrogressive approach to their enquiries, using accurate evidence of a late date as a starting point for their search for earlier forms. In a letter to Fustel de Coulanges, written about 1885, Seebohm asked whether agrarian structures so clearly evident in Britain were in any way comparable with those in France. Fustel replied that he knew of no evidence that would indicate a similarity; so absorbed was he in the ancient texts, that he was able neither to read the all too familiar marks on the fields of northern France, nor to hear the familiar sound of the debates then proceeding in the *Chambre* on the issue of *vaine pâture*.[4] Since that time much attention has been paid to post-sixteenth-century records, and writers have come to rely increasingly on the tithe maps because of their detailed portrayal of small parcels and their demarcation of land sub-divisions among different occupiers. In 1897, for example, Walter Rye drew attention to the value of tithe maps in investigations of field systems and used the 1843 tithe survey of Cawston, Norfolk, in a study published the following year.[5]

Map evidence

Gilbert Slater described the peculiarities of the Wessex village community by reference to the types of tenures recorded in the tithe awards for

Grimstone and Fordington in Dorset.[6] He amplified his field studies of decayed open fields in the midlands by referring to tithe maps of Sutton in Northamptonshire, Soham in Cambridgeshire and Yattenden in Berkshire.[7] He also devoted several pages to exposing inaccuracies in the 'Return of the acreage of waste lands subject to rights of common and of common field lands in each parish in England and Wales in which tithes have been commuted under the Tithe Commutation Acts', dated 27 November 1873. Although the task of re-examining thousands of individual maps and awards to produce a correct statement of the remaining open fields appeared formidable, Slater regarded them as 'the richest mine of information' for such a study.[8] A source of this value could not be overlooked in future enquiries. Modern practitioners now claim that 'accurate topographic and cadastral maps are almost as essential a prerequisite for the study of field systems of the past as they are for the study of contemporary geographical problems'.[9]

Place-name evidence

The utilisation of place-name evidence for the study of past field systems has been greatly assisted by the work of the English Place-Name Society. The collection and interpretation of field and minor name elements was one of the first objectives of the Society's survey. The earliest volume referring to tithe apportionments as a source for field-names was the volume on Surrey, published in 1934. The editors explained that they had recourse to names listed in the tithe awards 'owing to the comparative poverty of the present-day materials'.[10] Tithe schedules for almost all parishes in Surrey and also in Middlesex preserved names from an era before urbanisation obliterated farms and fields.[11] The volume for Essex owes much to a pioneer work by W. C. Waller at the beginning of the century, probably the most complete list of field names for a single county abstracted from tithe material.[12] In 1943, F. T. Wainwright declared that field-name forms recorded in the tithe award schedules 'may contain evidence of the highest historical value', and he demonstrated their value by tracing an ancient 'moot hill' from names of fields on opposite sides of a boundary between the parishes of Brimstage and Thornton Hough in Cheshire.[13] A recent work by John Field considers tithe apportionments 'a sound basis for a collection' of field-names and illustrates the use of a tithe survey by reference to Preston Montford in Shropshire.[14]

The names of fields recorded in the tithe apportionments offer some indication of possible earlier conditions, such as the location of a piece of land enclosed by the mid-nineteenth century, in former open fields. For accurate dating, however, other evidence is required for the very reason that 'field names like other toponyms tend to be retained long after their descriptive names have been rendered inaccurate by agrarian and social change'.[15] Nor were open-field place-name elements such as *furlong, shott, rigg, gore* or *butt* exclusive to open-field areas, so that recognition of these and similar terms in tithe apportionments can be only indicative, not diagnostic, without other, generally earlier, supporting evidence.[16] One of the most successful ways of using the many millions of tithe survey field-names has been to plot the distribution of particular elements such as *breck, intake,* or *ffridd* over wide areas in order to reconstruct past agrarian patterns.[17] Such studies are based on the premise that the names of these cultural features were not given in a random or meaningless way. Second, tithe survey place-names provide valuable topographic reference points. Place-names are not always found immediately adjacent to the features to which they refer, but are good indicators of the location of features mentioned by name in other, perhaps much earlier, documents.[18]

English field systems

In a classic study of English field systems, H. L. Gray remarked that the tithe surveys 'picture exactly the conditions of townships at the time the rating was made', but their relevance for a study of medieval conditions is uncertain because 'that time is usually so late that the old field system of the township had already been much transformed'.[19] Late as they are, they yield fuller and more precise statements than early documents and for that reason cannot be ignored. Following Seebohm's example, Gray used a tithe survey to depict a typical open-field arrangement at Chalgrove in Oxfordshire.[20] His sketch of the field pattern, taken from the tithe map, is reproduced here as Fig. 5.1. The accompanying account discusses the shape of the strips, their length and breadth and their distribution among the open fields. The picture is completed by an abstract of the copyhold tenements of John Jones who held 41 separate parcels of about half an acre each, amounting in all to less than 22 acres.[21] Gray, perhaps more than Seebohm, appreciated the value of studying the complexities of field systems in well-documented periods and from this datum line would retrace the threads of development backward into the obscurity of the past. He considered 'it is often only by the aid of late survivals that the early evidence can be interpreted at all'.[22] An examination of the morphology of fields from maps and terriers lent support to views expressed by Meitzen and Maitland that distinctive field patterns characterised different regions of Britain. Gray considered evidence for the distinctiveness of two- and three-field systems to be clear enough to warrant the drawing of a boundary on a map separating the midland area from other areas. Gray was inclined to follow Meitzen in attributing morphological differences in field arrangements to ethnic origins. The western limit of the midland area corresponds closely with the limit of Anglo-Saxon and Scandinavian colonisation, the west lying in an area characterised by what is

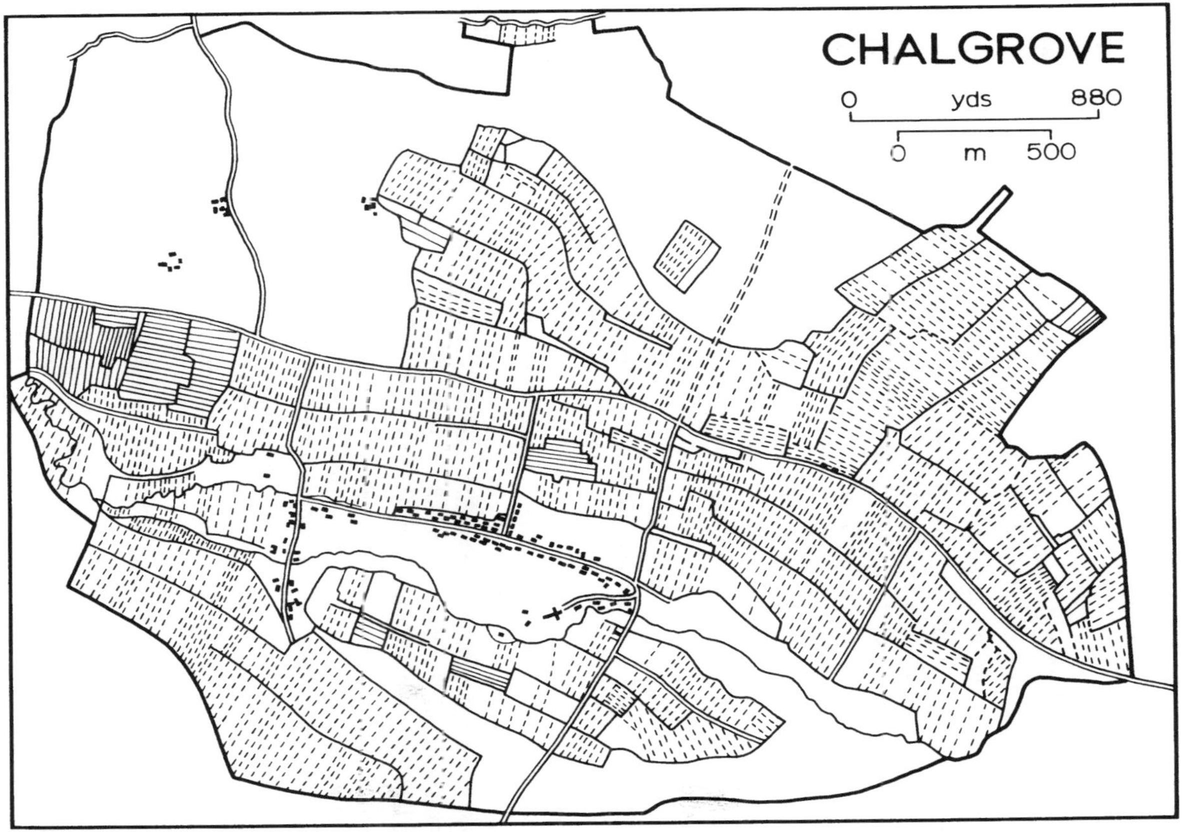

5.1 The open fields of Chalgrove in Oxfordshire. Source: H. L. Gray, *English field systems*, 1915.

termed the Celtic system. Whilst not disregarding differences between the physical conditions of farming in the midlands and in western Britain, the coincidence of linguistic and political divisions with the line of demarcation between the two- and three-field systems and the infield–outfield system suggested that ethnic differences were of greater significance.[23]

Open fields in England

For over twenty years Gray's work stood alone, unchallenged in broad essentials, and during the same period the tithe surveys were neglected for a variety of reasons. In the study of field systems some detailed early maps from the sixteenth and seventeenth centuries were brought to light among the muniments of Oxford and Cambridge colleges and this evidence was more directly relevant to an understanding of medieval agrarian structures than the later tithe surveys. The tithe documents were also very numerous and bulky to handle and it was difficult to gain access to them until they were moved to spacious premises in Finsbury Square after the establishment of the Tithe Redemption Commission in 1936. Neither J. H. Clapham's three-volume work on the economic history of nineteenth-century Britain, nor the essays of J. L. and Barbara Hammond contain references to them, and they are mentioned only briefly in the first study to dispute the validity of Gray's explanation of the origins of open fields.[24] C. S. and C. S. Orwin rejected the view that different types of field systems were developed independently by Celts and Anglo-Saxons. The differences noted by Gray were more apparent than real; they were differences of form not of function. The Orwins claimed that these variations could be explained more satisfactorily as variants of a single open-field system devised to serve the needs of medieval farming communities. 'There is very little', they asserted, 'in the characteristic features of the open fields which cannot be explained simply and naturally by the common sense of farming practice.'[25] *The open fields* is much less extensively documented than Gray's study. It is based largely on an examination of the husbandry of a single village, Laxton in Nottinghamshire, whose fields still lie open. The tithe survey for the parish was consulted to identify the names of owners and occupiers of the open fields, but no reference is made to the names of fields nor the state of cultivation.

Whilst the Orwins were examining in depth the archetypal arrangement of open fields at Laxton, F. G. Emmison surveyed the range of variation among open-field parishes in the country around Bedford, identifying multiple and composite forms of arrangements, where parts of parishes were enclosed and were operating two- or three-field courses over four, six, nine or twelve fields.[26] The tithe map of Yielden in Bedfordshire illustrates a typical form of three-field layout in a parish where half the land was already enclosed and the remainder lay in three open fields. An analysis of the apportionment shows that the three fields contained 635 acres in 511 strips belonging to only five proprietors.[27] Orwins' and Emmison's studies led later investigators to expect some diversity in open-field arrangements within the midlands and they also implied that within a framework of apparently different forms the same system might operate. The next step was to question whether open fields in the midland area formed, as Gray suggested, a unique and distinctive type or whether they were related to field systems in other parts of Britain.

Open fields in the south-west peninsula

The tithe surveys have yielded evidence of resemblances between field patterns in western Britain and those in the midlands. In Devonshire, a close examination by A. H. Shorter of the tithe surveys of a dozen townships in south Devon provided abundant traces of open-field arrangements.[28] A re-examination of the material relating to Braunton by A. H. Slee was equally rewarding.[29] The tithe apportionment of 1840 lists some 500 strips on which tithe was paid and these were cultivated by over 100 different occupiers. A further search in the tithe documents of another two dozen parishes chosen at random by H. P. R. Finberg showed that 'all but six displayed the characteristic vestiges of strip cultivation. In some cases the "church-town" from which the parish takes its name presented the appearance of a nucleated village like Braunton, with enclosed strip fields adjoining it on one or more sides. In others, outlying hamlets were surrounded by strip systems of their own.'[30] Finberg was confident that a thorough scrutiny of all tithe maps and other recent surveys 'would bring to light similar vestiges in scores of Devon parishes'.[31] The tithe maps for both Devon and Cornwall have been examined by H. S. A. Fox in the course of his studies of field systems in the south-west peninsula. His general conclusion is that the tithe evidence comes too late to provide a sound basis for making conclusive judgements; but it does indicate localities where further investigations might profitably be pursued.[32] Local studies by W. G. Hoskins and E. Gawne on the fringes of Dartmoor, by N. W. Alcock in east Devon, by A. H. Shorter on Brixham, by W. M. Williams on Ashworthy and D. J. Bonney on Challacombe have succeeded in tracing earlier evidence to support mid-nineteenth-century testimony and have encouraged wider speculation.[33] As evidence for open-field arrangements beyond Gray's limit has accumulated, searchers have ventured further west into Cornwall. N. J. G. Pounds' thesis touches lightly on the character of Cornish field patterns, whilst M. E. Witherick identifies remnants of open-field strips from the tithe documents in a re-evaluation of the origins of medieval boroughs in Cornwall.[34] The tithe maps for the whole of Cornwall are systematically but somewhat cursorily examined by Pierre Flatrès and a map of strip fields, reproduced here as Fig. 5.2, is constructed.[35]

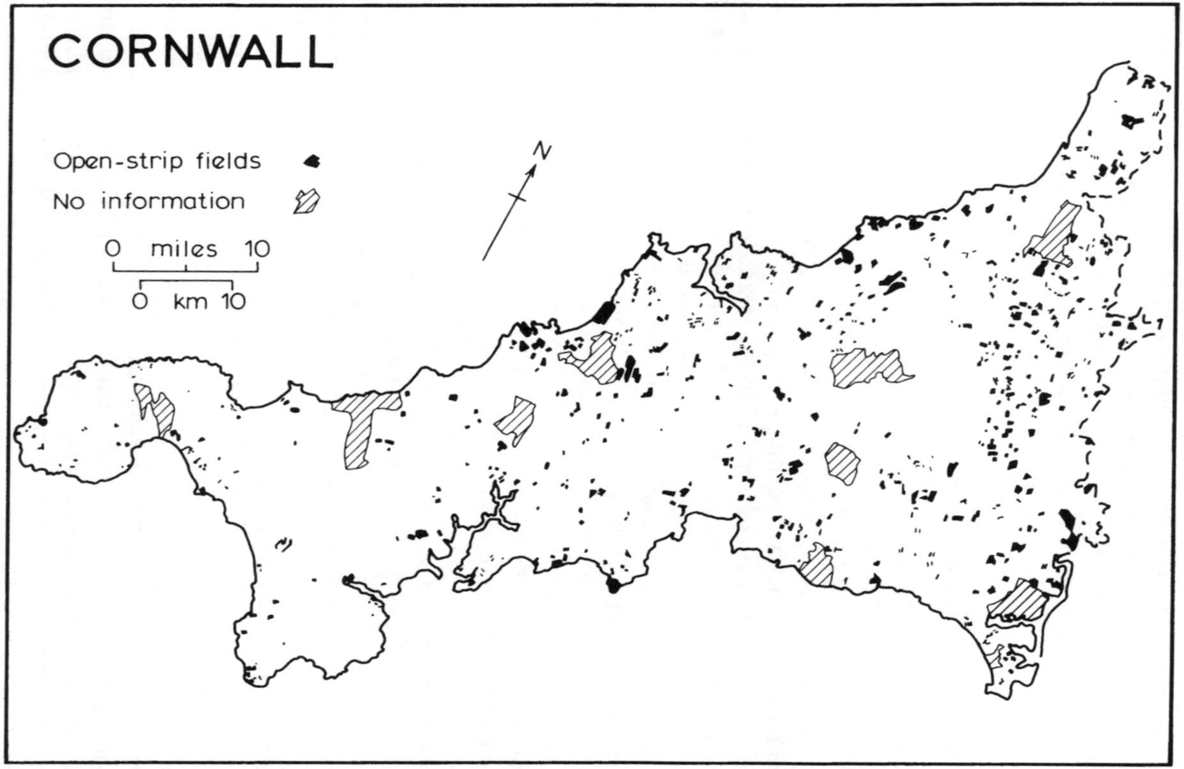

5.2 'Open fields' in Cornwall. Source: P. Flatrès, *Géographie rurale de quatre contrées celtiques . . .*, 1957.

Forms of settlements and fields in the Welsh borderland

While the south-western border of H. L. Gray's midland system has been decisively breached, fresh attacks have been mounted on the Welsh borderlands and advances have penetrated deep into Wales. Dorothy Sylvester's studies, making extensive use of tithe surveys for Cheshire, have led her to seek and to find traces of field arrangements similar to those in the midlands.[36] In reconstructing patterns of rural settlement in Anglesey, she declares: 'the first complete survey of habitations and fields, here as elsewhere, was the tithe survey made in the 1830s and 1840s'.[37] An examination of the tithe maps and apportionments of some eighty Flintshire townships formed the basis of an account of rural settlement in that county.[38] In addition to maps of field layouts in individual townships, such as Gwysaney, the article also presents a sketch map portraying, among other features, the distribution of open fields.[39] A similar study of eastern Montgomeryshire draws heavily upon tithe material and again mid-nineteenth-century surveys are relied upon for an account of township fields in the coastlands of Gwent.[40] In Gwent in Monmouthshire, vestiges of six open fields are identified on the tithe map for the parish of Undy in 1840, whilst the pattern of common meadows is illustrated from a map and apportionment for the parish of Redwick in 1846.[41] In other Welsh border counties, similar traces of open fields are delineated on many tithe maps.

The conclusions of these earlier studies are brought together and extended in a summary volume describing the rural landscape of the whole length of the Welsh borderlands.[42] A map locating open arable and common meadow lands in the district is constructed largely from tithe evidence.[43] These studies are flawed by a straining of the tithe evidence. The manner of interpreting several documents is open to doubt. For example, tithe areas represented on some maps depict whole farms, not separate fields, and yield little or no information of value in reconstructing sizes and shapes of fields or types of field boundary. The significance of lines, particularly dotted or broken lines on tithe maps, deserves careful attention if the maps are to be read correctly. But the most serious weakness in this work is that similarities in form are regarded as expressions of similar functions, such that all unenclosed strips are alike and alike share a common origin. But the forms under investigation are very late, possibly much altered, relics from systems from which they are supposed to have been derived. It is by no means certain that unenclosed strips delineated on nineteenth-century maps are directly related to strips in medieval common fields. Having made these reservations, it must be acknowledged that a great achievement of Dorothy Sylvester's monumental effort is to make a considerable advance beyond the simple division drawn by Gray. A reading of her book leaves no room to doubt that 'the heterogeneity of settlement and field patterns in the Borderland is such that it is impossible to categorise them simply nor, from the angle of field patterns in particular, is it desirable even if it were possible, to "type" them beyond a point'.[44]

Interpreting groupings of buildings

A notion that has impeded progress towards a recognition of the intertwining of Welsh and English cultural forms is F. W. Maitland's characterisation of the west as a land of hamlets and lowland England as a land of villages. Recent work based partly on map evidence makes it clear that the distinction is far less sharp and less critically important than it was formerly thought to be.[45] Dorothy Sylvester's work, for example, carries the map-reading exercise back from the present to the mid-nineteenth century, substituting a five-fold classification for Maitland's simple two-fold division, illustrated by a map showing a complex intermingling of settlement types.[46]

In detail, a variety of arrangements of buildings is depicted on large-scale plans of small areas. With the aid of tithe surveys for 28 parishes, D. H. C. Bennett examined settlement patterns in western Pembrokeshire.[47] An important revision to earlier work is that maps alone provide an incomplete record of building patterns. Fewer buildings are represented on the tithe maps than are listed in the apportionments and in all but one of the parishes fewer houses are listed in the apportionments than are recorded in the 1841 census enumeration books. Having located these additional houses, the relationship of isolated and nucleated settlements to landforms and to farm boundaries is examined with precision, particular attention being paid to sites of churches. Bennett concludes that the Celtic church has had a sustained impact on the morphology of Welsh settlements. In south-east Monmouthshire R. A. Worthington used tithe surveys to produce another account of settlement at that period.[48] He maps habitations and describes the sites and morphology of isolated and nucleated settlements, seeking explanations for their distribution in the nature of the physical environment. This points to the conclusion that availability of water is one key to their location.

The territorial basis of Welsh settlements

The study of settlement forms is taken a step forward by a fuller consideration of the relation of farm houses to farm holdings. A major advance in this direction is G. R. J. Jones' study of Welsh farming settlements based on an analysis of farms and farm boundaries indicated on the tithe surveys.[49] It is argued that a study of rural settlement should properly begin with an account of the landholdings and of the location and extent of different types of farmland. The groupings of buildings is not, by itself, an adequate indicator of cultural differences. An alternative concept proceeds from the view that 'overconcentration on distributions of dwellings has tended to mask the importance of the landholding necessary for the sustenance of every farm family'.[50] Jones concludes by explaining the settlement pattern of seven townships in terms of the distribution of open-field arable land. In the absence of accurate detailed maps from an earlier date, much reliance is placed upon the tithe material, which is assumed to portray the major lineaments of a medieval settlement pattern. Later studies use tithe surveys in a similar manner in reconstructing medieval rural settlements in Anglesey and on the Welsh border.[51] It remains to be demonstrated with reasonable assurance that medieval arrangements of farms and fields survived undisturbed during the long period that elapsed between the events under discussion and the compilation of tithe records in the mid-nineteenth century. Without documentation for intervening centuries the conclusions remain speculative. In recent studies G. R. J. Jones attempts to bridge this gap. Tithe files throw some light on the extent to which tribal lands in Wales were consolidated or remained dispersed.[52] Survivals of Celtic field arrangements and fragmented glebe lands in Arfon are traced back from the tithe surveys.[53] Fragmented holdings appearing in the nineteenth-century survey of Llanynys are similarly examined retrogressively[54] (Fig. 5.3). Some firm generalisations can now be made about the distribution of bond settlements in north-west Wales.[55] Careful use of tithe surveys in conjunction with much earlier evidence underpin two further essays of fundamental importance to understanding Welsh field systems and tenurial arrangements.[56]

Agrarian change in Wales

Whilst G. R. J. Jones draws upon tithe records for evidence of survivals, illuminating aspects of continuity in Welsh settlements, others turn to the same source in attempting to assess the extent of changes prior to the mid-nineteenth century. The aim of J. W. Edwards' study of the Vale of Clwyd is not so much to trace remnants of open fields as to measure the amount of improvement taking place in parishes undergoing enclosure.[57] The tithe maps and apportionments show the outlines of rectangular fields imposed on previously open marshland on the north-Wales coast. By 1840 this land was largely under the plough and tithe files testify to the excellence of its cultivation. In neighbouring townships vestiges of open fields appear on tithe surveys and these are plotted on a map.[58] In western Montgomeryshire, J. Gareth Thomas is likewise concerned with changes that occurred in the rural landscape between the date of enclosure and the tithe surveys.[59] A map of changes in settlement from 1826 to 1846 indicates the disappearance of squatters' dwellings in that period, and it provides indirect confirmation of

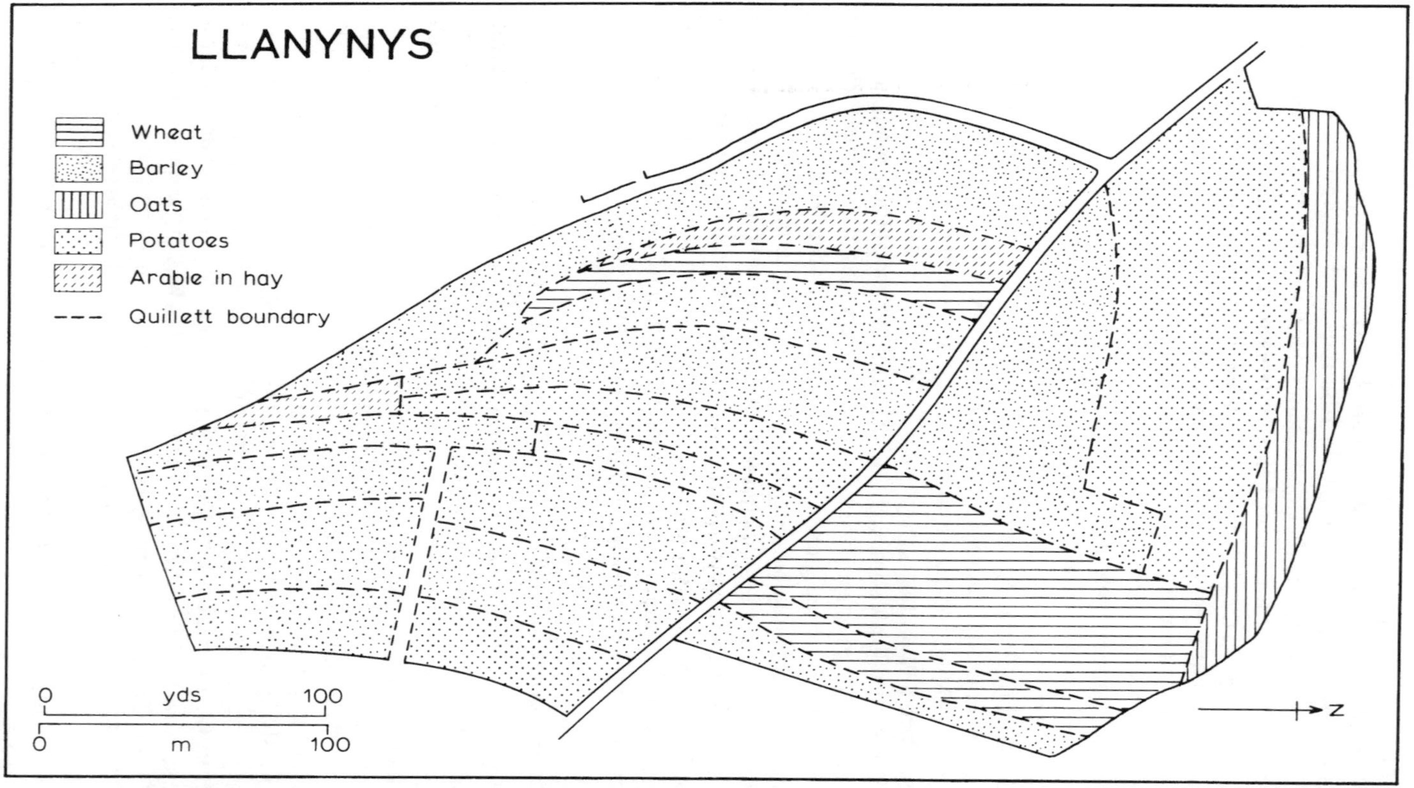

5.3 The Llanynys quilletts. Source: G. R. J. Jones, 'The Llanynys quilletts: a measure of landscape transformation in North Wales', 1964.

the former extent of common fields. As Colin Morgan notes in his study of the effects of parliamentary enclosure on the landscapes of Caernarvonshire and Merioneth, for parishes where there is both an enclosure and a tithe map, the tithe maps can be particularly valuable as they record the pattern of fields and farmsteads that actually emerged after an enclosure award rather than the intended landscape indicated by an enclosure map.[60] Similar work has been carried out in the Banwy valley by W. T. R. Pryce.[61] Further south, a study of the open fields of Rhossili and neighbouring parishes by Margaret Davies is based largely on a tithe survey of 1845[62] (Fig. 5.4). A comparison between the tithe maps and a survey of the manor of Rhossili in 1780 indicates that there was little change in the field pattern during the 65-year period.[63] Strip fields are again found in the parish of Laugharne at the time of the tithe survey of 1842.[64] Examination of other tithe maps from 1838 to 1844 brings to light similar features in many localities in Gower and adjoining parts of south Wales. These studies indicate that unenclosed strip fields similar in appearance to those of midland England were once present in different parts of Wales.

'Celtic' fields in Wales

A comprehensive account of rural landscapes in the four Celtic countries of Ireland, Wales, Cornwall and the Isle of Man by Pierre Flatrès contains many maps based on the tithe surveys illustrating field patterns and settlement types.[65] Amongst them are maps of open-strip fields in Cornwall (Fig. 5.2 above) and also one of strip fields in Wales. The method of compiling these maps recalls the method, severely criticised by Slater, used to prepare the 1873 'Return of commons and common field lands'. In Wales almost every township had widely scattered open strips intermixed with its enclosed fields, and many of the enclosed fields themselves were similar in shape and size to the unenclosed strips. Many strips were held by farmers resident in hamlets and many were arable in 1840; but at this time Wales possessed very few large continuous tracts of open fields comparable with those in the midlands. Flatrès refuses to identify the scattered remnants in Wales with the strips of midland open fields. He prefers to interpret them as vestiges of an extinct field system indigenous to the Celtic lands. The course of development from an original Celtic system changing through time (partly as a result of independent processes and partly through modifications brought by contacts with the English) to produce a pattern resembling, if only superficially, that of the midlands, is scarcely hinted at in Flatrès' account. But his approach to the problem is attractive because it makes an appeal to history, asking how the mid-nineteenth-century pattern emerged, what changes brought it into being, and how its development differed from that of other systems. Historical reasoning seeks to identify common

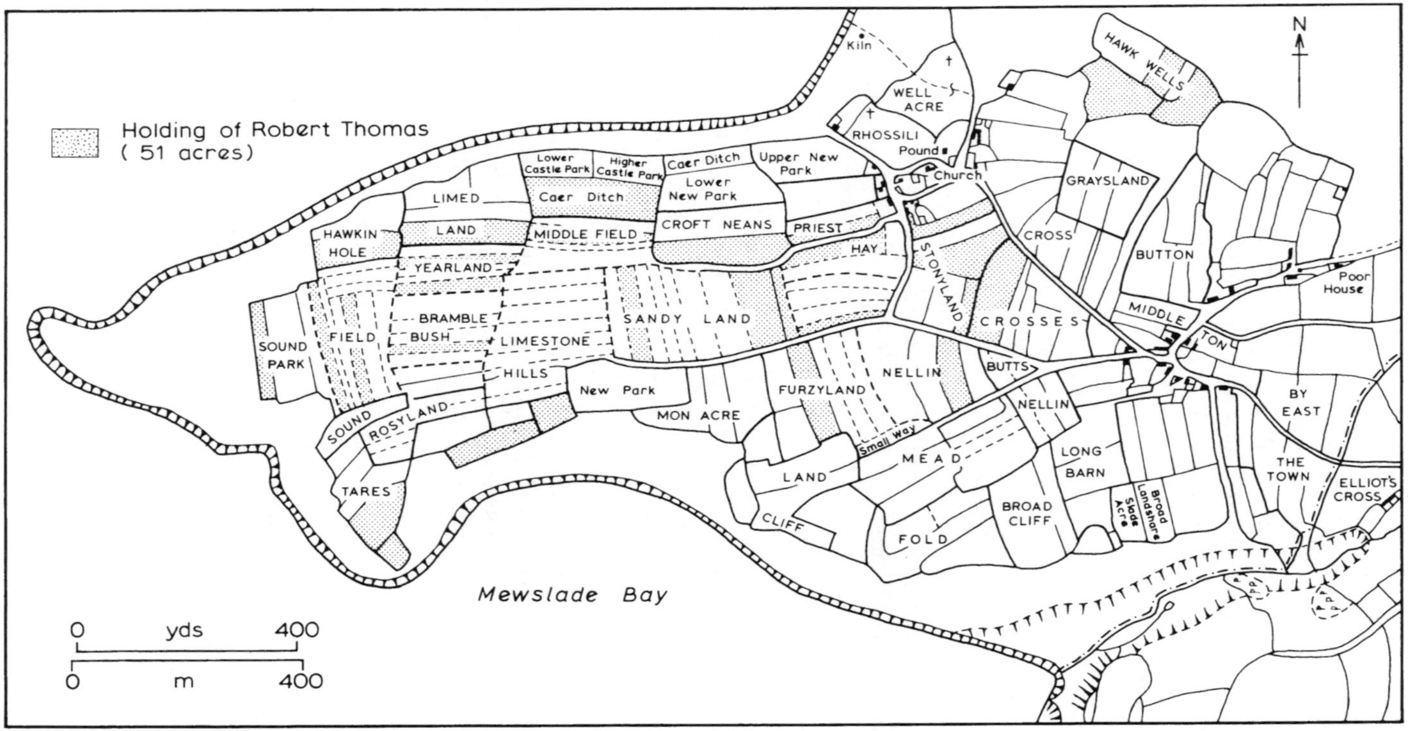

5.4 The open fields of Rhossili, south Wales. Source: Margaret F. Davies, 'Rhossili open fields and related South Wales field patterns', 1956.

elements in the processes at work and is less concerned with the forms produced. Morphologists are faced with the challenge of showing that similar forms have similar origins. Specifically, a suspension of the attack on the autonomy of Welsh agrarian structures is called for, until their history has been more fully examined. Gray's line may have to be redrawn but the case for abandoning it has not been justified.

A single or multiple field system in England?

In 1959, Joan Thirsk announced that there was no county in England in which some traces of open-field cultivation had not been found.[66] It proclaimed a triumph for a uniformitarian view of English field systems, vindicating an assertion made by the Orwins that there is nothing in the basic organisation of open fields that cannot be explained by the common sense of farming practice. All fields are open fields, some more open than others, and local variants are not only to be expected but may readily be attributed to local differences in climate, terrain, soils and to inequalities in the operation of market forces. The legal niceties which Seebohm, Vinogradoff and Maitland treated with respectful care are counted as of little relevance; the imprints of ethnic characteristics laboriously deciphered by Meitzen and Gray are dismissed as mostly illusory; and the cataclysmic events which allegedly altered the course of medieval and modern history scarcely appear to have ruffled the surface of that one enduring system to which all but a few traditional farming practices in England owe their existence. Over a decade of patient study, however, has not succeeded in reducing all the outstanding irregularities in English field systems to fit a uniform mould.[67] On the contrary, non-conforming characteristics have assumed greater importance in recent investigations. Ambiguities surrounding the origins of Celtic field systems have not been dispelled and the diversity of field arrangements in northern England has yet to be satisfactorily elucidated. Within midland England itself wide variations in local practices reported in recent local histories impose severe strains on a uniformitarian view. Close correspondence between form and function among features in highlands and lowlands, on heavy and light soils and in arable and pastoral districts is being called in question and a thorough re-examination of Kentish fields lends stronger support to Gray's notion of separate development than to a uniformitarian interpretation. In the Chilterns and in East Anglia decisive results are not being achieved by either party, but everywhere important historical questions are being raised with little prospect of obtaining satisfactory answers from uniformitarians. Among questions that remain unanswered are when and how was an open-field system first formed; were open fields planted on freshly cleared sites; were they extended by medieval reclamation into the wastes; did an open-field system re-assert itself after villages had been devastated or depopulated; when was the last open field in England created; did the open-field system in the nineteenth century function in the same way that it had done in the twelfth century? The tithe material cannot be expected to yield much evidence towards unravelling the remoter antecedents of nineteenth-century field patterns except as a source for field names and as a guide to the location of significant features. Some studies have suffered from an uncritical dependence on tithe surveys to the neglect of earlier sources.

Field systems in northern England

In northern England several writers have found evidence among the tithe surveys for the former existence of field patterns closely resembling those in the midlands described by Gray.[68] Some of this evidence derives from tithe surveys. In the Durham region the earliest detailed records of field boundaries, upon which Harry Thorpe based his investigation of rural settlement types, are tithe surveys.[69] The origin of field patterns is less certain than in districts where enclosures took place more recently and the evidence suggests a greater heterogeneity of forms than those prevailing in the midlands. On the other hand, traces of strip fields occur in most localities and a regular two-field arrangement is exhibited on the Heighington map.[70] Tithe maps are the main source of plans of village forms for J. S. Ingleson's study of settlement, agrarian systems and field patterns in central Durham, whilst both D. A. Alexander and B. K. Roberts have used tithe maps to identify 'town fields' in that county.[71] In the Lake District a tenuous relationship with midland field systems is construed from mapped forms. Commenting on the tithe survey of Askham Town Field in Westmorland, T. H. Bainbridge observes that it was divided into open arable strips or 'dales' cultivated by farmers residing in a compact hamlet, laid out like a miniature midland open-field village, its fields containing only thirty-five dales.[72] Part of the tithe map for Dalton illustrates the arrangement of dales, forming a pattern very unlike that of strips in a midland parish, and no connection between the two systems can be secured with this flimsy thread. In Cumberland, some 204 tithe maps and apportionments are examined by G. Elliott in a search for 'quilleted fields'.[73] These appear on tithe maps as strips enclosed by dotted lines and are distinguished readily from unfenced tracts of mossland recorded as pasture or moor in the state of cultivation column in the apportionments. Again, their relationship with a midland system is uncertain; they are associated with small groups of farms and are widely scattered throughout townships. A full review of their early history is needed before firm conclusions are reached.

Other studies have explored the extent to which an open-field system was transferred to the English uplands. In Derbyshire J. C. Jackson traces evidence for open-field cultivation at altitudes over 800 feet above sea level by studying field-names on tithe and other recent surveys.[74] An 1820 tithing map of Holmesfield indicates two open fields. To the west of the village four adjacent closes bear the name 'Town Field' and beyond them lie Far and Near Hugh Flatt, whilst to the south of the village stretches what was probably another open field called Dale Field. Extensive use is made of field-name evidence derived from later tithe commutation surveys. An apportionment for Ashleyhay in 1842, for example, yields four name-elements indicating the former presence of open-field arable farming.[75] Field patterns shown on tithe maps are also examined. In the parish of Thorpe the pattern of strip fields in 1850 is compared with the distribution and orientation of ridge-and-furrow on the ground. Alan Baker takes Jackson to task for his lack of caution, not only because his work leans too heavily on nineteenth-century evidence but also because it fails to investigate critically the functions performed within the framework of forms represented on these late maps.[76] The characteristic modes of colonisation have yet to be analysed, the organisation of communal grazing and of communal crop husbandry remain unaccounted for, and the essential workings of traditional farming in the uplands remain obscure. As it now stands, the enquiry offers little more than a well-matched assemblage of identikit features to link fields in Derbyshire with the midland system.

The tithe surveys may make a small contribution to a deeper understanding of the agrarian history of the uplands. They furnish the fullest and most comprehensive records of field and minor names, elements of which may be studied as indicators of dates of colonisation. S. R. Eyre exploits this source in tracing the extension of cultivation on the edge of the Derbyshire moorlands before the time of parliamentary enclosure.[77] Names containing the elements 'ridding', 'stubbing' and 'intake' are presumed to date from the time of initial land clearance from woods and wastes. Localities where fields have remained undisturbed since being reclaimed are indicated on a map showing the distribution of these elements.[78] In John Chapman's study of the North York Moors a map of 'intake' name-elements illustrates not only an upward advance of cultivation, pushing back the moorland edge, but also a simultaneous attack on obdurate pockets of unimproved land at lower levels.[79] In Ribblesdale in Lancashire Alan Digby considers 'flatt', 'moor' and 'moss' names of medieval origin, to be distinguished from name-elements indicating improvements in later times.[80] A frequent characteristic of later improvements is that fields once broken by the plough, bearing names such as 'barley croft' and 'wheat field', were converted to meadow or pasture by the time their state of cultivation came to be recorded in tithe apportionments. On Dartmoor, field-names in tithe apportionments suggest the former existence of 'strip fields' but maps and apportionments reveal a pattern of small tenements in nucleated settlements surrounded by their own fields.[81] In short, pictures of the uplands as scenes being transformed by several different phases of occupance are emerging from recent studies, and the transplanting of midland open fields appears to be a rather shadowy episode in most of these histories.

Infield–outfield arrangements on light soils

The English lowlands have ceased to be the exclusive domain of the two- or three-field system. Exact counterparts of the infield–outfield system, identified in Gray's account as a peculiarly Celtic practice, have been found in many localities in lowland England. A number of Norfolk parishes are discovered from the tithe surveys by J. E. G. Mosby to have practised this form of cultivation.[82] The arrangement and organisation of fields in two such parishes, at Caldecote and Bircham Tofts both in the sandy region of west Norfolk, are examined in detail; the brecks of Bylaugh are similarly investigated from the tithe survey.[83] Mosby's map of the fields of Caldecote is reproduced here as Fig. 5.5. The tithe survey shows this to have been a one-farm parish in 1851 with an arrangement of fields characteristic of an infield–outfield system of cultivation. In the west of the parish are fen pastures and a few arable closes on low-lying land. Situated around the homestead of Caldecote farm are the home meadows and arable closes, whilst stretching away to the east on higher ground are five open brecks, beyond which lie unbroken sheep-walks. The presence of a 'breck' element in field and minor names serves as a guide to the location of infield–outfield cultivation. All 'breck' names mentioned in the tithe awards for the county

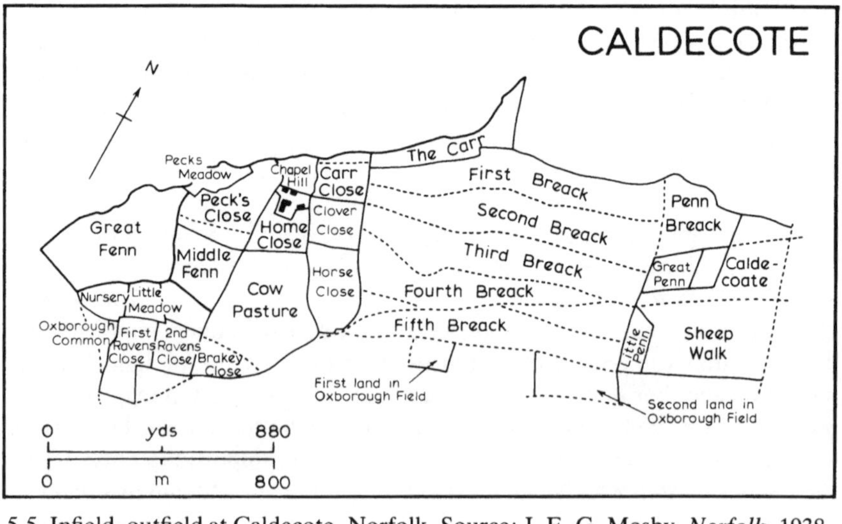

5.5 Infield–outfield at Caldecote, Norfolk. Source: J. E. G. Mosby, *Norfolk*, 1938.

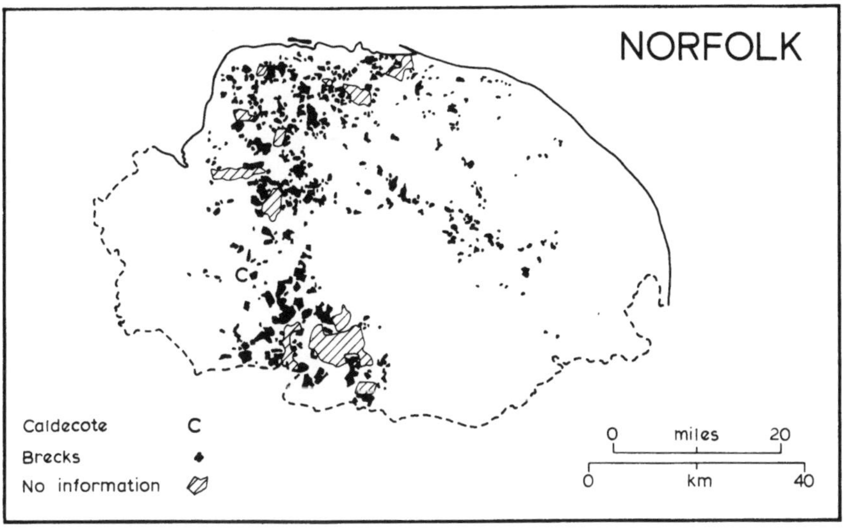

5.6 Norfolk brecks. Source: as Fig. 5.5.

are mapped.[84] A map based on this work (Fig. 5.6) shows that almost all brecks are concentrated on the lighter soils of Norfolk with a preponderance in Breckland itself and in the Good Sand region. Another map of mid-nineteenth-century brecks illustrates Malcolm Postgate's thesis on the historical geography of the Breckland.[85] In this and his subsequent studies, special care is exercised in interpreting field-name evidence and in defining finer shades of meaning among different types of 'intake' and 'breck'.[86]

The former existence of infield–outfield cultivation has been recognised in many parts of the country outside Norfolk, but few studies have made use of field-names recorded in tithe apportionments. In neighbouring Suffolk, P. Armstrong considers that tithe maps, such as that of the parish of Eyke, with designations 'common field in parts' indicate holdings in the process of reorganisation.[87] Another study relating to the Fylde region of Lancashire is mentioned by Wilfred Smith.[88] Another by Norman Hilton includes a map of fluctuating cultivation in the Land's End peninsula in 1840.[89] Here the term 'croft', which appears frequently in apportionments, is understood to refer to a temporarily cultivated field, a relic of a 'Celtic Outfield'.[90] In a comprehensive review of infield–outfield survivals in western and central Europe Harald Uhlig makes reference to the use of tithe evidence by workers in western Britain.[91] For districts of light, hungry soils in lowland England tithe maps and apportionments will undoubtedly add many more examples of the kind illustrated by a map of Carburton in Nottinghamshire (Fig. 5.7) to which B. R. Dittmer's attention was drawn by an account of the parish written by J. D. Chambers.[92]

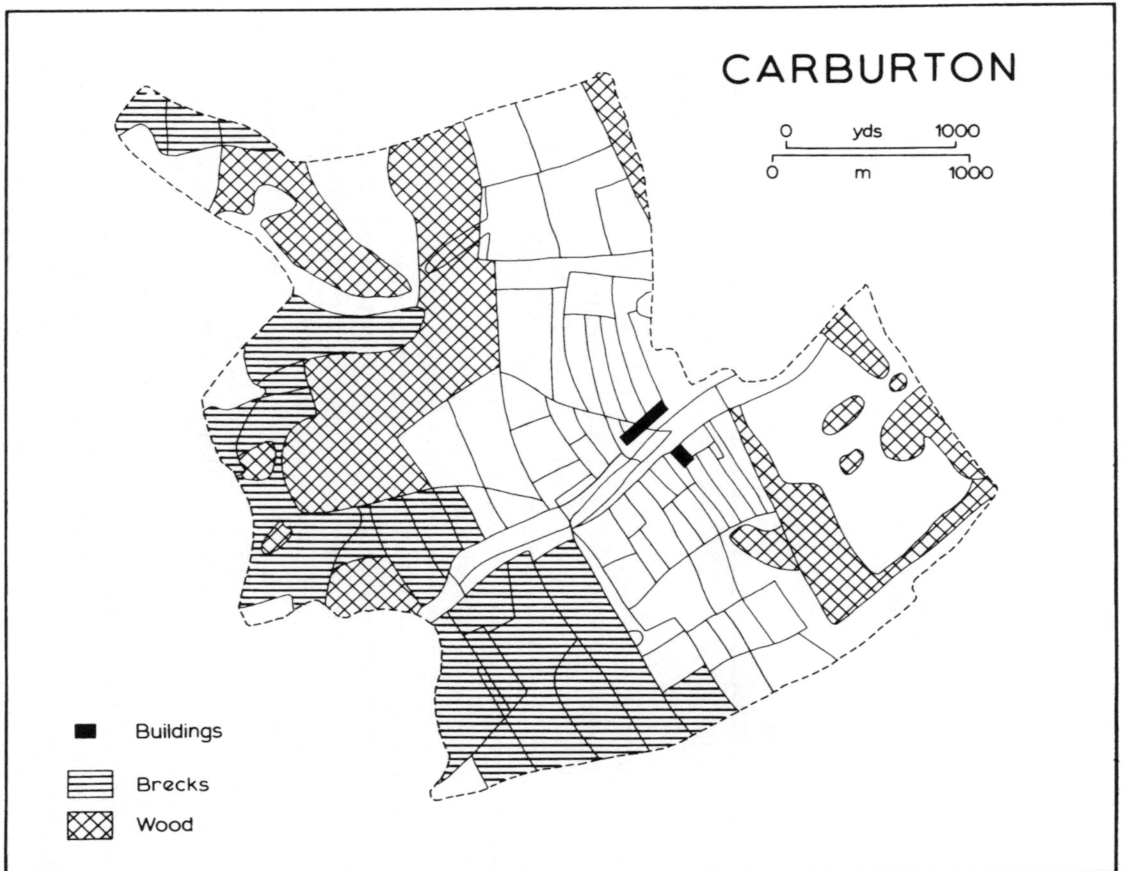

5.7 Infield–outfield at Carburton, Nottinghamshire. Source: information supplied by Mr B. R. Dittmer.

Variations on two- and three-field arrangements in the midlands

Within the midland area itself tithe surveys continue to yield evidence for a great variety of local field arrangements and associated settlement types. Gray's own detailed studies in Oxfordshire and Herefordshire have brought to light important exceptions to the prevailing order of two or three open fields, and his method of enquiry has been followed by many small-scale studies in other counties. Much attention has been devoted to Cheshire. Among recent studies of that county are four which make use of tithe material. Differing field systems in several townships are illustrated by tithe maps in C. S. Davies' history of agriculture, and a tithe map of Snelson shows open-field strips still unenclosed in 1848.[93] In a study of field-names in Amounderness hundred, F. T. Wainwright compares philologically elements recorded in the tithe schedules with those referred to in earlier sources.[94] Tithe evidence is embodied in the fullest and most penetrating survey of Cheshire place-names by J. McN. Dodgson.[95] A rich diversity of local practices is suggested by field-name elements from sand, clay and upland districts. More specifically, in an account by Vera Chapman, tithe maps serve to confirm that open fields once extended into west Cheshire.[96] In Yorkshire, another intensively studied county, G. R. J. Jones has extracted from tithe maps and apportionments field-names, property and township boundaries throwing fresh light on the origins of villages, on the emergence of Leeds before the founding of Kirkstall Abbey, and on the beginnings of the city of Leeds.[97] A study of the evolution of settlement in Nidderdale by P. A. Harris also exploits tithe material. In Worcestershire B. D. Giles bases an account of changes in field patterns in five parishes on enclosure and tithe map evidence, and an examination of common fields and enclosure in parts of Berkshire by R. I. Hodgson and Paul Laxton is partly derived from tithe sources.[98] As more localities are studied in greater detail the less uniform the midlands and the south appear, but unfortunately, tithe evidence is least abundant for those counties within the midlands where parliamentary enclosures were most numerous.

Kentish field systems

In appraising H. L. Gray's contribution to the study of field systems A. R. H. Baker reaffirms the value of a retrogressive approach.[99] Recent studies have succeeded repeatedly in making sense of early evidence by first grasping the significance of late survivals. In interpreting field systems in Kent the tithe surveys provide a firm datum line from which investigations proceed backward into the past. In many Kentish townships M. D. Nightingale found ample evidence from the tithe surveys and from other sources to demonstrate the existence of open fields, but unequivocal indications that these were common fields of a midland type are not elicited.[100] The problem of identity assumed a new importance when Alan Baker began a retrogressive study of field systems at three Kent manors, using tithe maps as starting points for his enquiries.[101] In the vale of Holmesdale, a tithe map for the manor of Wrotham indicates one arable field of seven acres called 'common field' but this was enclosed and, according to the apportionment, was in the hands of a single owner-occupier.[102] The tithe map also presents a contrast in field patterns between large, rectangular fields on chalky marls on either side of Wrotham village and much smaller, irregular parcels lying to the north and to the south of the village. A comparison of eighteenth- and early nineteenth-century estate maps with the tithe maps reveals that 'here many field boundaries were being removed to increase the size of fields at a time when many townships in the midlands saw an extension of the hedgerow by parliamentary enclosure'.[103] A tithe map of the east Kent parish of Deal in 1843 exhibits a pattern of open arable strips with most, but not all, enclosed fields in pasture.[104] The tithe map, however, is a misleading guide to the open or enclosed state of the fields, for all boundaries are marked by continuous lines and they signify property boundaries, not field boundaries. The tithe file of 1842 makes it clear that cereal production was of paramount importance, implying that prairie farming without permanent hedges and fences was introduced to improve efficiency in grain growing and that divisions within ring-fenced holdings were likely to be shifted from time to time. At Gillingham, on the dip slope of the North Downs, the tithe map represents all farms and all fields as enclosed at this time.[105] Baker notes that seven fields, depicted as 'sub-divided', are enclosures internally sub-divided without fences. And these subdivisions are not held by separate occupiers: the apportionment records them as belonging to single farms.

In these three localities in Kent, wide differences in field arrangements are observable and still wider differences, reflected in field patterns and management in the later settled Weald and in the coastal marshlands, separate arable from pastoral systems. But from a close examination of a variety of unenclosed strip fields in Kent, a fresh appreciation of the effects of gavelkind tenure and of a partly free market in land has been gained. Partitioning of almost compact family holdings has produced field systems superficially resembling those in the midlands, but with three important differences. First, more farmers live in hamlets and isolated farms than in nucleated villages; secondly, unenclosed strips created by partitioning arable fields are scattered unevenly among many fields and are not grouped in two or three identical open fields; thirdly, and without exceptions, communal grazing over fallow arable land is not exercised by customary right but only by private agreement. Baker's findings vindicate H. L. Gray's conclusion that field systems in Kent differ in their essential characteristics from those in the midlands. While explorations in the south-west and on the Welsh borderland suggest that the frontier of a midland common-field province should be moved some distance west of the line proposed in 1915, the position in the north and in the eastern counties is still far from clear. Until recently it seemed likely that Gray's divisions would be discarded entirely, but now it is evident that open fields similar in appearance to those in the midlands originated in different ways and served different functions in Kent. At last a limit has been reached, and traditional farming practices both in Kent and in the midlands have been redefined with a new precision and patent clarity. The notion, implicit in the Orwins' account, that all open fields are alike calls for revision. New questions are raised concerning the essential characteristics of common fields. Whereas F. D. Hartley simply traces from the tithe surveys a map of all unenclosed fields in the Chilterns, David Roden compares field arrangements in that area in tithe times with those of earlier dates.[106] The focus of interest has shifted towards elucidating the nature of internal divisions in one or two fields and to discovering the significance of these divisions for traditional farming in the Chilterns. The method employed by Baker and Roden discriminates sharply between form and function and probes in depth the workings of field systems.

The intrinsic value of tithe surveys for studies of field systems

Whilst much effort has been expended on tracing field patterns back to periods remote from tithe times, the intrinsic value of the surveys as a record of the mid-nineteenth-century landscape and its relic features has been partly lost sight of. In southern England much of the traditional agrarian landscape has vanished but among its most persistent relict features are vernacular buildings. A recent study in Hampshire by Gwyn I. Meirion-Jones uses tithe surveys to locate buildings dating back to a pre-railway age and also to distinguish dwellings from other structures.[107] As an incidental reward two deserted village sites at Dogmersfield and Hartley Mauditt are identified.[108] In tracing the origin of what are now relict features of past landscapes in England, Maurice Beresford makes use of tithe maps and awards, and shows that field-names recorded in apportionments may assist in the identification of lost villages: 'where the village survives only as a field name this source is useful for locating the name, or for seeing whether there were any "Town Fields"'.[109] The tithe map may also throw light on some local peculiarity of a deserted village such as Whitchurch in Warwickshire, depopulated in the sixteenth century but having a daughter settlement, Crimscote, whose open fields persisted until tithe times.[110] In the West Riding of Yorkshire, a settlement called Claverlay is referred to in medieval documents as an area within the vill of Upper Whitley. No such place exists today but the tithe survey records a field called Clover Leys in the general area where the documents locate this 'lost' settlement.[111] Tithe maps are also an important source of evidence for studies such as that conducted by W. S. G. Thomas into lost villages in south-west Carmarthenshire.[112] He uses the tithe map of Llandawke, for example, to show that in 1841 Llandawke Farm consisted of three large fields, a fact he adduces in support of Maurice Beresford's contention that the pastures of lost villages were markedly larger than fields resulting from later enclosure.[113] M. G. Jarrett and S. Wrathmell have reconstructed the extent of two farmsteads at the deserted site of West Whelpington, Northumberland, using the 1844 tithe map and supporting archaeological, parish register and hearth tax evidence.[114]

Fields and field boundaries have also been much studied as relict features themselves rather than as expressions of particular agrarian systems, and the tithe surveys provide a probably unequalled record of their sizes and shapes around the year 1840.[115] Tithe surveys have assisted with the identification of relict fields relating to many past societies, even to the work of the now distant Roman *agrimensores* who were responsible for what little regular, rectilinear land division was practised in this remote province of the Roman Empire.[116] O. A. W. and Margaret Dilke consider that the most convincing example of Roman centuriation in Britain is to be found at Cliffe near Rochester, a pattern which they investigated with the aid of the 1840 tithe map.[117] For J. A. Yelling, tithe maps and apportionments help distinguish between different field patterns that resulted from either piecemeal or general enclosure and indicate the amount of open land that still remained in his study parishes around 1840.[118]

Perhaps the most remarkable testimony of the tithe surveys is not their record of landscape features such as fields and habitations, essential though this is for retrogressive studies of field systems, but their disclosure of surviving elements of social orders, economic systems, and political and religious institutions that are unmistakably medieval. Little over a century ago in Sherwood Forest the men of Carburton practised a primitive form of shifting cultivation and in Norfolk a gentleman farmer at Caldecote also possessed five brecks. At that time, too, the villagers of Braunton in Devon collectively depastured their flocks and herds on common wastes and on fallow arable, and grazing was organised in a similar manner by commoners at Ashdon and Bartlow in north-west Essex and at Heighington in County Durham. At Levisham on the edge of the North York Moors, as on the fringes of Exmoor or around Delamere Forest, piecemeal reclamation was adding an intake here and there to the cultivated area. The cutting of trees and the grubbing up of roots, the paring and burning of turf, the digging of ditches and spreading of marl were ageless ordeals as familiar to nineteenth-century labourers as they were to Anglo-Saxons. Only during the past hundred years have these arduous efforts ceased. Yet a present-day investigator must exercise considerable powers of imagination to recapture a sense of living in those Victorian rural communities that were closer to the middle ages than to the present. There is still much to be learned about that forgotten England and those silent people who worked in the fields and gathered the harvests and paid their rents to extinct lordships and colleges and city companies.

6

Land use

In the 1930s, when Dudley Stamp conducted the first Land Utilisation Survey of Great Britain, the extent of land under the plough had fallen to a minimum. It had shrunk to a smaller acreage than in the trough of the previous depression in arable farming in the 1890s. Indeed, from the records of official agricultural statistics, an almost unbroken decline may be traced back to the 1870s. That decade marked a watershed in the economics of British wheat growing. Until 1873 home production of wheat exceeded the quantity imported, and not until 1879 did the price of wheat slump below 45s per quarter in response to a world glut of grains.[1] Whilst it is evident that the arable area diminished without remission after the flood of cheap foreign wheat entered the British market, it is much less certain that the decline originated at that date or was caused solely by falling prices. If an earlier origin is to be sought, the first question to be raised is how much earlier had the arable acreage reached its maximum extent? The enquiry must proceed without the aid of official agricultural statistics which were first collected on a national basis in 1866.[2] The previous half century had been taken up with wordy debates on the Corn Laws, the Anti-Corn-Law League complaining that grain growing in Britain was grossly over-protected and that areas better suited to other types of farming were kept under crops.[3] The repeal of the Corn Laws in 1846 exposed inefficient producers to the threat of foreign competition and some may have been induced to convert their arable into grass.[4] But there is no indication of widespread laying down to grass. On the contrary, much publicised technical innovations, including tile draining and harvesting machines, made possible an extension of cereal cultivation not only on heavy, poorly drained soils, but also in western districts, where a harvest had to be snatched during a few dry days in autumn.[5] The line on James Caird's map of 1852 dividing England into corn-growing and pastoral districts may possibly represent the furthermost advance of arable farming, at the height of what Caird himself described as an age of high farming[6] (see Fig. 3.17). Essays on farming in different counties published in the *Journal of the Royal Agricultural Society* between 1845 and 1869 report ploughing on claylands in many parts of the country and also describe the raising of cash crops in western districts.[7] On the other hand, traces of ridge and furrow in midland pastures and remnants of intake walls above northern dales provide firm evidence that large tracts of permanent grassland were once ploughed and have lain undisturbed since their conversion to pasture.[8] It might be argued from these visible remains that the maximum extent of arable cultivation was reached at the time of parliamentary enclosure.[9] But that impression is repeatedly belied by the most reliable estimates of the arable acreage from Arthur Young's in 1770 to the abstract of the Agricultural Statistics in 1872.

Arable maximum between 1840 and 1870

The estimates presented in Table 6.1 give little indication that acreages of land under crops and under grass changed much relative to one another during the first quarter of the nineteenth century. The figures imply that conversion of arable to grass was either much less widespread than traces of ridge and furrow would lead a present-day observer to believe or else that losses to pasture were more than fully compensated by gains from wasteland reclamation.[10] In the middle of the nineteenth century, however, an appreciable change in the opposite direction is clearly indicated by the statistical evidence. The arable acreage shows a considerable expansion, while the grassland acreage shows a corresponding diminution. In 1872, when meadow and pasture occupied approximately the same amount of land as arable had occupied in 1801, the arable area was greater than the area of meadow and pasture seventy years earlier.

The exact date at which the arable acreage in England and Wales attained its greatest extent remains an open question, but within a span of time extending from the Napoleonic wars to the onset of continuous decline in grain farming in the 1870s, the most likely period for an occurrence of the maximum is around mid-century, in the third quarter rather than in the second quarter of the century.[11] From this point of view it may be inferred that the greater part of the tithe survey was completed a few years before the maximum. H. C. K. Henderson's comparison of information drawn from the tithe surveys with that recorded in the area books for the first edition 1:2,500 Ordnance Survey plans in 1875 indicates that both in Sussex and in Derbyshire the arable area in 1875 was slightly greater than in 1840.[12] Similar comparisons elsewhere have yielded similar results (Fig. 6.1). In Denbighshire, for example, the area of farmland appears to have been smaller in 1840 than in 1870, and for England and Wales the total area under crops is greater in 1872 than in any of the six preceding years for which agricultural statistics were collected.[13] Some or all of these apparent dif-

Table 6.1 *Area of arable, meadow and pasture in England and Wales 1801–72*

Date	Source	Arable land (acres)	Meadow and pasture (acres)	Cultivated area (acres)	Ratio of arable: grass
1801a	B. P. Capper	11,350,501	16,796,458	28,146,959	0.68
1801b	Crop return	7,860,000 (excluding fallow etc.)	–	–	–
1808	W. T. Comber	11,575,000	17,495,000	29,070,000	0.66
1827	W. Couling	11,143,370	17,605,630	28,749,000	0.63
1840	Tithe files	15,092,555 (excluding seeds in western counties)	16,363,409 (includes some 'rough grazings')	31,455,964	0.92
1851	James Caird	13,667,000	13,332,000	26,999,000	1.02
1872	Agricultural Statistics	18,136,369	11,522,712	29,659,081	1.57

Sources: *1801a* – B. P. Capper, *A statistical account of the population and cultivation, produce and consumption of England and Wales* (London, 1801)
1801b – M. Turner, 'Arable in England and Wales: estimates from the 1801 crop return', *Journal of Historical Geography*, 7 (1981), 291–302
1808 – W. T. Comber, *An inquiry into the state of national subsistence*, (London, 1808); on Capper and Comber see also H. C. Prince, 'England c. 1800', in H. C. Darby (ed.), *A new historical geography of England* (Cambridge, 1973), 403
1827 – W. Couling, 'Evidence to House of Commons Select Committee on emigration from the United Kingdom, 1827', cited in G. R. Porter, *The progress of the nation*, 2nd edition (London, 1847), 155–8
1840 – Estimates of land use in the tithe files. Only those data covering more than 90 per cent of the tithe district are included; county figures have been obtained by multiplying the sum of the available tithe file acreages by weighting factors equivalent to total county area: area of county with tithe-file data; county figures were then aggregated to produce national figures
1851 – J. Caird, *English agriculture in 1850–51*, (London, 1852)
1872 – L. D. Stamp, *The land of Britain, its use and misuse*, 3rd edition (London 1962), appendix 8.

ferences may be attributed to differences in methods used for recording and compiling data and it would be unwise to accept them at their face value as firm evidence for agricultural change.[14] A useful, although not infallible, check might be made by comparing states of cultivation recorded in a tithe apportionment of the 1840s with those recorded in a later altered apportionment. In the light of our present knowledge, it may be stated that none of these findings is inconsistent with a peak in arable cultivation having been reached at any time between 1840 and 1875.[15] For purposes of comparison with the results of the Land Utilisation Survey in the 1930s the date of the tithe survey is

6.1 Arable land in the river Wey valley above Guildford, Surrey, *c.* 1840 to 1939. Source: D. W. Shave, 'The distribution of arable land in the upper Wey basin . . .', 1941.

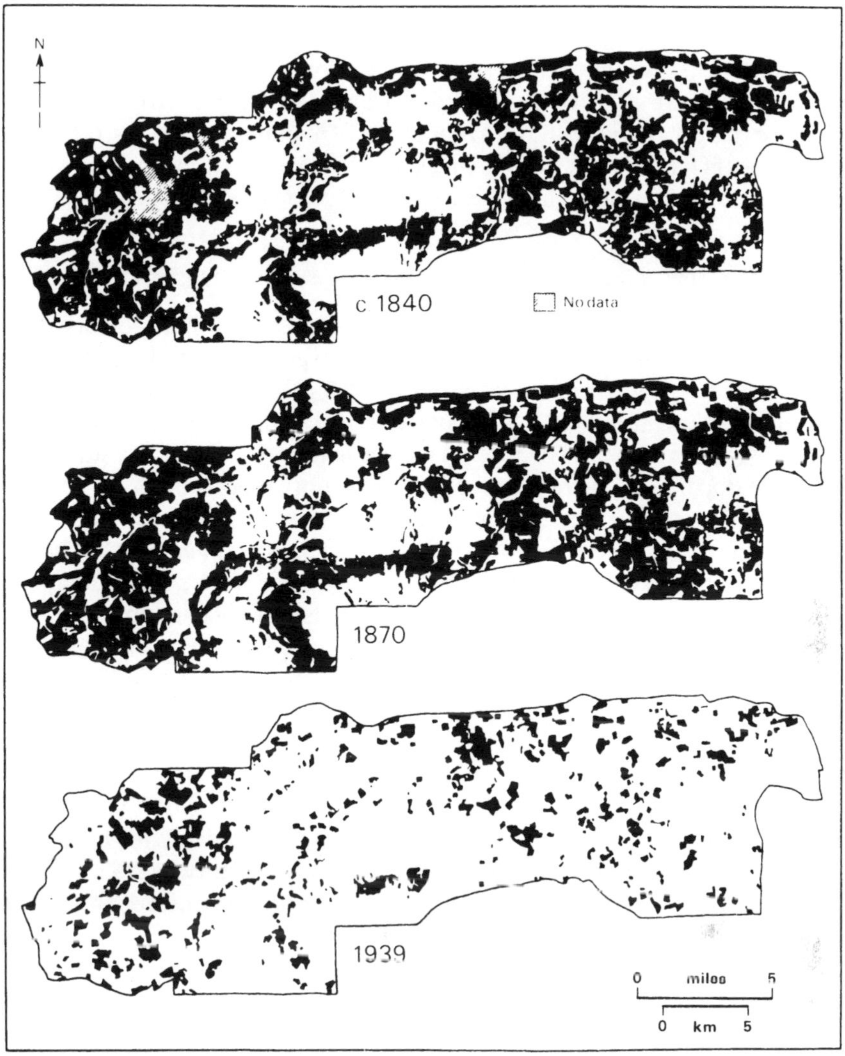
N
c.1840
No data
1870
1939
0 miles 5
0 km 5

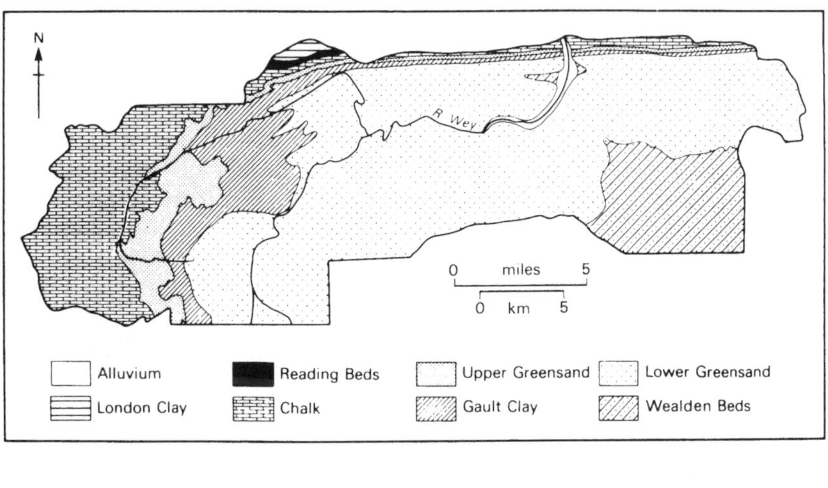
N
R. Wey
0 miles 5
0 km 5
Alluvium
Reading Beds
Upper Greensand
Lower Greensand
London Clay
Chalk
Gault Clay
Wealden Beds

sufficiently close in time to the ultimate limit of ploughing up to provide a reliable guide to the pattern of the widest arable distribution. To compare the land use pattern of the 1840s with that of the 1930s not only demonstrates the direction of change and affords a measure of the extent of change but it also indicates in detail where change was greatest and where it was least.

Land Utilisation Survey of Great Britain

Reviewing the great volume of work done by the Land Utilisation Survey of Great Britain, Dudley Stamp emphasised the value of comparing the land use of different regions at different times and for this purpose he considered the tithe surveys to be the first accurate record of land use in England and Wales.[16] Many detailed accounts of land use in the 1840s, based on studies of the tithe documents, were prepared for the county reports published by the Land Utilisation Survey. Summarising the results of these local studies by drawing a broad comparison between land use in tithe times and that in the 1930s, Dudley Stamp concluded that 'there has been outstanding stability of land use on the *best* land and on the *poorest* lands and a maximum of change, dictated by economic vicissitudes, on land of intermediate quality'.[17]

Sample parishes: E. C. Willatts' method

The first study of its kind, made by E. C. Willatts, secretary to the Land Utilisation Survey, appeared in 1933.[18] For a long time Willatts had known of the existence of the tithe surveys since the apportionment for his native parish of Wraysbury had been reproduced in a local history in 1862. He had come across the map that accompanied the apportionment, mounted and heavily varnished, in the office of an estate agent in Windsor.[19] The firm had been engaged to carry out not only the Wraysbury survey but also others in the district, and through the kindness of one of the partners to whom Willatts was personally known he was allowed to make tracings. Then, in the autumn of 1932, the secretary to the tithe commissioners, having had his interest aroused in the work of the Land Utilisation Survey, drew Stamp's attention to the significance of the tithe records. Following this introduction, Stamp accompanied by Willatts went to view the archives and they were granted permission to pursue their searches among the documents free from the usual charges. Recognising the value of the material, Willatts immediately prepared a paper on the subject which was read at the British Association meeting in Leicester in September 1933.

The essence of this paper was published in the December number of the *Geographical Journal*. It declared the tithe surveys 'our best data' for a study of land utilisation in the past, and outlined a method whereby information for each field recorded in the state of cultivation column of an apportionment might be transferred to a modern base map with the aid of a tithe map. Land-use maps for four small blocks of parishes to the south-west of London were constructed, the districts being selected to illustrate strong geological contrasts. It was assumed that differences in land use were to be explained by differences in the character of rocks or at least by a complex of terrain, soil and hydrology viewed together as a physical basis for agriculture. At Ashtead and Headley a survey of 1638 showed only the best soils under cultivation. In 1840, approximately 63 per cent of the chalk was cultivated and about the same amount was recorded as arable in a survey in 1887. However, by 1933, cultivation on the chalk had shrunk to nearly half the area it occupied a century earlier. In most parishes and on most soils the area of woodland and heathland showed little change, but everywhere there is evidence of the spread of houses and gardens, and everywhere a marked decrease in the arable acreage is indicated. A map showing areas converted from arable to grass 'tells the agricultural story more truthfully than does a comparison of the two maps of arable areas' because much of the arable was taken for housing development and thus represented a permanent loss to agricultural uses.[20] Evidently the physical characteristics of a site had less influence on its use or change of use than either its proximity to London or the profitability of new farming enterprises. An appreciation of the strength of social and economic forces promoting change was the first lesson to be learned from this essay.

In the Land Utilisation Survey report for Middlesex and the London region Willatts extended the scope of his investigation to 25 sample parishes.[21] For each of these he calculated the percentages of different geological outcrops occupied by arable, grass, heath, woods, market gardens and houses. Everywhere, regardless of the nature of the bedrock, the acreage under the plough is found to have declined, and in some localities almost to have disappeared. The four maps of Ashtead and Headley are illustrated here as Fig. 6.2. Fig. 6.3 is a land-use map of Wye in Kent demonstrating a method of plotting six categories of land use from the tithe survey on the same map.

Arable tracts: H. C. K. Henderson's method

Concurrently and independently of Willatts' pioneer exploration, neither being aware of the other's converging train of discovery, H. C. K. Henderson began a study of the tithe surveys relating to the Adur basin in Sussex. As a schoolboy during the First World War, Henderson had witnessed the ploughing up of large areas of downland and also of permanent pastures on the Weald Clay lowlands apparently never before cut by ploughshares. He soon learned from studying tithe maps in parish chests and from Ordnance Survey 'Area Books' that many of those fields had been tilled and had raised

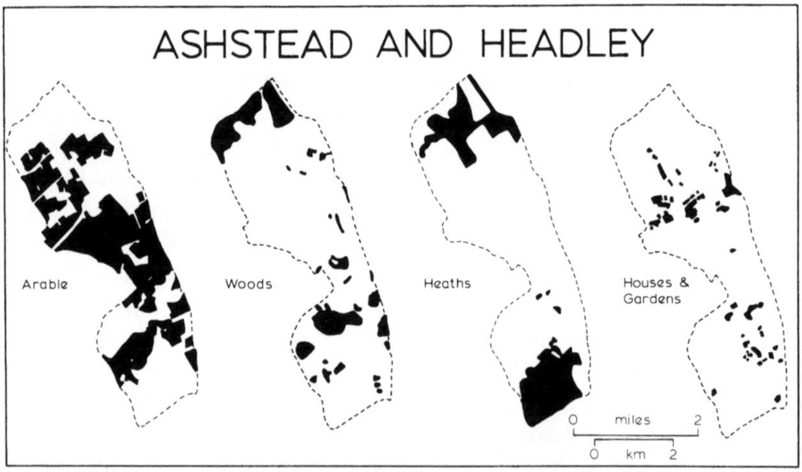

6.2 Land use of the sample parishes of Ashtead and Headley, Surrey. Source: E. C. Willatts, 'Changes in land utilization in the south-west of the London Basin, 1840–1932', 1933.

crops less than half a century earlier. Some years later, his attention was directed towards the main repository of tithe records by Edward Lynam, curator of maps at the British Museum. Before the Tithe Redemption Commission was established in 1936, the British Museum received many enquiries from house purchasers and farmers about the tithe surveys and Lynam realised that these records might also be of use in reconstructing the former state of cultivation of a large part of the country. He suggested to Henderson that he should visit the collection and examine the documents. Shortly after that introduction Henderson embarked on a major research project that was to engage him and a number of research students at Birkbeck College London until the outbreak of war. The arable areas were abstracted from entries in apportionments and transferred to tracing paper laid over tithe maps. Because of the vast, unwieldy size of the tracings, the information had to be reduced to a one-inch scale as work proceeded. It was a laborious task.

Henderson's study of the changing distribution of arable land in the Adur basin covers a compact block of country instead of sample parishes.[22] Comparisons are made with the 1931 Land Utilisation Survey of the area, with area books for the first edition 1:2,500 Ordnance Survey plans of 1875 and also with Yeakell and Gardner's map of 1780. The account is illustrated by three maps covering an area of about 300 square miles showing, field-by-field, the distribution of arable land in 1931, in 1875 and at the time of the tithe surveys in 1837–56. A fourth map shows the distribution of meadow and woodland in 1780. A map of arable land from tithe data is redrawn in

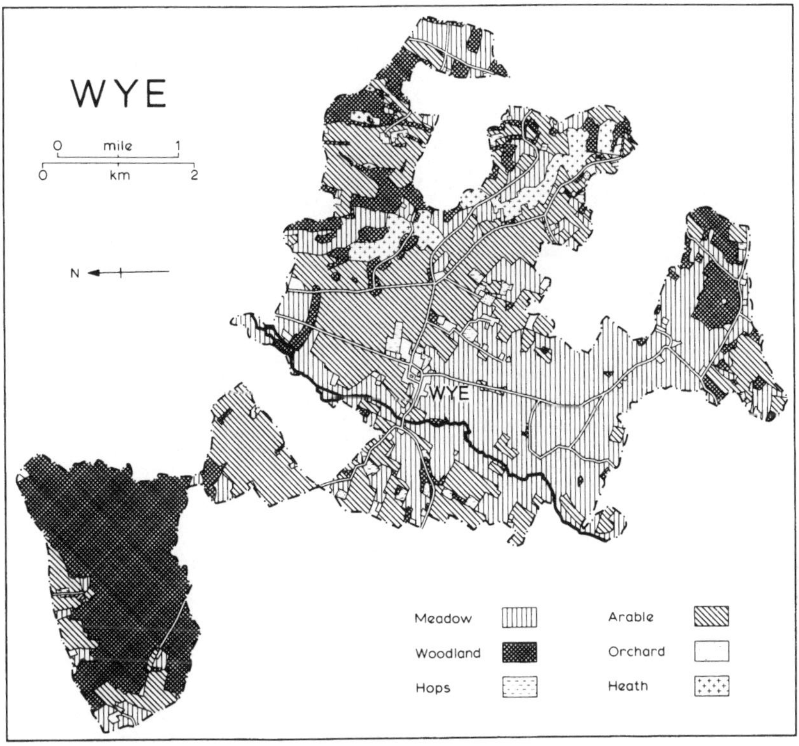

6.3 Land use in the parish of Wye, Kent. Compiled in 1955 by H. C. Prince with the assistance of students from University College London.

Fig. 6.4. Despite the fact that the tithe surveys are incomplete for this area and also span a long period of time, they do provide a reliable basis for comparison with the two later field surveys. They show that there was more arable land in the Adur basin around 1845 than today but not as much as in 1875. Henderson's account avoids the pitfall of prejudging a particular mode of causation in agricultural development. It examines a number of intermediate stages in the course of change from an arable to a grassland regime. It attempts to identify the mechanisms bringing about changes. It was reported that similar studies of changing arable land were being carried out in eight counties and it was hoped that eventually all the available evidence might be interpreted and mapped. Much of this work has been published subsequently in the Land Utilisation Survey reports. The Sussex report summarises the work of H. C. K. Henderson, E. W. H. Briault and H. B. Smith covering about 500 square miles. It concludes, 'the tithe commutation record shows on the whole the maximum extent of arable cultivation ever reached in the Weald; on the chalk this comes later'.[23] The Derbyshire report contains an analysis by Henderson of changes in arable

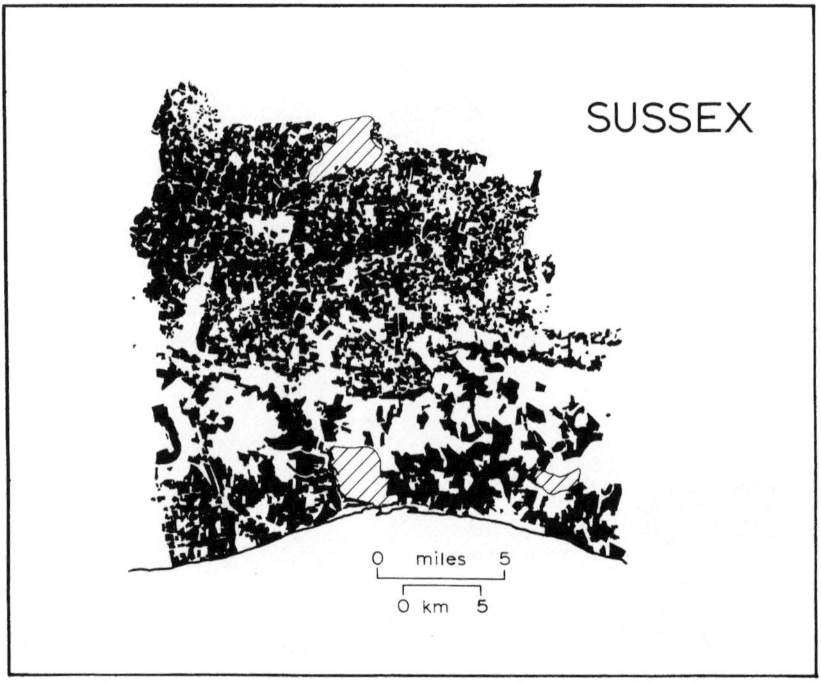

6.4 Arable land in the Adur Basin, Sussex. Source: H. C. K. Henderson, 'Our changing agriculture: the distribution of arable land in the Adur Basin . . .', 1936.

land in relation to geological outcrops in a 162-square-mile strip from the crest of the Pennines to the eastern county border.[24] As in south Sussex the greatest extent of arable land occurred at the time of the compilation of the Ordnance Survey area books.

Farm studies: J. E. G. Mosby's method

Meanwhile, in Norfolk a very remarkable survey was being carried out with the help of hundreds of schoolchildren and other volunteers under the direction of J. E. G. Mosby. The breadth of Mosby's approach to the tithe surveys reflects his own many-sided professional interests – as a practising geographer, as a teacher at one of the county's leading grammar schools, as assistant commissioner for Boy Scouts, later as principal of Wymondham College and, in his retirement from teaching, as a Church of England clergyman and rector of Mulbarton. In its scope and methods his use of the tithe material represents a considerable advance on the pioneer works of Willatts and Henderson, partly because it covers a larger area and partly because it relates land use not only to soil conditions and changes in the prices of farm produce but also to conditions of land tenure and farming practice.[25] It makes a serious attempt to discover the nature of processes bringing about changes, by examining in detail the character of Norfolk farms and the changing character of Norfolk farming. On the one hand, it presents a map of arable land in an area of about a thousand square miles in west Norfolk, the largest single tract of country so mapped in the reports. On the other hand, it explains changes of land use within sample parishes and sample farms in terms of soil, size of holding, field arrangement, field size, field shape and the nature of land tenure. The originality of the work lies in its examination of tenurial questions such as those affecting the use of fold courses and outfields and also in its attention to details of farm management such as crop rotations and the introduction of special crops. The extent of changes in the area of arable land throughout the county between 1840 and 1935 is shown on a map made by comparing the parish estimates of land use in the tithe apportionments with the parish statistics collected by the Ministry of Agriculture. A map of arable land in the Good Sand region in tithe times is redrawn as Fig. 6.5.

Later reports of the Land Utilisation Survey

The later reports have extended and added to our knowledge of the landscape of England and Wales in the mid-nineteenth century, mostly on the lines suggested in the first essays. Some follow the pattern of Henderson's essays by mapping only arable land within large and continuous tracts of country and computing the proportion of each geological outcrop occupied by it. In this way L. G. Cameron has covered 156 square miles of south-east Hertfordshire, D. W. Shave 182 square miles of the upper Wey basin in Surrey, and L. R. Hawkes about 200 square miles of the upper Exe basin in Devon and Somerset including an area of six square miles north of Tiverton treated in greater detail by W. W. French.[26] In south-east Hertfordshire, a map of arable at the time of the tithe surveys was compared with the Land Utilisation Survey of 1936 and with Dury and Andrews' map of 1766. This comparison shows that the arable acreage was at its greatest in 1840, especially on boulder-clay soils. In the Wey basin, little change occurred between the tithe survey and the 'area books' except on the chalk where the acreage appears to have increased by some 10.8 per cent during that thirty-year period. In Devon, Hawkes and French were faced with the problem that the tithe surveyors had classified long leys as arable in the state of cultivation column of the apportionments and, as a result, neither the arable nor the grass acreages could be compared with those for 1936.

Others follow Willatts' method of selecting sample parishes representative of different land-use regions and of examining different categories of land use in relation to geological outcrops. In this way, 3 sample parishes in

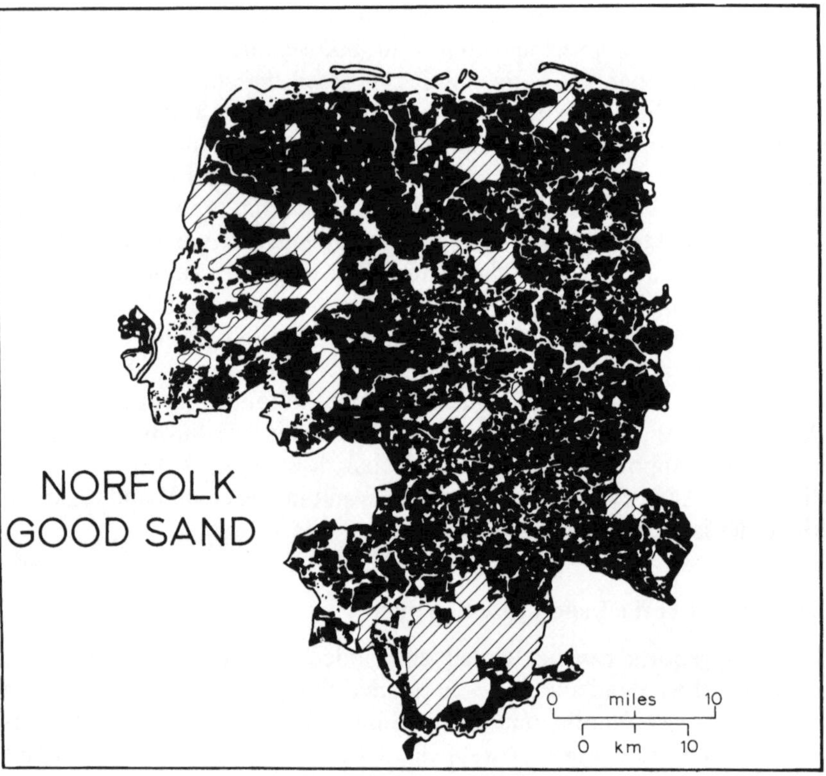

6.5 Arable land in the Good Sand district of Norfolk. Source: J. E. G. Mosby, *Norfolk*, 1938.

south-east Essex are mapped by Rupert Coles, who also presented uncritically a map of arable in the county based on the uncertain evidence of the parish summaries.[27] In Bedfordshire 8 sample parishes are mapped by C. E. Fitchett, in Worcestershire more than 20 are selected by K. M. Buchanan, in Warwickshire about 30 are sampled by A. W. McPherson and others, whilst Dudley Stamp includes 2 of Willatts' parishes in his report on Kent.[28] In all these reports acreages of arable land and sometimes of other land uses, such as hopyards in the Teme valley of Worcestershire, are measured and expressed as percentages of the surface area of a parish or of a geological formation within a parish. Some calculations, such as those involving small areas of orchard or meadow or heathland in single parishes, may give an impression of accuracy and precision not warranted by the tithe surveys themselves, but such flaws in individual calculations do not invalidate general conclusions drawn from a large number of parishes. A weakness in the method arises from selecting sample parishes on the basis of their geological variety. Repeatedly, reporters acknowledge that changes in land use they have been discussing are not related closely to geological factors. To the extent that samples succeed in reflecting differences in the incidence and rate of changes they may be said to be representative, but more by accident than by design. Beyond all doubt, regional contrasts in the distribution of arable land are distinct and measurable; differences in the extent of arable land in tithe times and in the 1930s are also capable of being measured reasonably accurately.

In the reports for the Welsh border counties and for Wales, use is made of tithe surveys in discussing two aspects of land use: the changing extent of moorland and the decline of arable land. Margaret Davies uses tithe documents to trace the retreat of the moorland edge in 2 Pembrokeshire parishes by comparing the position of enclosed fields and the limit of improved land about 1840 with those in 1932.[29] Emrys Howell examines the changing extent of moors, unimproved grazings and common wastes in Shropshire, large tracts of which were reported to be capable of cultivation in the tithe surveys.[30] In south-east Brecon the moorlands and heaths were more extensive in 1844 than in the 1930s but the diminution of the moorland has not been accompanied by an extension of the arable. On the contrary, many fields on the higher slopes between 500 and 1,000 feet which were then ploughed have since become permanent pastures.[31] In an area of 50 square miles in Montgomeryshire arable was everywhere much less extensive in 1930–4 than in 1840 but the decrease had been 'appreciably more in the lower land than on the higher'.[32] The later Welsh reports make fuller use of farm- and field-boundary information derived from the tithe surveys but the areas studied and mapped are much smaller. A map of land utilisation in 1847 covering 12 square miles of the Towy valley in south-east Carmarthenshire shows 5 categories of land use, field boundaries and land belonging to sample farms.[33] Another map of 12 square miles of land behind Aberystwyth shows all the land that was ploughed in 1845 but put to other uses in 1935.[34]

From this review of the work of the Land Utilisation Survey two distinct approaches to the treatment of the tithe material emerge. The first approach is based on studies of sample parishes following the method pioneered by Willatts in 1933. The second approach is based on the abstraction of tithe land-use data for tracts or blocks of country as exemplified by Henderson in 1936. On balance, more valuable results have been obtained by the latter approach. Tithe data gain in value by aggregation, when information for one parish is ranged alongside that for its neighbours. Possible errors introduced by ambiguous classifications in the state of cultivation columns and discrepancies in the dates at which different pieces of information were recorded are smoothed out when the data are gathered together.

Local land-use studies in the post-war era

Public interest in the tithe surveys was stimulated during the 1930s when the question of redeeming tithe rent-charges and finally extinguishing tithes was debated in parliament. In 1930, N. S. B. and E. Gras, writing an economic and social history of Crawley in Hampshire, found the tithe records most useful. 'The survey maps and descriptions which accompany them are among the most valuable sources for a study of agricultural and social history.'[35] The commutation proceedings are briefly reviewed, the structure of land tenure in the village is discussed in detail, and the schedule of apportionment is transcribed in full. From the mid-1930s, tithe surveys begin to figure as one of the 'standard' sources to which local historians turned for information on local land use. A. G. Ruston and D. Witney devote a chapter to the history of tithes and glebe in Hooton Pagnell, examining the steps leading to commutation and providing one of the most informative accounts of its effects on a rural community.[36] Another parish survey, that of Hexton in Hertfordshire, includes a coloured map showing the land use of each field at the time of the tithe survey, and acreages of arable, grass and wood are compared with those shown on maps of 1900, 1918 and 1930.[37] More superficially, a parish history of Tunstall in Lancashire reproduces estimated acreages of land use from the tithe apportionment and also furnishes abstracts from the preambles to awards for townships within the parish.[38]

The pervasive influence of the work of the Land Utilisation Survey of Great Britain on the writing of local studies in the post-war era is evident in the treatment of land-use data from the tithe surveys. Among accounts dealing almost exclusively with land use in small areas are M. E. Otter's survey of Llanrug in Caernarvonshire, and Margaret Davies' of Llantrithyd in Glamorgan, both of which compare agricultural uses at the time of the tithe surveys with those recorded by the Land Utilisation Survey.[39] For the parish of Hawne, Birmingham, I. Davies makes a comparison between land use in tithe times and that mapped in the field in 1951.[40] Another urban study, tracing the growth and changing functions of Exeter in the early nineteenth century, introduces tithe estimates of land-use acreages for the seven incorporated parishes.[41] In an excursion through London's countryside S. W. Wooldridge and G. E. Hutchings refer in passing to tithe surveys for the Hertfordshire parishes of Ridge and Shenley, noting that in the mid-nineteenth as in the mid-twentieth century the London Clay was predominantly under grass.[42] Also in Hertfordshire, the land use of Hatfield parish is reconstructed from the tithe survey by Gladys Brown.[43] Again, the tithe survey for Redbourn in Hertfordshire is heavily drawn upon in a local history prepared by members of the Workers' Educational Association. The tithe map itself is redrawn as an end paper to the work. Land-use information is abstracted and sizes of farms are compared with those recorded in the 1851 census enumeration.[44] In the neighbouring county of Middlesex, K. A. Smalley makes extensive use of the tithe survey in depicting Greenford in the mid-nineteenth century. A land-use map is based on tithe evidence.[45] One of the most comprehensive local studies exploiting tithe surveys is that of a group of parishes on the borders of Worcestershire and Herefordshire by Constance Pritchard. The locations and sizes of farms and estates are described and the dominant position held by three large landowning families is elucidated. Land-use information is derived from the parish estimates and from schedules of apportionment and attempts are made to explain the pattern in terms of soils, geology and terrain.[46]

Victoria History of the Counties of England

Geographers in their studies of mid-nineteenth-century land use frequently draw comparisons with present-day distributions. Historians, on the other hand, often use evidence from tithe documents to throw light on earlier conditions and for this the interpretation of field-name elements may be more illuminating than the analysis of land-use patterns. Contributors to the post-war volumes of the *Victoria County History* make use of the land-use information in the tithe surveys in two ways. First, in the tradition of earlier local studies influenced by the Land Utilisation Survey of Great Britain, many refer to the state of cultivation of parish lands, mostly derived directly from the parish land-use estimates. Secondly, and more innovatively, tithe maps and apportionments have been used to locate or to identify functions of individual buildings. Toll houses, almshouses, windmills, schools, smithies, forges, wheelwrights' shops, brick kilns, patent chair factories, smelt houses, beer shops, tanneries, lime kilns, tithe barns, market houses, chapels, workhouses, hospitals and other buildings are traced in this way. Extensive use of tithe evidence in *Essex*, volume 4, and *Shropshire*, volume 8, is notable.[47]

The Oxfordshire material, ignored for so long because of its fragmentary state, has been fully exploited by that county's historians. Neither have the land-use data been extracted simply because a tithe survey exists for a particular parish, a criticism that may be levelled at the work of some contributors to the Essex volumes.[48] In Oxfordshire tithe surveys are consulted where land-use information may throw light on processes of change or correct an impression conveyed by a literary account. In the parish of Holton, for example, quantitative data from the tithe surveys do not support Arthur Young's observation that the district was mainly arable. Both the tithe evidence and that of a survey in 1813 indicate that the parish contained a high proportion of grassland.[49] At Dorchester, a comparison with R. Davis' map of 1797 suggests that much of the east side of the parish had been converted to arable by the time of the tithe survey.[50] Increasing arable acreages are also indicated at Weston-on-the-Green where a tithe survey of 1848 recorded 1,089 acres of meadow and pasture and 1,215 acres of arable but where in 1867 two-thirds of the land lay in arable.[51] Comparisons between the tithe surveys and the Land Utilisation Survey indicate a widespread reversion to pasture before 1930. In parishes such as Noke and Harwick the extent of arable in the 1930s had been reduced to only one-third of its extent in the 1840s.[52] Land use at the time of the tithe surveys has also been related to variations in soil conditions and to agricultural improvements. Variations in the land-use pattern of Waterstock parish are described in detail, whilst in Ardley field-names indicate that the stonebrash soils of the lower oolites afforded only very rough grazing at the time of the tithe survey.[53]

The *Victoria County History*'s work is still continuing; it is engaged on the virtually endless task of providing a standard reference on English local history. Its recent accounts have paid more attention than earlier to local topography, and the usefulness of tithe survey land-use data is being increasingly appreciated. To date substantial references are made to this source in over twenty-five volumes of the *History*.[54]

Blocks of agricultural land: F. D. Hartley's contribution

Land-use data for many hundreds of parishes have now been extracted from the tithe surveys and plotted on parish maps after the manner of E. C. Willatts. Enquiries conducted along the lines of H. C. K. Henderson's method at Birkbeck College London were interrupted by the Second World War and were not resumed when the war ended.

After a lapse of some years, tithe studies found a new patron in H. C. Darby at University College London. Darby's interest in the tithe surveys had been kindled by references to them in the Land Utilisation Survey reports and he regarded them as a land inventory comparable in scope, in comprehensiveness and in uniformity with the Domesday survey of 1086.[55] By comparison with the Domesday evidence, the tithe records presented few serious problems in textual criticism and it seemed within the grasp of a team of workers to complete a tithe geography of England, county by county, region by region, tract by tract. A systematic treatment of all the data relating to a solid block of country was the favoured method of approach, and in 1953 a new generation of tithe studies was inaugurated by F. D. Hartley, a graduate student at University College London.

Hartley's work was a contribution to a detailed enquiry directed by J. T. Coppock into changing agriculture in the Chilterns. The survey covered an area of 1,300 square miles north and west of London. Information mapped from the tithe documents included not only arable land as in previous studies

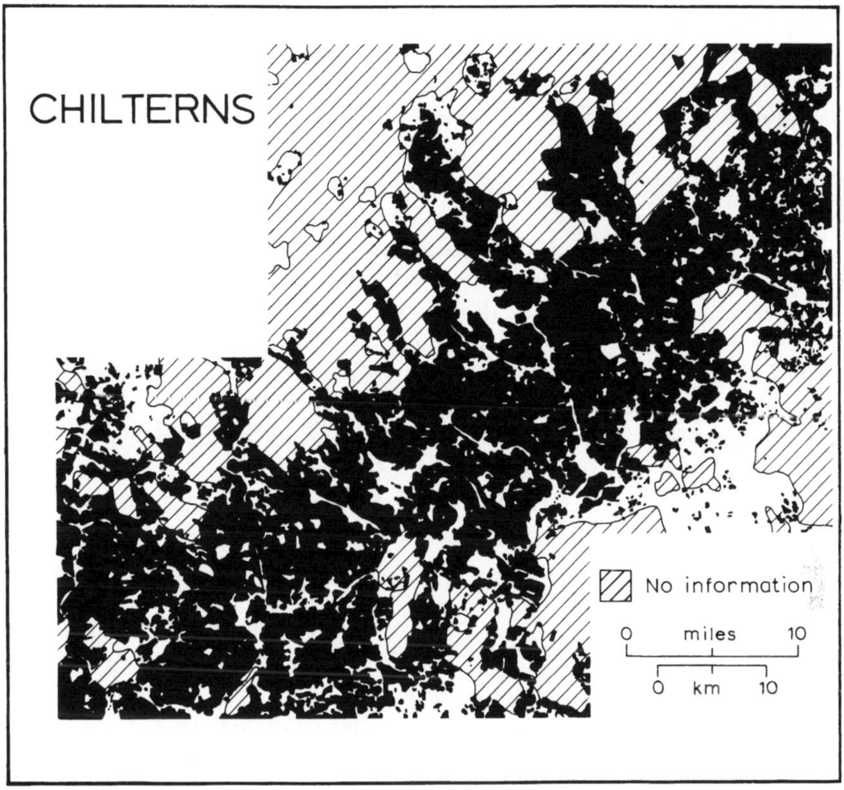

6.6 Arable land in the Chilterns. Source: F. D. Hartley, 'An agricultural geography of the Chilterns *c.* 1840', 1953.

of large areas but also the complementary pattern of grassland. The extent of arable land in the Chilterns in tithe times is represented on Fig. 6.6. In addition, woodland, heathland and settlements were mapped for good measure.[56] To handle this enormous quantity of data a new and efficient procedure for abstracting land-use information from apportionments had to be devised. The key to success lay in the preparation of a form on which numbers (representing tithe areas on the tithe maps) were printed in serial order. Against each number was a space and in that space an abstractor could enter a letter code indicating a category of land use, such as A for arable, M for meadow, H for heath, corresponding to the state of cultivation recorded in the apportionment. It was then a fairly simple operation to transfer the coded information from a form to a modern base map – an outline edition of the Ordnance Survey 1:25,000 map being ideal for the purpose – referring to the tithe map to find the locations of the numbered tithe areas. With coloured pencils an attractive fair draft of a finished map might be drawn directly from information on the forms. The procedure not only minimises the labour expended on cross-referencing between apportionments and tithe maps, with attendant risks of errors, but also it is automatically self-checking. Failure to abstract land-use classifications for all parcels of land is revealed by gaps on the form, whilst failure to transfer all information to the base map is revealed by blank patches on the coloured draft.

Within the limits of the large area covered by Hartley's study it is possible to examine contrasts not only between different soil types but also between different social and economic situations. The proportion of arable land and the degree of clustering of farms along village streets may be observed to have differed from place to place, from districts where open fields survived to districts enclosed by act of parliament, and both may be observed to have differed from old enclosed districts. Champion and woodland districts may be distinguished and other significant associations of land-use categories, such as parkland or market-gardening tracts, may be identified. Hartley's work has demonstrated the value of enlarging the scale and scope of tithe studies.

Diversity of land use in southern England

In 1960 another important step forward was taken by M. C. Naish, also a student of H. C. Darby at University College London. In a study of the changing agricultural landscape of the Hampshire chalklands Naish drew a picture of the countryside about 1840 based on the tithe surveys.[57] It presents a detailed likeness of the scene at the beginning of a period of prosperity following the extraordinary upheaval of the Napoleonic wars and the post-war slump that had plunged the region into deep distress between 1815 and 1836. Maps showing the extent of eight categories of land use – arable land, down pasture, water meadows, dry meadows and pasture, heathlands, commons, and woodland – illustrate the account. Naish was deeply interested in the diversity and varied combinations of agricultural land uses in the region. He was one of the first geographers to examine the tithe files and discover that they contain a 'questionnaire' dealing with crop acreages and with other aspects of farming. Following this lead, later students from University College London have systematically consulted the tithe files and have derived much valuable information from them. But that work is directed more towards an understanding of farming practices than of land use and will be treated in the next chapter.

A study of agricultural changes in a neighbouring part of Wiltshire conducted by another University College student, Brian Dittmer, concludes with a discussion of the mid-nineteenth-century agrarian landscape in which the pattern of land use is reconstructed from the tithe surveys.[58] The account is illustrated with maps showing the distribution of commons, arable land,

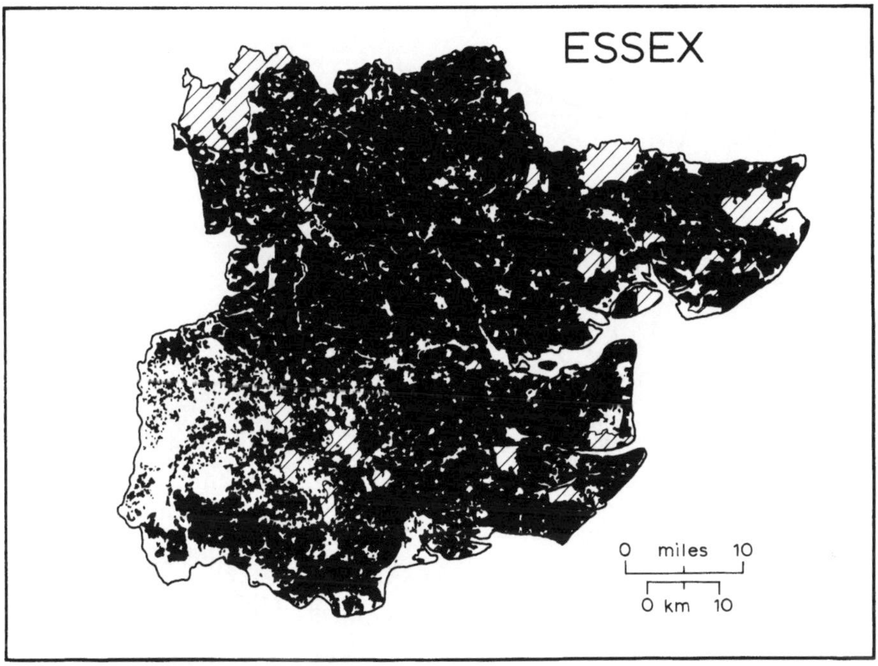

6.7 Arable land in Essex. Source: E. A. Cox, 'An agricultural geography of Essex, *c.* 1840', 1963.

meadow and pasture, and woodland. The most important feature to emerge from this survey of land use is that over 70 per cent of the heavy lands of north-west Wiltshire were recorded as being under grass at this time. Whilst Dittmer was working on agricultural change in a part of Wiltshire, a fellow student, Elwyn Cox, undertook a county-wide survey of Essex.[59] The million acres covered by Cox's study represent the largest block of territory yet completed for which field-by-field distribution maps of all categories of land use recorded in the tithe surveys have been compiled. The achievement is a great feat of efficient organisation and one that makes a substantial addition to our knowledge of the agricultural geography of the mid-nineteenth century. Cox's map of arable land in Essex is redrawn as Fig. 6.7. Comparison of Figs. 6.4–6.7 shows how the size of study areas has increased progressively since Henderson demonstrated the value of mapping blocks of country in 1936. Most recently, attention has turned away from the production of chorochromatic distribution maps of land use using the field-by-field data from apportionments and maps to exploiting parish/township estimates of land use in the tithe files[60] (Fig. 6.8). The work of A. D. M. Phillips is noted in the following section on the midland counties and a programme to map all the parish estimates for England and Wales is discussed in chapter 9.

Whilst these synchronic reconstructions of agricultural geography in 1840

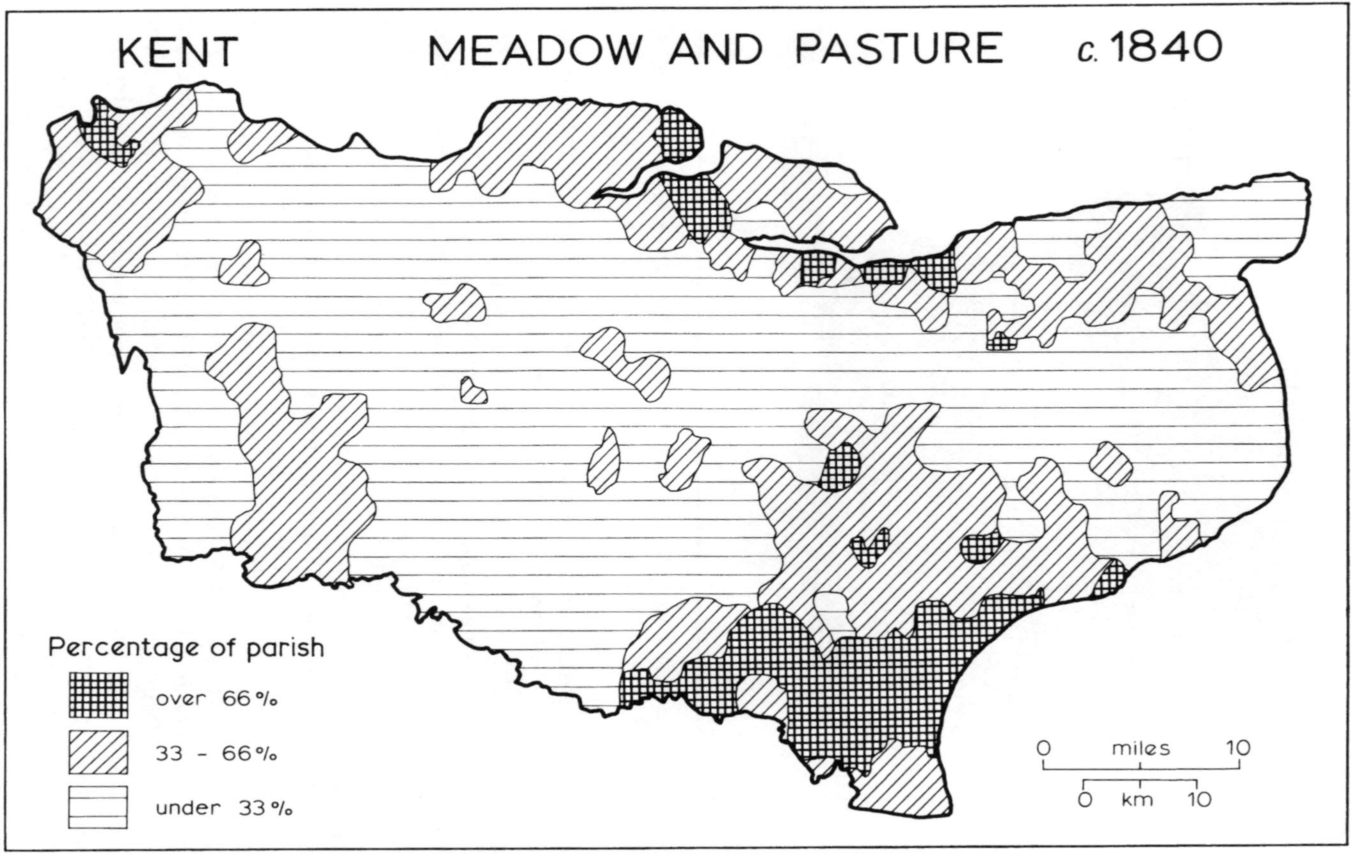

6.8 Meadow and pasture in Kent.

have been extended to larger and larger regions, diachronic studies of changing agriculture have tended to remain confined in scope to small areas. Following the method of Henderson, M. J. Frost has compared land use in the upper Mole basin from John Rocque's map, from the tithe surveys, from the Ordnance Survey area books and from a recent field survey.[61] The enquiry goes further than Henderson's Adur basin study by examining maps of all categories of land use to be extracted from the different sources, but the treatment of the tithe evidence is superficial when compared with the work of Dittmer and Cox. Aileen Carpenter's study of agricultural change in south Hertfordshire covers a very small area of 14 parishes and from the tithe surveys only the arable land is abstracted. The investigation concentrates on changes taking place after 1840 and for this purpose altered apportionments and their accompanying maps are used. Acquisition of land by the Midland Railway Company was followed by a re-apportionment in parts of Bushey and Aldenham parishes in 1883–4, and information from this survey has been used to construct a map of land use.[62] Among other studies of agricultural change in southern England in which evidence has been drawn from the tithe surveys are that of Dorset by R. F. J. Chiplen and that of Surrey by A. G. Parton.[63]

Land-use changes following enclosure in the midlands

In the midland shires where a high proportion of parishes had some or all of their tithes abolished under the terms of parliamentary enclosure awards, coverage of tithe commutation records is fragmentary and it is rarely possible to reconstruct land-use patterns on a field-by-field basis for large blocks of territory. Where field-by-field evidence is discontinuous or lacking, attempts have been made with varying degrees of caution and confidence to evaluate and interpret parish estimates of arable and grass acreages in the apportionments. Within counties the estimates may be used to assess broadly the magnitude of contrasts between land use regions and comparisons may be instituted with the 1801 crop returns and with parish data abstracted from the late nineteenth-century agricultural returns.

In an account of agriculture in the west midlands around 1840, Jean East uses the parish estimates to work out proportions of arable to grass from parish to parish and to construct a 'types-of-farming' map for the whole region.[64] It is pointed out that the estimates do not refer to all land within a parish but generally only to titheable lands. The ratio of arable to grass may be distorted by the exclusion of tithe-free areas. In newly enclosed midland parishes lands which had been exempted from tithes under enclosure awards often included a high proportion of former open-field arable. Where enclosure had occurred very recently the proportion of arable might be seriously under-represented in the estimates; for earlier enclosures it might be expected that some conversion of arable to grass would redress the balance. In compiling maps from the estimates Jean East was unable to find a satisfactory way of correcting this inherent source of inaccuracy.

In 1954 in an introduction to modern agrarian history in the *Victoria History of the County of Leicester*, Joan Thirsk compares the tithe estimates of arable land with the 1801 crop returns to indicate the extent of change that took place in the first four decades of the nineteenth century.[65] Both on cold clays in north-west Leicestershire and on lighter soils in the east acreages of arable appear to have increased. The Leicestershire evidence, for what it is worth, suggests that in 5 different parishes enclosures were not followed by conversion to pasture. Even on heavy soils at Desford, where in 1801 only 398 acres were returned as under crops, the tithe apportionment recorded 549 acres of arable and 1,400 acres of grass, whilst on light soils at Carlton Curlieu the arable acreage apparently increased from 30 to 140 between 1801 and the time of the tithe survey in 1850.

In a study of rural landscape changes in east Yorkshire Alan Harris also turns to parish estimates in the absence of field-by-field data from the apportionments.[66] Where large parts of parishes are tithe-free and not enumerated the problem of the representativeness of the information is squarely faced. For the purposes of computation parishes for which information is deficient are excluded. For Holderness a map of arable and grass acreages is constructed, 'derived from the tithe surveys, some of which cover only part of a parish, but only fairly complete surveys have been used in the compilation of the maps'.[67] For eight of the most complete parishes tithe acreages are compared with the 1801 crop returns.

In 1966 a fuller and much more detailed treatment of available evidence for east Worcestershire is included in J. A. Yelling's study of open fields, enclosure and farm production.[68] For some 119 parishes arable acreages in the tithe apportionment parish estimates are compared with those in the 1867 agricultural statistics. It is noted that for many parishes the estimates and the statistics do not refer to exactly the same areas and that the figures should be compared only in general terms. More detailed analysis is performed on tithe data relating to particular farms and estates.

Among the fuller accounts of mid-nineteenth-century land use in the midlands are county-wide studies by A. D. M. Phillips on Staffordshire, Nottinghamshire and Herefordshire, each of which is based on an analysis of all available parish land-use estimates for those counties.[69] Notwithstanding difficulties of data accuracy, he considers that 'the summaries in the preambles to tithe awards provide details of the major categories of land use around 1840 not available on such a scale from any other source'.[70] In Herefordshire he finds that a high proportion of land, 88 per cent, was cultivated at that date, that the acreage of grassland was greater than that of arable in most parts of the county, and that in detail the distribution of arable and grass within that county can be related to soil conditions. On the other hand, in the east midlands it was arable that dominated in Nottinghamshire *c.* 1840 but again 'distinct distributions of arable and permanent grassland were evident on different soil types'.[71] Similarly he considers that 'the distribution of arable and grassland reveals that distinctions in farming practices on light and heavy land in Staffordshire existed around 1840'.[72] Phillips investigates the relationship between agricultural systems and soil types in further detail by considering patterns of crops and their yields in Staffordshire and Nottinghamshire. For this his sources are reports on tithe agreements in tithe files; this important work is reviewed in the following chapter concerned with studies of mid-nineteenth-century farming.

Misleading evidence from the west

Tithe evidence from south-western England and from Wales is suspect because the classification of arable land and grass is often ambiguous, the source of ambiguity arising from the practice of laying down ploughland to long leys of three or more years' duration. In western districts the likelihood of obtaining a false picture from state of cultivation data and, above all, from parish estimates is much greater than in other parts of Britain.

An unwary step along this treacherous path was taken by N. J. G. Pounds in a study of the historical geography of Cornwall which makes reference to tithe surveys as a source for reconstructing land use in the mid-nineteenth century, without indicating the defects of the material.[73] In an appendix to an account of economic development in the lower Conway valley and on the Creuddyn peninsula D. Geraint Griffith transcribes land-use data from the parish estimates for 16 parishes. No critical examination is offered of the way in which acreages were compiled or how categories of use were defined before proceeding to draw inferences from the figures. It is adduced from the estimates that in 1840 arable husbandry dominated one side of the Conway whilst across the river a pastoral economy prevailed, and it is also concluded from a comparison of the estimates with statements in the Board of Agriculture reports that since the Napoleonic wars arable land had increased in all parts of the region.[74] A study by J. C. Grove of a small area, covering 9 parishes in west Gower, concludes that the area was predominantly arable in the 1840s.[75] Following this misleading trail yet further is a broad survey comparing agricultural changes in Pembrokeshire and Cornwall from the middle of the sixteenth to the end of the nineteenth century.[76] Among the sources from which parish acreages in different land-use categories are drawn are the 1801 crop returns, the tithe surveys and the 1870 agricultural statistics. Describing the tithe surveys for Pembrokeshire compiled between 1837 and 1843, T. R. B. Dicks states that 'each gives accurate information of the acreages in each parish under arable, meadow and pasture, waste and woodland. The method adopted in their study has been to construct isopleth maps of the ratio between the total area of the parish unit and the various elements of land utilisation.'[77] Without thorough checking against other contemporary sources and without detailed knowledge of the classes of land exempt from tithes in each parish this procedure cannot yield reliable results. To compound the errors tithe data are compared with 1801 and 1870 statistics without considering the methods by which the three sets of data were compiled and how far they are comparable. Turning to Cornwall the tithe estimates seem to indicate that arable land covered between 50 and 70 per cent of most parishes. Meadow and pasture, on the other hand, were of little importance, occupying less than 10 per cent of the surface in more than two-thirds of Cornish parishes. This impression is created largely by the designation of long-ley pastures as arable in the tithe apportionments in south-west England.

In the Land's End peninsula, N. Hilton considers that the maximum extent of arable farming can be dated to the 1840s though he is aware that arable acreages recorded in his main source, the tithe apportionments, did include long-ley rotation grasses.[78] Dr Dicks, on the other hand, appears to make no allowance for the inclusion of infrequently ploughed land in the arable category and thus the picture of arable farming that he draws is somewhat misleading. Fig. 6.9 is a map of arable excluding long-ley grasses in Cornwall compiled from data recorded in tithe file reports on tithe agreements. In only one Cornish parish with extant tithe file data did the annual acreage of land under crops exceed 40 per cent of total parish area and for many the figure was less than 20 per cent.[79]

Allowing for difficulties of definition, the parish estimates for western counties have some advantages over the field-by-field data in the schedules of apportionment. In an exceptional western county, Cheshire, where 'arable-type' agreement report forms were used, long leys are excluded from estimates of arable acreage. The accuracy of these has been tested in R. E. Porter's study of nineteenth-century farming and they are found to be quite reliable.[80] Township estimates are useful because from many Cheshire schedules of apportionment it is not possible to obtain field-by-field data, tithe areas being frequently returned as 'arable and pasture' by the apportioner. 'By using the estimates it has been possible to obtain a broad picture of land use for almost the whole county in the mid-nineteenth century, at the expense of only a small degree of accuracy.'[81]

Problems of mapping arable land from tithe surveys in the west and in Wales are clearly identified by P. E. Jones in his study of part of Caernarvonshire.[82] In two of his five parishes, high acreages of arable land are recorded in tithe apportionments by comparison with levels in the other three. This distinction is not found in later surveys. The apportionments of the two

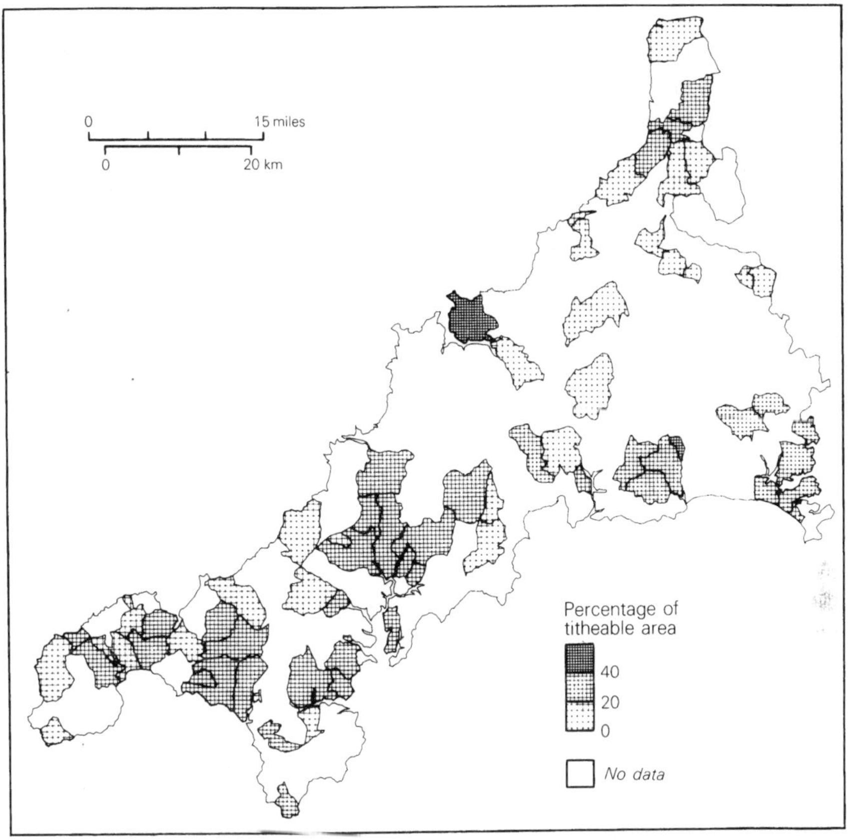

6.9 Arable land in Cornwall.

former parishes were made by Welsh valuers, while an Englishman, Francis Marston of Hopesay, Shropshire, valued the rent-charge in the other three.

It is evident that Marston's conception of arable land was at variance with that of the other surveyors. Coming from an English county he may not have regarded land laid down to grass for long periods as arable land, whereas it appears that all land capable of being ploughed was classified as arable by the Welsh surveyors.[83]

A similarly cautious and careful appraisal of the value of Welsh tithe estimates is made by J. M. Powell in a study of the changing economic geography of Montgomeryshire in the nineteenth century.[84] Powell considers that 'a discussion of the validity of the documents would by itself justify a considerable study'.[85] In practice, the estimates are subjected to tests in an attempt to verify and measure their accuracy whilst techniques for mapping the data are chosen to avoid presenting false impressions. Surface areas of parishes tabulated in the published abstract of the 1851 census are compared with total acreages recorded in the tithe estimates. In none of the Montgomeryshire parishes under review are the two quantities exactly the same but the difference between them is nowhere sufficiently large to invalidate the tithe surveyor's estimate. Different categories of land use are represented together on the same map so that relationships between one category and another may be observed simultaneously over the whole area. Acreages of arable, pasture, sheepwalk and common grazing, and wood are plotted as bars standing side by side within each parish. This map shows clearly a contrast between eastern vales and plateaux where arable is important and western and southern uplands where moorland is dominant. The land use of three blocks of parishes is analysed in greater detail and distribution maps of different land-use categories are compiled from schedules of apportionment. From an examination of these maps and a comparison with the 1801 crop returns, it would appear that the greatest change taking place in the first 40 years of the century was the enclosure of common wastes and the extension of arable cultivation. In south-west Carmarthenshire a detailed examination of the tithe documents has been carried out by W. S. G. Thomas.[86] This reveals that meadow and pasture are separately distinguished in the state of cultivation columns of the apportionments and it has been possible to draw separate maps of these categories. Inspection of these maps indicates that at the time of the surveys pasture dominated all parishes in the area under investigation, an impression confirmed by descriptions of farming reported in the tithe files. In conducting a search among tithe surveys relating to estates in Merioneth, C. Thomas claims that they are 'the foremost sources for a study of the agricultural geography of the mid-nineteenth century'.[87] But defects in the material are not overlooked. Among 30 apportionments examined only 12 record the state of cultivation for each field and from 10 maps field boundaries are omitted. Information for farms and estates is more complete.

Moorland edges

Since the completion of the Land Utilisation Survey, further studies have made use of the tithe surveys to trace the upward limit of cultivation in highland Britain. The early years of the nineteenth century witnessed a great extension of arable farming at the margins of cultivation, a process stimulated by high grain prices. Once broken up, these intakes from waste, moor and rough pasture appear to have remained in cultivation through to the 1840s and perhaps later.

Following the lead of the Welsh Land Utilisation Survey reports, the theme of the retreat of the moorland edge has been taken up in other highland regions. Evidence for these enquiries is derived, in the first place, from an interpretation and comparison of reports and surveys made at different dates. Norman Hilton's account of 86 square miles of the Land's End peninsula is illustrated by a series of maps indicating the extent of rough grazing at different periods, one of which is based upon the tithe surveys.[88] By making comparisons with earlier and later surveys, he establishes that the maximum extent of arable incursion into the moorlands occurred about 1840. T. H. Bainbridge reaches a similar conclusion in Cumberland.[89] A tithe apportionment for Latrigg (Applethwaite) shows that cultivation was carried on at higher altitudes in the 1840s than in later years. In the lower Conway valley 'the effect of the Hungry Forties', D. G. Griffith asserts, 'is best illustrated by the tithe records'.[90] Descriptions of land use written by George Kay 1794, Walter Davies 1810 and Edmund Hyde Hall 1809–11 are compared with the tithe estimates and it is inferred that a general expansion of cultivation had taken place in the intervening years. A detailed illustration of a township dominated by arable farming is provided by the tithe survey of Tre Garthmen, a place for which land use is plotted on a photostat of the original tithe map.

A fresh approach to the problem is taken in S. R. Eyre's study of the upward limit of cultivation on the east moor of Derbyshire.[91] It relies heavily upon a previously neglected source of moorland land use evidence in the record of field-names in the tithe apportionments. Names containing the elements 'ridding', 'stubbing' and 'intake' are abstracted both from the tithe apportionments and from terriers accompanying enclosure awards and their distributions are plotted on maps. Eyre considers that these names were given to fields and farms at the time they were reclaimed from waste, moor or wood. They provide a long-term record of moorland enclosures. Another research worker at the University of Leeds, Alan Digby, also uses field-name evidence to trace advances of cultivation into the moorlands of Ribblesdale in Lancashire since the late middle ages.[92] Digby compares evidence of field-name elements with land-use information for later periods and, where anomalies and discrepancies occur, he searches for other indications for changes in use. In particular, he seeks evidence for changes from waste or rough grazing to cultivation. The element 'flatt' is a fairly reliable indicator of medieval cultivation, but the occurrence of such elements as 'moor' or 'moss' in names of fields and farms that were enclosed at an early date may also bear witness to medieval colonisation. These and other elements often provide valuable evidence of more recent phases of occupance and reclamation. Among examples cited are the elements 'hazelhead' and 'hollins' in the names of fields no longer covered with bushes at the time of the tithe surveys. A change of a different kind is revealed by fields named 'barley croft' and 'wheat field' whose states of cultivation in 1842 are recorded as meadow and pasture. In mid-Ribblesdale 32 out of 53 indications of land-use changes pointed to a conversion of land to pasture. A map of 15 townships represents general directions in which land uses were being changed from the states implied by field-name elements to the states of cultivation recorded in the tithe apportionments. This analysis suggests that in the valley itself a tendency to lay down arable to grass, to change to a pastoral economy – as indicated by animal elements in later field-names – was both widespread and persistent, whilst the moorland edge was being pushed back by the plough.

The most searching and comprehensive enquiry into the changing position of the moorland edge is that conducted by John Chapman, first on the North York Moors and later in Monmouthshire.[93] In his study of the North York Moors, 'intake' name elements are plotted on a map to show the limit reached by improvements up to the time of the tithe surveys. The distribution indicates that intakes were not confined to areas high up adjoining the moor wall. In Fylingdales an 1843 tithe survey shows several such intakes situated some distance from the moorland edge and it is inferred that these pockets of waste land defied improvement when colonising movements were at their height. They remained to be brought into cultivation at later periods, perhaps in the course of farm consolidations. A map of land use in Levisham, where the moorland edge formed a continuous frontier in tithe times, is depicted on Fig. 6.10. In drawing a broad picture of the North York Moors Chapman uses a few parish estimates without critically examining their limitations as sources of information. In the Monmouthshire study, however, the problem of discerning general trends through time demands closer attention. It is a region where there are extensive gaps in the field surveys and where few parishes possess records of land use at more than one or two dates. Tithe estimates, with all their imperfections, cover almost all parishes and provide the best available basis for constructing a datum line against which changes may be measured. Differences in proportions of land in different land-use categories provide crude indices of change before and after the surveys. Comparisons with evidence for earlier periods suggest that the upward limit of cultivation in Monmouthshire was reached before the Napoleonic wars and in most localities the high point had been attained by 1750. In periods from 1780 to 1800 and from 1815 to 1835 there appear to have been more abandonment and more reversion to waste than intaking in the uplands. Fencing of new land from open moors was narrowly localised. On the other hand, considerable areas of land at lower altitudes enclosed before 1750 lay unimproved and it was on these old enclosed tracts that reclamation and improvement were most active, particularly in the years between 1835 and 1870. After 1870 recession and reversion were continuous and widespread.

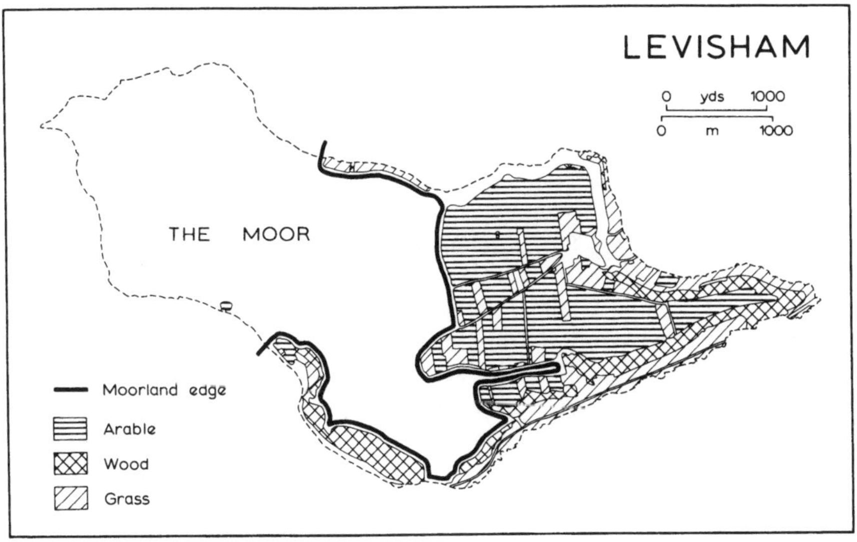

6.10 Land use at Levisham, North Riding of Yorkshire. Source: J. Chapman, 'Changing agriculture and the moorland edge in the North York Moors, 1750–1960', 1961.

Lowland heaths

It is clear that over most of highland Britain reclamation at the moorland edge had slowed down and in many districts it had come to a halt before 1840. On lowland heaths, however, it was still very active. Indeed, on the chalklands of southern England the arable acreage did not reach its greatest extent until the 1870s.

The overwhelming importance of arable farming and the continuing intensification of the use of land for raising crops in light soil areas of eastern England is illustrated by J. E. G. Mosby's map based on the tithe surveys[94] (Fig. 6.5 above). Between the time of Thomas Donald and Thomas Milne's map in 1797 and the time of the tithe surveys almost all remaining heaths and sheepwalks in the Good Sand region were brought under the plough. The only evidence that remained to bear witness to the formerly extensive practice of temporary cultivation was to be found in the widely prevalent 'breck' element in field-names in most sandy tracts in the country. In Lincolnshire, S. A. Johnson uses the tithe land use estimates to show that the great improving movement had lost none of its impetus on light soils, whereas elsewhere a traditional grassland economy persisted.[95] The extension of arable farming was especially characteristic on the wolds. A more recent study of 400 square miles in the Breckland by Malcolm Postgate contains several maps of land use derived from the tithe surveys.[96] In addition to distribution maps of various categories of land use defined in the state of cultivation columns of the apportionments, the parish estimates of land use acreages from the preambles to the awards are also mapped to provide generalised pictures of land use in the region as a whole. The tithe estimates for Breckland parishes dating from 1837 to 1846 are compared with relevant portions of late-eighteenth-century printed county maps – that for Norfolk surveyed by Donald and Milne in 1797, that for Suffolk by Joseph Hodskinson in 1783. The comparison suggests that about one-fifth of the former area of Breckland heath may have disappeared during a span of little more than half a century. Having traced the course of improvement in the Sandlings of east Suffolk from the early seventeenth century, Elizabeth Burrell pauses to summarise the results achieved by the mid-nineteenth century.[97] Areas of arable, pasture, heath and woodland are plotted from the tithe surveys. Again, improvement appears to have been most extensive on light loams and most active during the early nineteenth century.

In a critical examination of quantitative evidence for an agricultural revolution in south Lincolnshire, David Grigg makes extensive use of the tithe surveys to portray a 'new agricultural geography' of the region for a period following the main phase of improvement.[98] From an inspection of tithe apportionments he concludes that gorsy heaths remained a widespread feature in the landscape as late as the 1840s, whilst a tabulation of arable land as a percentage of all crops and grass derived from parish estimates indicates that over the region as a whole the amount of grass had been much reduced by mid-century. The highest proportions of meadow and pasture were still concentrated in traditional grazing districts in west and south-east Kesteven, the advance of arable cultivation having by this time penetrated farthest on light soils in the uplands in the centre. Evidence for south Lincolnshire indicates that the most far-reaching changes in agriculture, whose magnitude might be considered revolutionary, occurred only during the nineteenth century and not earlier. A peak of heath reclamation was reached during the middle years of the century, but somewhat later in parts of southern England than elsewhere. In Monmouthshire the force of expansion into the moorlands spent itself over a hundred years before it expired on lowland heaths. Indeed, small-scale reclamation continued on sandy soils until 1870. In the Suffolk Sandlings, P. Armstrong has elucidated from an examination of altered apportionments that up to the final years of the nineteenth century small tracts of heathland were being brought into cultivation whilst arable fields in the same locality were reverting to wild sheep walks; in Dorset, G. L. Cunningham considers that 'the years 1810–1850 were a period of quite significant change in the agricultural landscape of south-east Dorset. The heathland still dominated tracts of sand and gravel soils but in several areas heaths were being replaced by improved farmland.'[99]

Marshlands

The history of marshland draining is characterised by a wave-like alternation of crests of activity followed by troughs of neglect. In many marshland regions the mid-nineteenth century stands out as a high point of industrious improvement while at the same time over much of the English claylands investment in underdraining was heavier than at any previous period. Steam pumps made possible new feats of regulating levels of water in ditches while drain tiles provided durable and efficient means of conducting ground water into ditches. Concerted efforts by landowners and land-improvement companies extended the benefits of draining to marshes previously considered unprofitable to improve. Whilst in the history of draining in the Somerset Levels, Michael Williams speaks of 1830 as the beginning of 'the lost years', elsewhere it marks the commencement of a period of feverish activity.[100] Meres in Shropshire and Cheshire, mosses in Lancashire and coastal flats around Morecambe Bay were brought into cultivation for the first time and tithe surveys indicate progress that had been made by *c.* 1840.[101] In 1848 Whittlesey Mere in the Huntingdonshire fens was drained dry in six weeks by steam power. Other neglected pockets of waterlogged peat were similarly drained and drainage works that had latterly fallen into disrepair were restored. In the fenlands of Kesteven, Dennis Mills finds that by the time of the tithe surveys almost every available acre of land was under cultivation. In 1848 over 90 per cent of Martin Dales was arable, and in the 1,200 acres of Thorpe Tilney Fen only two closes were recorded as permanent pasture.[102]

Tithe surveys have contributed to the body of evidence supporting an anthropogenic origin of the Broads and have been compared with later Ordnance Survey maps and air photographs to indicate shrinkage of the Broads since tithe times.[103] For June Sheppard these documents helped locate the medieval meres of Holderness.[104]

On the lower Thames marshlands, three studies acknowledge the value of the land-use information furnished by the tithe surveys. B. E. Cracknell finds that the surveys present an accurate picture of the use of alluvial marshes in the estuary. A map showing changes in land use on Tilbury Levels between 1840 and 1861 is constructed by comparing land-use information in the tithe surveys with that recorded on later maps of the commissioners of sewers.[105] In a later study of Canvey Island the tithe schedule is used to create a complete picture of land use which shows that the greatest part of the island was under arable crops in 1840.[106] D. W. Gramolt in a history of the changes in the coastal marshes of east Essex draws maps of pasture and woodland around 1840. The pattern of drainage ditches on Clements Marsh is traced from a 1796 survey, from the tithe maps and from an 1867 survey. The extension of drainage channels serves to indicate an expansion in the improved area. By the middle of the nineteenth century there was little room for fresh additions to the arable acreage.[107]

Woodland and parkland

In the 1840s no great changes in the woodland area were taking place. The long-term reduction in standing timber for constructional and shipbuilding purposes was slowing down as increasing volumes of iron, steel and imported softwoods were substituted. The consumption of wood and charcoal for domestic fires, for iron smelting and for a variety of industrial processes was also diminishing as coal and coke replaced the older fuels. The unceasing attrition of ancient woods slackened as sawmills closed, as charcoal burning became extinct, as the rights of villagers to gather winter fuel and to depasture their pigs and cows were abolished by enclosure acts. Regions that had been stripped almost bare of trees by the end of the Napoleonic wars began to recover a wooded appearance. In addition to the growth that occurred spontaneously as seedlings established themselves on cut-over ground, the planting of timber trees among quickset hedges following enclosure and the making of vast plantations to adorn parks and landscape gardens contributed to giving the landscape a newly wooded aspect. Planting schemes initiated at the beginning of the nineteenth century were still being implemented in the 1870s. By the end of the Second World War, when trees planted a hundred years earlier had begun to grow old and were being felled, probably more than one-third of the nation's timber reserves stood in hedgerows and parks.

The replacement of ancient woods by new plantations and by natural regeneration did not, in all places, occur on sites continuously occupied by woodland. Whilst comparisons between total acreages under woods at different dates may indicate very small net changes, it does not follow that either the location or the floristic composition of woodlands remained unchanged. In south Buckinghamshire much evidence gathered from maps and from estate records by A. J. Mansfield points to a different conclusion.[108] A careful inspection of maps from the seventeenth century onwards indicates extensive shifts in the location of woods as old stands were cleared and new ones raised. The presence of wood or clearing elements in field names testifies to the former extent of woodland. In tithe apportionments many parcels of land bearing wood names are recorded in state of cultivation columns as arable or grass. Conversely, some parcels described as fields are recorded as being used for plantations or coppices or woods. Comparisons between descriptions of woods noted in inventories and schedules at different periods frequently reflect changes in composition such as from wood to coppice or from oak-wood to beech plantation. Occasionally, tree symbols on maps imply a change from hardwoods to conifers.

Names and descriptions of parcels of land entered in tithe apportionments may throw light on functions, as for example 'Ice-house Wood', or personal associations, as for example 'Lord Howe's Plantation', or the intended visual effects, as for example 'Arnos Grove', or features in landscape gardens. They may also yield information leading to the identification of former parks. A series of articles on medieval deer parks by L. M. Cantor uses this source of evidence. There is a bibliography of his published lists and descriptions of the medieval parks in Dorset, Staffordshire, Leicestershire and Buckinghamshire in an article on the medieval parks of England written jointly by Cantor and J. Hatherly.[109]

For reconstructing the former extent of woodland, tithe maps are a somewhat unwieldy and inaccessible source and difficulties are compounded in areas where timber trees were exempt from tithe. Other maps surveyed at this time, including some that were published, represent woods in forms that may be copied directly on tracing paper. Parks, in particular, are represented more clearly both on private estate maps and on printed maps than they are on tithe maps. In most studies of land use based on tithe records, agricultural uses are emphasised whilst woods and parks are treated as minor elements in the rural economy. Maps of woodland derived from tithe surveys are included in these studies to fill in spaces between scenes of farming activity. In other studies the changing extent of woodland is traced through time. As an illustration of this process, M. J. Frost compiles a series of maps showing woodland changes in the upper Mole basin in Surrey between the mid-eighteenth century and the present time.[110] The tithe surveys provide data for one period. In another account of woodland in Surrey, devoted entirely to woods in the parish of Great Bookham, J. A. Evans uses the tithe survey of 1839 to bring the history to an end with a full and exact inventory of all the woods and their acreages.[111]

In recent years botanists with historical inclinations have turned to the tithe surveys to aid their enquiries into the chronology of woodland growth and succession.[112] G. F. Peterken's detailed examination of the history of the Thicks in Staverton Park in Suffolk leads him to conclude that the ancient oaks surviving there 'originated naturally over a long period and that the existing trees are the product of natural regeneration between the sixteenth century or earlier and the early nineteenth century'.[113] A key to the reconstruction is provided by the tithe maps of 1846 and the accompanying schedule of apportionment. John Sheail has used tithe maps, apportionments and files to identify plantations of trees established in the Breckland for shelter, timber and amenity.[114] On Exmoor, Olive Hallam attempts an ambitious direct comparison of acreages of woodland recorded in the tithe surveys of 24 parishes in the Somerset part of the National Park with 'acreages' computed from Domesday Book.[115] Her conclusion is that overall the acreage of woodland had changed little, that in 16 parishes it had increased but had decreased in 8. The propriety of conducting such comparisons is not questioned though she does admit that 'the converted Domesday figures can only be considered as approximations, it is an extraordinary coincidence that the acreages should be so nearly equal'.[116]

Another area of investigation in which tithe documents have played an essential part is the study of hedgerows, as pioneered by N. W. Moore, Max Hooper and B. K. Davis.[117] A method for determining the age of hedgerows by counting the number of different shrub and tree species present is tested by examining accurately dated field boundaries. The tithe surveys provide an invaluable guide to the alignment, position and length of field boundaries in the 1840s, and in a few instances information from maps and apportionments may indicate whether a live hedge formed the boundary.

Settlements

Houses with gardens and other built-up sites occupy small areas of land but their location provides a vital key to an understanding of all aspects of land use. The morphology of rural settlements throws light on the history of colonisation, on the organisation of the rural economy and on changes in population. The tithe surveys have provided material for settlement studies carried out both by geographers and by historians. Some studies of settlements in conjunction with field systems which use the tithe surveys as a source of evidence have been reviewed already in chapter 5. In this section studies which consider settlement primarily as a type of land use are considered.

Jean East's study of the form and function of settlements in the west midlands ranks as one of the first to recognise the value of the tithe surveys as a source for reconstructing a geography of settlements at a regional scale.[118] The distribution of buildings and houses with gardens in tithe times is compared with that recorded by the Land Utilisation Survey. A few parishes are selected for detailed investigation and maps of the built-up area are drawn for both dates. Among these are maps of settlement in Offenham, 1841, Preston Wynne, 1839, Ryton, 1839, and Elmbridge, 1841. Other parishes situated at the edges of urban areas, including Cheadle, 1842, and Bishop's Castle, 1843, illustrate some effects of town growth on rural settlements. An abandonment of an early industrial site is indicated by a comparison of a tithe survey for Dawley, 1845, with a Land Utilisation Survey map of 1935. On the earlier survey collieries and blast furnaces are represented, whereas the later map marks them as disused collieries and classifies the site as rough grazing.

In the first of a number of published articles on the settlement geography of north Wales and the Welsh borderland, Dorothy Sylvester declares that 'the tithe maps alone give a complete picture of rural settlement'.[119] In

Anglesey, as elsewhere, they provide the earliest complete delineation of habitations and fields. The ground plans and arrangement of buildings in the 1830s and 1840s may be compared with their present layouts. Maps illustrating morphological variations in settlement types within different localities accompany each of her articles. The results are brought together and summarised in a general account of the historical geography of the Welsh borderland.[120] Rural settlements are classified into five types and the distributions of these types, whose characteristics are identified from evidence in the tithe surveys, are plotted on maps. Many of the inferences drawn by Dorothy Sylvester are challenged by G. R. J. Jones (see chapter 5 above) who considers the location of dwellings inseparable from the larger question concerning the location of landholdings from which they draw their sustenance. A knowledge of social structures and of field systems is essential to a proper understanding of settlement patterns. In practice, the tithe surveys furnish some evidence for all these subjects of enquiry.

Amongst workers whose principal concern has been to examine systems of farming and agricultural land use in different regions, but who have also examined patterns of settlement portrayed on tithe maps, are F. D. Hartley, who has compiled a map of houses and gardens for the Chiltern area, Elizabeth Burrell, who has illustrated an agricultural geography of the Sandlings in Suffolk with a map of settlements, and R. Allison, who has constructed a similar map for south-west Essex.[121] E. A. Cox has discussed the distribution of buildings in a chapter dealing with unfarmed land in Essex in tithe times, whilst B. R. Dittmer has prepared a composite map of buildings, gardens and non-agricultural land in north-west Wiltshire.[122] M. C. Naish presents a map of settlements on the Hampshire chalklands from tithe surveys, and also uses tithe maps to illustrate the forms of selected village plans in greater detail.[123] G. I. Meirion-Jones compiles maps from tithe surveys to distinguish regions characterised by villages, hamlets and dispersed settlements, and this analysis serves as a starting-point for a study of vernacular building in rural England. A handlist of houses has been compiled from tithe surveys for Selborne and Odiham in Hampshire and surviving examples have then been inspected in the field. This enquiry, incidentally, confirms that nucleated settlements were still bound together by persistent open-field arrangements in the nineteenth century.[124] Local historians have consulted tithe maps to identify the sites and plans of old houses, have traced inns from names and descriptions of premises recorded in tithe apportionments and are using tithe maps and apportionments as starting-points for tracing histories of individual buildings.[125]

Tithe surveys have also been used to examine the changing character of settlements on urban fringes. The most interesting studies are those which relate building development to earlier cadasters, showing new estates designed to fill spaces delimited by ancient property boundaries (see chapter

8). Their focus of interest is upon landownership. A morphological approach to the study of the changing geography of three settlements on the southern edge of London by Bessie Taylor uses tithe maps principally to show the detailed arrangements of buildings in the villages of Beckenham, West Wickham, Bromley, Hayes and Keston in metropolitan Kent.[126] A study by P. E. Jones of Bangor and its environs at the time of the tithe survey in 1840 shows the city in embryonic form before the railway transformed it. The network of mid-nineteenth-century roads and the pattern of field boundaries, however, are clearly discernible in the modern street plan.[127] A very detailed investigation into the progress of suburban building in outer west London in the middle years of the nineteenth century by Michael Jahn makes extensive use of tithe maps and apportionments.[128] Again, the legacy of relict features from a pre-urban cadaster is readily identified and appears to be substantial.

In addition, tithe records have assisted a search for sites of former industrial activities. Names and descriptions of premises on apportionments have provided valuable information, as have names and symbols inscribed on maps. Tithe surveys may also be the only available source for names of owners and occupiers of industrial sites. In accounting for the location of lime kilns in Surrey, D. J. Robinson and R. U. Cooke have consulted tithe surveys for evidence concerning ownership.[129] Other studies have used tithe maps and schedules of apportionments to trace sites and owners of early cotton mills in Derbyshire, Cheshire and the West Riding.[130]

7

Farming

A consideration of land use alone affords a very incomplete view of mid-nineteenth-century farming. A fuller picture takes account of farmers' assessments of their soils, methods of tillage, use of marls, manures and artificial fertilisers, courses of cropping, yields and prices, numbers and kinds of livestock kept and markets served. A comprehensive survey would also include assessments of the quality of local farming practices and a critical appraisal of James Caird's notion of 'high farming'.[1]

Agricultural writers at this period were unanimous in welcoming advances made by applying science to agriculture and most observers condemned common rights, family settlements, corn laws and tithe payments as impediments to progress. Caird in his county-by-county survey in *English Agriculture in 1850–51* and the prize essays on the farming of different counties published in the *Journal of the Royal Agricultural Society of England* between 1845 and 1869 praised efforts by enterprising landowners and farmers directed towards increasing agricultural productivity.[2] Among innovations singled out for special praise were Justus von Liebig's work demonstrating the benefits to yields of arable crops gained from spreading Chilean nitrates, potash and phosphates.[3] The advantages to be gained for large-scale grain growing from the use of mechanical reapers and threshing machines were quickly appreciated.[4] In Norfolk, Lincolnshire, Yorkshire, Lancashire and Cheshire, improvements obtained from marling and liming light soils were applauded.[5] In districts as far apart as Dorset and Northumberland, long leases convenanting regular courses of cropping and stipulating soil-conservation measures were greeted as leading steps to reclaiming wastes and improving lands already in cultivation.[6] In different parts of England clay soils were reported to be newly drained by tiles; tracts of peat soils were reclaimed by steam pumps; and alluvial soils were improved by irrigation and warping.[7] While costly improvements were recommended in the journals, farmers complained that farm incomes were being depressed by imports of cheap wheat from Ireland and they felt unjustly burdened by tithes.

A House of Commons select committee to enquire into the state of agriculture in 1836 received many complaints about the burden of tithes from different localities. Several Buckinghamshire witnesses were of the opinion that 'the commutation of tithe would be a very great thing' and that abolition 'would benefit the land in the long run because there would be no chill to improvement'.[8] A Suffolk farmer who had invested in an improved system of husbandry felt aggrieved that, where tithes had not been reduced, 'the clergyman has taken advantage of the improvements', and a witness from Lincolnshire asserted that an improving landlord 'would be charged with a perpetual tithe arising out of a tenant's good management'.[9] A Sussex farmer considered that any improvements producing a return of 10 per cent would be nullified by tithe payments and a Gloucestershire farmer estimated that tithe, 'taken at the gross tenth, might have been in some cases more than the rent'.[10] Many witnesses reached the conclusion expressed by a Somerset farmer that tithe 'operates as a very great drawback to agriculture in general'.[11] That opinion was endorsed by professional agriculturalists, including Caird, and it was given wide publicity in J. R. McCulloch's *A statistical account of the British empire*, where tithes were described as 'a very serious obstacle to the progress of agricultural improvement'.[12] The passage argued that 'the subjecting of land to so heavy a tax as *a tenth of the gross produce*, without any deduction for any part of the expenses incurred in cultivation, must be a very great discouragement to the outlay of capital upon it'.[13] While many improving farmers endured increased liabilities to tithes, some obtained agreements from the tithe owners remitting payments on increments earned from capital investments and others compounded for fixed money rents (see also the section in chapter 1: 'Tithe and agricultural improvement').

Tithing maps, accounts and cause papers

Under the provisions of most enclosure acts tithe owners were compensated for the abolition of tithes by allotments of land or by regular money payments. Farmers took advantage of every other pretext such as the appointment of a new incumbent or the accession of a new patron of the living to negotiate fresh terms on which their tithes would be collected, and wherever possible they sought to dismiss the tithing man.[14] Records of these transactions often include detailed surveys and inventories of the crops grown on particular farms or fields. Where copies of the documents were deposited in parish chests or in estate archives they have subsequently come to light and have provided a valuable source of information about farming in the period before the Tithe Commutation Act of 1836.

In 1924, J. H. Clapham called attention to the late-eighteenth-century tithing surveys of Prescot which were used to reconstruct the economic and social conditions of a south-Lancashire parish during that period.[15] The documents reveal the presence of smallholdings, the importance of arable farming, the yields of several crops and the extent to which waste land had been reduced between the time of the first survey in 1775 and the last in 1794. A parallel study was being made at this time by J. A. Venn using the tithing surveys for the parish of Mattishall in Norfolk, also indicating the paramount importance of crop husbandry.[16] Clapham hoped that a systematic search for similar surveys would throw light on 'the problem of the size of the agricultural unit and that of the ratio of "entrepreneurs" to "proletarians" at different dates'.[17] But his own three-volume work on the economic history of modern Britain contains no reference either to these early surveys or to the more comprehensive mid-nineteenth-century tithe surveys as sources for agrarian history. The appeal did not pass entirely unheeded, although only after an interval of thirty years were the tithing surveys of Mattishall discussed in detail in an article by M. F. Lloyd-Pritchard.[18] Among other accounts dealing with the local histories of tithe payments and surveys of farming carried out in connection with them are studies of Nevern and of Mathry in Pembrokeshire, North Somercotes in Lincolnshire, Luton in Bedfordshire, Hatfield in Hertfordshire and Fetcham in Surrey.[19]

Disputes over tithe payments were frequently occasioned by changes in cropping, when tithe owners demanded payment for land that had not previously been cultivated or had been assessed only for small tithes, or when farmers substituted green crops for grain and refused to pay great tithes. Tithe disputes, or *causes* as they were known, were also frequent in areas where lay impropriators held the tithe rights of former monastic houses and pressed their claims to the full. Records of the court proceedings concerned often contain data on crop and livestock production.[20] Caution has, of course, to be applied in interpreting these data as the documents do not usually tell the whole story of a cause, and facts presented by the opposing parties rarely coincide. Tithe causes increased in frequency after the dissolution of the monasteries as also does the richness of the information that they contain on local farming.[21] P. K. Mitchell has used this source to assess the proportions of various crops cultivated on the enclosed fields of the west Cleveland district of Yorkshire.[22] His thesis on agriculture in this area from the sixteenth to the nineteenth centuries contains an exemplary model of the kind of detailed analysis which can be undertaken with pre-1836 tithe records. He uses yields quoted in late eighteenth-century tithe causes as a check on those entered in the 1801 crop return and for one township, Ingleby Barwick, he reconstructs the yields of wheat and oats, 1814–18, from surviving tithe accounts[23] (Table 7.1).

Other, more local, studies of farming have been made using the pre-1836 tithe documents of Ecclesfield in Yorkshire, Rossendale in Lancashire and

Table 7.1 *Wheat yields at Ingleby Barwick, Yorkshire, 1814–18*

	1814	1815	1816	1817	1818
Number of farms tithed	3	4	5	7	7
Wheat acreage	95	114	228	252	281
Maximum yield (bushels)	24	20	24	22	22
Minimum yield (bushels)	9	7	6	8	11

Source: Mitchell, 'West Cleveland land use, c. 1550–1850', 377.

Sheldon in Warwickshire.[24] The cultivation of intakes newly won from moorlands has been inferred from additions to tithe assessments in some townships in west Cumberland and in north Staffordshire.[25] Conversely, a nineteenth-century retreat from the upper limit of cultivation on Dartmoor may be traced from a comparison of late-eighteenth-century maps with tithe maps and apportionments for Widecombe, Challacombe and adjoining parishes.[26] A complaint from the vicar of Castle Acre in Norfolk provides the earliest evidence for the introduction of turnips and clover in crop rotations in that parish.[27] The letter of complaint also throws light on the reorganisation of farms, in that land formerly subject to tithes ceased to pay when it was amalgamated with Abbey Farm, a holding exempt from tithes. A record relating to a similar dispute at Droitwich in Worcestershire states that 66 acres of closes were 'commonly sown with wheat or with peas and beans and some years grass'.[28] The same succession of crops and ley grass was followed at the time of the tithe surveys.

Unlike the later tithe commutation surveys, early tithing maps and records of tithe disputes are too unevenly scattered through time and space for an agricultural geography of England and Wales at a particular period to be reconstructed. A survey of the 1,200 or so parishes of Norfolk and Suffolk by Nesta Evans reveals that only 40 Suffolk and 48 Norfolk parishes possess tithe books dating from before 1836, that those which do survive are mostly for places in the eastern parts of those counties, and that for only one parish, Fressingfield in Suffolk, is there a pre-Reformation tithe book.[29] In England and Wales, pre-1836 tithe cause papers, account books and tithing maps are, despite their relative rarity, especially valuable as sources of detailed information about crops, fields and farms that may be compared with evidence from tithe commutation surveys of the 1840s. It seems unlikely, however, that tithe evidence will be as useful a measure of pre-industrial agricultural production in England and Wales as it has proved on the European continent, particularly in France, Spain, Italy and Switzerland.[30]

Crop maps

The work of the Land Utilisation Survey of Great Britain was almost completed before tithe apportionments recording crops instead of land-use categories in the state of cultivation column were brought to light. Among the earliest discoveries was that of J. E. G. Mosby, who reported that crops were listed in a tithe apportionment for Narford in Norfolk.[31] Another discovery was made by J. B. Jarvis who mapped arable land for 70 square miles around Wrexham in Denbighshire.[32] In that area, a tithe map for Erbistock was coloured and labelled to indicate crops growing in fields, whose boundaries appear to have changed scarcely at all since 1840. Percentages of arable derived from estimates in the apportionment summaries are compared with percentages derived from agricultural statistics for 1870. The comparison illustrates the depressed state of farming at the time of the tithe survey. A study by Jean East of farming types, including crop rotations, in the west midlands draws evidence from tithe surveys, but apportionment lists or crop maps are not specifically referred to.[33] Early studies of tithe surveys summarised in the county reports of the Land Utilisation Survey left little impression of the amount of evidence on crops still waiting to be collected.

As recently as 1970, lists of crops in tithe apportionments and crop maps were regarded as exceptional rarities. A passing reference in a guide to parish records by G. H. Tupling describes the apportionment for Ormskirk in Lancashire as 'specifying in the case of arable land the crops grown on it'.[34] A study of the mid-nineteenth-century agricultural geography of the vale of Clwyd in Denbighshire by J. Wynne Edwards includes a map of crops grown at Ysgeibion in Llanynys drawn from a tithe survey[35] (Fig. 7.1). In a tithe apportionment for South Warnborough in Hampshire, M. C. Naish found that actual crops grown on the arable were listed for each parcel, and from this information he compiled a map showing the field-by-field distribution of crops[36] (Fig. 7.1). The map confirms statements in the tithe file for the parish that wheat, oats, barley, turnips and clover were sown in roughly equal proportions. The discovery of a wealth of evidence on crops in questionnaires in the tithe files diverted attention away from the apportionments and maps. In 1973, an undergraduate at University College London was surprised to find a hitherto unreported list of crops entered in the state of cultivation column of the apportionment for Paulerspury in Northamptonshire.[37] In the absence of direct evidence for cropping in Hartlebury in mid-Worcestershire, B. D. Giles resorted to inference. Field-names such as 'wheatlands', 'wheat field', 'flax pit', 'potato ground' indicated that soils in the vicinity were suitable for growing the crops named. As a cautionary note, Giles added: 'It is not suggested that such names signify that these crops were growing in these particular fields, but the fact that the names

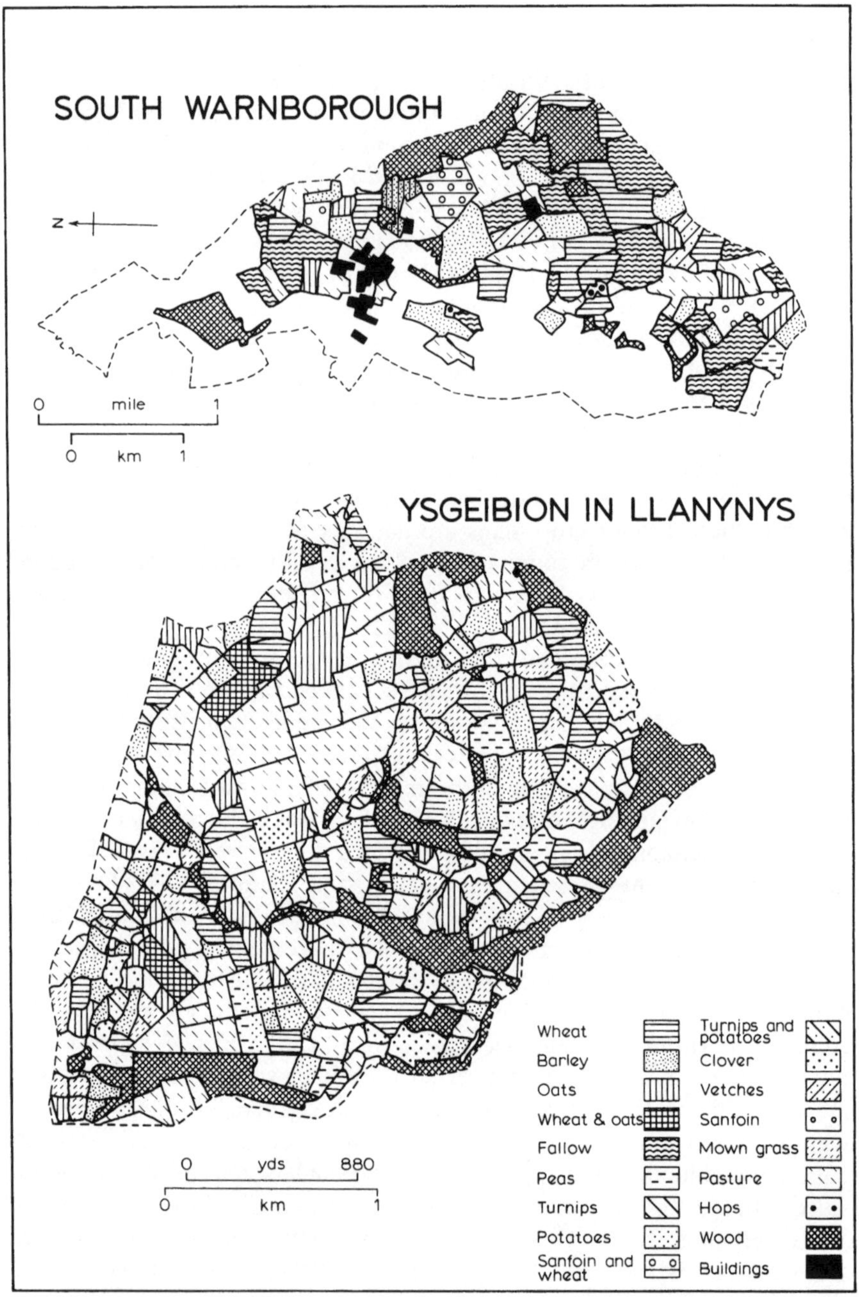

7.1 Crops at South Warnborough in Hampshire and Ysgeibion in Llanynys, Denbighshire. Sources respectively: M. C. Naish, 'The agricultural landscape of the Hampshire chalklands, 1700–1840', 1961; and J. W. Edwards, 'Enclosure and agricultural improvement in the Vale of Clwyd, 1750–1875', 1963.

have been preserved in field names suggests that these crops were at one time locally important.'[38] At about the same time, quite independently, A. D. M. Phillips, working at the University of Keele, and Regina Porter at the University of Liverpool discovered unexpectedly large numbers of apportionments listing crops.

In a study of farming practices and soil types in Staffordshire around 1840, Phillips found no fewer than 12 out of 239 tithe apportionments recorded crops in the state-of-cultivation column.[39] By far the largest number of crop listings has been discovered among the apportionments for Cheshire: 44 out of 448 apportionments specify crops under the state of cultivation. The data are widely scattered across the county. In Merseyside, Hale, Speke, Woolton, Toxteth and possibly other townships possess apportionments listing crops.[40] An extensive search through apportionments and maps for Lancashire might bring to light further examples. Crop data from apportionments and maps are doubly valuable, first, because crops are located within particular fields and their cultivation may be related to local variations in soils, slopes, drainage conditions and micro-climates, secondly, because field survey evidence may be compared with valuers' estimates recorded in tithe files. Crop maps afford a means of testing the reliability of the more abundant tithe-file evidence (see above chapter 4).

Tithe files

An important advance in the study of mid-nineteenth-century farming was made in the late 1950s when several workers turned their attention to the wealth of information on cropping, crop yields, prices, markets, livestock husbandry, manuring and soil characteristics contained in the tithe files. At the University of Leeds, G. R. J. Jones gained fresh insights into farming practices in the Welsh borderland from an examination of material in the files, while at University College London, a concerted effort by a group of graduate students disclosed the immense richness and diversity of a source that previously had been neglected.[41]

In 1961, M. C. Naish completed his thesis on the Hampshire chalklands.[42] He considered the quantitative information in the tithe files too generalised and for many places too inaccurate to serve as a basis for constructing maps. But the assistant commissioners' and local agents' descriptions of parishes were of great value. Among other features, they testified to the general poor quality of downland pasture at this period. They also described water meadows, often not identified on the maps or named in the apportionments, adjudging few to be of good quality. Elizabeth Burrell agreed with Naish that file data on cropping were not sufficiently accurate to provide material for cartographic representation. On the other hand, observations on crop rotations, yields, manures and fertilisers offered detailed and authoritative information on important aspects of farming in the Suffolk Sandlings.

Synoptic statements by assistant commissioners, such as the description of Aldringham-with-Thorpe in 1837, where 'everything in agriculture' was 'subservient to the flock', are particularly illuminating.[43] In a study of changing agriculture and the moorland edge in the North York Moors, John Chapman drew heavily upon the assistant commissioners' descriptions and explanatory remarks. These included some pertinent comments on over-stocking the moorlands in the early nineteenth century.[44] D. W. Gramolt also used the comments of the assistant commissioners to describe and explain farming practices on the Essex marshlands. The tithe files yield evidence for changes in land use resulting from disputes between farmers and rectors over tithe payments. At Mundon, a farmer laid down all his arable to marsh pasture because he considered the impropriate tithes too high.[45] Malcolm Postgate not only examined local differences in soil fertility and progress in agricultural improvements from assistant commissioners' statements but also compiled a map showing the distribution of seven crops in the Breckland of Norfolk and Suffolk.[46] In addition to general descriptions of agriculture in different parishes in the vale of Clwyd, Wynne Edwards constructed maps of the average annual rentable values of arable and pasture based on assessments in the tithe-file questionnaires.[47] Another study completed at University College London at this time, A. R. H. Baker's investigation of field systems in Kent, referred to the assistant commissioner's description of Deal.[48]

In 1963, E. A. Cox and B. R. Dittmer took a bold initiative in drawing maps covering very extensive areas from quantitative data on crops and livestock recorded in a more or less uniform manner in questionnaires in the tithe files. By abstracting data for large numbers of parishes and by grouping wide ranges of quantities into single size-categories, errors and deficiencies which had severely restricted the use of data at the scale of individual parishes were subsumed in broader descriptions at a regional level. With the aid of crop and livestock maps at a county or half-county scale crude contrasts between different land-use categories could be amplified and refined. In a study of the mid-nineteenth-century agricultural geography of Essex, Elwyn Cox first examined the qualitative, contemporary descriptions and appraisals of soils contained in the files.[49] He then related statements drawn from the files on the management of grassland to data from the apportionments and maps, comparing estimates of acreages of grass mown for hay in the file questionnaires with acreages under grass recorded in the apportionment summaries. An account of livestock farming is augmented with information from the files on livestock numbers and animal produce. In analysing regional variations in crop husbandry, the tithe files yield basic data for answering two crucial questions: they indicate where different crops were grown and what rotations were followed in different districts. From information abstracted from 296 tithe files for the whole county of Essex,

Cox mapped distributions of crops and fallows, rotations and yields. His map of barley as a percentage of arable (Fig. 7.2) highlights the contrast between agriculture on lighter soils in north and east Essex and that on the southern claylands, a distinction that is completely masked by the crude land-use classification of tithe apportionments and maps (see above Fig. 6.7). A survey of farming regions is illustrated by observations of assistant commissioners on leases, draining, embanking, manuring, marling, burning and building. This was the most extensive and also the most penetrating analysis of tithe file data to have been carried out up to 1963.

In north-west Wiltshire, Brian Dittmer found that the tithe file questionnaires contained not only information about crops grown on the arable but specified and enumerated animals grazed on the pasture.[50] Maps based on these statistics portray significant regional concentrations in livestock enterprises (Fig. 7.2). Dittmer also attempted to assess the quality of pasture in different localities by calculating stocking densities: the number of acres of meadow and pasture grazed per head of livestock. Finally, maps showing average annual rentable values indicate contrasts between arable and pasture land, confirming the superiority of farming productivity in the clay vales compared with the Cotswold region. Cox and Dittmer's most original contributions to the advancement of tithe studies were to demonstrate the value of mapping crop and livestock distributions over areas large enough to conceal the imperfections of individual parish data.

In 1965 appeared the first and still one of the most valuable introductions to the tithe files as a source for reconstructing the agricultural geography of mid-nineteenth-century England and Wales. Cox and Dittmer describe the contents of the files, critically assess the accuracy of the evidence and show, with reference to Essex and north-west Wiltshire, how the evidence may be interpreted.[51] They conclude that 'any work that uses the tithe maps and apportionments would be incomplete without reference to the tithe files and the unofficial, supplementary tithe documents in the county record offices'.[52] Critical evaluation of internal and external evidence has cast doubt on the previously unexamined presumption that land-use classifications and measurements of parcels in the apportionments are more reliable than the apportionment summaries or the file estimates. Research at University College London in the early 1960s showed that none of the sources of data is free from error or ambiguity.

In the 1960s, outside University College London, the tithe files were mostly consulted for descriptive comments. In 1965, W. S. G. Thomas submitted a thesis on south-west Carmarthenshire.[53] The 1801 crop returns were compared with tithe-file data for selected parishes to demonstrate a decline in the cultivation of barley and oats and a replacement of grains by potatoes and turnips. Neither Thomas' study nor Allison's thesis on the changing landscape of south-west Essex present farming data from the file

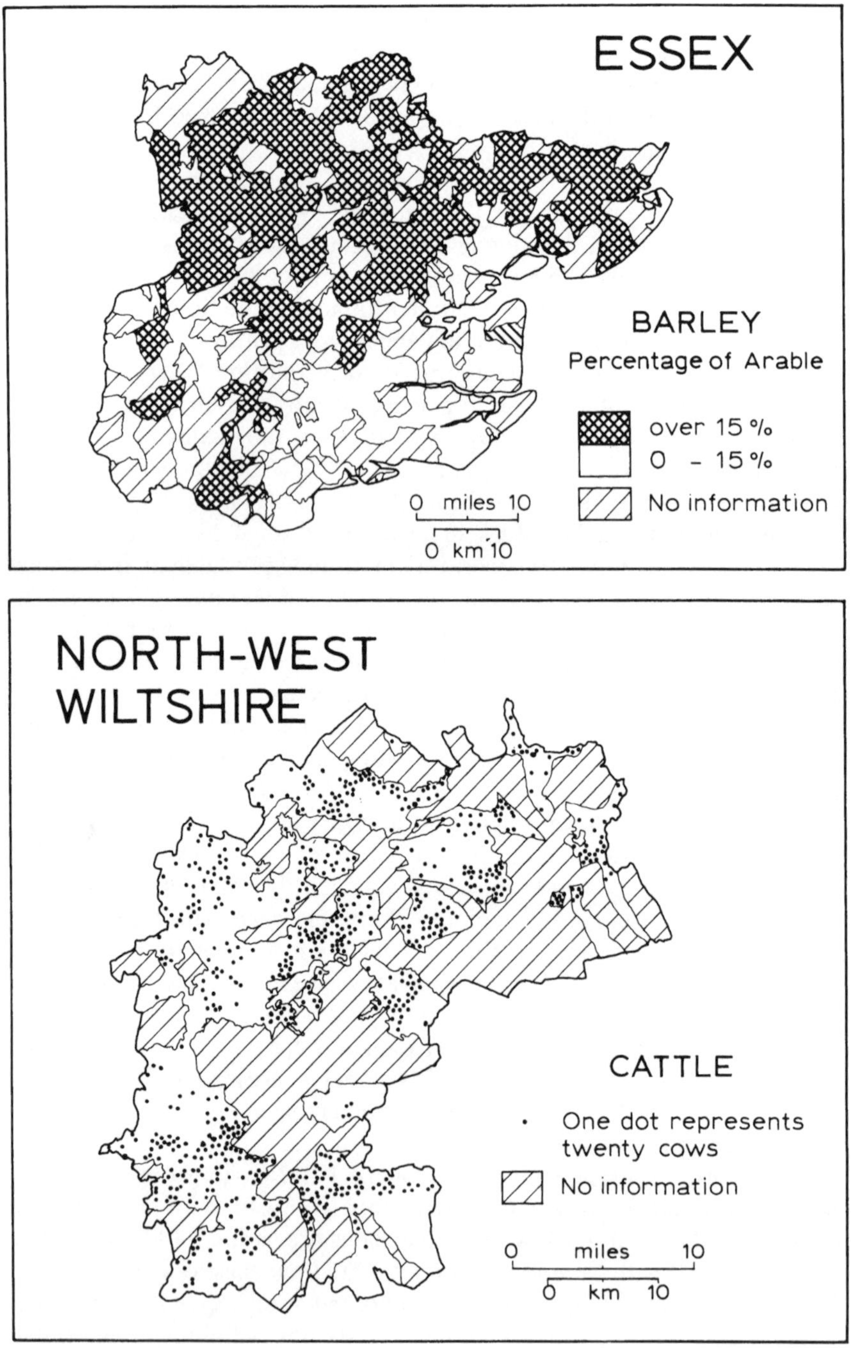

7.2 Barley in Essex and cattle in north-west Wiltshire. Source: E. A. Cox and B. R. Dittmer, 'The tithe files of the mid-nineteenth century', 1965.

questionnaires in cartographic form.[54] Allison drew extensively on the files for descriptive and explanatory comments, noting in particular the region's apparent diversity of crop rotations, all, however, variants on the same basic principle of four courses of winter cereal, spring cereal, leguminous crop and fallow. The tithe file data for the west Cleveland district of Yorkshire have been subjected to a most detailed and comprehensive examination by P. K. Mitchell.[55] Proportions of cropland growing wheat, oats, barley, pulses, seeds, turnips, potatoes and lying in fallow are mapped for each parish. The problem of variations in reliability is surmounted by using different symbols to represent data thought to be less reliable than the norm. Wheat growing and bare fallows still dominated courses of cropping over much of Cleveland, but longer rotations were gaining ground and livestock enterprises were expanding. Differences in crop acreages between 1801 and 1841 are measured and yields of grain crops over the period 1833–41 are analysed. An attempt is made to map crop-combination regions for the 1840s. Also in Yorkshire, in a survey of Wensleydale farming, R. T. Fieldhouse of the University of Leeds uses comments in the tithe files on acreages of corn crops and their yields, sheep breeds, cheese making and marketing, and the general question of the effect of tithe payments on agricultural improvement.[56] A reading of descriptions of local farming in the Cheshire tithe files helped Regina Porter frame her general conclusion that in the nineteenth century 'Cheshire farmers also adapted their stocking and cropping procedures in response to the expansion of the markets for produce. The productivity of livestock farming, both in terms of yield per cow and density of stock kept per acre increased, encouraged by the nearby markets for cheese and particularly liquid milk.'[57]

In 1973, John Chapman traced the changing extent of wastes in Monmouthshire from 1750 to the present.[58] The study maps the cultivated area from apportionment summaries and makes passing references to information from file questionnaires. Another thesis completed in 1973 by Alan Parton traces the encroachment of the metropolitan built-up area into Surrey from 1800 to 1870.[59] Choropleth maps are drawn from the apportionment summaries and a crop-combination map is constructed from data out of the file questionnaires.

A logical extension of Cox and Dittmer's argument about the accuracy of tithe file information has led to a critical reappraisal of the reliability and potential usefulness of all tithe survey data, whether drawn from maps, apportionments or files. Before embarking on yet another transcription of land-use categories from the apportionments, Roger Kain reviewed the state of tithe studies in 1973. He concluded that they had reached a cul-de-sac, and declared:

> Field-by-field studies of land use, estate and farm boundaries have yielded about as much useful information on the agricultural geography of 1840 as may be expected.

But the labour of scores of workers over the past forty years has not yet provided an adequate description, let alone an explanation, of the geography of the whole of rural England and Wales in the middle of the last century. A few problems concerning the reliability of the source remain unresolved but, setting these aside, it is the sheer bulk of the tithe material which is so daunting.[60]

To exploit the material efficiently and to draw statistically valid conclusions about the agricultural geography of Kent, it was decided to sample the data, sorting, tabulating, correlating and mapping the sampled statistics with the aid of a computer. The initial tasks of selecting and testing appropriate sampling procedures and setting up computer programmes were time-consuming but results have fully justified the effort and the preparatory work will not have to be repeated in future studies. Crop data for 174 sampling points, and ownership and farm-tenure data for 120 estates are processed and mapped by a SYMAP interpolation algorithm. A few maps are presented here to illustrate the scope of the investigation.

Analyses of cropping, crop yields and rotations are much more precise than in earlier studies. About 1840 barley occupied 11.3 per cent of the arable in Kent. Little was grown on heavy soils in the Weald, on Romney Marsh or in Sheppey or Hoo, but in Thanet and north-west Kent it occupied over one-fifth of the arable and produced high yields in those districts (Fig. 7.3). Barley was grown less extensively in 1801 than in 1840; indeed, it was the only grain crop to expand in acreage during the early nineteenth century, the largest increases occurring in north Kent and in the north-west. An examination of the distribution of individual crops associates particular crops with particular soils, but around 1840 monoculture, apart from hop and fruit growing, was negligible. Crops were grown in succession and their distribution may be explained as much by rotations as by soils. Assistant commissioners experienced great difficulties in identifying typical courses of cropping. Kentish farmers were staunchly individualistic and little restrained by leasehold covenants. A six-course rotation, generally turnips followed by a spring grain, clover and seeds, wheat, peas or beans and wheat again, was widely adopted in north and east Kent where it served as a basis for corn–sheep husbandry (Fig. 7.4). On light soils clover took the place of beans as a preparation for a second wheat crop, and on kind clay soils a second crop of beans was taken instead of clover. On the most productive soils in the county seven- or eight-shift rotations were followed; on the heaviest soils four or five courses prevailed, whilst on the poorest soils up to a quarter of the ploughland was laid down to fallow. The traditional Wealden three-course of wheat, beans and dead fallow had almost disappeared by 1840 but fallows still occupied large areas. In a county dominated by various systems of convertible husbandry it is unrealistic to separate ploughland from grassland management. As the cultivation of root and green crops expanded and increasing quantities of animal feeding stuffs were imported, livestock numbers increased without causing a correspond-

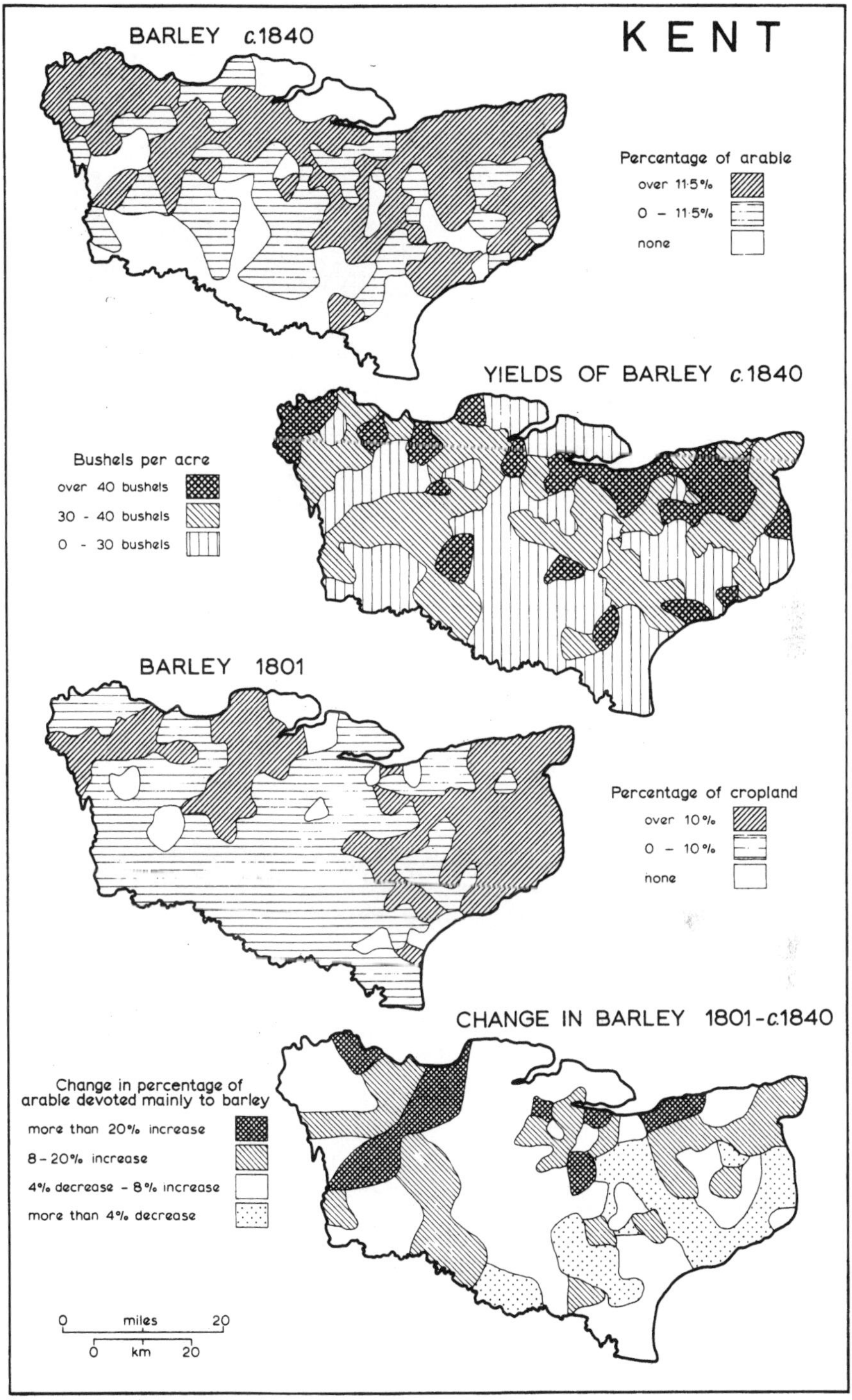

7.3 Barley in Kent.

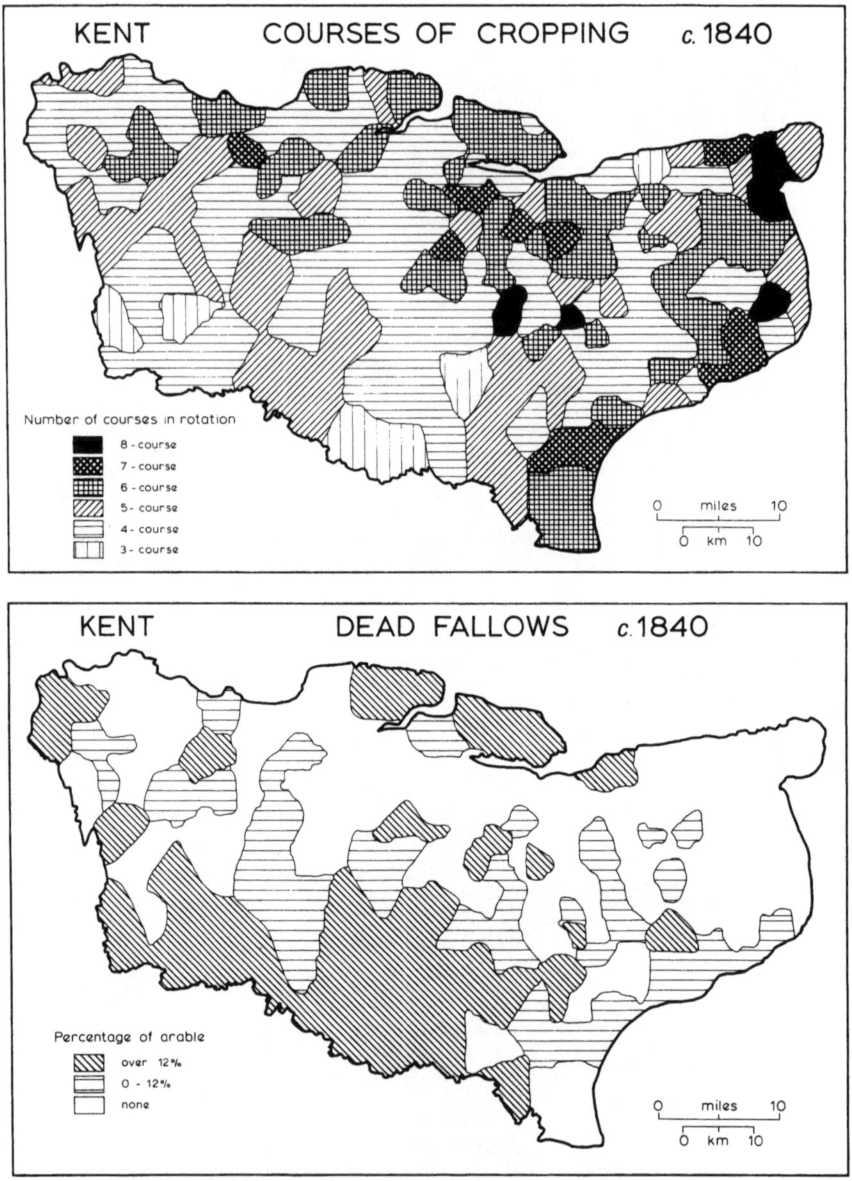

7.4 Crop rotations in Kent and bare fallow as a percentage of arable.

ing increase in the area of grassland. On the contrary, in Romney Marsh and elsewhere, considerable areas of permanent grass were broken up. Between 1840 and 1875 the proportion of the county under grass decreased from 32.1 per cent to 23.3 per cent. The general term 'grass' rarely appears in the tithe documents. Both files and apportionments distinguish between pasture,

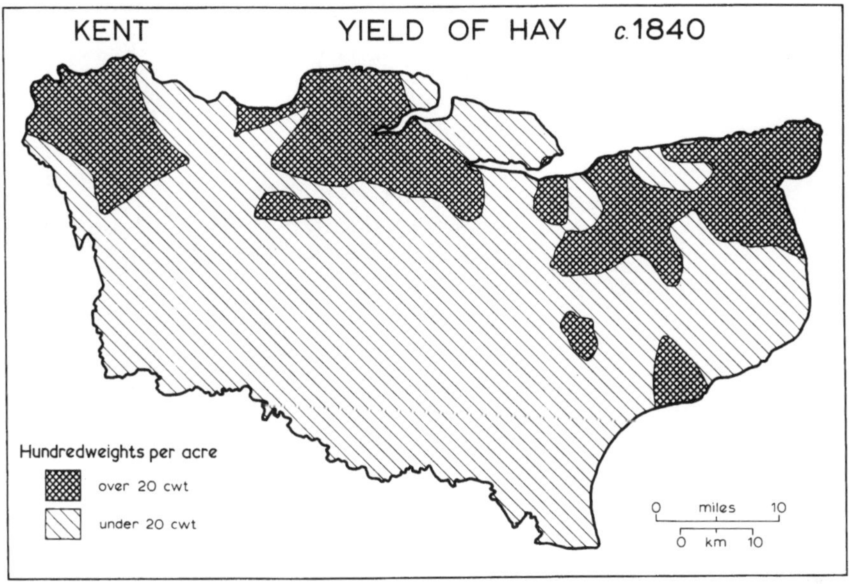

7.5 Yield of hay in Kent.

downland, meadow, marsh and saltings, each assessed on a different scale of rent-charges. Yields of hay clearly indicate that the most productive meadows lay in north Kent, whilst the highest proportions of pasture lay in and around Romney Marsh (Fig. 7.5).

Farming on light and heavy soils

In 1973, A. D. M. Phillips at the University of Keele published results of the first of two important projects using tithe survey data to test a hypothesis advanced by agricultural historians that agricultural practices, as reflected in rotations and yields, were relatively advanced on light soils in England, while clayland agriculture was still a backward sector in 1840.[61] For Staffordshire and later for Nottinghamshire he has mapped the assistant commissioners' classifications of soils, has plotted arable and grass as proportions of total acreages covered by apportionment summaries, has plotted wheat, barley, oats, turnips, beans and peas, clover and seeds, and fallow as percentages of arable recorded in the file questionnaires, has mapped crop yields and also the distribution of leading livestock enterprises[62] (Fig. 7.6). In both counties he recognises a clear dichotomy in agricultural practices about 1840 which is correlated with light and heavy land.

Light-land farming systems were more flexible and structurally better balanced. Mixed-farming practices had been widely adopted, giving farmers the choice of both cereals and livestock as saleable products. Heavy-land farming revealed many of the

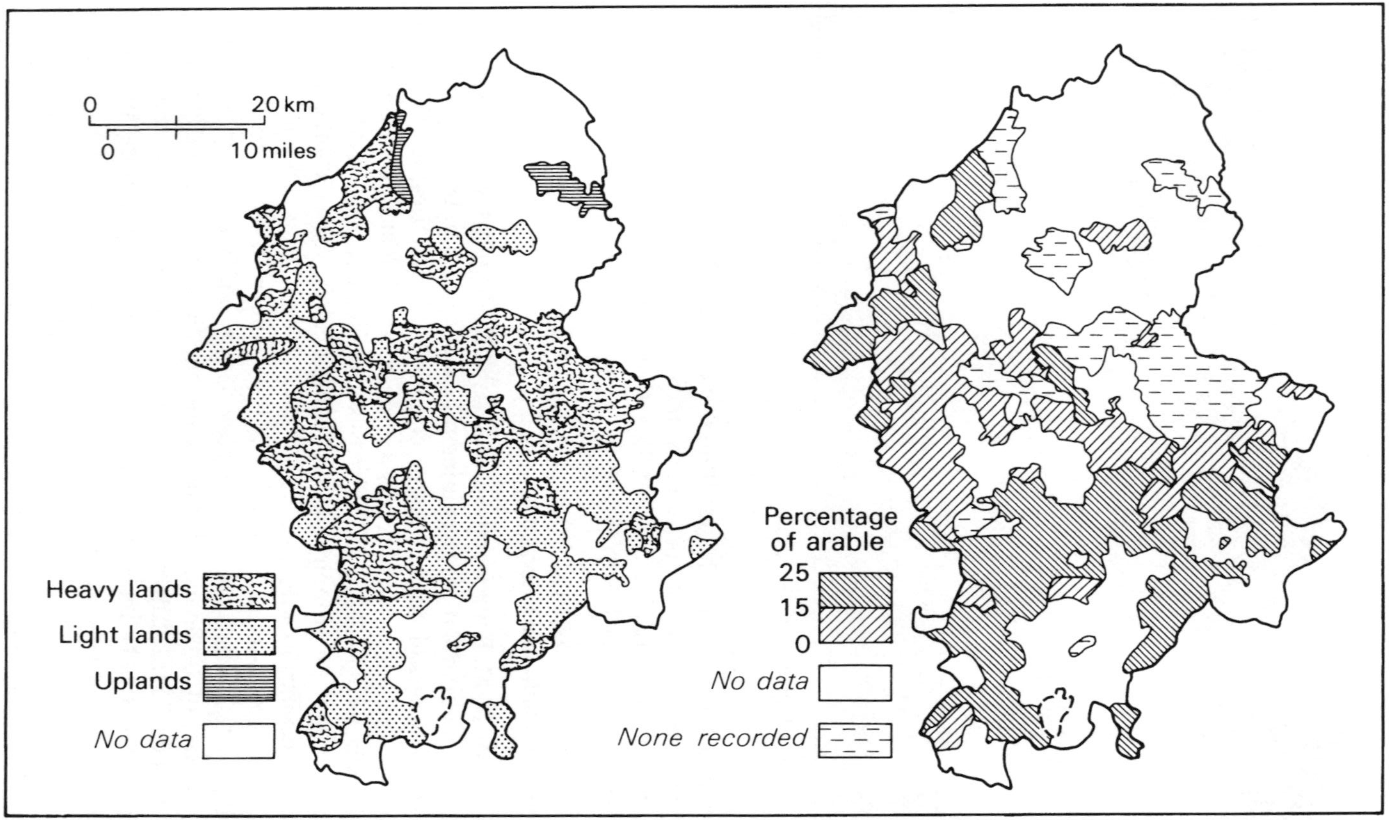

7.6 Soil divisions and distribution of barley in Staffordshire. Source: A. D. M. Phillips, 'A study of farming practices and soil types in Staffordshire around 1840', 1973.

features attributed to it in this period: wheat was the main cash crop, while fallows persisted and were areally significant.[63]

Phillips' findings have been confirmed in a recent study of Suffolk where evidence from tithe files not only highlights the differentiation of agricultural systems on light and heavy land but also suggests that there were distinctive farming systems on the claylands of southern Suffolk compared with farming on heavy soils elsewhere in the county. In respect of the proportions of bare fallows, pulse crops, roots and clover and yields of wheat, this southern area of clay soils appears no longer a laggard sector by about 1840 but rather its agriculture was more akin to that practised on light soils in the east of the county[64] (Fig. 7.7).

The fact that tithe file data on crops, yields, and livestock are available for small units (parishes in southern England and townships elsewhere) means that they are ideally suited for assisting in the delineation of types of farming areas. They permit, for example, a much more detailed analysis of farming systems than do the 1854 crop returns for Poor Law Unions (18 Unions in Suffolk compared with 355 tithe districts with reports on agreements, 269 of which contain data covering more than 90 per cent of tithe district area). The exploitation of the 1854 return, which was collected for some eleven counties, owes much to the work of J. P. Dodd.[65] For Norfolk his calculation of 62 per cent arable in 1854 corresponds almost exactly with J. E. G. Mosby's figure of 63 per cent arable in the 1840s calculated from the tithe surveys.[66] In a study of Gloucestershire, Dodd comments on the tithe files as follows: 'by virtue of the sheer volume of material to sift through, these impose limitations on the degree of use possible'.[67] There is no doubt that transcribing data from tithe files is time-consuming but it is also clear that boundaries of large Poor Law Unions rarely coincide with boundaries of either soil or types of farming regions. While providing an excellent basis from which to produce county-wide aggregations of crop acreages, acreages for Poor Law Unions do not permit the kind of detailed analysis of farming on different soil types pioneered by Phillips with tithe surveys.

Gardens, orchards and hops

Most studies using land-use data from the apportionments have been concerned with the overall structure of land use or with the extent of arable land, but a few studies have focused on specific categories of land use, mostly minor categories. At the time of the tithe surveys, market gardening was concentrated at the fringes of urban areas. In a thesis on the changing landscape of rural Middlesex, G. B. G. Bull observes 'an almost complete coincidence between the market-gardening belt of south-west Middlesex and the Flood Plain Terrace'.[68] A map based on apportionment listings

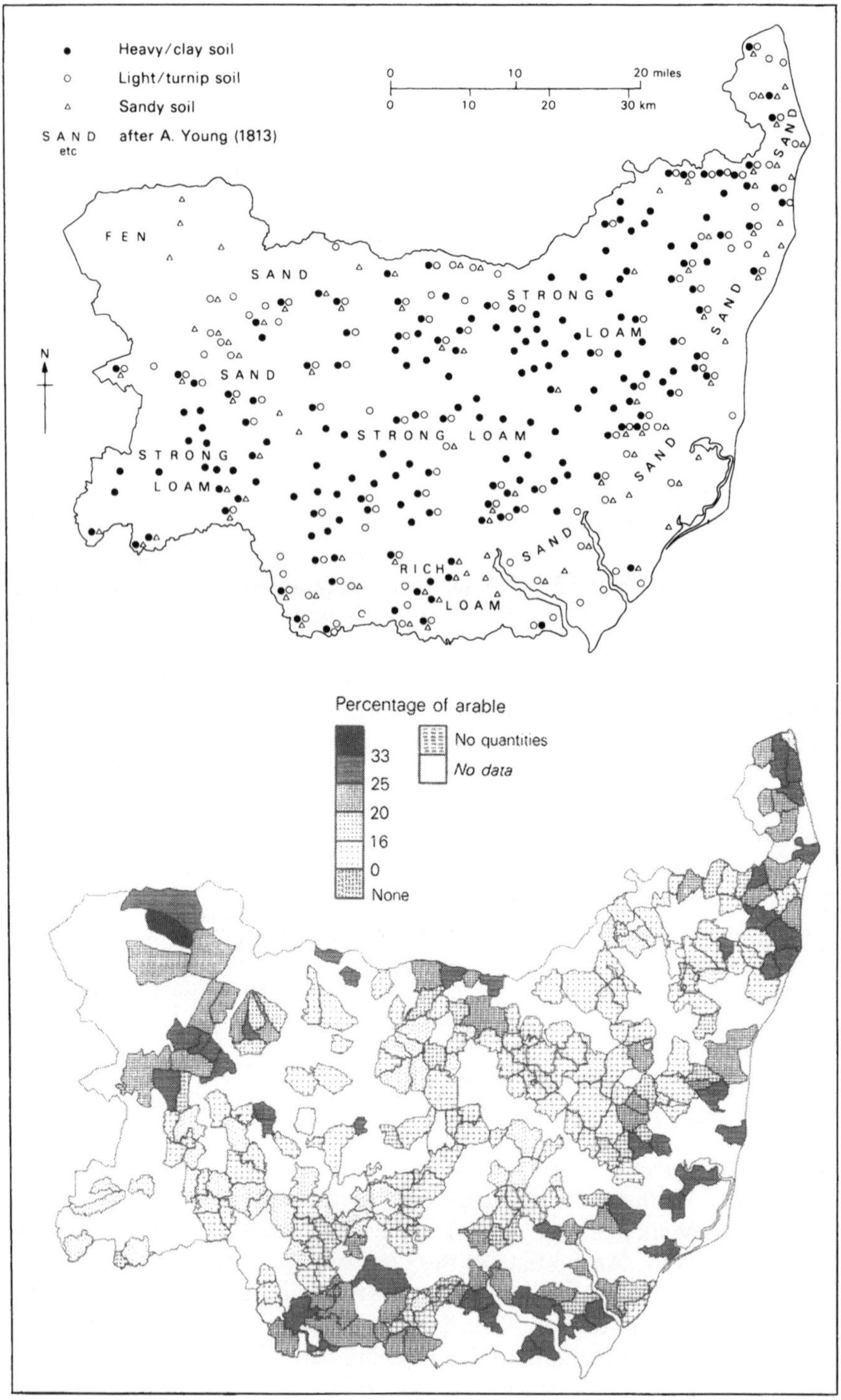

7.7 Soil types and distribution of turnips in Suffolk.

illustrates the distribution. Later studies by Parton and P. G. Atherall have extended the mapping of market gardens into Surrey, Kent and up the Lea valley in Essex.[69] M. R. G. Conzen uses evidence from tithe and other surveys to demonstrate the persistence of allotments and nurseries in the urban fringe belt of Alnwick in Northumberland, especially to the south-east of the town on light soils.[70]

Acreages of hop gardens, bearing an extraordinary rent-charge while in this state of cultivation, are often recorded at the end of a summary in a schedule of apportionment. Tithe apportionments for central Kent, examined by Bruce Winter, indicate that hops occupied less than 2 per cent of the area of most parishes and rarely more than 5 per cent.[71] A search through apportionments for the whole county by D. W. Harvey yields a very different result.[72] In several mid-Kent parishes, over 15 per cent of the area was under hops. The study correlates hop acreages with rental values, owner occupation, size of holding and distance from London. The location of hop gardens is noted in studies by Giles, Kain and Phillips.[73]

A major study of fruit cultivation in nineteenth-century Kent has been conducted by David Harvey, based partly on data from the tithe apportionments and maps.[74] He considers that the nineteenth century was the formative period for the Kent industry, relates changes in acreage and type of crop to changing and increasing national demand and uses the tithe surveys as a basis for a cross-sectional summary of the extent and distribution of the industry at about 1840.

An atlas of agriculture *c.* 1840

In 1978 Roger Kain and a small group of co-workers at the University of Exeter began to compile a computer atlas of agriculture in England from tithe file data with the support of a grant from the Social Science Research Council.[75] The production of such an atlas had often been mooted in the past but modern cartographic and analytical techniques have rendered it no longer a pipe-dream. A total of more than a thousand maps of key crop, yield and livestock distributions have been compiled for 31 counties with 20 per cent or more of their parishes/townships with tithe file data. All the quantitative data on crops and livestock have been transcribed from every tithe file and the complete data set is deposited in machine-readable form on magnetic tapes in the ESRC Archive.[76] An atlas of about 700 of the maps and an index is to be published as a companion volume to this book by Cambridge University Press. As work on the atlas has progressed, reports on material of unusual interest in Cornwall, Suffolk and Cheshire have been published.[77] Fig. 7.7 is an example of one of the county maps produced for the atlas and Fig. 7.8 is a map of the yield of oats in England and Wales based on data aggregated from all the extant parish/township figures. In Table 7.2, tithe district data on crop acreages and yields are aggregated and

Table 7.2 *Crop acreages as percentages of county arable acreages and crop yields, as recorded by assistant commissioners and local agents in their reports on tithe agreements. An explanatory key follows the table*

County	Estimated arable acres	Wheat a	Wheat b	Barley a	Barley b	Oats a	Oats b	Pulses a	Pulses b	Turnips a	Turnips b	Seeds a	Seeds b	Bare fallow
England														
Bedfordshire	177,557	22.8	22.7	13.2	31.4	7.4	36.9	13.6	21.8	11.4	3.5	16.5	21.0	16.0
Berkshire	263,956	24.0	24.2	15.6	34.7	8.4	40.3	5.7	29.4	17.7	2.7	23.3	22.7	5.0
Buckinghamshire	260,405	23.3	21.0	14.8	28.4	10.0	34.7	7.2	25.5	13.8	3.6	20.5	19.1	6.9
Cambridgeshire	367,370	23.1	22.4	10.8	30.0	13.6	39.6	5.5	23.9	5.0	3.4	28.2	21.5	10.8
Cheshire	180,344	31.4	20.6	3.6	29.4	32.1	26.2	–	–	2.5	2.7	–	–	16.4
Cornwall	206,096	32.7	17.9	29.5	28.2	10.2	31.0	–	–	–	–	–	–	–
Cumberland	–	–	–	–	–	–	–	–	–	–	–	–	–	–
Derbyshire	166,426	24.4	22.3	6.4	29.4	24.2	30.6	2.3	27.6	6.7	3.2	21.1	24.6	14.3
Devonshire	373,120	34.2	15.6	23.8	25.9	12.4	28.3	–	–	–	–	–	–	–
Dorset	135,599	34.0	20.4	25.1	29.7	11.0	32.8	–	–	–	–	–	–	–
Durham	341,828	22.4	17.1	4.6	27.3	22.3	26.7	2.5	20.4	5.1	3.1	21.8	19.0	20.8
Essex	768,156	25.6	24.6	18.5	34.5	6.2	41.1	8.8	25.8	7.3	3.2	17.9	22.8	15.5
Gloucestershire	257,805	31.6	19.6	20.5	27.1	1.2	27.5	6.4	23.2	–	–	–	–	–
Hampshire	688,576	20.6	21.5	15.2	27.9	5.7	35.0	2.2	24.3	16.4	2.5	33.8	17.6	4.4
Herefordshire	212,456	33.8	–	15.7	–	1.1	–	8.0	–	–	–	–	–	–
Hertfordshire	260,638	23.4	21.6	20.1	29.4	6.7	33.6	5.3	22.2	13.1	2.5	19.6	21.0	11.9
Huntingdonshire	114,986	23.7	22.0	16.6	31.4	6.0	35.1	11.3	22.8	2.7	2.6	15.8	22.5	21.1
Kent	505,030	27.6	25.6	13.3	33.7	10.6	39.1	11.0	26.2	12.0	3.0	19.2	22.1	5.7
Lancashire	330,290	26.8	22.9	2.2	28.3	27.5	30.7	2.6	24.0	–	–	–	–	–
Leicestershire	–	–	–	–	–	–	–	–	–	–	–	–	–	–
Lincolnshire	865,678	24.9	22.9	10.3	31.1	13.8	38.0	5.6	22.7	12.1	2.5	24.2	22.5	7.7
Middlesex	–	–	–	–	–	–	–	–	–	–	–	–	–	–
Monmouthshire	106,217	–	–	–	–	–	–	–	–	–	–	–	–	–
Norfolk	864,264	23.5	23.3	22.3	31.5	2.8	35.7	1.9	26.5	24.2	2.8	24.9	23.1	2.1

Northamptonshire	–	–	–	–	–	–	–	–	–	–	–	–	–	–
Northumberland	580,264	19.3	19.5	4.9	30.7	22.6	31.7	1.6	26.4	6.4	3.1	26.3	–	16.9
Nottinghamshire	–	–	–	–	–	–	–	–	–	–	–	–	–	–
Oxfordshire	264,041	24.0	22.9	17.2	33.3	6.6	38.7	7.0	30.0	13.9	2.5	23.9	21.3	7.1
Rutland	36,610	19.5	23.5	19.2	33.6	6.0	40.0	10.7	22.0	13.0	2.5	23.1	23.8	8.3
Shropshire	388,386	23.6	19.5	9.9	26.4	14.7	25.7	0.8	21.1	9.7	2.6	24.1	20.8	14.4
Somerset	255,943	34.1	21.0	17.3	31.3	2.7	30.8	6.2	29.6	–	–	–	–	–
Staffordshire	326,252	21.9	21.3	12.7	28.8	13.0	27.9	1.3	23.3	12.1	2.6	27.7	21.9	9.9
Suffolk	665,716	23.9	23.2	23.3	32.4	1.6	36.9	5.9	25.1	14.0	2.7	19.4	21.9	9.8
Surrey	233,401	23.2	20.9	9.2	31.6	14.3	35.6	5.0	22.9	9.3	2.8	25.2	20.7	12.7
Sussex	409,633	22.6	25.6	6.1	34.4	18.7	35.6	1.8	26.0	7.4	2.6	24.8	–	13.5
Warwickshire	268,049	22.4	23.1	12.0	32.6	10.3	37.4	7.4	24.3	7.7	3.0	26.6	22.8	12.8
Westmorland	–	–	–	–	–	–	–	–	–	–	–	–	–	–
Wiltshire	303,833	34.5	22.0	28.1	30.2	5.0	28.9	2.5	28.7	–	–	–	–	–
Worcestershire	201,722	36.2	22.5	9.5	34.0	1.7	32.0	14.8	19.0	–	–	–	–	–
York City & Ainsty	1,247	–	–	–	–	–	–	–	–	–	–	–	–	–
Yorkshire, E. Riding	503,821	22.0	18.6	10.4	28.0	16.6	32.5	5.5	19.6	10.3	2.7	21.2	2.09	13.6
Yorkshire, N. Riding	434,768	23.6	19.4	7.5	30.4	17.0	29.4	4.8	18.6	9.1	2.9	19.0	23.6	16.9
Yorkshire, W. Riding	512,276	22.6	21.0	13.6	30.5	12.1	33.2	2.9	22.3	12.5	2.9	22.2	21.1	11.5
Wales														
Anglesey	66,978	9.4	–	19.7	–	43.8	–	–	–	–	–	–	–	–
Brecon	84,007	–	–	–	–	–	–	–	–	–	–	–	–	–
Caernarvonshire	51,724	–	–	–	–	–	–	–	–	–	–	–	–	–
Cardiganshire	126,772	–	–	–	–	–	–	–	–	–	–	–	–	–
Carmarthenshire	157,725	–	–	–	–	–	–	–	–	–	–	–	–	–
Denbighshire	92,167	24.5	16.0	24.9	20.0	31.5	32.0	0.8	14.0	–	–	–	–	–
Flintshire	56,550	32.0	–	18.9	–	28.2	–	1.3	–	–	–	–	–	–
Glamorgan	150,393	–	–	–	–	–	–	–	–	–	–	–	–	–
Merionethshire	24,832	13.9	–	18.4	–	47.0	–	–	–	–	–	–	–	–
Montgomeryshire	71,379	26.1	–	20.9	–	33.0	–	1.3	–	–	–	–	–	–

County	Estimated arable acres	Wheat		Barley		Oats		Pulses		Turnips		Seeds		Bare fallow
		a	b	a	b	a	b	a	b	a	b	a	b	
Pembrokeshire	101,170	–	–	–	–	–	–	–	–	–	–	–	–	–
Radnorshire	38,021	–	–	–	–	–	–	–	–	–	–	–	–	–

(i) The symbol '–' is used where data are unavailable, where individual crops cannot be distinguished, and where data relate to very small samples (fewer than 10 per cent of tithe districts).
(ii) County units are those employed by the Tithe Commission.
(iii) The estimate of arable acreage in each county is obtained by multiplying the total acreage enumerated in tithe file reports on agreements by a weighting factor equivalent to the ratio of county area: sample area. County areas are those calculated from tithe maps under the direction of R. K. Dawson and recorded in the 1851 census of population.
(iv) Under columns 'a' are the mean percentages of the sample sown with each crop or left in bare fallow in the years of average, 1829–35. Sample sizes vary for each crop; samples smaller than 10 per cent of districts are omitted.
(v) Under columns 'b' are the mean yields for each crop. For wheat, barley, oats and pulses these are in bushels/acre; for turnips the figure is an expression of the titheable value in £/acre; for seeds in cwts/acre.
(vi) In all the Welsh counties and in Cornwall, Devonshire, Dorset, Gloucestershire, Herefordshire, Monmouthshire, Somerset and Worcestershire, arable land excludes seed crops. (See chapter 3: 'quantitative data on farming in tithe file reports on agreements'.)

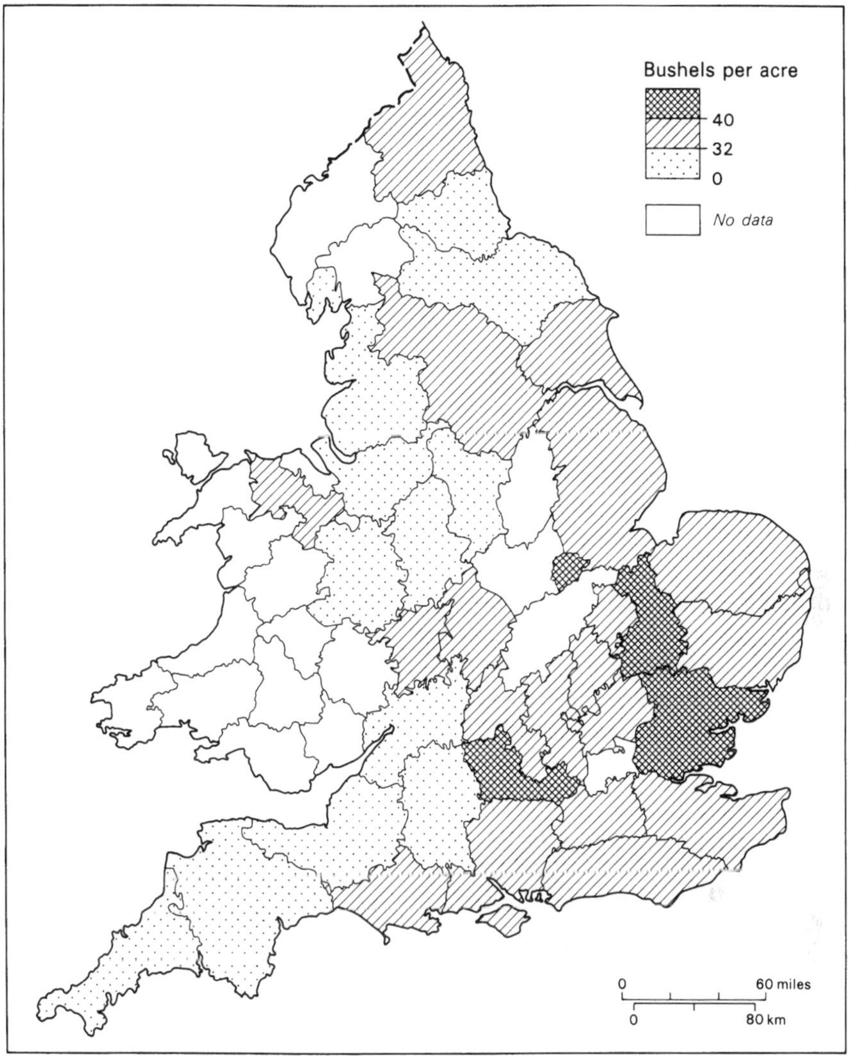

7.8 Yield of oats in England and Wales.

percentaged to form a set of county statistics. These are being compared with the 1801 Crop Return and post-1866 Agricultural Statistics by Dr Mark Overton for his contribution to the *Atlas of the Industrial Revolution*, a project jointly sponsored by the Economic History Society and the Historical Geography Research Group.

8

Farms, landowners and rural social structure

One of the more recent developments in tithe studies is the analysis of landownership and occupation data from the surveys. Agricultural historians find apportionment lists of occupiers of every plot of titheable land valuable in understanding patterns of land use and crops. Social historians use tithe surveys when tracing the descent of manors and estates, in studies of landowners and the structure of landowning society and, most recently, for house repopulation and community reconstruction. Urban historians find tithe surveys which pre-date much nineteenth-century urban expansion a useful source for reconstructing pre-urban cadasters in investigating the effect of landownership on urban morphology.

The layout of farms

Using a modern base map in conjunction with a tithe map and apportionment, it is possible to reconstruct boundaries of farm units *c.* 1840 by locating all tithe areas, usually fields, listed under the name of each occupier in the apportionment. As this is a laborious task, most researchers have employed some form of sampling, usually selecting a few 'typical' farms. A range of farm layouts *c.* 1840 is illustrated in Fig. 8.1. The two extremes of fragmentation are indicated by the 63-acre holding of William Hussey in the open fields of Winterborne Kingston, Dorset and the compact, ring-fence farm of Reach Court at Cliffe in east Kent. Oxenhoath and East Court farms, also in Kent, display intermediate states of fragmentation.

J. E. G. Mosby produced one of the first analyses of the relationship between land use and farm layout in his report on the Land Utilisation Survey of Norfolk.[1] In a section dealing with specific farm types he produced a series of land-use maps of Summerfield Farm in the Good Sand region at various dates, one being at the time of the tithe survey of 1845. Jean East advanced the method in 1947 by careful selection of sample farms to ensure that they are representative.[2] She identified 'types of farming' regions in the

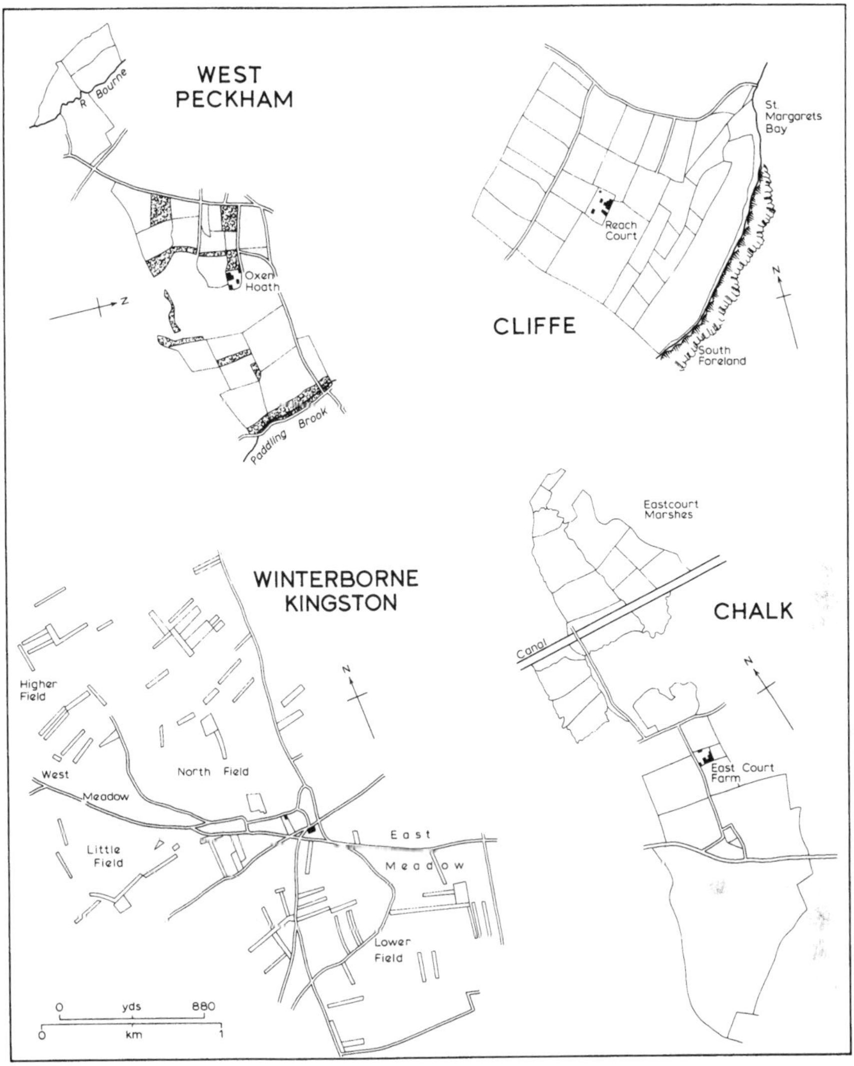

8.1 Farm layout at Winterborne Kingston, Dorset, and West Peckham, Cliffe and Chalk in Kent.

west midlands and within these regions studied sample parishes, producing maps of farm boundaries for comparison with the National Farm Survey of 1941. A further series of maps summarises changes in farm boundaries around urban areas.

A review has been made of sources available for the study of changes in field and farm boundaries by J. T. Coppock in which the value of the tithe surveys is discussed. As an example, a map of farm boundaries for the parish of Tewin is constructed (Fig. 8.2). When interpreting such a map Coppock cautions that 'farm boundaries do not necessarily coincide with parish boundaries, and some of the apparently small holdings around the borders of the parish are in fact parts of farms which lie mainly in adjacent parishes'.[3]

The first study concerned with farm patterns over a wider area was carried out by D. H. C. Bennett.[4] He presents a map of farms in west Pembrokeshire from the tithe surveys and recognises two major categories, 'townreds' or lands of intermixed ownership and occupation associated with clustered settlement, and 'isolated farmsteads', lands of consolidated ownership and occupation with single farmsteads. For each parish he provides a map of farm boundaries and a description of fragmentation and consolidation of farms about 1840. In a search for explanations, he compares farm boundaries on the few eighteenth-century maps of the area with those of the tithe surveys, indicating a trend towards consolidation of holdings in the townreds at the same time as compact holdings were being sub-divided. Both processes imparted greater uniformity to the settlement pattern. Finally, he compares farms in the 1840s with those of 1954, clearly demonstrating effects of rural depopulation and amalgamation of holdings. A similar study has been conducted by J. C. Grove.[5] In addition, by a simple, effective and so far unique method he maps the size of holdings in west Gower. He locates each farmstead by reference to the tithe map and then allocates to each a symbol according to a size classification.

Also in Wales, Elwyn Davies has investigated a system of seasonal transhumance which survived into the nineteenth century, particularly in the northern counties. He draws evidence on the layout of the *hendre* (permanent farm on the lowland) and *hafod* (summer dairy in the mountains) from tithe surveys. A detailed study of tithe surveys of Llanrug and Landwrog in Caernarvonshire reveals those *hafodydd* which had developed into independent farms by the mid-nineteenth century.[6] A map of the Hiraethog Moors of Denbighshire compiled from tithe surveys of its constituent parishes indicates surviving *hendre* and *hafod* farms about 1840; Davies contends that 'the tithe survey which was carried out in the middle of the nineteenth century provides an almost complete coverage of the agricultural holdings in the country and make it possible to illustrate *hafodydd, hafotai* and *lluestydd* in their various forms and stages of development'.[7]

Many of the agricultural geographies reviewed in chapters 6 and 7 include sections dealing with the layout of farms, usually placed after a discussion of land use and cropping patterns. M. J. Frost follows the method of analysis by parishes set out by Coppock for a study of land-use changes in the Mole valley of Surrey.[8] He presents maps of farms at different periods, one set derived from the tithe surveys. W. S. G. Thomas, in a chapter of his thesis on agriculture in south-west Carmarthenshire based on studies of sample farms, looks back at the outline of these farms on maps drawn from the tithe

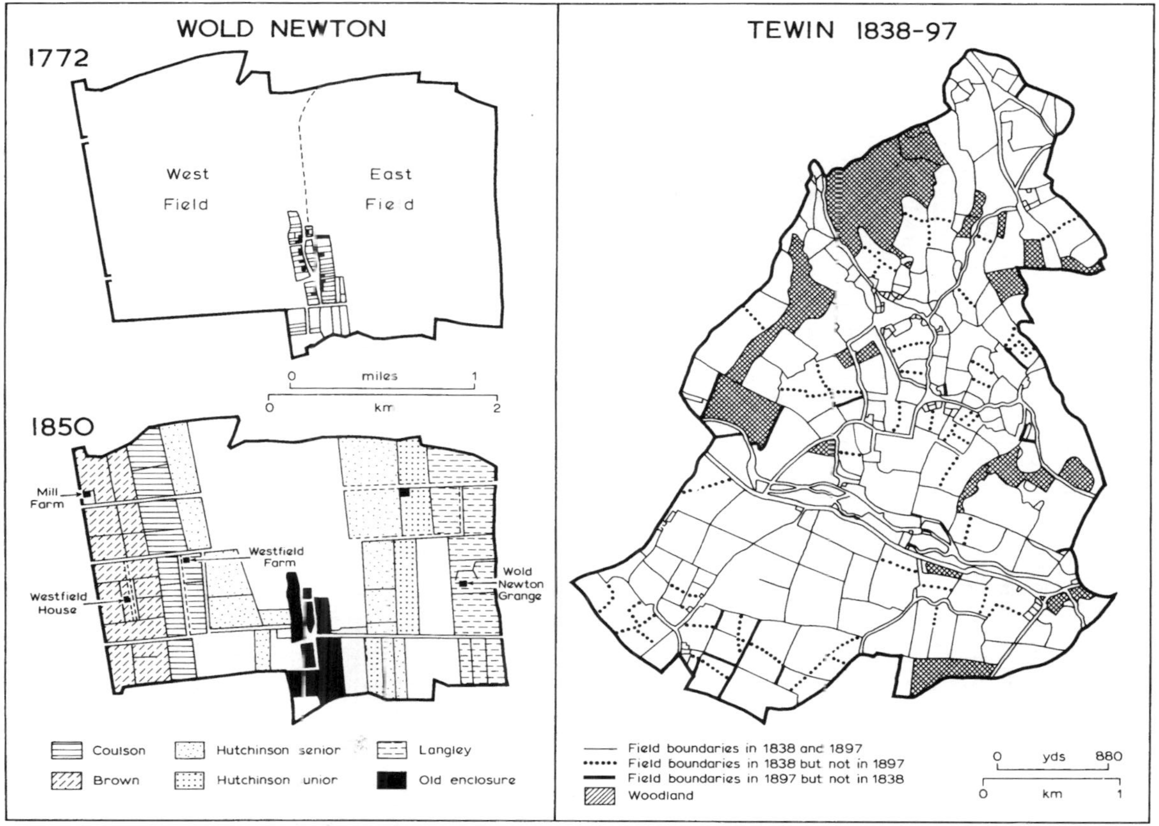

8.2 The pattern of farms after enclosure at Wold Newton, Yorkshire, and field and farm boundaries at Tewin, Hertfordshire. Sources respectively: M. B. Gleave, 'Dispersed and nucleated settlements in the Yorkshire Wolds, 1770–1850', 1962; and J. T. Coppock, 'Changes in farm and field boundaries in the 19th century', 1958.

survey to show changes between 1841 and 1961.[9] M. C. Naish examines farm layout and size in 9 sample parishes, Elizabeth Burrell produces 2 farm maps and one of dispersed holdings in Snape, Suffolk, and John Chapman one of 3 sample holdings in the parish of Lastingham, Yorkshire.[10] Brian Dittmer combines a study of sample farms with maps showing selected farm holdings in 5 tithe districts, while D. W. Gramolt produces a map of land occupation in 5 east-Essex parishes.[11] John Chiplen discusses the rural landscape of the Blackmore Vale physical region by physical region with some description of the layout of sample farms in each.[12]

Enclosure, particularly parliamentary enclosure, usually produced sweeping changes in the layout of holdings in a parish (Fig. 8.2). The enclosure-award map shows a planned landscape, the landscape as it was intended to be; whether this landscape actually emerged depended on various factors, but particularly on sales and exchanges of land after the award.[13] In parishes where tithe was not extinguished at enclosure, a tithe commutation map of the 1840s can be profitably studied in conjunction with an earlier enclosure award.[14] Of one Montgomeryshire parish, J. G. Thomas says: 'Twenty years had elapsed between the Award and the date of the tithe survey, so that the evidence of the tithe map and apportionment will show how the award was working out in practice, and also whether any marked changes had occurred since it was made.'[15] A map of farm units in 1846 shows a great contrast in form between early enclosed lands and farms created by parliamentary enclosure, a conclusion supported by J. M. Powell's later study of the same county.[16] Also in north Wales, Colin Morgan has used tithe survey data to gauge the effect of parliamentary enclosure on former commons in Caernarvonshire and Merioneth.[17] With the aid of a sample of tithe surveys he demonstrates the consolidation of farms. From a comparison of tithe maps and enclosure maps he considers that farms emerged in three ways: some were entirely new creations, some had their origin in pre-enclosure squatters' holdings which maintained their identity to form small farms post-enclosure, and a third group evolved by the addition of land to a pre-existing nucleus.

All these studies are characterised by non-quantitative analyses of layout and farm shape. In a study of Kentish farming, Roger Kain uses some simple quantitative indices, notably Cole's coefficient of compactness to measure shape and a fragmentation index measured by the ratio of land contiguous to a farmstead to total farm area.[18] Tables 8.1 and 8.2 illustrate some results of this study of 87 randomly selected farms.[19] Table 8.1 suggests that in Kent in the 1840s there was a consistent relationship between farm shape and the proportion of arable, pasture and woodland. The proportion of arable land on farms increases as compactness of the farm land increases, whilst the highest proportions of pasture are found on the least compact farms. The proportion of woodland on farms consistently declines as compactness

Table 8.1 *The shape of farms and their land use in Kent c.1840*

Cole's shape index	Mean percentages of farm under:					
	arable	pasture	wood	hops	fruit	buildings
Under 25.0	48.3	41.7	4.0	1.4	0.5	2.2
25.1–50.0	53.8	34.9	3.1	2.6	0.5	2.4
Over 50.0	70.6	23.6	1.2	0.7	0.6	2.9

Table 8.2 *The fragmentation of farms and their land use in Kent c.1840*

Fragmentation index	Mean percentages of farm under:					
	arable	pasture	wood	hops	fruit	buildings
Under 25.0	46.8	46.9	0.7	0.6	0.1	2.2
25.1–50.0	62.7	27.9	2.9	2.8	0.0	1.1
50.1–75.0	47.9	34.9	6.4	6.6	3.0	1.6
Over 75.0	55.0	32.9	4.4	2.0	0.4	1.9

increases. Hops, fruit and land covered by buildings, however, show little relationship with farm shape. With the crude classification of land use provided by the tithe apportionments, no clear relationship between land use and fragmentation of farms emerges in Table 8.2. Very fragmented farms with less than 25 per cent of land contiguous to the farmstead perhaps form a separate group characterised by high proportions of pasture.

In another study based in Kent, Clare Lukehurst has worked with a contiguous block of 36 parishes in the area of the Stour marshes.[20] She has compiled a complete farm-boundary map of the area, analyses the fragmentation of farms and the relative importance of marsh to upland farms, and compares farm boundaries of 1840 with those of 1964. Counties such as Kent with almost complete tithe survey coverage permit an examination of questions which can be but partially answered or not even addressed in areas where documentation is incomplete. A case in point is the large-scale study of connections between landholdings in complementary farming ecosystems, as between marshes and uplands, for example. The unique record of land occupiers that tithe surveys provide has enabled Roger Kain to examine the extent of the practice of running Romney Marsh holdings in conjunction with land in the Kentish uplands.[21] Using a computer, he compares names of farmers with holdings in the marsh with a list of names of all land occupiers in Kent. He concludes that there were 232 holdings of more than 10 acres in Romney Marsh and that more than half the marshland was held by persons occupying land outside it. The pattern of these linkages is illustrated on Fig. 8.3. This shows that, although most upland parts of holdings linked with Romney Marsh were situated south and east of a line through Capel-le-Ferne, Waltham, Charing, Cranbrook and Hawkhurst, some lay much further afield in the western Weald. It also shows that upland parts of holdings tended to be localised on particular soil types; there is no straightforward decline in the number of linkages with distance away from Romney Marsh. Soil types identified on the map are those recognised by assistant tithe commissioners and recorded in the tithe files. Over three-quarters of all upland parts of holdings were located in the Ragsoil and Wealden areas where the proportion of grassland to arable was above the county average. These areas were also relatively accessible to Romney Marsh compared, for example, with the clayland area of north Kent where there were also extensive tracts of upland pasture. Some qualitative evidence in the tithe files suggests that these north-Kent uplands bore a similar relationship to the Thames and Stour marshes as the Weald did to Romney Marsh, a relationship confirmed by Clare Lukehurst's independent analysis.[22]

The tithe surveys permit identification of landholders bearing the same name and enable acreages to be calculated but they do not provide precise information on the relationship between separate parts of holdings. It is likely that some of the hypothesised fragmented holdings on Fig. 8.3 were run as quite separate farms but the tithe surveys do not illuminate this point. Nor is it possible to be certain that quite separate individuals who happen to bear the same name have not entered the analysis. Brian Short has also conducted a highly quantitative study of farm fragmentation with tithe-survey data for 13 Kent and Sussex High Weald parishes.[23] He entered these with further data from sale catalogues, estate surveys and other manuscript sources.

Farm size and tenure

From the summaries to schedules of apportionment a picture of sizes of holdings in a parish can be obtained. Though a tedious task if a group of parishes is being studied – unless computerised data storage and sorting procedures are available – it is possible to extend the scope of enquiry to regional or county scales, providing a fairly complete coverage of tithe surveys is available. Table 8.3 provides an example; it is a summary of the size of farms in Kent about 1840. The tithe surveys show that some 900,000 acres enumerated in the tithe surveys were divided into 6,100 holdings of 10 acres and over. The largest holding in the hands of a single person was 3,500

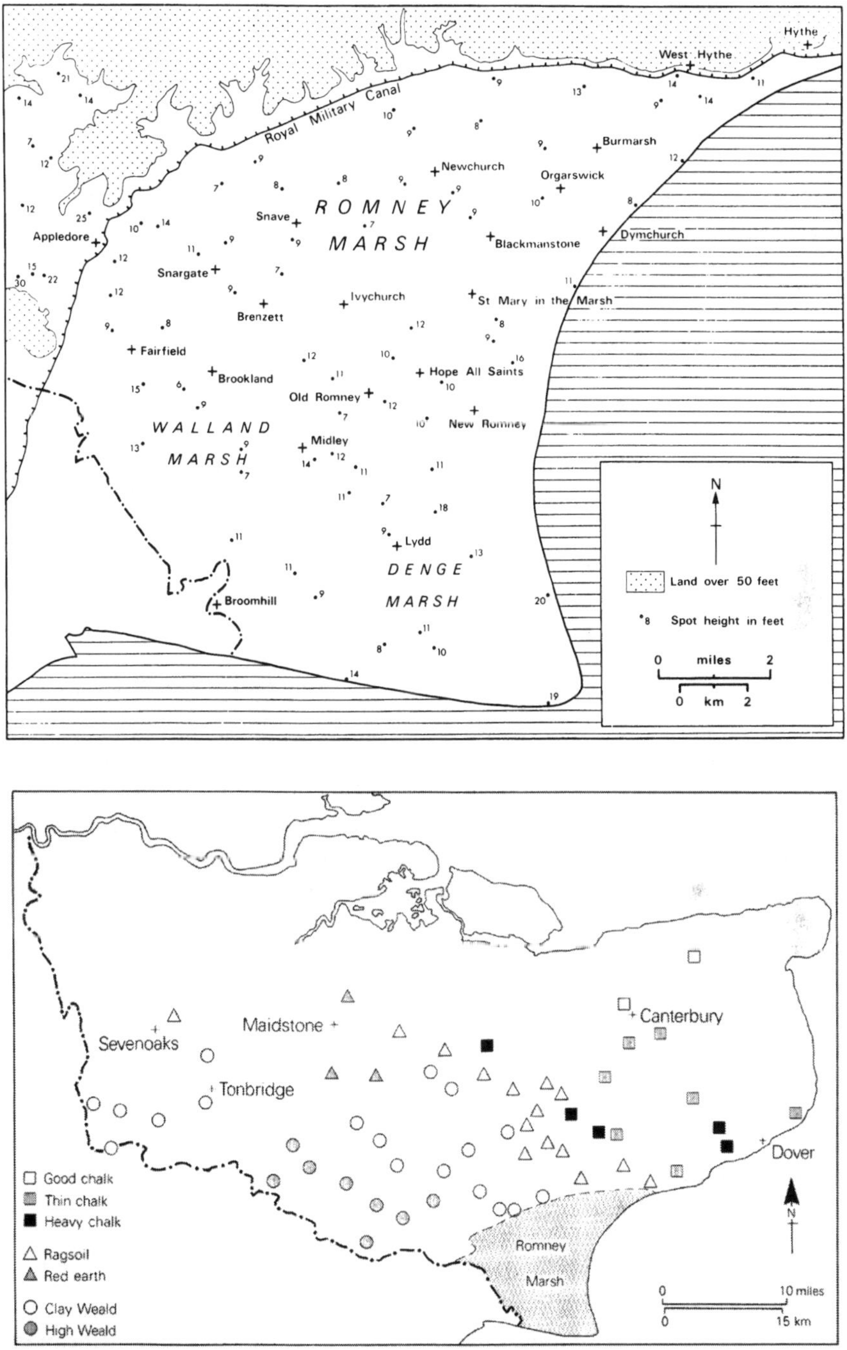

8.3 The topography of Romney Marsh and the farming links between marsh and upland Kent.

Table 8.3 *The size of farms in Kent c.1840*

Size class (acres)	Number of farms	Total acreage	Percentage of total acreage	Average size in acres
10–50	2,670	64,102	7.1	24
51–100	1,072	77,994	8.7	72
101–500	2,016	440,587	49.0	218
501–1,000	250	169,959	18.8	679
1,001–2,000	75	103,077	11.5	1,374
over 2,000	17	43,917	4.9	2,583
Totals	6,100	899,636	100	147

acres. The average size of farms, excluding those less than 10 acres, was just under 150 acres. Thirty-four per cent of farms were in the 101–500 acres size group and their operators occupied 49 per cent of the county. Nearly two-thirds of the county was farmed in units of less than 500 acres. Although reports of the assistant tithe commissioners in the tithe files are mainly concerned with soils, crops and yields, some did comment on the size of farms. They also observed that most Kentish farms were of 100 to 300 acres and that farms of more than 350 acres were exceptional.

This example illustrates the potential value of the tithe surveys as a datum for studies concerned with the size of farms. Few of these cover large areas; most are concerned with farm size in single, or a series of 'typical' parishes. Most of the studies listed in notes 8–17 above analyse farm size as well as farm shape using data from the tithe surveys. Additionally, farm sizes are reconstructed in many recent volumes of the *Victoria History of the Counties of England.*[24] In some local studies the number of farms in various size categories is listed, little more than a transcript of tithe apportionments. Indeed, some local historians go no further than to print lists of occupiers' and owners' names.[25] On the other hand, R. E. Sandell's transcript of Wiltshire tithe apportionments is at an entirely different scale.[26] He lists names and acreages of all those holding more than 50 acres from every one of the county's tithe surveys, providing a valuable research tool for future historians. More interesting still is the work of those who use tithe surveys as a quantitative base to be related to earlier, fragmentary information on farm sizes. Amongst local historians, V. H. T. Skipp was an early pioneer of the careful combination of tithe survey and earlier data on farm sizes.[27]

One of many farm studies is that of Francis Leeson who located a map of Coulsdon, Surrey, made in 1762 which he compared with the 1837 tithe survey.[28] Pre-1836 tithing maps and records are also valuable comparative sources where they are extant. Michael Havinden has compared a tithe map of East Lockinge, Berkshire, made in 1769 with the 1840 tithe survey and other documents to measure the consolidation of farms over the period.[29] No study of farm size, consolidation, or tenure can now ignore the tithe survey where this is extant.

Landed estates and their owners

The record of names of landowners and acreages of their estates which tithe surveys contain is unequalled for any other period of our history. At a local scale, the body of tithe surveys represents some 11,800 fairly comprehensive parish and township land inventories. At a county scale, in those parts of the country where tithe coverage is fairly complete, the tithe apportionments are a similarly comprehensive regional cadaster. For students with interests as diverse as genealogists and econometricians, they are an equal fund of data on people who owned land around the year 1840. Their contribution varies from providing perhaps one single piece of information in a complicated unravelling of the descent of a particular manor, or perhaps a single statistic of the number of acres owned by an individual whose changing landowning fortunes are being examined, to one of providing many millions of individual items of data for processing and aggregating by computer. Examples of the former include Russell Howes' study of Joseph Pitt, a Gloucestershire landowner; that of J. D. Marshall on the Cavendish family in Furness; Sue Farrant's work on estates in the Sussex Ouse Valley; Wyn Ford's and L. W. Lloyd's respective reconstructions of the descent of Boltro Farm, Cuckfield, from 1663–1966 and Corsygedol, the principal estate of Ardudwys in Merioneth; and the Architects in Agriculture Group's study of the Coleshill–Buscot estate in Oxfordshire.[30] Many studies in agrarian history include maps of estate boundaries for single parishes or small groups of parishes compiled from tithe surveys in a similar manner to those of farm boundaries described above.[31] Aileen Carpenter has reviewed the value of such maps and the utility of tithe surveys as a source of estate boundary data.[32] Fig. 8.4 is a map of parish, estate, holding and field boundaries in Shoreham, Kent, reconstructed from the 1842 tithe survey. In 1961 Malcolm Postgate pioneered the use of tithe surveys to produce maps of landownership over wider areas.[33] His map of landownership in the Breckland *c.*1840 is reproduced here as Fig. 8.5. In his account of the composition and management of estates he uses tithe apportionments to work out the percentage of land held by great landowners.

A map of estate boundaries is both laborious to construct and limited in its usefulness. There is little justification in producing maps of boundaries for this date simply because tithe surveys make it possible. Regional variations of sizes of landed estates can be shown more easily and more precisely by plotting apportionment data at a parish scale. One of the simplest ways of showing such variations is to divide the number of owners of land in a parish

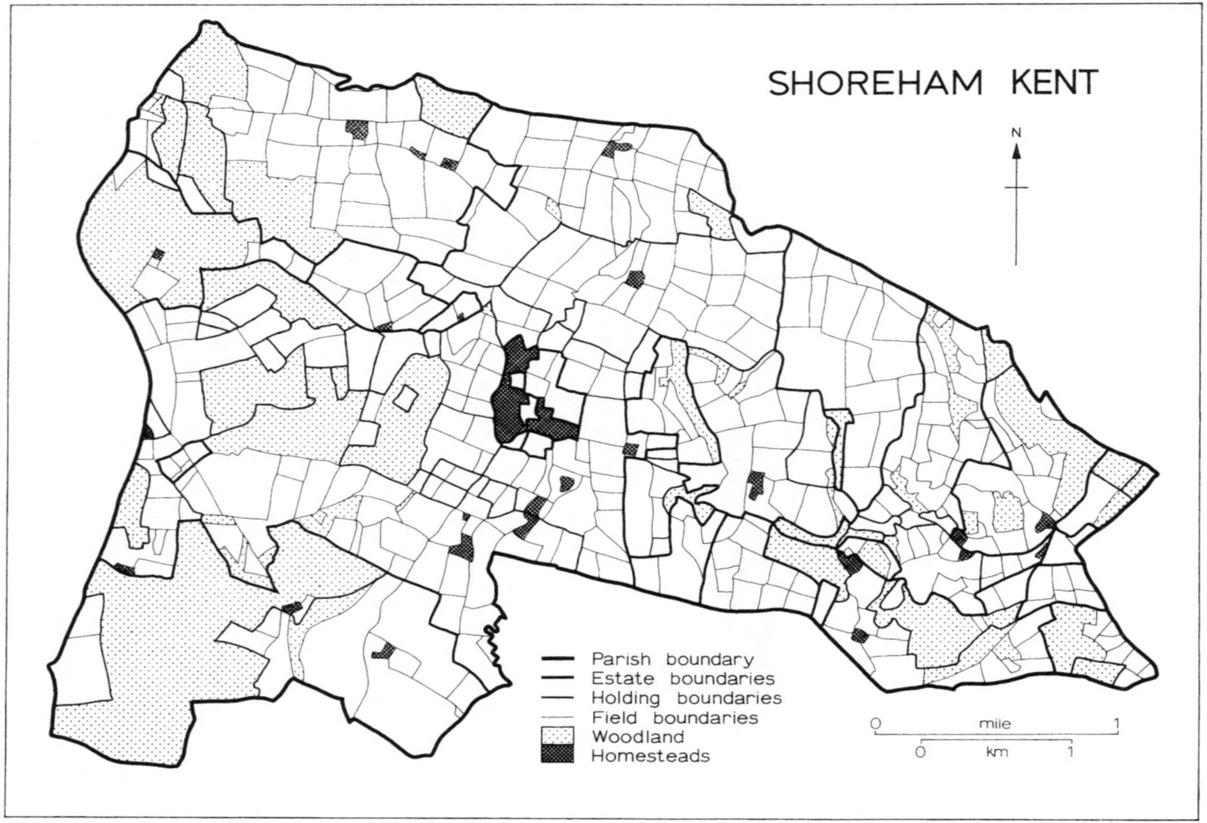

8.4 Field, farm and estate boundaries at Shoreham, Kent.

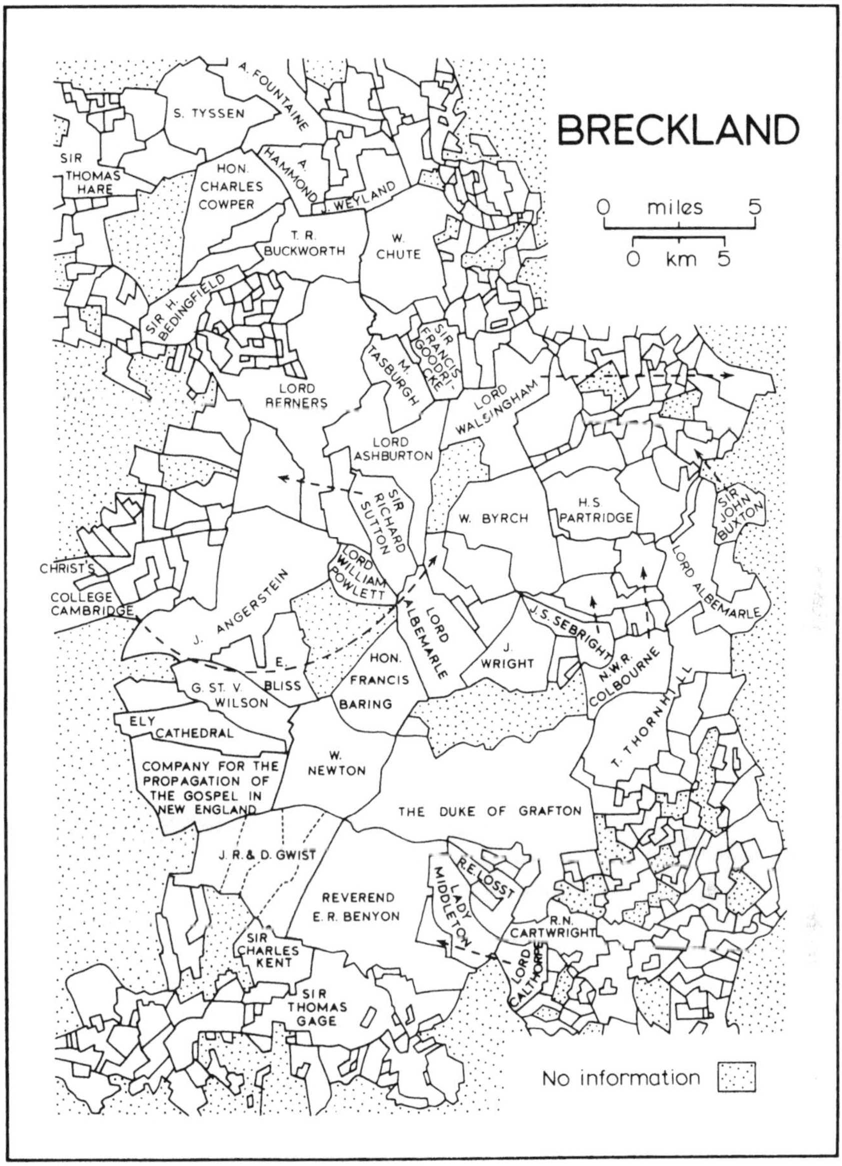

8.5 Landed estates in the Breckland. Source: M. R. Postgate, 'Historical geography of the Breckland, 1600–1850', 1961.

into the total acreage of the parish and then to plot the results by a choropleth technique. This technique was used by Dennis Mills to produce a map of the density of owners (number of owners divided by the area of the parish) for the whole of Leicestershire, identifying 'open' and 'closed' parishes on the basis of their landownership structure.[34] As the tithe survey coverage of Leicestershire is imperfect, Mills also obtained numbers of owners from land tax assessments. From these analyses he derived a four-fold classification: squire's township, absentee landlord township, freehold *morcellement* and divided township.

Refinement of analysis has since been introduced. J. A. Yelling produced a map of estate structure in east Worcestershire by mapping the proportion of the cultivated acreage of parishes held in estates exceeding 150 acres.[35] This analysis shows that the largest estates occur where the parishes themselves are largest. Although it does not completely describe the estate structure of a region, it provides a check on regional contrasts. For example, Yelling detects a relationship between non-parliamentary enclosure and the presence of large estates in the tithe surveys in one part of his study area and considers that concentration of ownership was ultimately the most important local factor determining the distribution of non-parliamentary enclosure. Other studies of regional patterns of landownership in the middle years of the nineteenth century include those by J. S. Ingleson in central Durham, and Heather Fuller in Lincolnshire.[36]

In Essex, a count of owners of land in the tithe surveys and at the time of the Return of Owners of Land, 1873, has been made by F. M. L. Thompson and reported in *English landed society in the nineteenth century*.[37] Thompson found 20 owners in the group of the 'greater gentry' in Essex at both dates and in the group of the 'squires' 111 at the time of the tithe surveys and 115 in 1873. A comparison of their names reveals that this appearance of stability is deceptive because among the 'greater gentry' four families represented in the 1840s owned no land by 1873 and three families listed in 1873 had not been Essex landowners in the 1840s. Markedly different degrees of fluidity are observed when changes in ownership amongst lesser landowners are taken into account. The rising price of land and the restricted availability of property made it easier for mercantile and industrial entrepreneurs to buy themselves into these groups. In 1872, no fewer than 38 per cent of the owners of 'lesser-yeomen' sized estates and 23 per cent of the 'greater-yeomen' group were newcomers since the 1840s. Comparison of the names of landowners in the tithe surveys with those in the 1873 return shows that only 60 per cent of owners in the two yeomen groups survived as landowners through the thirty-year period. Throughout the spectrum, a continuous contraction and expansion of estates occurred, with the result that in Essex the proportion of the county owned in estates of over 1,000 acres increased only very slightly.

Table 8.4 shows that similar changes in the structure of landownership

Table 8.4 *Landownership in Kent in 1873 and changes 1840–73*

Categories of owner	Size class (acres)	Number of owners 1873	Percentage change in number of owners 1840–73	Acreage owned 1873	Percentage of total area 1873	Percentage change in acreage 1840–73	Average acreage 1873
Small proprietors	1–100	6,347	−14	114,482	12	−13	18
Lesser yeomen	101–300	1,047	+3	148,544	16	−13	142
Greater yeomen	301–1,000	403	−9	205,374	22	−9	509
Squires	1,001–3,000	108	+1	185,692	20	+8	1,719
Greater gentry	3,001–10,000	49	+53	242,667	25	+47	4,952
Nobility	over 10,000	4	0	53,839	5	+8	13,460
Totals		7,958	−11	950,598	100	0	119

Sources: Tithe apportionments *c.*1840; W. E. Baxter's edition of the 1873 Return of Owners of Land published as, *The Domesday Book for the County of Kent*, Lewes, 1877.

occurred in Kent in the generation between the tithe surveys and the 1873 return.[38] It is compiled by entering on a computer file the names of each landowner and the acreage of his estate from summaries of schedules of tithe apportionments for every parish in the county. The table represents an aggregation of these data and statistics derived from the 'New Domesday' and shows that by 1873 the total number of owners had decreased by some 11 per cent overall but that this aggregate figure masks changes in both directions within the spectrum of estate sizes. The number of estates of less than 1,000 acres decreased and the total area occupied by such estates also decreased. The acreage of estates belonging to small proprietors and lesser yeomen decreased more than the acreage held by greater yeomen. Conversely, the number and size of gentry estates showed a marked increase. The number of greater gentry increased by 53 per cent and their territory expanded by 47 per cent. The numbers of nobility remained constant yet extended their territory by about 8 per cent.

The names of landowners in the computer file of owners in Kent about 1840 were compared with those in the 1872–3 return. The comparison indicates which types of estate continued in the ownership of the same family throughout the period and also indicates which changed hands. Differing rates of entry to and exit from the body of landowners can be clearly illustrated. Only 54 per cent of the numerous lesser-yeomen group of 1840 survived as landowners in 1873 and of these 27 per cent found themselves owning diminished estates while only 13 per cent expanded their territory. The survival rate for larger estates was much higher. As many as 70 per cent of the squirearchy of 1840 survived to 1873. Of the lesser gentry, possessing 3,000- to 5,000-acre estates, 77 per cent survived the generation to 1873 but 26 per cent of them owned less land than in 1840. A similar percentage also increased their estates; that of the Conyngham family, for example, more than doubled to just under 10,000 acres. All the greater gentry with 5,000- to 10,000-acre estates in 1840 still owned some land in the county in 1873. Of the largest estates of more than 10,000 acres, only one decreased in size. The acreage of land owned by corporate institutions showed great stability through the period. The 67,000 acres enumerated in the tithe surveys is matched by 69,000 acres in the 1873 return.

In Kent, as in Essex, estates were both contracting and expanding during this period. The net result of these changes in Kent was an increase from 42 per cent to 50 per cent in the proportion of the county occupied by estates of more than 1,000 acres. The territorial expansion of gentry estates seems to have taken place more at the expense of small proprietors and lesser yeomen than of greater yeomen.

Tithe surveys and parish land tax assessments

In the early years of the present century, considerable public concern was expressed about the plight of the nation's small landowners. A number of social historians at that time attempted to chart the long-term fortunes of these classes, particularly of owner-occupier farmers.[39] The question of the effect of enclosure on small landowners was re-opened after the Second World War and the debate continues today.[40] From the start, parish land tax assessments have provided an important source of data while tithe surveys have not been brought to bear as much as their value warrants.[41]

David Grigg has been among the first to study landownership changes by combining land tax and tithe data. For twelve parishes in the Holland division of Lincolnshire he compares the percentage of total parish areas owned by owner-occupiers in the tithe apportionments with earlier land tax data.[42] In four parishes no change occurred, in seven the importance of owner-occupation declined, while in one it increased. The tithe apportionments show that the owner-occupier still held an important place in fenland farming in the mid-nineteenth century. Furthermore, he suggests that the proportion of land owner-occupied is related to the date of enclosure; old enclosed parishes had smaller numbers of owner-occupiers. Williams' study of Ashworthy extends forward in time from the tithe survey.[43] He compares the ownership structure at the time of the tithe survey with that in 1873, 1922, and 1960, and finds that as estates broke up the number of owner-occupied farms increased.

As a cautionary note, it may well be dangerous to infer too much from owner-occupation as defined in the columns of the tithe apportionments. The repetition of a landowner's name in the occupier's column does not necessarily mean owner-farming. Some farms might be temporarily 'in hand'. In mid-nineteenth century Kent, for example, the tithe surveys record some 32 per cent of land in the occupation of its owners. This figure includes not only owner-occupied farms, but farms in hand and also woods, parks and pleasure grounds. Colin Thomas' analysis of the Merioneth tithe apportionments draws the conclusion that 'there can be no doubt that the tenant farm dominated the landscape and was the keystone of social relationships in all Merioneth parishes at this time'.[44] He does not question, however, the propriety of assuming that every tithe-survey occupier listed as holding land owned by another person is in every case a tenant farmer.

The land tax returns present even more serious problems of interpretation than the tithe surveys, notably the validity of 'acreage equivalents' calculated by equating the proportion of each listed owner's monetary contribution to the acreage he owned in the parish.[45] Reassessments, voluntary redemption, the rating of 'non-land' items, and variations in rent per acre within parishes can upset the simple ratio of tax paid to acres owned. Tithe surveys can be used to provide a check on these acreage equivalents and can help establish the degree of error which might arise from their use.

The most exhaustive comparative test of land tax acreage equivalents with tithe survey acreages is that by Sarah Banks.[46] For 89 west Norfolk parishes she compares the percentage of land owned by the largest owner, the four largest owners, the average size of estate and the total number of landowners as calculated from the 1831 tax assessment and the tithe surveys. The overall structure of landownership derived from each source is quite similar but for some estate-size categories, and especially at the scale of individual holdings, the land-tax assessments are found to be fallible. If anything, comparison with the tithe surveys suggests that the land tax, at least in west Norfolk, is most likely to be reliable in parishes containing a substantial number of estates of comparable size than where land is concentrated into only a few hands.

Urban cadasters

F. W. H. Sheppard, in a review of the sources and methods used for the *Survey of London*, remarked that he had formed an impression that the tithe surveys had not been used as extensively as they might have been as a source for the history of urban areas.[47] In the discussion following Dr Sheppard's paper at the Urban History Group conference in Leicester in 1966, Professor W. G. Hoskins, Dr G. H. Martin and other participants commented on the role of maps in urban history and censured scholars who neglected this source of evidence. The usefulness of nineteenth-century tithe maps was not specifically mentioned, although their value for identifying streets, buildings, landowners and occupiers has since been confirmed in J. B. Harley's review of map sources for historians.[48] For purposes of analysing building plans and property boundaries in medieval towns, earlier and more detailed maps are preferred, but in the absence of reliable alternative sources, T. R. Slater has measured dimensions of medieval burgage plots from tithe maps.[49] M. W. Beresford has identified the selions of a thirteenth-century new town at Warkworth, Northumberland, from blocks of parcels named on a tithe survey 'The Tens' and 'New Town Butts'.[50]

Tithe surveys have proved particularly helpful for reconstructing pre-urban cadasters. The size of properties and tenurial structures of landholdings were of crucial importance in the selection of sites for urban development. David Ward has examined the thesis that landholdings as the unit of purchase acted as a framework within which subsequent building in Leeds was planned.[51] He finds that field boundaries were quite unrelated to the pattern of building except where they were also boundaries of ownership. On the other hand, he finds a very close relationship between the shape of properties and the pattern of nineteenth-century urban development. This is clearly demonstrated in the Potternewton district of Leeds, some maps of which are reproduced as Fig. 8.6. Studies of Bradford by M. J. Mortimore, of Croydon by R. C. W. Cox, by Michael Jahn in outer west London, by J. M. Rawcliffe in Bromley, Kent, and of Lewisham in south-east London by R. W. Pepper illustrate for other areas a close correlation between pre-urban cadasters and subsequent urban morphology, identical with that observed by Ward in Leeds.[52] In five Scunthorpe parishes, D. C. D. Pocock attributes differential rates of growth to differences in sizes of estates, whilst in the Calder Darwen valley of Lancashire, K. L. Wallwork finds that where large landowners controlled townships they often refused to permit industrial building, at least before the 1840s.[53] Jane Springett has investigated the nature and intensity of urban development in Huddersfield in relation to the spatial pattern of landownership, reconstructed in part from parish tithe surveys.[54]

Urban historians have studied the characteristics and behaviour of urban estates of different sizes. H. J. Dyos' analysis of the structure of landownership in Camberwell from a tithe apportionment of 1837 shows that the seven largest landowners held two-thirds of the titheable land scattered throughout the parish.[55] A table showing how titheable land was distributed among estates in Dyos' size categories in Hampstead in 1838 provides a basis for F. M. L. Thompson's detailed account of the character, location and prospects for building development of different types of estates.[56] Martin Daunton uses tithe apportionment data for 27 towns to examine relationships between proportions of land held by the three largest landowners in each town, their tenurial systems and housing conditions. Results of the analysis indicate little more than 'a tenuous connection between concentrated ownership and short leasehold, and between fragmented ownership and freehold'.[57] Neither were quality of housing nor levels of rent related closely to the structure of landownership.[58]

In his book on the impact of railways on Victorian cities, J. R. Kellett comments, 'in spite of the importance of a comprehensive knowledge of property titles as a sound basis for all urban history, no research work has yet been done to piece together maps of the comparative ownership patterns in our major cities'.[59] His map of property ownership and railways in Birmingham, for example, based partly on tithe maps, and his analysis of its pattern clearly demonstrate the need to consider landowners' influences on routes taken by railway companies through urban and suburban areas.

For almost all towns in England and Wales there are one or more tithe surveys which depict the built-up area. Urban parishes are usually small and numerous and contain garden ground and occasional plots of farm land on which tithes were payable. But relatively few urban historians have used tithe surveys in studies of morphological change, preferring instead large-

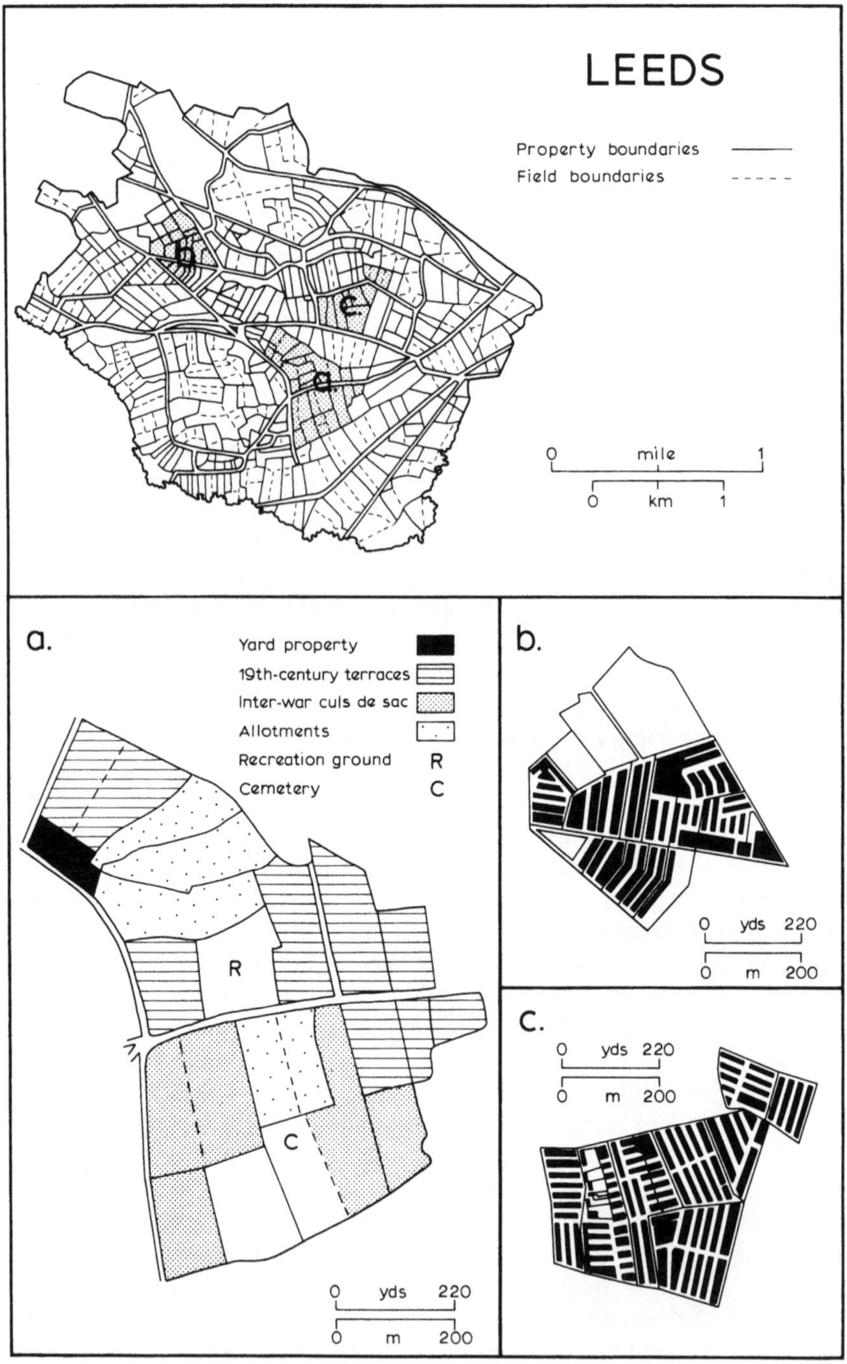

8.6 The pre-urban cadaster and urban development in the Potternewton district of Leeds. Source: D. Ward, 'The pre-urban cadaster and the urban pattern of Leeds', 1962.

scale maps by the Ordnance Survey. Among the exceptions is J. D. Marshall's discussion of the role of the 'detached colony' in the urbanisation of north-west England.[60] He finds that in Preston, despite the fact that comparatively few houses were owned by mill firms in the pre-1840 period, the tithe map shows factories congregated along Moor Brook, with a 'colony' of a few rows of terraced dwellings. The tithe map of Freetown, a 'detached colony' of Bury, Lancashire, shows that it must have housed a considerable proportion of Bury's population at that date. Later maps show that, although the colony had been absorbed into the general urban framework, it still retained a measure of its identity.

Other morphological cross-sections using tithe surveys include M. E. Witherick's investigation of stages in the growth of some sixteen urban settlements in central Cornwall.[61] This contains a series of cross-sections of urban extent; a final one is based on tithe-map evidence. Similar cross-sections have been reconstructed by, amongst others, F. S. Ottrey for Wirksworth in Derbyshire, by F. Hewitt for parts of Bristol, by B. C. D. Nokes of industrial settlements in north-east Worcestershire, by R. D. F. Bromley of Chulmleigh in Devon, and by K. A. Cowlard in Wakefield.[62] As well as mapping the boundaries of properties and the limits of building from the tithe survey, Cowlard also links the names of owners from the tithe survey with the 1841 pollbook to investigate political affiliations. He finds that the supposed Toryism of the landowning classes did not hold true of Wakefield in the early 1840s: there was an equal balance between the parties.

P. S. Richards is particularly fortunate as an altered apportionment of his study town, Wolverton, Buckinghamshire, was made in the 1880s.[63] Re-apportionment was usually occasioned by some traumatic event which radically altered the existing pattern of tithe areas, such as the purchase of land by a railway company or the parcelling out of tithe areas for building. Comparison of original and altered maps and Ordnance Survey large-scale town plans can provide a useful measure of nineteenth-century transformation.

Rural social structures

In 1962, in the first of a series of articles on nineteenth-century social structure in parts of Wales, Spencer Thomas initiated a particularly fruitful line of enquiry with tithe surveys, linking tithe-survey personal names and acreages with occupation and other data from the 1841 and 1851 population census enumerators' returns.[64] He considers that problems of defining farms from the holding units of the tithe surveys can be resolved by cross-checking with the census and that the accuracy with which the latter records the occupation 'farmer' can be ascertained by reference to the tithe apportionment. From differences found between the census and tithe apportionment of Llansantffraid, a parish which he has studied closely, he concludes that no standard criterion for defining the occupation of 'farmer' was applied in the 1841 census. More recently he has tested the 1851 census of a group of south-west Carmarthenshire parishes against the tithe survey and parish rate books and finds that the 1851 data are much more reliable in respect of occupation. By contrast, it is the tithe survey that he criticises: 'occupation in the Tithe Apportionment did not necessarily mean that the people named lived there. Neither did it guarantee that the occupiers worked the farm as tenants because they might well have been agricultural labourers in the employ of another tenant farmer working more than one farm.'[65] Other studies of Welsh villages – such as that by G. J. Lewis of Bow Street, 4 miles north of Aberystwyth, and Colin Thomas' work with communities in the lower Teifi valley – include comparisons of tithe and census data with respect to occupation structure.[66]

In 1971, Adrian Henstock of Nottinghamshire Record Office published the first results of work that he and an adult-education class carried out with the tithe surveys and the census.[67] He has coined the phrase 'house repopulation' to describe this work which links households enumerated in the census with actual buildings on the tithe map. 'Depending on circumstances it may be found that no more than one in four or even six households can be placed with certainty at first, but, having once established these "hooks", the remainder can be pinned up in between.'[68] For the Wiltshire town of Bradford in 1841, house repopulation has been pursued to the fullest extent that complementary evidence from census enumerators' books, Pigot's directory and local newspapers will permit. Gee Langdon has drawn from the tithe map and other sources a faithful portrait of a rural market town.[69]

The technique has been refined and extended to embrace 'community reconstruction' by Dennis Mills and provides one of the tools for his penetrating studies of social structure in the village of Melbourn in Cambridgeshire in the nineteenth century. In an exploratory article describing work in progress he says,

> while the Tithe Award presents a considerable amount of evidence of social solidarity, the data within it cannot be fully utilized without recourse to the other major documents available for the period. Kinship links between owners and occupiers will become much more certain when the Tithe Award data are fully integrated with those from the Family Reconstitution forms. The lynchpin in this exercise will be the Census Enumeration Schedules of 1841, which give a static picture of each household at that date, while the Tithe Award makes it possible to place the households both spatially and within the socio-tenurial networks within the village.[70]

He presented some house repopulation results in 1978 in a map of the central

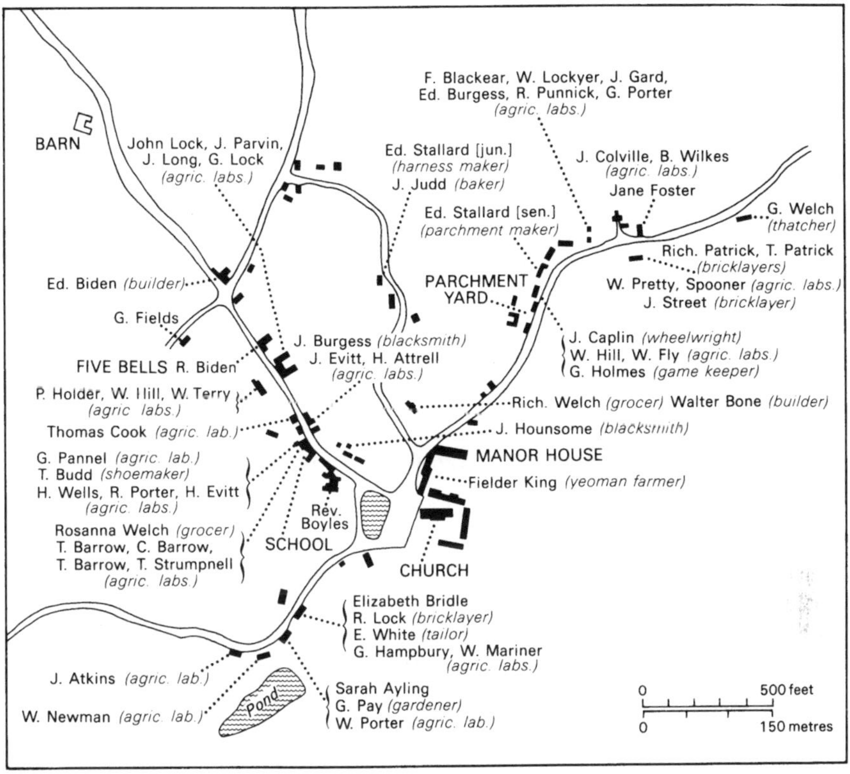

8.7 House repopulation of Buriton, Hampshire. Source: E. M. Yates, 'The evolution of the English village', 1982.

part of Melbourn and a schedule listing people resident in each tenement, their occupations, and some references to the twentieth century illustrated by photographs of the High Street in the 1930s and in 1977.[71] Fig. 8.7 is a map of Buriton, Hampshire, in 1841 compiled using similar techniques by E. M. Yates.[72] It is based on the tithe map and the 1841 census and identifies heads of households, their residences and employment. Once houses have been repopulated, the residential pattern can be analysed. For Melbourn, Dennis Mills has examined kinship networks by measuring the residential propinquity of kin as a contribution to understanding mobility and segregation in nineteenth-century society.[73]

9

Summary and prospect

National and regional enquiries: land use and farming *c.* 1840

The middle years of the nineteenth century have been acclaimed as a period of 'high farming', the historiography of which is summarised by P. J. Perry.[1] These decades have been considered to mark the culmination of two centuries or more of great technical improvement in agriculture, of improvements made possible by the introduction of new farm implements, of improved breeds of livestock and of new methods of conserving and increasing soil fertility by adopting new crop rotations and applying new kinds of fertilisers. Changes in farming technique were accompanied by an intensification of farming on land already occupied, and by an extension of cultivation to land that was formerly waste. At the beginning of Queen Victoria's reign the new husbandry was an accomplished fact. In most parts of England, communal grazing on the fallow field and on the stubble after harvest had disappeared; the exchange and consolidation of scattered holdings in open fields was nearing completion; the reclamation of many tracts of heath, waste and unimproved grazings was approaching its furthest limit; draining and embanking were proceeding in the remaining waterlogged areas; while in parks and on land of little value for agriculture, hundreds of acres of woodland were being planted every year.

Soon after the tithe survey of England and Wales was completed, fresh stimuli to agricultural change appeared. From about 1840 onwards, a number of developments tended to improve the competitive position of the clayland farmer and began to diminish the previously marked distinction between cold, heavy claylands and warmer, light-soil areas. Effective drainage, the only feasible technical solution to the expense, uncertainty and inefficiency of the old three-course clayland arable system, was made possible with the production of cheap tile drains and the availability of financial assistance. Also, in the middle years of the nineteenth century, a sound scientific base for agriculture was being developed and increasing use of bone meal, importation of guano and the purchase of feedstuffs showed that farmers were beginning to heed the advice so readily made available to them by the Royal Agricultural Society of England, founded in 1838, and by dozens of local agricultural societies.[2] Finally, the extension of the railway network after 1840 had far-reaching effects on agriculture: markets for products were widened and regional specialisation facilitated, whilst manures and fertilisers could be more efficiently and cheaply distributed.

The tithe surveys picture the nation's rural landscape just before these later transformations occurred and before the great Victorian expansion of the urban area over the countryside. Indeed, the post-1840 advance in agriculture was in no small measure assisted by the Tithe Commutation Act which removed an iniquitous tax on the produce of the land and so dismantled a further barrier to improvement.

In the 1930s the writers of the county reports of the First Land Utilisation Survey of Britain demonstrated the effectiveness of plotting information from the tithe surveys on to modern small-scale maps and also the greater returns to be obtained by plotting tithe surveys for large tracts of country rather than for sample parishes (chapter 6). For L. D. Stamp, the director of the survey, the tithe surveys represented 'an invaluable source of information' for constructing 'a Land Utilisation map of approximately a century ago'.[3]

In a retrospective commentary on the *Historical geography of England before 1800* (1936), Professor H. C. Darby noted that among the 'sources that cry aloud for attention is the body of Tithe Surveys made on a parish basis in the years around 1840'.[4] He reviewed a number of pioneer analyses of the tithe documents and commented in 1960, 'Well would it be if such work could be extended to give us as complete a map of England around about 1840 as possible.'[5]

Since the Second World War and particularly since about 1960, considerable advances have been made with this source and, indeed, *A new historical geography of England*, (1973) contains a number of maps based on tithe survey evidence.[6] Broad regional contrasts in land utilisation at mid-century can now be recognised but the greater part of England and Wales still awaits detailed, local research to establish exact patterns of farming. In about 50 regional-scale studies land-use information, particularly the field-by-field distribution of arable land, has been plotted from the tithe surveys. Fig. 9.1 shows those areas of England for which arable land has been mapped by both field-by-field (chorochromatic) and parish summary (choropleth) techniques. It indicates a concentration of activity in East Anglia, the Home Counties and southern England which reflects both the good coverage of tithe surveys in these areas and the interests of the Department of Geography, University College London, where many studies have been conducted.

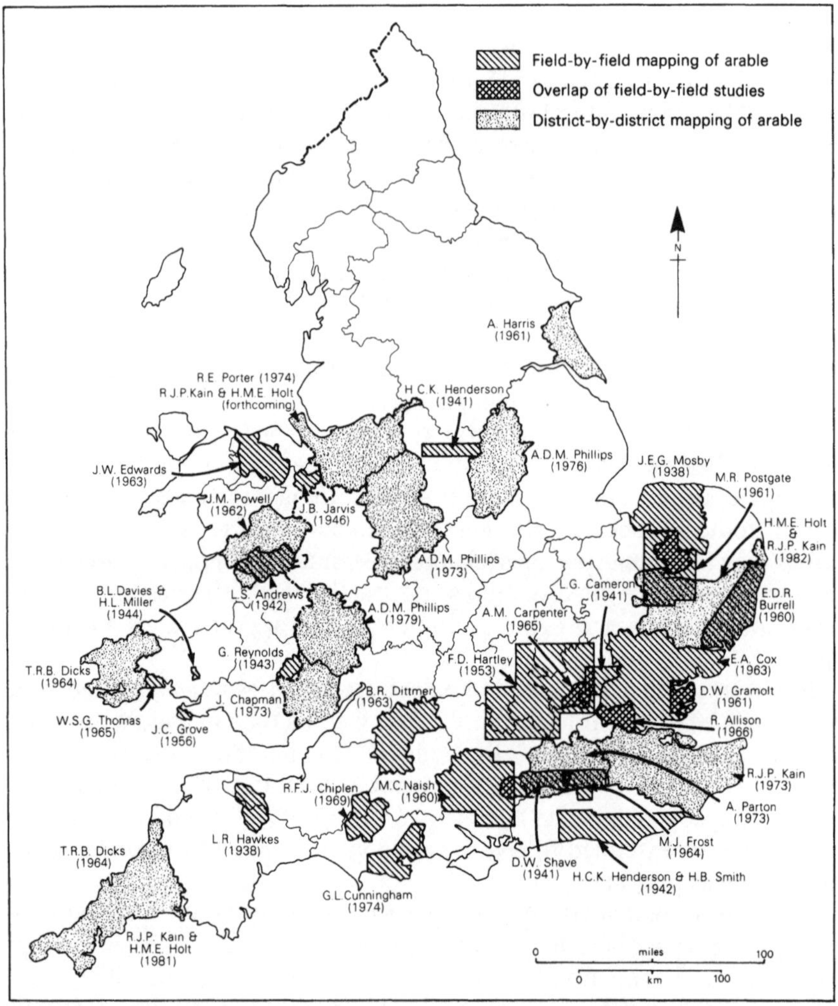

9.1 Areas of England and Wales for which arable land has been plotted from tithe surveys.

The preparation of field-by-field maps is a very tedious task (chapter 6) and beyond a certain point the repetition of studies of detailed interdigitations of land use declines in usefulness. With the land use of some six million acres in 18 counties already plotted, it may be considered that this point has now been reached. Furthermore, although a map of England and Wales showing every field recorded as arable in the tithe surveys may appear very precise, it would be of questionable value. 'Arable' as a category was defined in at least two ways in the tithe apportionments (see chapter 4) and it is not possible to determine which criteria were used at a particular place without careful checking in tithe files. As a result, to compare a map of arable compiled from tithe apportionments of a western pastoral county such as Cornwall with, say, Norfolk from the arable east of the country could be very misleading, as in the west of England long leys of ten years or more were commonly classed as arable in the apportionments. On the other hand, tithe file information on land use, crops and yields is susceptible to treatment at a national scale because consistent classifications can be made. The data are quantitative and, although formidable in bulk, they are eminently suited to computer processing. They are also sufficiently detailed to provide a clear picture of many elements in the rural landscape and can throw more light on the nature of farming at mid-century than a field-by-field map of arable land. As noted in chapter 7, in 1978 Roger Kain and a small group of co-workers at the University of Exeter began transcribing these data from the tithe files, and it is planned that an atlas of maps of English and Welsh counties will be published as a companion volume to this book.

Local enquiries: relict features and changing landscapes

One of the values, then, of the tithe surveys is the way they can provide a 'sheet-anchor' source for broadly painted, mid-nineteenth century cross-sections. But only a relatively small number of users of tithe surveys declare this as the aim of their enquiries; studies reviewed in chapters 5–8 confirm that the tithe surveys have been used mainly to examine conditions at some earlier date or as one of a series of sources consulted for evidence of change through time. Furthermore, such studies are usually conducted at a quite different order of resolution from period pictures, usually focusing on small areas, often single parishes, estates or farms, rather than extending over whole counties or the entire country.

In many studies reviewed, tithe surveys have been used to make good deficiencies in earlier records, to provide details of early methods of cultivation, land tenure, village forms and especially of field systems. It was an interest in field systems that first drew historians to the tithe maps, although that path has not been without pitfalls. A tithe map can indicate the shape and size of fields, apportionments list their owners and occupiers, but the temptation to leap directly from the mid-nineteenth century to the middle ages must be strongly resisted. Tithe surveys, for example, cannot tell us whether the strip fields they indicate were ever subject to common-field husbandry (chapter 5). If earlier maps of comparable accuracy are available, the tithe survey might properly be passed over. Indeed, H. L. Gray, himself a pioneer of the use of tithe maps in retrogressive study of field systems, asserts that 'had the tithe maps been made in the middle of the eighteenth century they would have been a boon to the student; dating as they do from the middle of the nineteenth, they are only of occasional assistance'.[7] In studies of early field systems and other relict features, tithe surveys are of most use where earlier sources of information are lacking and only then if their recent date is respected.

In studies of changing landscapes the tithe surveys have been much used to provide temporal perspectives for modern land-use surveys. This was the objective for many workers in the 1930s whose purpose was generally 'to evaluate correctly the various factors which have been at work influencing agricultural geography'.[8] Essentially these are investigations of changing land use in relation to land quality. Their limitation is that they attempt to measure change in terms of crude categories of land use which are often not comparably defined in each of the sources used. It is also questionable whether anything approaching measures of real rates and directions of change may be obtained by analysing data from only two or three widely spaced dates. The broad state of cultivation classification employed in most tithe apportionments masks changes in cropping systems and intensity of land use (chapter 7). Tithe surveys have been used, for example, to chart the advance of arable farming onto moorlands in highland Britain and into heaths and marshes in lowland England, but the maps and apportionments do not reveal the intensity of use of these newly reclaimed lands. Tithe files may help answer the question of how significant a contribution to agricultural output these extensions really made. But such questions will be answered properly only if, at a local scale, it is possible to correlate landscape changes with some detailed input–output data obtained perhaps from farm accounts or estate papers.

Tithe surveys as a source of historical evidence

The great strength of the tithe surveys is the sheer volume of apposite, synchronic data they contain, from which patterns of land use, crops, fields, farms and estates can be reconstructed. Their weakness is that, with the exception of the relatively little used descriptive comments in the tithe files, the surveys are silent on the processes of agrarian change.[9] Furthermore, many studies based on them reveal a landscape singularly devoid of people. This deficiency is now being remedied by linking tithe surveys with census returns. In recent reconstructions of social structure, tithe data are used to provide a precise spatial dimension to population data (chapter 8).

Although by no means perfect in accuracy or ideal in content, there can be no doubt that their comprehensiveness, opportune timing, and extensive coverage of the country earn the tithe surveys pride of place amongst nineteenth-century manuscript sources. After the great Domesday Book of the eleventh-century, they represent the most detailed and important national inventory to be taken before our own time. In 1959, in the first major article which called attention to the tithe surveys as a historical source, Hugh Prince set out a list of questions which the surveys can help answer.[10] They provide a record of parish boundaries before major changes took place; of estates at a time when many of them had reached their greatest extent. They represent every type of holding from fragmented open-field tenements to compact ring-fence units; of fields, both enclosed and unenclosed, in every variety of shape and size. They provide a record of the use of land; whether cultivated or uncultivated, arable or grass, orchard or hop ground, heath or marsh, wood or agriculturally unproductive. They also provide a record of the names of landowners and occupiers, and of the fields belonging to them. They can tell us how much titheable land belonged to estates of various sizes and how much was owned by the church, the universities, the railway companies, and by the nobility, the gentry and the peasantry. They can tell us how much arable land remained unenclosed in 1840, where it was situated and who owned it. From them we can discover what land was farmed by owner-occupiers or by tenant farmers, how much woodland or cottage property was occupied by owners or by tenants, and how much land was occupied by commons or highways. They can tell us whether farmsteads were situated in the midst of their own fields, or if not, whether they were attached to villages or hamlets. They show what size and shape farms were in different parts of the country, and what proportion of a farm was arable or grass.

Many of these questions are still only partially answered, a few are no longer topics for debate, but since historical enquiry has embraced new themes, the list could now be extended as it was after the discovery of the tithe files and a first discussion of their crop, yield and livestock data by Elwyn Cox and Brian Dittmer.[11] The tithe surveys, fully exploited in conjunction with early Ordnance Survey maps, the 1841 and 1851 census enumerators' books, the land-tax assessments, private-estate accounts and surveys, farmers' notebooks and diaries, and the Royal Agricultural Society of England's *prize essays* on county farming, can present a vivid picture of many aspects of the condition of rural and urbanising England in the middle years of the nineteenth century and provide solid points of reference for retrogressive enquiries.

Notes

Introduction

1 J. H. Andrews, *A paper landscape. The Ordnance Survey in nineteenth-century Ireland* (Oxford, Clarendon Press, 1975); H. D. Clout and K. Sutton, 'The cadastre as a source for French rural studies', *Agricultural History*, 43 (1969), 215–23; H. B. Johnson, *Order upon the land: the U.S. rectangular land survey and the upper Mississippi country* (New York, Oxford University Press, 1976).

2 E. J. Hobsbawm and G. F. E. Rudé, *Captain Swing* (Lawrence and Wishart, 1969); J. P. D. Dunbabin, *Rural discontent in nineteenth-century Britain* (London, Faber, 1974); A. Charlesworth, *Social protest in a rural society: the spatial diffusion of the Captain Swing disturbances 1830–1831*, Historical Geography Research Series No. 1 (Norwich, Geobooks, 1979); A. Charlesworth (ed.), *An atlas of rural protest in Britain, 1548–1900* (London, Croom Helm, 1983).

3 E. J. Evans, *The contentious tithe. The tithe problem and English agriculture, 1750–1850* (London, Routledge and Kegan Paul, 1976); E. J. Evans, *Tithes and the Tithe Commutation Act 1836*, Standing Conference for Local History (London, Bedford Square Press, 1978).

1 The nature of tithes

1 J. A. Venn, *The foundations of agricultural economics*, 2nd edn (Cambridge, Cambridge University Press, 1933), 150–82; R. E. Prothero (Lord Ernle), *English farming past and present*, 6th edn (London, Heinemann and Frank Cass, 1961), 332–48.

2 A. Young quoted in J. D. Chambers and G. E. Mingay, *The agricultural revolution, 1750–1880*, (London, Batsford, 1966), 45.

3 P. W. Millard, *The law relating to tithes and payments in lieu thereof*, 3rd edn (London, Butterworth, 1938).

4 E. Kerridge, *The agricultural revolution* (London, Allen and Unwin, 1967), 272.

5 Venn, *Agricultural economics*, 158.

6 A. G. Little, 'Personal tithes', *English Historical Review*, 60 (1945), 67–88.

7 Evans, *Contentious tithe*, 17–18; C. Hill, *Economic problems of the Church, from Archbishop Whitgift to the Long Parliament* (Oxford, Clarendon Press, 1956), 86.

8 Evans, *Contentious tithe*, 7; Hill, *Economic problems of the Church*, 78.

9 E. J. Evans, 'Tithing customs and disputes: the evidence of glebe terriers, 1698–1850', *Agricultural History Review*, 18 (1970), 17–35.

10 R. J. P. Kain, *An atlas and index of the tithe files of mid-nineteenth century England and Wales* (Cambridge, Cambridge University Press, forthcoming).

11 Anon, 'Tithing customs at North Somercotes, A.D. 1588', *Lincolnshire Historian*, 10 (1952), 375 and 381; D. M. Barratt (ed.), *Ecclesiastical terriers of Warwick parishes* (Dugdale Society Publications, 22, 1955); R. M. Barton, *Life in Cornwall in the nineteenth century* (Truro, Bradford Barton, 1970), 105–6, 110, 119–20, 128–9, 202–3; B. Charles, 'The vicarage and tithes of Nevern in Pembrokeshire', *Journal of the Historical Society of the Church in Wales*, 1 (1947), 26–39; J. C. Cox, 'Ancient documents relating to tithes in the Peak', *Journal of the Derbyshire Archaeological and Natural History Society*, 5 (1883), 129–64; R. F. Dickinson, 'Tithing customs in west Cumberland in the eighteenth century', *Transactions of the Cumberland and Westmorland Antiquarian and Archaeological Society,* new series, 60 (1960), 130–4; F. G. Emmison, 'Tithes, perambulations and sabbath-breach in Elizabethan Essex', in F. G. Emmison and R. Stephens (eds.), *Tribute to an antiquary: essays presented to Marc Fitch by some of his friends* (London, Leopard's Head Press, 1976), 177–215; Evans, 'Tithing customs and disputes', 17–35; Nesta Evans, 'Tithe books as a source for the local historian', *Local Historian*, 14 (1980), 24–7; W. E. Godfrey, 'A Staveley tithe book of the Rev. James Gisborne', *Journal of the Derbyshire Archaeological and Natural History Society,* 71 (1951), 38–46; R. H. Worth, 'The tenants and commoners of Dartmoor', *Report and Transactions of the Devonshire Association*, 76 (1944), 187–214; S. F. Hockey, 'The pattern of tithes in the Isle of Wight', *Proceedings of the Hampshire Field Club and Archaeological Society*, 21 (1960), 145–55; C. A. F. Meekings, 'St Teath's tithes – 1295', *Devon and Cornwall Notes and Queries*, 32 (1972), 168–70; F. C. Morgan, 'Bosbury tithes and oblations, 1635 to 1641', *Transactions of the Woolhope Naturalists' Field Club*, 38 (1965), 140–8; C. S. and Christabel S. Orwin, *The open fields* (Oxford, Clarendon Press, 1938), 183–5; W. A. Pemberton, 'A parson's account book', *Local Historian*, 13 (1978), 397–405; D. G. Thomas, 'The Gelligaer parish tithe customs', *Gelligaer*, 7 (1970), 11–17; A. V. Woodman, 'Dunton tithe procedure', *Records of Buckinghamshire*, 16 (1960), 363–4. Further examples are cited in Evans, *Contentious tithe* and 'Tithing customs and disputes'; G. F. A. Best, *Temporal Pillars* (Cambridge, Cambridge University Press, 1964); Hill, *Economic problems of the Church*.

12 Hill, *Economic problems of the Church*, 132–67.

13 H. Grove, *Alienated tithes . . .* (London, privately printed, 1896); Evans, *Contentious tithe*, 8.

14 Hill, *Economic problems of the Church*, 132–46.

15 W. G. Hoskins, *The midland peasant* (London, Macmillan, 1957), 130–4.

16 Hill, *Economic problems of the Church*, 95.

17 Evans, *Contentious tithe*, 21–2; Prothero, *English farming past and present*, 341.

18 Evans, *Contentious tithe*, 21.

19 Quoted in Evans, *Contentious tithe*, 21.

20 W. R. Ward, 'The tithe question in England in the early nineteenth century', *Journal of Ecclesiastical History*, 16 (1965), 67–81.

21 Quoted in Evans, *Contentious tithe*, 18.

22 PRO IR 18/13853.

23 E. J. Evans, 'A nineteenth-century tithe dispute and its significance: the case of Kendal', *Transactions of the Cumberland and Westmorland Antiquarian and Archaeological Society*, new series, 74 (1974), 159–85.

24 Venn, *Agricultural economics*, 154–62; Evans, 'Tithing customs and disputes', 17–35 and 'A nineteenth-century tithe dispute', 159–83; E. J. Evans, 'Some reasons for the growth of English rural anti-clericalism, c.1750–c.1830', *Past and Present*, 66 (1975), 84–109. See also, C. Stella Davies, *The agricultural history of Cheshire 1750–1850* (Manchester, Chetham Society, 3rd series, 10, 1960), 104–6; R. W. Greaves, *The Corporation of Leicester, 1689–1836* (Oxford, Oxford University Press, 1970); Hoskins, *Midland peasant*, 134–40; A. K. R. Kiralfy, 'The Star Chamber litigation of vicar Richard Levitt in 1609', *Proceedings of the Leatherhead and District Local History Society*, 1 (1951), 21–3; F. Jones, 'The Mathry tithe suit', *Journal of the Historical Society of the Church in Wales*, 2 (1950), 97–102; J. S. Purvis, *Select XVI century causes in tithe from the York Diocesan Registry*, Yorkshire Archaeological Society Record Series, 114 (1949); J. A. F. Thomson, 'Tithe disputes in later medieval London', *English Historical Review*, 78 (1963), 1–17; W. R. Ward, *Religion and Society in England, 1790–1850* (London, Batsford, 1972); A. Wharham, 'Tithes in country life', *History Today*, 22 (1972), 426–33; V. Williams, 'Tithing troubles. Farmers' revolt against tithes, 1747/8', *Gelligaer*, 9 (1972), 24–30.

25 R. C. Gaut, *A history of Worcestershire agriculture and rural evolution* (Worcester, Littlebury, 1939).

26 Hill, *Economic problems of the Church*, 81–2.

27 Cited in Venn, *Agricultural economics*, 151–2.

28 Holkham MSS, 'Castleacre Register for Briefs and Offerings distributed each Sacrament and for Doles of Charity, Anno Domini 1709 to 1749, Amb: Pimlowe, Vicar', Castleacre Deeds 1700–1800, Bundle 11, No. 116.

29 A. Young, *Travels during the years 1787, 1788, and 1789 . . . with a view of ascertaining the cultivation . . . of the kingdom of France* (Bury St Edmunds, Rackham, 1792).

30 Best, *Temporal pillars*, 66.

31 Evans, *Contentious tithe*, 44.

32 Evans, 'Some reasons for the growth of English rural anti-clericalism'; Evans, 'A nineteenth-century tithe dispute and its significance'; Evans, *Contentious tithe*, 42–66.

33 A valuable account of the part played by opponents to tithes in the English Revolution is Margaret James, 'The political importance of the tithes controversy in the English Revolution, 1640–60', *History*, 26 (1941), 1–18. The objections of tithes by Quakers are discussed in B. Reay, 'Quaker opposition to tithes 1652–1660', *Past and Present*, 86 (1980); 98–120: A. D. Gilbert, *Religion*

and society in industrial England, church, chapel and social change, 1740–1914 (London, Longman, 1976); Evans, *Contentious tithe*, 58–62.

34 A. B. Anderson, 'A study in the sociology of religious persecution: the first Quakers', *Journal of Religious History*, 9 (1977), 247–62.

35 N. C. Hunt, *Two early political associations. The Quakers and the Dissenting Deputies in the age of Sir Robert Walpole* (Oxford, Clarendon Press, 1961), 62–112; E. J. Evans, 'A history of the tithe system in England, 1690–1850, with special reference to Staffordshire', unpublished University of Warwick Ph.D. thesis (1970), 178–239.

36 F. M. L. Thompson, *Chartered surveyors: the growth of a profession* (London, Routledge and Kegan Paul, 1968), 100–3; tithe payment is also regarded as unimportant in Chambers and Mingay, *Agricultural revolution*, 45–6.

37 J. Tuke, *General view of the agriculture of the North Riding of Yorkshire* (London, McMillan, 1800), 322–8.

38 J. Billingsley, *General view of the agriculture of the county of Somerset* (Bath, R. Cruttwell, 1797), 35; N. Kent, *General view of the agriculture of the county of Norfolk* (Norwich, Norfolk Press, 1796), 153–5.

39 Thomas Rudge, *General view of the agriculture of the county of Gloucester* (London, Richard Phillips, 1807), p. 60.

40 J. Boys, *General view of the agriculture of the county of Kent* (London, Sherwood, Neely and Jones, 1813), 43.

41 D. Walker, *General view of the agriculture of the county of Hertford* (London, W. Bulmer, 1795), 24, 74, 78.

42 W. Pitt, *General view of the agriculture of the county of Stafford* (London, G. Nicol, 1796), 27.

43 PRO IR 18/12734.

44 PRO IR 18/12865.

45 PRO IR 18/11142.

46 PRO IR 18/2050.

47 J. Caird, *English agriculture in 1850–51*, 2nd edn (London, Longman, Brown, Green and Longmans, 1852), 80.

48 R. J. P. Kain, 'Contemporary opinion concerning the possible conversion of pasture to arable after tithe commutation', *Cantium*, 6 (1974), 77–9.

49 PRO IR 18/3694.

50 PRO IR 18/3406.

51 PRO IR 18/3533, 3406, 3483.

52 R. J. P. Kain, 'The land of Kent in the middle of the nineteenth century', unpublished University of London Ph.D. thesis (1973), 323–8.

53 Evans, *Contentious tithe*, 69.

54 E. L. Jones, 'The changing basis of English agricultural prosperity, 1853–73', *Agricultural History Review*, 10 (1962), 102–19.

55 Evans, *Contentious tithe*, 163. See also G. E. Mingay, *Rural life in Victorian England* (London, Heinemann, 1977) and his *The agricultural revolution. Changes in agriculture, 1650–1880* (London, Black, 1977).

56 R. C. Russell, *The enclosure of Barton-upon-Humber, 1793–1796*, (Barton-upon-Humber, Workers' Educational Association, 1968); R. C. Russell, *The enclosures of East Halton, 1801–1804 and North Kelsey, 1813–1840* (North

Lindsey Branch of Workers' Educational Association, 1974); T. W. Beastall, *The agricultural revolution in Lincolnshire* (Lincoln, History of Lincolnshire Committee, 1978), 35–41.

57 Evans, *Contentious tithe*, 94.

58 V. Lavrovsky, 'Tithe commutation as a factor in the gradual decrease of landownership by the English peasantry', *Economic History Review,* 4 (1933), 273–89. See also G. E. Mingay, *Enclosure and the small farmer in the age of the industrial revolution* (London, Macmillan, 1968) 22, 24.

59 Chambers and Mingay, *Agricultural revolution*, 85–8.

60 Cited in Chambers and Mingay, *Agricultural revolution*, 87.

61 Ward, 'The tithe question', 72.

62 E. C. K. Gonner, *Common land and enclosure* (London, Macmillan, 1912), 316–18. See also W. H. R. Curtler, *The enclosure and redistribution of our land* (Oxford, Clarendon Press, 1920), 162, 200.

63 British Parliamentary Papers [BPP] House of Commons (HC), 1836, XLIV, 'A Return from the Inclosure and other Private Acts in which provisions are included for the Commutation of Tithes, of the Proportion in Land, Yearly Money Payment, or Corn Rent, allotted in Lieu of Tithe . . .', 344 pp.

64 Ward, 'The tithe question', 71.

65 BPP (HC) 1831–2, XXX, 'A return of the several parishes in England and Wales, in which Commutations of the whole Great and Small Tithes of such Parish have been authorised under any Act of Parliament . . .', 178 pp. This return was compiled by searching only those Private Acts contained in the Library of the House of Commons which were printed as Bills when pending in parliament.

66 Millard, *Law relating to tithes*, 12. Ward also cites these figures in 'The tithe question in England', 70; Evans' calculations from the 1836 'Return from the Inclosure and other Private Acts' puts the proportion of acts which dealt with tithes at a lower figure of about 60 per cent of all 3,700 acts. See *Contentious tithe*, 111.

67 Millard, *Law relating to tithes*, 12, 16, 18, cites as examples of these: Brinklow Inclosure Act, 1741, 14 Geo. II, Cap. 14; Vicar's Rate in Halifax Act, 1830, 10 Geo. IV, Cap. 14; Kendal Corn Rent Act, 1834, 4 & 5, Will. IV, Cap. 16.

68 Billingsley, *General view . . . of Somerset*, 199.

69 W. Cobbett, *Rural rides* (London, Everyman edition, Dent, 1912), Vol. 2, 124.

70 G. F. E. Rudé, 'English rural and urban disturbances on the eve of the First Reform Bill, 1830–1', *Past and Present*, 37 (1967), 87–102; Hobsbawm and Rudé, *Captain Swing*; Dunbabin, *Rural discontent in nineteenth-century Britain*; Charlesworth, *Social protest in a rural society*; J. Stevenson, *Popular disturbances in England, 1700–1870* (London, Longman, 1979); R. A. E. Wells, 'The development of the English rural proletariat and social protest, 1700–1850', *Journal of Peasant Studies*, 6 (1979), 115–39.

2 The Tithe Commutation Act of 1836

1 J. A. Symon, *Scottish farming past and present* (Edinburgh, Oliver and Boyd, 1959), 81–3; Christabel S. Orwin and Edith H. Whetham, *History of British*

agriculture 1846–1914 (London, Longmans, 1964), 183–6; R. C. Simington, 'The tithe composition applotment books', *Analectica Hibernica*, 10 (1941), 295–8; J. H. Johnson, 'The Irish tithe composition applotment books as a geographical source', *Irish Geography*, 3 (1958), 254–62.

2 Ward, 'The tithe question', 67–81.

3 Evans, *Contentious tithe*, 116.

4 Evans, *Contentious tithe*, 119.

5 Evans, *Contentious tithe*, 121.

6 *Hansard's Parliamentary Debates [Hansard]*, 3rd series, XVII, 273–6.

7 *Hansard*, 3rd series, XVII, 273–6; XIX, 275–82.

8 *Hansard*, 3rd series, XXII, 822.

9 *Hansard*, 3rd series, XXII, 818–39; XXVII, 170–8,

10 *Hansard*, 3rd series, XXVII, 180–4.

11 *Hansard*, 3rd series, XXVII, 190–1.

12 *Hansard*, 3rd series, XXVII, 194.

13 *Hansard*, 3rd series, XXXI, 185–6.

14 *Hansard*, 3rd series, XXXI, 721.

15 P. O'Donoghue, 'Opposition to tithe payments in 1832–3', *Studia Hibernica*, 12 (1972), 77–108.

16 E. J. Evans, *Tithes and the Tithe Commutation Act 1836* (London, Bedford Square Press, 1978), 13–14.

17 6 and 7 Will. IV, cap. 71; W. Eagle, *The acts for the commutation of tithes in England and Wales*, 3rd edition (London, Saunders and Benning, 1840).

18 W. Vamplew, 'Tithes and agriculture: some comments on commutation', *Economic History Review*, 2nd series, 34 (1981), 115–19.

19 The administrative model of the new Poor Law is discussed in A. E. Davies, 'The New Poor Law in a rural area, 1834–1850', *Ceredigion*, 8 (1978), 246–90, and R. N. Thompson, 'The working of the Poor Law Amendment Act in Cumbria, 1836–1871', *Northern History*, 15 (1979), 117–37.

20 D. Spring, *The English landed estate in the nineteenth century: its administration* (Baltimore, Johns Hopkins, 1963), 166; Evans, *Contentious tithe,* 136.

21 Quoted in Spring, *The English landed estate*, 167.

22 Spring, *The English landed estate*, 167.

23 For example, R. Jones, *Remarks on the manner in which tithe should be assessed to the poor's rate . . .* (London, Shaw and Sons, 1838).

24 Evans, *Contentious tithe*, 137.

25 Evans, *Contentious tithe*, 137.

26 H. M. Chichester, 'Robert Kearsley Dawson', *Dictionary of National Biography*, XIV (London, Smith Elder, 1888), 228; J. E. Portlock, *Memoir of the life of Major-General Colby* (London, Seeley, Jackson and Halliday, 1869); J. H. Andrews, 'The Ordnance Survey in nineteenth-century Ireland', unpublished Trinity College Dublin M.Litt. thesis (1971), 190–1, and 258–9; Rosemary L. Harris, 'The Ordnance Survey Memoirs', *Ulster Folklife*, 1 (1955), 43–52; Sir Charles Close, *The early years of the Ordnance Survey*, new edition with an introduction by J. B. Harley (Newton Abbot, David and Charles, 1969), 82–92.

27 R. K. Dawson, *Plans of the cities and boroughs of England and Wales shewing their boundaries as established by the Boundaries Act, passed 11th July 1832 . . .*,

in 2 vols. (1832); W. Porter, *History of the Corps of the Royal Engineers* (London, Longman Green, 1889), Vol. 2, 243.

28 Barbara de Vries, 'The role of the land surveyor in the development of New Zealand, 1840–76', unpublished Victoria University of Wellington M.A. thesis (1966), 31–5.

29 Harriet M. E. Holt, 'Assistant commissioners and local agents: their role in tithe commutation, 1836–1854', *Agricultural History Review* (in the press).

30 Evans, *Tithe Commutation Act*, 15.

31 R. J. P. Kain, *An atlas and index of the tithe files of mid-nineteenth century England and Wales*.

32 R. J. P. Kain, 'The tithe files of mid-nineteenth century England and Wales', in M. A. Reed (ed.), *Discovering past landscapes* (London, Croom Helm, 1984), 56–84.

33 PRO IR 18/1206.

34 PRO IR 18/1340.

35 A. Clapham, *A short history of the surveyor's profession* (London, Royal Institution of Chartered Surveyors, 1949).

36 Bucks. RO Townsend MSS D85/16/1–6. Farm and household accounts, diaries, rentals, stock books, valuations, relating to Wood End, Medmenham, Great Marlow, Bucks. (1830–56); D85/17/1–22. Dispute over title to Finnemoor (1832–4); D85/18/1–6. Apprenticeship indenture and correspondence, Joseph Townsend to Stephen Godson, land surveyor, Hook Norton, Oxon. (1813); for an account of the family and estate, see A. H. Plaisted, *The manor and parish records of Medmenham* (London, Longmans Green, 1925).

37 Bucks. RO Townsend MSS D85/Business Archives Council, British Archives Committee (BAC) II. Letter from Joseph Townsend to Tithe Commissioners for England and Wales (17 September 1836).

38 Bucks. RO Townsend MSS D85/BAC IV. Letter from Joseph Townsend to Mr Hovenden (6 October 1836), 2.

39 Letter from Joseph Townsend (6 October 1836), 1.

40 Bucks. RO Townsend MSS D85/BAC III. Letter from Lord Downshire to Joseph Townsend (24 September 1836).

41 Bucks. RO Townsend MSS D85/15/11/2. Letter from Richard Jones to Joseph Townsend (1 July 1837), 1.

42 Letter from Richard Jones (1 July 1837), 2.

43 Bucks. RO Townsend MSS D85/15/11/77. Letter from Marquis of Downshire to Joseph Townsend (6 October 1837), 2.

44 Bucks. RO Townsend MSS D85/BAC V. Letter from G. H. Whalley to Joseph Townsend (7 August 1839).

45 PRO IR 18/11505, Brantingham; 11566, Faxfleet; 11763 Thorpe-le-Street.

46 PRO IR 18/3635.

47 Bucks. RO Townsend MSS D85/15/11/81 (1). Extracts from the Official File of papers in the Tithe Office relating to the compulsory commutation of tithes of the parish of Manchester (1844–9).

48 Extracts from the Manchester Tithe File (25 July 1844), 5–6.

49 Extracts from the Manchester Tithe File (9 September 1847), 6–7.

50 Bucks. RO Townsend MSS D85/15/38/1–6. Letters from Joseph Townsend to Lord Carrington, asking for the inclusion of his name in the Bucks. Commission

of the Peace (1849–51); Clerk of the Peace MSS Q/JQc 4. Confidential correspondence of Acton Tindal, Clerk of the Peace, with Lord Carrington, Lord Lieutenant and Custos Rotulorum, regarding the suitability of Mr Townsend, land surveyor, for appointment to the Marlow bench (1847–53).

51 F. M. L. Thompson, *English landed society in the nineteenth century* (London, Routledge and Kegan Paul, 1963), 109.

52 Confidential correspondence of Acton Tindal (1850, 1851); further information supplied by Hugh Hanley, Bucks. County Archivist, in a letter dated 10 May 1973.

53 Bucks. RO Townsend MSS D85/15/39. Letter from Acton Tindal, asking Joseph Townsend whether he wishes to qualify for nomination to the Commission of the Peace (16 February 1850).

54 Bucks. RO Townsend MSS D85/15/11/1. Letter to Lord John Russell from Joseph Townsend (27 March 1851), 1–2.

55 Bucks. RO Townsend MSS D85/15/11/79. Letter from Arthur Russell to Joseph Townsend (8 April 1851), 1–2.

56 G. H. Whalley, *The Tithe Act, and the Tithe Amendment Act . . .* (London, Shaw and Sons, 1838), 304–6.

57 Whalley, *The Tithe Act*, 201–4.

58 Transcripts of these are printed in Whalley, *The Tithe Act*. Similar examples are occasionally found in tithe files and more frequently among the papers of solicitors who acted for tithe owners and tithe payers. See, for example, the papers of Thomas Salt, solicitor, in the Shropshire Record Office, and Burrow and company, solicitors of Cullompton, in the Devon Record Office. We are grateful to Harriet M. E. Holt for drawing our attention to these collections.

59 Evans, *Contentious tithe*, 129.

60 Our enquiries at the Public Record Office, the Tithe Redemption Commission, the Board of Inland Revenue and other government departments have failed to discover the unpublished papers of the Tithe Commission for England and Wales for the period between the passing of the Tithe Commutation Act and the late 1850s when the business of commutation was virtually complete. Their discovery would be a matter of the first importance for understanding further the organisation of commutation, much of which at present must be inferred from the one side of correspondence preserved in parochial tithe files.

61 Evidence from Table 2.1 and Holt, 'Assistant commissioners and local agents'.

62 Evans, *Contentious tithe*, 145.

63 Evans, *Contentious tithe*, 141.

64 Shropshire Record Office 3651/T/1, Tithe commutation papers, records of proceedings, and draft agreements.

65 PRO IR 29 17/406.

66 Whalley, *The Tithe Act*, 291.

67 Whalley, *The Tithe Act*, 295–6, 312.

68 Quoted in Evans, *Tithes and the Tithe Commutation Act*, 25.

69 Evans, *Contentious tithe*, 151.

70 Evans, *Contentious tithe*, 152.

71 Whalley, *The Tithe Act*, 320.

72 BPP (HC), 1837, VI, 'Report from the Select Committee on Survey of Parishes (Tithe Commutation Act); with the Minutes of evidence', 52.

73 Andrews, *The Ordnance Survey in nineteenth-century Ireland*, 36–7.
74 See the 'correspondence' in H. Barty-King, *Scratch a surveyor . . .* (London, Heinemann, 1975), 109–11.
75 Devon Record Office 2165A/PB59–102 – Correspondence, 1838–41, from Snell, assistant overseer, Drewsteignton; Jole, surveyor, Plymouth; landowners of Drewsteignton; Tithe Commission and others. We are indebted to Dr J. B. Harley for directing out attention to these papers.
76 PRO IR 18/3774.
77 R. J. P. Kain, 'The tithe commutation surveys', *Archaeologia Cantiana*, 89 (1974), 101–18.
78 We owe the information from which Fig. 2.11 is compiled to Mr Paul Laxton.
79 E. A. Cox, 'An agricultural geography of Essex *c.* 1840', unpublished University of London M.A. thesis (1963), 24.
80 B. R. Dittmer, 'An agricultural geography of northwest Wiltshire, 1773–1840', unpublished University of London M.A. thesis (1963), 30–2.
81 Thompson, *Chartered surveyors*, 106.
82 J. Farncombe, 'On the farming of Sussex', *Journal of the Royal Agricultural Society of England*, 11 (1850), 75.
83 BPP (HC), 1857, IV, 363.
84 BPP (HC), 1837–8, XXXVIII, 'Return of Agreements for the Commutation of Tithes', 189.
85 *Hansard*, 3rd series, 36, 585.
86 'Report on the Survey of Parishes', 25.
87 BPP (HC), 1837, XLI, 'Copy of Papers Respecting the Proposed Survey of Lands Under the Tithe Act', 9.
88 BPP (HC), 1839, XVI, 335.
89 BPP (HC), 1844, XXI, 419; D. W. Howell, *Land and people in nineteenth-century Wales* (London, Routledge and Kegan Paul, 1978), 83–5.
90 PRO IR 18/4420 Great Claybrook, Leicestershire.
91 BPP (HC), 1839, XVI, 335.
92 BPP (HC), 1840, XXVIII, 139.
93 BPP (HC), 1843, XXIX, 391.
94 BPP (HC), 1849, XXII, 549; Evans, *Contentious tithe*, 143.
95 BPP (HC), 1849, XXII, 549.
96 BPP (HC), 1857 second session, XXI, 350.
97 Act of 49 and 50 Vict., cap. 54 (1886).
98 Act of 54 and 55 Vict., cap. 8 (1891).
99 Act of 8 and 9 Geo. V., cap. 54 (1918).
100 Act of 15 and 16 Geo. V, cap. 87 (1925).
101 Act of 26 Geo. V and 1 Edw. VIII, cap. 43 (1936).
102 C. Fox, *The countryside and the law* (Newton Abbot, David and Charles, 1971), 111.

3 Tithe maps, apportionments and files

1 BPP (HC), 1837, XLI, 'Copy of papers respecting the proposed survey of lands under the Tithe Act'.
2 'Copy of papers', 10.
3 'Copy of papers', 9.

4 BPP (HC), 1837, VI 'Report from the select committee on survey of parishes (Tithe Commutation Act); with the minutes of evidence', 47–57.
5 'Copy of papers', 5.
6 'Copy of papers', 11–16.
7 'Copy of papers', 11.
8 'Copy of papers', 12.
9 F. Hull (ed.), *Catalogue of estate maps, 1590–1840, in the Kent County Archives Office* (Maidstone, Kent County Council, 1973).
10 'Copy of papers', 12–13.
11 'Copy of papers', 14.
12 'Copy of papers', 13.
13 'Copy of papers', 14.
14 Article 28 of Colby's 'Instructions for the Interior Survey of Ireland' reproduced by Andrews, 'Ordnance Survey in nineteenth-century Ireland,' Appendix B, 521–37.
15 An Act for the Commutation of Tithes in England and Wales, 6 & 7 Will. IV, cap. 71.
16 BPP (HC) 1837–8, XXXVIII, 'Return of Agreements for the commutation of tithes . . .'
17 'Report on survey of parishes', 47–8.
18 'Copy of papers', 16.
19 'Copy of papers', 17.
20 'Copy of papers', 4.
21 'Report on survey of parishes', 66 pp. of evidence and report.
22 'Report on survey of parishes', 15, 24, 27.
23 'Report on survey of parishes', 47.
24 'Report on survey of parishes', 13.
25 *Journal of the House of Commons*, 92 (1837), 14 and 18 April.
26 'Report on survey of parishes', 6.
27 An Act to Amend an Act for the Commutation of Tithes in England and Wales, 1 Vict. cap. 69; 2 & 3 Vict. cap. 62 extended the amendments to maps accompanying compulsory awards.
28 R. J. P Kain, 'R. K. Dawson's proposal in 1836 for a cadastral survey of England and Wales', *Cartographic Journal*, 12 (1975), 81–8.
29 Thompson, *Chartered surveyors*, 105.
30 Quoted in Close, *The early years of the Ordnance Survey*, 92.
31 BPP (HC), 1824, VIII, 'Report from the select committee appointed to consider the best mode of apportioning equally the local burthens collected in Ireland, to provide for a general survey and valuation . . .', 77.
32 BPP (HC), 1852–3, LXXXV, Appendix pp. clvii–clxi.
33 BPP (HC), 1844, XVII, 'Minutes of evidence taken before the commission inquiring into the state of large towns and populous districts', 371.
34 Tithe Commission, 'Instructions as to forms of apportionment and maps', issued 31 July 1837; a transcript of these instructions is printed in Whalley, *The Tithe Act, and the Tithe Amendment Act*, 194–8.
35 Copies of the 'instructions' have occasionally found their way into parish tithe files; for example, PRO IR 18/4323. They may also be found among the papers of solicitors and land surveyors in county record offfices.

36 We are grateful to Dr J. B. Harley for drawing our attention to the correspondence concerning the Drewsteignton tithe map in Devon Record Office (2165A/PB59–102).
37 PRO IR 18/1276.
38 Devon Record Office 2165A/PB62.
39 Devon Record Office 2165A/PB71.
40 Devon Record Office 2165A/PB96.
41 Devon Record Office 2165A/PB96.
42 Devon Record Office 2165A/PB60, 61, 63, 64.
43 PRO IR 18/1276.
44 'Instructions as to forms of apportionment and maps', 31 July 1837.
45 'Instructions as to forms of apportionment and maps', 31 July 1837.
46 Eagle, *The acts for the commutation of tithes in England and Wales*, 138.
47 Leicestershire Record Office DE380/36 and DE380/25/8.
48 Leicestershire Record Office DE380/30/1.
49 Leicestershire Record Office DE380/30/2.
50 Whalley, *The Tithe Act*, 313.
51 BPP (HC), 1852–3, LXXXV, clvii–clxi. Letter from Major Dawson, RE, to the Registrar General, 20 July 1852.
52 BPP (HC), 1854, XLI, 'Correspondence respecting the scale for the Ordnance Survey. . .' Letter dated 24 February 1854 from James Walker, FRS, to the Master General of Ordnance, 333.
53 B. R. Dittmer, 'An agricultural geography of northwest Wiltshire, 1773–1840,' unpublished University of London M.A. thesis (1963), 30.
54 F. D. Hartley, 'The agricultural geography of the Chilterns *c*.1840', unpublished University of London M.A. thesis (1953), chapter 1.
55 BPP (HC), 1837 second session, XXI. Letter dated 30 October 1854 from H. Pyne, Clerk to the Board of Copyhold and Tithe Commissioners to the Royal Commission on Registration of Title and Sale and Transfer of Land, 347.
56 A. D. M. Phillips, 'A study of farming practices and soil types in Staffordshire around 1840', *North Staffordshire Journal of Field Studies*, 13 (1973), 30, 34.
57 'Royal Commission on Registration of Title', evidence of William Blamire, 259.
58 Secretary of the Tithe Redemption Commission, 'The records of the Tithe Redemption Commission', *Journal of the Society of Archivists*, 1 (1957), 136; E. A. Cox and B. R. Dittmer, 'The tithe files of the mid-nineteenth century', *Agricultural History Review*, 13 (1965), 1–16; Kain, 'The tithe files of mid-nineteenth century England and Wales'.
59 Cox and Dittmer, 'The tithe files', 3–9.
60 PRO IR 18/454.
61 Harriet M. E. Holt, 'The tithe files of Norfolk', *Norfolk Research Committee Bulletin*, 23 (1980), 6–7.
62 PRO IR 18/14266.
63 The full index in machine-readable form is deposited in the Economic and Social Research Council's Archive at the University of Essex. Those parts relating to agriculture and the rural landscape are contained in Kain, *An atlas and index of the tithe files*.

64 G. Slater, *The English peasantry and the enclosure of common fields* (London, Constable, 1907), 189.
65 BPP (HC), 1857, second session XXI, 'Report of the commissioners appointed to consider the subject of the registration of title with reference to the sale and transfer of land', 297.
66 List and Index Society, *Inland Revenue tithe maps and apportionments* (London, Swift (P. and D.), 1971 and 1972), Vols. 68 and 83.
67 Kain, *An atlas and index of the tithe files*.

4 The accuracy of the tithe surveys

1 Janet M. Hooke and R. J. P. Kain, *Historical change in the physical environment: a guide to sources and techniques* (London, Butterworth, 1982), 68–94; see also J. B. Harley's comments on the evaluation of the whole 'family' of privately produced estate, enclosure and tithe maps in *Maps for the local historian. A guide to the British sources* (London, National Council of Social Service, 1972), 36–9.
2 Reply of John Meadows White to a Treasury circular concerning the scale for future Ordnance Survey maps printed in BPP (HC), 1854, XLI 'Correspondence respecting the scale for the Ordnance Survey and upon contouring and hill delineation', 107–10.
3 BPP (HC), 1856, XIV, 'Report from the select committee on Ordnance Survey of Scotland together with the proceedings of the committee, minutes of evidence, appendix and index', evidence of Lieutenant-Colonel R. K. Dawson, 31.
4 P. W. Millard, *The law relating to tithes and payments in lieu thereof*, 3rd edition (London, Butterworth, 1938), 84–6.
5 Ordnance Survey, *Account of field surveying and the preparation of the manuscript plans of the Ordnance Survey* (Southampton, Ordnance Survey, 1873).
6 Thompson, *Chartered surveyors*, 98.
7 BPP (HC), 1857, second session, XXI, 'Report of the commissioners appointed to consider the subject of the registration of title with reference to the sale and transfer of land', 256.
8 'Report . . . registration of title . . . sale and transfer of land', 256.
9 BPP (HC), 1844, XVII, 'Minutes of evidence taken before commissioners of inquiry into the state of large towns and populous districts', 371.
10 BPP (HC), 1850, XXXII, 'Report from the registration and conveyancing commission', 21.
11 PRO IR 18/1683.
12 'Minutes of evidence . . . state of large towns', 371.
13 PRO IR 18/10406.
14 BPP (HC), 1841, XII, 'Report of the tithe commissioners for England and Wales', dated 9 February 1841.
15 'Report of the tithe commissioners', 9 February 1841.
16 'Report of the tithe commissioners', 9 February 1841.
17 'Report . . . on Ordnance Survey of Scotland', 31.

18 BPP (HC), 1844, V, 'Report of select committee on commons enclosure and minutes of evidence', 159.
19 'Report . . . on commons enclosure', 159.
20 'Report . . . registration of title . . . sale and transfer of land', 261.
21 'Correspondence respecting the scale for the Ordnance Survey', 104.
22 'Report . . . on Ordnance Survey of Scotland', 32.
23 'Report . . . on Ordnance Survey of Scotland', 32.
24 BPP (HC), 1861, XIV, 'Report from the select committee on the cadastral survey', 54.
25 'Report . . . on the cadastral survey', 58.
26 'Correspondence respecting the scale for the Ordnance Survey', 205.
27 'Correspondence respecting the scale for the Ordnance Survey', 216; see also statement in 1861 by Lieutenant-Colonel G. A. Leach, at that date officer in charge of the map department of the Tithe Commission, in which he summarised Dawson's views on the possibility of combining existing tithe surveys into a national cadastral map, 'Report . . . on the cadastral survey', 29.
28 'Correspondence respecting the scale for the Ordnance Survey', 222.
29 'Correspondence respecting the scale for the Ordnance Survey', 325.
30 Janet M. Hooke and R. A. Perry, 'The planimetric accuracy of tithe maps', *Cartographic Journal*, 13 (1976), 177–83.
31 Information kindly supplied by Mr R. A. Perry.
32 Inconsistency and ambiguity are likely where landowners adopted units other than individual parcels of land as the basis for apportionment; A. R. H. Baker, in 'The field system of an east Kent parish (Deal)', *Archaeologia Cantiana*, 78 (1963), says on p. 99, 'The tithe map here is an unreliable guide to the open or enclosed state of the fields, for all the boundaries are shown as continuous lines. These boundaries are ownership rather than field boundaries.' In the Chilterns, dotted lines were also used to demarcate one person's lands from another's where this division was not marked adequately on the ground; see F. D. Hartley, 'The agricultural geography of the Chilterns *c.* 1840', unpublished University of London M.A. thesis (1953), 115.
33 For example: J. E. G. Mosby, *Norfolk*, Report of the Land Utilisation Survey of Britain, part 70 (1938), 144; B. L. Davies and H. Miller, *Carmarthenshire*, Report of the Land Utilisation Survey of Britain, part 39 (1944), 549; Hartley, 'The agricultural geography of the Chilterns', 20–1; A. Harris, *The rural landscape of the East Riding of Yorkshire, 1750–1850, a study in historical geography* (Oxford, Oxford University Press, 1961), 112; M. R. Postgate, 'Historical geography of the Breckland, 1600–1850', unpublished University of London M.A. thesis (1961), 272; E. A. Cox, 'An agricultural geography of Essex *c.* 1840', unpublished University of London M.A. thesis (1963), 39; J. M. Powell, 'Tithe surveys and schedules: some Montgomeryshire examples', *Journal of the National Library of Wales*, 16 (1969), 87–96; J. Chapman, 'Agriculture and the "waste" in Monmouthshire from 1750 to the present day', unpublished University of London Ph.D. thesis (1973), 21–6; Kain, 'The land of Kent in the middle of the nineteenth century', 93–102; A. D. M. Phillips, 'A study of farming practices and soil types in Staffordshire around 1840', *North Staffordshire Journal of Field Studies*, 13 (1973), 33–4.

34 PRO IR 18/3603, 3710.
35 PRO IR 18/3560, 3407, 3711.
36 PRO IR 18/3506, 3699.
37 Eagle, *The acts for the commutation of tithes in England and Wales*, 6.
38 Cox, 'An agricultural geography of Essex', 39.
39 Cox, 'An agricultural geography of Essex', 41.
40 Hartley, 'The agricultural geography of the Chilterns', 20–1.
41 Postgate, 'Historical geography of the Breckland', 272, 275.
42 Powell, 'The tithe surveys and schedules: some Montgomeryshire examples', 89.
43 Chapman, 'Agriculture and the "waste" in Monmouthshire', 22–6, 419–24.
44 S. Siegel, *Nonparametric statistics for the behavioral sciences* (New York, McGraw-Hill, 1956), 75–83.
45 Phillips, 'Farming practices and soil types in Staffordshire', 34.
46 Regina E. Porter, 'Agricultural change in Cheshire during the nineteenth century', unpublished University of Liverpool Ph.D. thesis (1974), 64.
47 PRO IR 18/572.
48 PRO IR 18/572.
49 PRO IR 18/742, 753, 769.
50 PRO IR 18/118–79, 11951–2, 11967, 12008, 12041, 12099, 12241.
51 See, for example, Howard's comments at Yeadon, PRO IR 18/12962.
52 Eagle, *The acts for the commutation of tithes*, 83–4; the quotation is from G. H. Whalley's discussion of the Tithe Commission's 'Form of Instructions No. 6 "Form of agreement . . . with form of schedule annexed" ', in *The Tithe Act and the whole of the Tithe Amendment Acts, with explanatory notes*, 2nd edition (London, Shaw and Sons, 1848), 245.
53 See, for example, the problems encountered in Dicks, 'The south-western peninsulas of England and Wales' discussed in this book on pp. 193–6.
54 R. J. P. Kain and Harriet M. E. Holt, 'Agriculture and land use in Cornwall *circa* 1840', *Southern History*, 3 (1981), 142–3.
55 Hartley, 'The agricultural geography of the Chilterns', 12.
56 PRO IR 18/3830.
57 PRO IR 18/3531.
58 PRO IR 18/3828.
59 PRO IR 18/3794.
60 PRO IR 18/3501, 3792.
61 PRO IR 18/9983.
62 PRO IR 18/7335, 7419, 7553, 7487.
63 PRO IR 18/5472, 5507.
64 Cox and Dittmer, 'The tithe files of the mid-nineteenth century', 1–16.
65 Phillips, 'Farming practices and soil types in Staffordshire', 34–5.
66 A. D. M. Phillips, 'Agricultural land use, soils and the Nottinghamshire tithe surveys *circa* 1840', *East Midland Geographer*, 6 (1976), 288.
67 PRO IR 18/454.
68 PRO IR 18/1407.
69 PRO IR 18/3074.
70 Cox and Dittmer, 'The tithe files of the mid-nineteenth century', 1–16.

71 'Report from the registration and conveyancing commission', 5.
72 'Report from the registration and conveyancing commission', 21–3.
73 'Report . . . registration of title . . . sale and transfer of land', 257.
74 R. E. Sandell (ed.), *Abstracts of Wiltshire tithe apportionments* (Devizes, Wiltshire Record Society, 1975), 10.
75 'Report . . . registration of title . . . sale and transfer of land', 260.
76 June A. Sheppard, 'East Yorkshire's agricultural labour force in the mid-nineteenth century,' *Agricultural History Review*, 9 (1961), 43–54.
77 C. Thomas, 'Rural society in nineteenth century Wales: south Cardiganshire in 1851', *Ceredigion*, 6 (1971), 388–414.
78 S. Thomas, 'The agricultural labour force in some south-west Carmarthenshire parishes in the mid-nineteenth century', *Welsh History Review*, 3 (1966), 63–73; also his 'The enumerators' returns as a source for a period picture of the parish of Llansantffraid, 1841–51', *Ceredigion*, 4 (1963) 408–21.
79 J. Harvey, 'A short history of Bookham, Surrey – part IX', *Proceedings of the Leatherhead and District Local History Society*, 2 (1962), 187–93.
80 J. T. Coppock, 'The statistical assessment of British agriculture', *Agricultural History Review*, 4 (1956), 66–79, reference on p. 78.
81 J. T. Coppock, 'The changing arable in the Chilterns, 1875–1951', *Geography*, 43 (1957), 217–29, Fig. 3; Aileen M. Carpenter, 'The value of the tithe surveys to the study of land ownership and occupancy in the mid-nineteenth century, with special reference to south Hertfordshire', *Hertfordshire Past and Present*, 7 (1967), 48–52.

5 Evidence of field systems

1 F. Seebohm, *The English village community* . . . (London, Longmans, 1883), 3. The map of Hitchin faces p. 6, and the field arrangements are described on pp. 1–4.
2 R. Dymond, 'Devonshire fields and hedges', *Journal of the Bath and West of England Society*, 4 (1856), 132–148.
3 A. Meitzen, *Wandesungen, Anbau und Agrarrecht der Völker Europas nördlich der Alpen, erste Abteilung: Siedlung und Agrarwesen der Westgermanen und Ostgermanen, der Kelten, Römer, Finnen und Slawen*, 3 vols. and atlas (Berlin, Wilhelm Hesty, 1895).
4 M. Bloch, *French rural history, an essay on its basic characteristics* (translation of *Les caractères originaux de l'histoire rurale française*, 1931) (London, Routledge and Kegan Paul, 1966), xxvii.
5 W. Rye, *Records and record searching: a guide to the genealogist and topographer*, 2nd edition (London, George Allen, 1897), 23; and *An account of the church and parish of Cawston, in the county of Norfolk* (Norwich, privately printed, 1898).
6 Slater, *The English peasantry*, 20–2, 32–4.
7 Slater, *The English peasantry*, 46, 61, 68.
8 Slater, *The English peasantry*, 187.
9 A. R. H. Baker and R. A. Butlin (eds.), *Studies of field systems in the British Isles* (Cambridge, Cambridge University Press, 1973), 1.

10 J. E. B. Gover, A. Mawer and F. M. Stenton, *The place names of Surrey*, English Place-Name Society, XI (Cambridge, Cambridge University Press, 1934), vi.
11 J. E. B. Gover, A. Mawer and F. M. Stenton, *The place names of Middlesex*, English Place-Name Society, XVIII (Cambridge, Cambridge University Press, 1942), 195–217.
12 W. C. Waller, 'Essex field names', *Transactions of the Essex Archaeological Society*, new series, 5 (1895), 114–81; 6 (1898), 60–84, 258–77; 7 (1900), 65–92, 285–327; 8 (1903), 76–103, 199–222, 295–323; 9 (1903), 68–100, 156–79; cited in P. H. Reaney, *The place names of Essex*, English Place-Name Society, XII (Cambridge, Cambridge University Press, 1935), 574.
13 F. T. Wainwright, 'Field-names', *Antiquity*, 17 (1943), 57–66, references on 59 and 64–5.
14 J. Field, *English field names: a dictionary* (Newton Abbot, David & Charles, 1972), xxii, xxv.
15 Baker and Butlin (eds.), *Studies of field systems*, 33.
16 Baker and Butlin (eds.), *Studies of field systems*, 33–4; J. Field, 'Progress in field names studies', *Local Historian*, 13 (1978), 388–96; A. Mawer, *The study of field-names in relation to place-names*, reprinted from J. G. Edwards, V. H. Galbraith (eds.), *Historical essays in honour of James Tait* (Manchester, printed for the subscribers, 1933), 189–206; M. Gelling, *Signposts to the past. Place names and the history of England* (London, J. M. Dent, 1978), 209.
17 Mosby, *Norfolk*; S. R. Eyre, 'The upward limit of enclosure on the east moor of north Derbyshire', *Transactions of the Institute of British Geographers*, 23 (1957), 61–74; C. Thomas, 'Place-name studies and agrarian colonization in North Wales', *Welsh History Review*, 10 (1980), 155–71.
18 Margaret L. Faull, 'Problems in the use of place-names', in P. Brandon and R. Millman (eds.), *Recording historic landscapes, principles and practices* (London, Polytechnic of North London, Department of Geography, 1980), 81–7.
19 H. L. Gray, *English field systems* (Cambridge, Mass., Harvard University Press, 1915), 15.
20 Gray, *English field systems*, 19–22.
21 Gray, *English field systems*, 22.
22 Gray, *English field systems*, 16.
23 Gray, *English field systems*, 3–16.
24 J. H. Clapham, *An economic history of modern Britain*, 3 vols. (Cambridge, Cambridge University Press, 1926–38); J. L. and Barbara Hammond, *The village labourer, 1760–1832* (London, Longman, 1912); Orwin and Orwin, *The open fields*.
25 Orwin and Orwin, *The open fields*, 14.
26 Emmison, *Types of open-field parishes*.
27 Emmison, *Types of open-field parishes*, 5.
28 A. H. Shorter, 'Landscore, stitch and quillett fields in Devon', *Devon and Cornwall Notes and Queries*, 23 (1949), 372–80.
29 A. H. Slee, 'The open fields of Braunton. Braunton Great Field and Braunton Downs', *Report and Transactions of the Devonshire Association*, 84 (1952), 142–9.

30 H. P. R. Finberg, 'The open field in Devon', in W. G. Hoskins and H. P. R. Finberg, *Devonshire studies* (London, Cape, 1952), 279.
31 Finberg, 'The open field in Devon', 280.
32 H. S. A. Fox, 'A geographical study of the field systems of Devon and Cornwall', unpublished University of Cambridge Ph.D. thesis (1971); 'The study of field systems', *Devon Historian*, 4 (1972), 3–11; 'The chronology of enclosure and economic development in medieval Devon', *Economic History Review*, 2nd series, 28 (1975), 181–202.
33 W. G. Hoskins, 'Three studies in family history', in W. G. Hoskins and H. P. R. Finberg, *Devonshire studies* (London, Jonathan Cape, 1952), 78–119, esp. 80 and 118; Elizabeth Gawne, 'Field patterns in Widecombe parish and the Forest of Dartmoor', *Report and Transactions of the Devonshire Association*, 102 (1970), 49–69; N. W. Alcock, 'Fields and farms in an east Devon parish', *Report and Transactions of the Devonshire Association*, 107 (1975), 93–172; A. H. Shorter, 'Field patterns in Brixham parish, Devon', *Report and Transactions of the Devonshire Association*, 82 (1950), 271–80; W. M. Williams, *A west country village, Ashworthy: family, kinship and land* (London, Routledge and Kegan Paul, 1963); D. J. Bonney, 'Former farms and fields at Challacombe, Manaton, Dartmoor', in K. J. Gregory and W. L. D. Ravenhill (eds.), *Exeter essays in geography* (Exeter, University of Exeter, 1971), 83–91.
34 N. J. G. Pounds, 'The historical geography of Cornwall', unpublished University of London Ph.D. thesis (1945); M. E. Witherick, 'Stages in the growth of urban settlement in central Cornwall', unpublished University of Birmingham Ph.D. thesis (1963).
35 P. Flatrès, *Géographie rurale de quatre contrées celtiques: Irlande, Galles, Cornwall et Man* (Rennes, Plihon, 1957).
36 Dorothy Sylvester, 'Rural settlement in Cheshire, some problems of origin and classification', *Transactions of the Historic Society of Lancashire and Cheshire*, 101 (1949), 1–37; 'The open fields of Cheshire', *Transactions of the Historic Society of Lancashire and Cheshire*, 108 (1956), 1–33.
37 Dorothy Sylvester, 'Rural settlement in Anglesey', *Anglesey Antiquarian Society and Field Club Transactions* unnumbered series (1949), 9.
38 Dorothy Sylvester, 'Settlement patterns in rural Flintshire', *Flintshire Historical Society Publications*, 15 (1954–5), 6–42.
39 Sylvester, 'Settlement patterns in rural Flintshire', 21, 32.
40 Dorothy Sylvester, 'The rural landscape of eastern Montgomeryshire', *Montgomeryshire Collections*, 54 (1955–6), 3–26; 'The common fields of the coastlands of Gwent', *Agricultural History Review*, 6 (1958), 9–26.
41 Sylvester, 'The common fields of the coastlands of Gwent', 16, 19.
42 Dorothy Sylvester, *The rural landscape of the Welsh borderland, a study in historical geography* (London, Macmillan, 1969).
43 Sylvester, *The rural landscape of the Welsh borderland*, 220–1.
44 Sylvester, *The rural landscape of the Welsh borderland*, 230.
45 F. W. Maitland, *Domesday Book and beyond: three essays in the early history of England* (Cambridge, Cambridge University Press, 1897); B. K. Roberts, *Rural settlement in Britain* (Folkestone, Dawson, 1977); B. K. Roberts, 'Planned villages from medieval England', in A. R. H. Baker and J. B. Harley (eds.),

Man made the land (Newton Abbot, David and Charles, 1973), 46–58; Pamela Allerston, 'English village development, findings from the Pickering district of north Yorkshire', *Transactions of the Institute of British Geographers*, 51 (1970), 95–109.

46 Sylvester, *The rural landscape of the Welsh borderland*, 190–217.

47 D. H. C. Bennett, 'Settlement patterns and farm units in western Pembrokeshire: a study in historical geography', unpublished University of Wales M.A. thesis (1955).

48 R. A. Worthington, 'The growth of rural settlement in south-eastern Monmouthshire', unpublished University of Wales M.A. thesis (1956).

49 G. R. J. Jones, 'Some medieval rural settlements in north Wales', *Transactions of the Institute of British Geographers*, 19 (1953), 51–72.

50 Jones, 'Some medieval rural settlements in north Wales', 51.

51 G. R. J. Jones, 'The distribution of medieval settlement in Anglesey', *Anglesey Antiquarian Society and Field Club Transactions*, unnumbered series (1955), 27–96; 'The pattern of settlement on the Welsh border', *Agricultural History Review*, 8 (1960), 66–81.

52 G. R. J. Jones, 'The tribal system in Wales: a re-assessment in the light of settlement studies', *Welsh History Review*, 1 (1961), 111–32.

53 G. R. J. Jones, 'Early settlement in Afron: the setting of Tre'r Ceiri', *Caernarvonshire Historical Society Transactions*, 24 (1963), 1–20.

54 G. R. J. Jones, 'The Llanynys quillets: a measure of landscape transformation in north Wales', *Transactions of the Denbighshire Historical Society*, 13 (1964), 133–58.

55 G. R. J. Jones, 'The distribution of bond settlements in north-west Wales', *Welsh History Review*, 2 (1964), 19–36.

56 G. R. J. Jones, 'Field systems of north Wales', in Baker and Butlin (eds.), *Studies of field systems*, 430–79; 'Early customary tenures in Wales and open-field agriculture', in T. Rowley (ed.), *The origins of open-field agriculture* (London, Croom Helm, 1981), 202–25.

57 J. W. Edwards, 'Enclosure and agricultural improvement in the Vale of Clwyd, 1750–1875', unpublished University of London M.A. thesis (1963).

58 Edwards, 'Enclosure and agricultural improvement in the Vale of Clwyd', 237.

59 J. G. Thomas, 'Some enclosure patterns in central Wales, a study in landscape modification', *Geography*, 42 (1957), 25–36.

60 C. Morgan, 'The effect of parliamentary enclosure on the landscape of Caernarvonshire and Merioneth', unpublished University of Wales M.Sc. thesis (1959), 165.

61 W. T. R. Pryce, 'Enclosure and field pattern in the Banwy Valley', *Montgomeryshire Collections*, 57 (1961–2), 23–32.

62 Margaret F. Davies, 'Rhosili open fields and related south Wales field patterns', *Agricultural History Review*, 4 (1956), 80–96.

63 Davies, 'Rhosili open fields', 84.

64 Margaret F. Davies, 'The open fields of Laugharne', *Geography*, 40 (1955), 169–77.

65 Flatrès, *Géographie rurale de quatre contrées celtiques*.

66 Joan Thirsk, *Tudor Enclosures*, Historical Association pamphlet, 41 (1959), 4.

67 H. S. A. Fox, 'Approaches to the adoption of the midland system', in Rowley (ed.), *The origins of open-field agriculture*, 64–111.

68 G. Elliot, 'Field systems of northwest England', in Baker and Butlin (eds.), *Studies of Field Systems*; R. A. Butlin, 'Field systems of Northumberland and Durham', in Baker and Butlin; June A. Sheppard, 'Field systems of Yorkshire', in Baker and Butlin, 41–187.

69 H. Thorpe, 'The geography of rural settlement in the Durham region', unpublished University of Durham M.Litt. thesis (1936), 124–43.

70 *ibid*, 133.

71 B. K. Roberts, *The green villages of County Durham: a study in historical geography* (Durham, Durham County Council, 1977), 24–38; J. S. Ingleson, 'Settlement, agrarian systems, and field patterns in central Durham, 1600–1850: a study in historical geography', unpublished University of Durham M.A. thesis (1972); D. A. Alexander, 'Settlement, field systems and landownership in Teesdale between 1600 and 1850: a study in historical geography', unpublished University of Durham M.A. thesis (1972); B. K. Roberts, 'Townfield origins: the case of Cockfield, County Durham', in Rowley *The origins of open field agriculture*, 145–61.

72 T. H. Bainbridge, 'Land utilisation in Cumbria in the mid-nineteenth century as revealed by a study of the tithe returns', *Transactions of the Cumberland and Westmorland Antiquarian and Archaeological Society*, new series, 43 (1943), 87–95.

73 G. Elliott, 'Changing agricultural landscapes in Cumberland', unpublished University of Liverpool M.A. thesis (1956).

74 J. C. Jackson, 'Open field cultivation in Derbyshire', *Derbyshire Archaeological Journal*, 82 (1962), 54–72.

75 Jackson, 'Open field cultivation in Derbyshire', 24.

76 A. R. H. Baker, 'Open fields in Derbyshire: some reservations about recent arguments', *Derbyshire Archaeological Journal*, 83 (1963), 77–81.

77 Eyre, 'The upward limit of enclosure', 61–74.

78 Eyre, 'The upward limit of enclosure', 70.

79 J. Chapman, 'Changing agriculture and the moorland edge in the North York Moors, 1750–1960', unpublished University of London M.A. thesis (1961).

80 A. Digby, 'Regional variations in land use in mid-Ribblesdale since late medieval times', unpublished University of Leeds M.A. thesis (1960).

81 Gawne, 'Field patterns in Widecombe parish and the Forest of Dartmoor', 49–69

82 Mosby, *Norfolk*, 128–34.

83 Mosby, *Norfolk*, 128–9, 134.

84 Mosby, *Norfolk*, 131.

85 M. R. Postgate, 'Historical geography of the Breckland, 1600–1850', unpublished University of London M.A. thesis (1961), 294.

86 M. R. Postgate, 'The field systems of Breckland', *Agricultural History Review*, 10 (1962), 81–101; 'Field systems of East Anglia', in Baker and Butlin (eds.), *Studies of field systems*, 281–324.

87 P. Armstrong, *The changing landscape: the history and ecology of man's impact on the face of East Anglia* (Lavenham, Dalton, 1975).

88 W. Smith, *An economic geography of Great Britain* (London, Methuen, 1949) on p. 16 refers to the work of Miss A. M. Moss.
89 N. Hilton, 'The Land's End peninsula: the influence of history on agriculture', *Geographical Journal*, 119 (1953), 55–72.
90 Hilton, 'The Land's End peninsula', 68.
91 H. Uhlig, 'Old hamlets with infield and outfield systems in western and central Europe', *Geografiska Annaler*, 43 (1961), 285–312.
92 J. D. Chambers, *Nottinghamshire in the eighteenth century*, 2nd edition (London, Frank Cass, 1966), 155–6.
93 C. Stella Davies, *The agricultural history of Cheshire, 1750–1850* (Manchester, Chetham Society, 3rd series, 10, 1960), 54–7, 225.
94 F. T. Wainwright, 'Field-names of Amounderness Hundred', *Transactions of the Historic Society of Lancashire and Cheshire*, 97 (1945–6), 71–116.
95 J. McN. Dodgson, *The Place-names of Cheshire*, English Place-Name Society, XLIV–XLVIII (Cambridge, Cambridge University Press, 1970–2).
96 Vera Chapman, 'Open fields in west Cheshire', *Transactions of the Historic Society of Lancashire and Cheshire*, 104 (1952), 35–59.
97 G. R. J. Jones, 'Some medieval rural settlements in north Wales', *Transactions of the Institute of British Geographers*, 19 (1953), 51–72; G. R. J. Jones, 'To the building of Kirkstall Abbey', in M. W. Beresford and G. R. J. Jones (eds.), *Leeds and its region* (Leeds, British Association for the Advancement of Science, 1967), 125.
98 B. D. Giles, 'Mid-Worcestershire in the first half of the nineteenth century: the enclosure and tithe awards of five parishes', *Transactions of the Worcestershire Archaeological Society*, 3rd series, 4 (1974), 35–66; P. Laxton, 'Common fields and enclosure in part of central Berkshire', *Journal of the Durham University Geographical Society*, 9 (1967), 44–56.
99 A. R. H. Baker, 'Howard Levi Gray and *English field systems*: an evaluation', *Agricultural History*, 39 (1965), 86-91.
100 M. D. Nightingale, 'Some evidence of open field agriculture in Kent', unpublished University of Oxford B.Litt. thesis (1952).
101 A. R. H. Baker, 'The field systems of Kent', unpublished University of London Ph.D. thesis (1963).
102 A. R. H. Baker, 'Field systems in the Vale of Holmesdale', *Agricultural History Review*, 14 (1966), 1–24.
103 Baker, 'Field systems in the Vale of Holmesdale', 5.
104 Baker, 'The field system of an east Kent parish (Deal)', 96–117.
105 A. R. H. Baker, 'Open fields and partible inheritance on a Kent manor', *Economic History Review*, 2nd series, 17 (1964), 1–23.
106 Hartley, 'The agricultural geography of the Chilterns c. 1840'; D Roden, 'Studies in Chiltern field systems', unpublished University of London Ph.D. thesis (1965); 'Field systems in Ibstone, a township of the south-west Chilterns, during the later middle ages', *Records of Buckinghamshire,* 18 (1966), 43–57; and 'Field systems of the Chiltern Hills and their environs', in Baker and Butlin (eds.), *Studies of field systems*, 325–76.
107 G. I. Meirion-Jones, 'A contribution to the historical geography of north-east Hampshire c. 1600-1850', unpublished University of London M.Phil. thesis (1969).

108 G. I. Meirion-Jones, 'The use of hearth tax returns and vernacular architecture in settlement studies with examples from north-east Hampshire', *Transactions of the Institute of British Geographers*, 53 (1971), 133–60.
109 M. W. Beresford, 'The lost villages of medieval England', *Geographical Journal*, 117 (1951), 140.
110 M. W. Beresford, *The lost villages of England* (London, Lutterworth, 1954), 226.
111 Margaret L. Faull, 'Place-names and past landscapes', *English Place-Name Society Journal*, 11 (1978–9), 24–46.
112 W. S. G. Thomas, 'Lost villages in south-west Carmarthenshire', *Transactions of the Institute of British Geographers*, 47 (1969), 191–203.
113 Thomas, 'Lost villages in south-west Carmarthenshire', 197.
114 M. G. Jarrett and S. Wrathmell, 'Sixteenth- and seventeenth-century farmsteads: West Whelpington, Northumberland', *Agricultural History Review*, 25 (1977), 108–19.
115 C. Taylor, *Fields in the English landscape* (London, Dent, 1975); R. Workman, 'Analysing a tithe map in depth', *Local Historian*, 14 (1981), 262–9.
116 O. A. W. Dilke, *The Roman land surveyors. An introduction to the agrimensores* (Newton Abbot, David and Charles, 1971).
117 O. A. W. and Margaret S. Dilke, 'Surveyors who measured by centuries', *Geographical Magazine*, 44 (1972), 630–6.
118 J. A. Yelling, *Common field and enclosure in England 1450–1850* (London, Macmillan, 1977), esp. 71–93, 120–45.

6 Land use

1 Prothero, *English farming past and present*; Orwin and Whetham, *History of British agriculture 1846–1914*; P. J. Perry (ed.), *British agriculture, 1875–1914* (London, Methuen, 1973).
2 Coppock, 'The statistical assessment of British agriculture', 4–21, 66–79; R. H. Best and J. T. Coppock, *The changing use of land in Britain* (London, Faber and Faber, 1962).
3 D. G. Barnes, *A history of the English Corn Laws from 1660–1846* (London, Routledge, 1930).
4 E. L. Jones, *The development of English agriculture, 1815–1873* (London, Macmillan, 1968), 17–25.
5 A. G. Street, *Farmer's glory* (London, Faber and Faber, 1932).
6 Caird, *English agriculture in 1850–51*.
7 The complete list of Prize Essays is in O. R. McGregor, 'Introduction part two: after 1815', in R. E. Prothero (Lord Ernle), *English farming past and present*, 6th edition, (London, Heinemann and Frank Cass, 1961), lxxix–cxlv.
8 Harrison, Mead and Pannett, 'A midland ridge-and-furrow map', 365–9; C. Taylor, *Fields in the English landscape* (London, Dent, 1975).
9 Chapman, 'Changing agriculture and the moorland edge in the North York Moors'; Eyre,'The upward limit of enclosure on the east moor of north Derbyshire', 61–74.
10 A. Harris, 'Changes in the early railway age: 1800–1850', in H. C. Darby (ed.), *A new historical geography of England* (Cambridge, Cambridge University

Press, 1973), 465–526; L. de Lavergne, *The rural economy of England, Scotland and Ireland* (Edinburgh and London, Blackwood, 1855).

11 L. D. Stamp, *The land of Britain, its use and misuse*, 3rd edition (London, Longman Green, 1962), 55–61.

12 H. C. K. Henderson, 'Our changing agriculture: the distribution of arable land in the Adur Basin, Sussex, from 1780 to 1931', *Journal of the Ministry of Agriculture*, 43 (1936), 625–33; 'Changes in land utilisation in Derbyshire 1837–1937', in A. H. Harris, *Derbyshire*, Report of the Land Utilisation Survey of Great Britain, part 63 (1941), 71–4.

13 J. B. Jarvis, 'Changes in land use in south east Denbighshire', in E. J. Howell, *North Wales*, Report of the Land Utilisation Survey of Great Britain, parts 41–3 (1946), 734–43.

14 J. T. Coppock, 'Maps as sources for the study of land use in the past', *Imago Mundi*, 22 (1968), 37–49; Helen Wallis, 'The history of land use mapping', *Cartographic Journal*, 18 (1981), 45 8.

15 H. C. K. Henderson, *Our changing agriculture* (London, University of London inaugural lecture, 1966).

16 Stamp, *Land of Britain*, 57–8.

17 Stamp, *Land of Britain*, 64.

18 E. C. Willatts,'Changes in land utilization in the south-west of the London Basin, 1840–1932' *Geographical Journal*, 82 (1933), 515-28, esp. 516–17.

19 Personal Communication from Dr Willatts, 1 May 1982; G. W. J. Gyll, *History of the parish of Wraysbury* (London, H. G. Bohn, 1862), 160–71.

20 Willatts, 'Changes in land utilization in the south-west of the London Basin' 525, 527.

21 E. C. Willatts, *Middlesex and the London region*, Report of the Land Utilisation Survey of Britain, part 79 (1937).

22 Henderson, 'Our changing agriculture: the distribution of arable land in the Adur Basin, Sussex'; personal communication from Professor Henderson, 14 June 1982.

23 E. W. H. Briault, *Sussex (East and West)*, Report of the Land Utilisation Survey of Great Britain, Parts 83–4 (1942), 83–4, 498–9, 504–6.

24 Harris, *Derbyshire*, 71–3.

25 Mosby, *Norfolk*, 128–51.

26 L. G. Cameron, *Hertfordshire*, Report of the Land Utilisation Survey of Great Britain, part 80 (1941), 328–9; D. W. Shave, 'The distribution of arable land in the upper Wey Basin in 1840, 1870, and 1939', in L. D. Stamp and E. C. Willatts, *Surrey*, Report of the Land Utilisation Survey of Great Britain, part 81 (1941), 392; L. D. Stamp, *Devonshire*, Report of the Land Utilisation Survey of Great Britain, part 92 (1941) refers to L. R. Hawkes, 'A regional study of the agricultural landscape of the north Exe Basin', unpublished University of London M. A. thesis (1938), and on p. 530 to the work of W. W. French.

27 R. Coles, 'Changes in land utilisation in three typical Essex parishes (c. 1840 to 1933)', in N. V. Scarfe, *Essex*, Report of the Land Utilisation Survey of Great Britain, part 82 (1942), 458; see also R. Coles, 'The historical geography of south-east Essex', unpublished University of London Ph.D. thesis (1934), 233.

28 C. E. Fitchett, *Bedfordshire*, Report of the Land Utilisation Survey of Great Britain, part 55 (1943), 181–9; K. M. Buchanan, *Worcestershire*, Report of the

Land Utilisation Survey of Great Britain, part 68 (1944), 515ff; A. W. McPherson, *Warwickshire*, Report of the Land Utilisation Survey of Great Britain, part 62 (1946), 789–837, acknowledges the work of Miss M. Talamo, Mrs Olga J. Garrett, and J. E. Spalton; L. D. Stamp, *Kent*, Report of the Land Utilisation Survey of Britain, part 85 (1943), 598, 600.

29 Davies, *Pembrokeshire*, 114, 120, 122.

30 E. J. Howell, *Shropshire*, Report of the Land Utilisation Survey of Great Britain, part 66 (1941), 292.

31 E. J. Howell, 'Land use and agriculture in Brecon and Radnor, 150 years ago, in Rosalynde M. Whyte, *Brecon*, Report of the Land Utilisation Survey of Great Britain, part 37 (1943), 383–94.

32 J. May and S. F. Wells, *Montgomeryshire*, Report of the Land Utilisation Survey of Great Britain, part 36 (1942), 352, based on the unpublished work of L. S. Andrews.

33 Davies and Miller, *Carmarthenshire*, 550.

34 E. J. Howell, *Cardiganshire*, Report of the Land Utilisation Survey of Great Britain, part 40 (1946), 606.

35 N. S. B. and Ethel C. Gras, *The economic and social history of an English village, Crawley, Hampshire, A.D. 909–1928* (Cambridge, Mass., Harvard University Press, 1930), 634.

36 A. G. Ruston and D. Witney, *Hooton Pagnell, The agricultural evolution of a Yorkshire village* (London, Arnold, 1934).

37 R. J. Whiteman (ed.), *Hexton: a parish survey* (Bradford, Cummins, 1937).

38 W. H. Chippindall, *A history of the parish of Tunstall*, Manchester, Chetham Society, new series, 104 (1940), 108–10.

39 M. E. Otter, 'The land utilisation of Llanrug parish', *Transactions of the Caernarvonshire Historical Society*, 7 (1946), 55–83; Margaret F. Davies, *Wales in maps* (Cardiff, University of Wales, 1951), 44–5.

40 I. Davies, 'The agriculture of the west midlands conurbation', unpublished University of Birmingham M.A. thesis (1955).

41 N. M. Simmonds, 'The functions and growth of the city of Exeter, 1800–1841', unpublished University of Exeter M.A. thesis (1959).

42 S. W. Wooldridge and G. E. Hutchings, *London's countryside* (London, Methuen, 1957), 187.

43 Gladys N. Brown, 'Scottish farmers in Hatfield', *Hertfordshire Past and Present*, 2 (1961), 41–8.

44 Workers' Educational Association, Redbourn Local History Tutorial Class, *The story of Redbourn* (Redbourn, WEA, 1962), 35–7 and endpaper.

45 K. A. Smalley, *Greenford – the historical geography of a northwest London parish* (Ealing, Ealing Local History Society Members' Papers, 3, 1963), 33–5.

46 Constance Pritchard, 'Changes in the agricultural geography of the parishes of Bockleton, Kyre Magna, Tenbury township and Foreign (Worc.) and Hampton Charles (Hereford) from 1841 to 1958', unpublished University of Birmingham M.A. thesis (1965), 57–104.

47 *Victoria History of the County of [VCH] Essex*, Vol. 4 (1956); *VCH Shropshire*, Vol. 8 (1968).

48 *VCH Essex*, Vol. 4, pp. 46, 59, 64, 75, 98, 105, 116.

49 *VCH Oxford*, Vol. 5 (1957), 173.
50 *VCH Oxford*, Vol. 7 (1962), 50.
51 *VCH Oxford*, Vol. 6 (1959), 350.
52 *VCH Oxford*, Vol. 6, pp. 171, 273.
53 *VCH Oxford*, Vol. 6, p. 7; Vol. 7, p. 225.
54 *VCH Cambridge*, Vols. 4, 6; *VCH Essex*, Vols. 4, 6, 7; *VCH Gloucester*, Vols. 6, 8, 11; *VCH Leicester*, Vol. 4; *VCH Middlesex*, Vols. 3, 5; *VCH Oxford*, Vols. 5, 6, 7; *VCH Shropshire*, Vol. 8; *VCH Somerset*, Vol. 4; *VCH Stafford*, Vols. 5, 8, 17; *VCH Warwick*, Vols. 3, 4, 8; *VCH Wiltshire*, Vols. 4, 6, 8; *VCH East Riding of Yorkshire*, Vol. 3.
55 H. C. Darby, 'An historical geography of England: twenty years after', *Geographical Journal*, 126 (1960), 147–59.
56 Hartley, 'The agricultural geography of the Chilterns *c.* 1840'.
57 M. C. Naish, 'The agricultural landscape of the Hampshire chalklands 1700–1840', unpublished University of London M.A. thesis (1961).
58 Dittmer, 'An agricultural geography of north-west Wiltshire, 1773–1840'.
59 Cox, 'An agricultural geography of Essex *c.* 1840'.
60 Kain, 'The land of Kent in the middle of the nineteenth century'.
61 M. J. Frost, 'The changing land use in the upper basin of the river Mole', unpublished University of London M.Sc. thesis (1964).
62 Aileen M. Carpenter, 'Changes in the agricultural geography of the south Hertfordshire plateau, 1750–1888', unpublished University of London M.A. thesis (1965).
63 R. F. J. Chiplen, 'The rural landscape of the Blackmore Vale, *c.* 1840', unpublished University of Exeter M.A. thesis (1969); A. G. Parton, 'Town and country in Surrey *c.* 1800–1870: a study in historical geography', unpublished University of Hull Ph.D. thesis (1973).
64 Jean East, 'The form and function of settlements in relation to types of farming in England and Wales (with an analysis of specific examples chosen from the west midlands and elsewhere)', unpublished University of London Ph.D. thesis (1947).
65 Joan Thirsk, 'Agrarian history, 1540–1950', in *Victoria History of the County of Leicester*, 2 (1954), 199–264.
66 Harris, *Rural landscape of the East Riding*.
67 Harris, *Rural landscape of the East Riding*, 112.
68 J. A. Yelling, 'Open field, enclosure and farm production in east Worcestershire 1540–1870', unpublished University of Birmingham Ph.D. thesis (1966).
69 Phillips, 'A study of farming practices and soil types in Staffordshire around 1840', 27–52; 'Agricultural land use, soils and the Nottinghamshire tithe surveys *circa* 1840', 284–301; 'Agricultural land use and the Herefordshire tithe surveys, *circa* 1840', *Transactions of the Woolhope Naturalists Field Club*, 43 (1979), 54–61.
70 Phillips, 'Agricultural land use and the Herefordshire tithe surveys', 56.
71 Phillips, 'Agricultural land use, soils and the Nottinghamshire tithe surveys', 290.
72 Phillips, 'A study of farming practices and soil types in Staffordshire', 38.
73 Pounds, 'The historical geography of Cornwall'.

74 D. G. Griffith, 'A study of the economic development of the lower Conway valley and the Creuddyn peninsula, 1750–1914', unpublished University of Wales M.A. thesis (1954).
75 J. C. Grove, 'Land use changes in west Gower 1840–1950', unpublished University of Wales M.A. thesis (1956).
76 T. R. B. Dicks, 'The south-western peninsulas of England and Wales; studies in agricultural geography, 1550–1900', unpublished University of Wales Ph.D. thesis (1964).
77 Dicks, 'The south-western peninsulas', 83.
78 N. Hilton, 'The Land's End Peninsula: the influence of history on agriculture', *Geographical Journal*, 119 (1953), 57–72.
79 R. J. P. Kain and Harriet M. E. Holt, 'Agriculture and land use in Cornwall *circa* 1840', *Southern History*, 3 (1981), 139–81.
80 Regina E. Porter, 'Agricultural change in Cheshire during the nineteenth century', unpublished University of Liverpool Ph.D. thesis (1974).
81 Porter, 'Agricultural change in Cheshire', 65.
82 P. E. Jones, 'Changes in land utilisation in Uwchgwyrfai, Caernarvonshire 1750 to 1956', unpublished University of Wales M.A. thesis (1959).
83 Jones, 'Changes in land utilisation in Uwchgwyrfai', 129.
84 J. M. Powell, 'An economic geography of Montgomeryshire in the nineteenth century', unpublished University of Liverpool M.A. thesis (1962); his map of arable land from the tithe surveys is also in 'Tithe surveys and schedules, some Montgomeryshire examples', 87–96.
85 Powell, 'An economic geography of Montgomeryshire'.
86 W. S. G. Thomas, 'Changing land utilisation, occupation and ownership in south-west Carmarthenshire from earliest times to the present', unpublished University of London Ph.D. thesis (1965).
87 C. Thomas, 'Estate surveys as sources in historical geography', *Journal of the National Library of Wales*, 14 (1966), 451–68; the uses and limitations of tithe surveys for studying nineteenth-century land improvement in mid-Wales, illustrated by a map showing variations in information recorded, are further examined in C. Thomas, 'Colonization, enclosure and the rural landscape', *National Library of Wales Journal*, 19 (1975), 132–46.
88 Hilton, 'The Land's End peninsula'.
89 Bainbridge, 'Land utilisation in Cumbria in the mid-nineteenth century as revealed by a study of the tithe returns', 87–95.
90 Griffith, 'A study of the economic development of the lower Conway valley', 40.
91 Eyre, 'The upward limit of enclosure'.
92 Digby, 'Regional variations in land use in mid-Ribblesdale since late medieval times'.
93 Chapman, 'Changing agriculture and the moorland edge'; Chapman, 'Agriculture and the "waste" in Monmouthshire from 1750 to the present day'.
94 Mosby, *Norfolk*, 143.
95 S. A. Johnson, 'Enclosure and the agricultural landscape of Lindsey from the sixteenth to the nineteenth century', unpublished University of Liverpool M.A. thesis (1957); 'Enclosure and agricultural landscapes in Lindsey', *Agricultural History Review*, 11 (1963), 95–102.

96 Postgate, 'Historical geography of the Breckland, 1600–1850'.

97 Elizabeth D. R. Burrell, 'An historical geography of the Sandlings of Suffolk 1600 to 1850', unpublished University of London M.Sc. thesis (1960).

98 D. B. Grigg, *The agricultural revolution in south Lincolnshire* (Cambridge, Cambridge University Press, 1966).

99 Armstrong, *The changing landscape: the history and ecology of man's impact on the face of East Anglia*; G. L. Cunningham, 'The changing landscape of the Dorset heathlands since 1700', unpublished University of London Ph.D. thesis (1974).

100 M. Williams, *The draining of the Somerset Levels* (Cambridge, Cambridge University Press, 1970).

101 A. D. M. Phillips, 'Mossland reclamation in nineteenth century Cheshire', *Transactions of the Historic Society of Lancashire and Cheshire*, 129 (1980), 93–107.

102 D. R. Mills, 'Population and settlement in Kesteven (Lincolnshire) *c.*1775–*c.*1885', unpublished University of Nottingham M.A. thesis (1957).

103 Joyce M. Lambert, J. N. Jennings, C. T. Smith, C. Green and J. N. Hutchinson, *The making of the Broads. A reconsideration of their origin in the light of new evidence* (London, Royal Geographical Society Research Series, 3, 1960); J. N. Jennings and Joyce M. Lambert, 'The shrinkage of the Broads', *New Naturalist*, 6 (1949), 26–7.

104 June A. Sheppard, 'The medieval meres of Holderness', *Transactions of the Institute of British Geographers*, 23 (1957), 75–86.

105 B. E. Cracknell, 'The alluvial marshlands of the lower Thames estuary: a study in changing use patterns', unpublished University of London Ph.D. thesis (1953).

106 B. E. Cracknell, *Canvey Island: the history of a marshland community* (Leicester, University of Leicester Department of English Local History, occasional paper 12, 1959).

107 D. W. Gramolt, 'The coastal marshland of east Essex between the seventeenth and mid-nineteenth centuries', unpublished University of London M.A. thesis (1961).

108 A. J. Mansfield, 'An historical geography of woodlands of the southern Chilterns, 1600–1947,' unpublished University of London M.Sc. thesis (1952).

109 L. M. Cantor and J. Hatherly, 'The medieval parks of England', *Geography*, 64 (1979), 71–85.

110 Frost, 'The changing land use in the upper basin of the river Mole'.

111 J. A. Evans, 'The woodlands of the Great Bookham area, 1790 to 1840', *Proceedings of the Leatherhead and District Local History Society*, 3 (1967), 27–32.

112 O. Rackham, 'Documentary evidence for the historical ecologist', *Landscape History*, 1 (1979), 29–33; *Ancient woodland: its history, vegetation and uses in England* (London, Edward Arnold, 1980); J. Sheail, *Historical ecology: the documentary evidence* (Cambridge, Institute of Terrestrial Ecology, 1980).

113 G. F. Peterken, 'Development of vegetation in Staverton Park, Suffolk', *Field Studies*, 3 (1969), 1–39; the passage quoted appears on p. 16.

114 J. Sheail, 'Documentary evidence of the changes in the use, management and

appreciation of the grass-heaths of Breckland', *Journal of Biogeography*, 6 (1979), 277–92.

115 O. Hallam, 'Vegetation and land use on Exmoor', *Somerset Archaeology and Natural History*, 122 (1978), 37–51.

116 Hallam, 'Vegetation and land use on Exmoor', 47.

117 N. W. Moore, M. D. Hooper and B. N. K. Davis, 'Hedges I. Introduction and reconnaissance studies', *Journal of Applied Ecology*, 4 (1967), 201–20; E. Pollard, M. D. Hooper and N. W. Moore, *Hedges* (London, Collins, 1974).

118 East, 'The form and function of settlements'.

119 Sylvester, 'Rural settlement in Anglesey', 9.

120 Sylvester, *The rural landscape of the Welsh borderland.*

121 Hartley, 'The agricultural geography of the Chilterns'; Burrell, 'An historical geography of the Sandlings of Suffolk'; R. Allison, 'The changing landscape of south-west Essex from 1600 to 1850', unpublished University of London Ph.D. thesis (1966).

122 Cox, 'An agricultural geography of Essex'; Dittmer, 'An agricultural geography of northwest Wiltshire'.

123 Naish, 'The agricultural landscape of the Hampshire chalklands'.

124 Meirion-Jones, 'A contribution to the historical geography of north-east Hampshire'.

125 W. Branch Johnson, 'Some sources of inn history', *Amateur Historian*, 6 (1963), 18–21; D. Iredale, 'How can I trace the history of my house?', *Amateur Historian*, 7 (1967), 182–9; J. H. Harvey, *Sources for the history of houses* (London, British Records Association, Archives and the User, 3, 1974).

126 Bessie Taylor, 'Bromley, Beckenham and Penge, Kent, since 1750: a comparative study of the changing geography of three towns on the southern fringe of the metropolis', unpublished University of London Ph.D. thesis (1966).

127 P. E. Jones, 'The city of Bangor and its environs at the time of the tithe survey, 1840', *Caernarvonshire Historical Society Transactions*, 31 (1970), 64–77.

128 M. A. Jahn, 'Railways and suburban development in outer west London 1850–1900 (Acton, Chiswick, Ealing and Hanwell)', unpublished University of London M.Phil. thesis (1971).

129 D. J. Robinson and R. U. Cooke, 'Lime-kilns in Surrey: a reconstruction of a rural industry', *Surrey Archaeological Collections*, 59 (1962), 19–26.

130 K. Swindell, 'The Cromford cotton mills: their site and location', *East Midland Geographer*, 3 (1965), 461–9; M. F. Ward, 'Industrial development and location in Leeds north of the river Aire, 1775–1914', unpublished University of Leeds Ph.D. thesis (1972).

7 Farming

1 J. Caird, *High farming under liberal covenants, the best substitute for protection* (Edinburgh, Blackwood, 1849).

2 H. C. Darby, 'Some early ideas on the agricultural regions of England', *Agricultural History Review*, 2 (1954), 41–7; Harris, 'Changes in the early railway age: 1800–1850', 473–86; J. B. Harley, 'England circa 1850', in Darby, *A new historical geography*, 534–52.

3 J. von Liebig, *Organic chemistry in its applications to agriculture and physiology*, ed. Lyon Playfair (London, Taylor and Walton, 1840).
4 P. Pusey, 'On the progress of agricultural knowledge during the last four years', *Journal of the Royal Agricultural Society of England*, 3 (1842), 169–217; P. Pusey, 'On the progress of agricultural knowledge during the last eight years', *Journal of the Royal Agricultural Society of England*, 11 (1850), 381–438.
5 J. Caird, *English agriculture in 1850–51*, 2nd edition (London, Longmans, 1852), 163; P. Pusey 'On the agricultural improvements of Lincolnshire', *Journal of the Royal Agricultural Society of England*, 4 (1843), p. 287; H. Prince, 'Victorian rural landscapes', in G. E. Mingay (ed.), *The Victorian countryside* (London, Routledge & Kegan Paul, 1981), Vol. 1, pp. 23–4; R. B. Grantham, 'A description of the works for reclaiming and marling parts of the late Forest of Delamere in the county of Cheshire', *Journal of the Royal Agricultural Society of England*, 25 (1846), 369–80.
6 Caird, *English agriculture in 1850–51*; Lavergne, *The rural economy of England, Scotland and Ireland*.
7 Frederick Law Olmsted, *Walks and talks of an American farmer in England* (Ann Arbor, University of Michigan Press, n.d.), esp. 105, 134, 154, 156, 247, 258–62; Gaut, *A history of Worcestershire agriculture and rural evolution*, 254; H. C. Darby, 'The draining of the English clay-lands', *Geographische Zeitschrift*, 52 (1964), 190–201; A. D. M. Phillips, 'Underdraining and the English claylands, 1850–1880: a review', *Agricultural History Review*, 17 (1969), 44–55; H. C. Darby, *The changing fenland* (Cambridge, Cambridge University Press, 1983); J. A. Clarke, 'On the Great Level of the fens, including the fens of south Lincolnshire', *Journal of the Royal Agricultural Society of England*, 8 (1847), 80–133.
8 BPP (HC), 1836, VIII, 'First report from the select committee to inquire into the state of agriculture; with minutes of evidence and appendix', Evidence of John Houghton, Q.702; John Rolfe, Q.1481.
9 'First report . . . the state of agriculture', Evidence of John Houghton, Q.791; 'Second report . . . the state of agriculture', Evidence of Robert Atkinson, Q.5925.
10 'Second report . . . the state of agriculture', Evidence of John Ellman, Q.4739; George Webb Hall, Q.4968.
11 'Third report . . . the state of agriculture', Evidence of John Hancock, Q.11443.
12 J. R. McCulloch, *A statistical account of the British empire: exhibiting its extent, physical capacities, population, industry, and civil and religious institutions*, 2 vols. (London, Charles Knight, 2nd edition, 1839), Vol. 2, p. 274.
13 McCulloch, *A statistical account of the British empire*, Vol. 2, p. 275.
14 Ward, 'The tithe question in England in the early nineteenth century', 67–81, esp. 70; Evans, *Contentious tithe*, esp. 94–114.
15 J. H. Clapham, 'Tithe surveys as a source of agrarian history', *Cambridge Historical Journal*, 1 (1924), 201–8.
16 J. A. Venn, 'The economy of a Norfolk parish in 1783 and at the present time', *Economic History*, 1 (1926), 76–88.
17 Clapham, 'Tithe surveys as a source of agrarian history', 207.

18 M. F. Lloyd-Pritchard, 'The vicar of Mattishall and his tithes, 1781–1803', *Agricultural History*, 27 (1953), 141–7.

19 Charles, 'The vicarage and tithes of Nevern in Pembrokeshire', 26–39; Jones, 'The Mathry tithe suit', *Journal of the Historical Society of the Church in Wales*, 2 (1950), 97–102; Anon., 'Tithing customs at North Somercotes, A.D. 1588', 375–81; J. F. Dyer, F. Stygall and J. Dony, *The story of Luton* (Luton, White Crescent Press, 1964); J. G. W. Lewarne, 'A cartographic survey of the area: 10. The Fetcham parish tithe map of 1791', *Proceedings of the Leatherhead and District Local History Society*, 2 (1965), 257–9.

20 R. J. P. Kain, 'Les dîmes, les relevés de dîmes et la mesure de la production agricole dans la Grande-Bretagne préindustrielle', in J. Goy and E. Le Roy Ladurie (eds.), *Prestations paysannes, dîmes, rente foncière et mouvement de la production agricole à l'époque préindustrielle* (Paris, Mouton, 1982), 713–32.

21 J. S. Purvis, 'A note on XVI century farming in Yorkshire', *Yorkshire Archaeological Journal*, 36 (1944–7), 435–54; Purvis, *Select XVI century causes in tithe from the York Diocesan Registry*.

22 P. K. Mitchell, 'West Cleveland land use, *c.*1550–1850', unpublished University of Durham Ph.D. thesis (1965).

23 Mitchell, 'West Cleveland land use', 359–89.

24 D. Hey, *The village of Ecclesfield* (Huddersfield, The Advertiser, 1968); G. H. Tupling, *The economic history of Rossendale* (Manchester, University of Manchester, Economic History Series, 4, 1927); V. H. T. Skipp (ed.), *Discovering Sheldon* (Birmingham, University of Birmingham Extra-Mural Department, 1960).

25 R. W. Sturgess, 'A study of agricultural change in the Staffordshire moorlands, 1780–1850', *North Staffordshire Journal of Field Studies*, 1 (1961), 77–85; Dickinson, 'Tithing customs in west Cumberland in the eighteenth century', 130–4.

26 Gawne, 'Field patterns in Widecombe parish and the Forest of Dartmoor', 49–69.

27 Holkham MSS Castleacre Deeds 1700–1800, 'Castleacre Register for Briefs and Offerings distributed each Sacrament and for Doles of Charity, Anno Domini 1709 to 1749, Amb: Pimlowe, Vicar'. Bundle 11, no. 116; 'Survey and Particulars of the Lands in the Manors and Town of Castle Acre' (1713–26). Bundle 11, nos. 119–24, cited in H. C. Prince, 'The origins of pits and depressions in Norfolk', *Geography*, 49 (1964), 15–32, references on p. 22.

28 J. A. Yelling, 'Changes in crop production in east Worcestershire, 1540–1867', *Agricultural History Review*, 21 (1973), 18–34.

29 Evans, 'Tithe books as a source for the local historian', 24–7.

30 R. J. P. Kain, 'Tithe as an index of pre-industrial agricultural production', *Agricultural History Review*, 27 (1979), 73–81; E. Le Roy Ladurie and J. Goy, *Tithe and agrarian history from the fourteenth to the nineteenth centuries* (Cambridge, Cambridge University Press, 1982).

31 Mosby, *Norfolk*, 142.

32 Jarvis, 'Changes in land use in south-east Denbighshire', 734–43.

33 East, 'The form and function of settlements in relation to types of farming in England and Wales'.

34 G. H. Tupling, 'Terriers and tithe and enclosure awards', *Amateur Historian*, 1 (1954), 361–4.
35 Edwards, 'Enclosure and agricultural improvement in the Vale of Clwyd, 1750–1875'.
36 Naish, 'The agricultural landscape of the Hampshire chalklands'.
37 R. A. Sinfield, 'The distribution of tithe surveys in England', unpublished University College London B.A. course paper (1969).
38 Giles, 'Mid-Worcestershire in the first half of the nineteenth century', 35–66, ref. on p. 38.
39 Phillips, 'A study of farming practices and soil types in Staffordshire around 1840', 27–52.
40 Porter, 'Agricultural change in Cheshire during the nineteenth century'.
41 The first reference to evidence from tithe files appears in G. R. J. Jones, 'The pattern of settlement on the Welsh border', *Agricultural History Review*, 8 (1960), 66–81 (the reference is to the tithe file for Meliden, p. 73); also G. R. J. Jones, 'The Llanynys quillets', 133–58, for details of farming practice.
42 Naish, 'The agricultural landscape of the Hampshire chalklands'.
43 Burrell, 'An historical geography of the Sandlings of Suffolk, 1600 to 1850', 195.
44 Chapman, 'Changing agriculture and the moorland edge in the North York Moors, 1750–1960'.
45 Gramolt, 'The coastal marshland of east Essex between the seventeenth and mid-nineteenth centuries', 391.
46 Postgate, 'Historical geography of the Breckland, 1600–1850', 312.
47 Edwards, 'Enclosure and agricultural improvement in the Vale of Clwyd', 181–3.
48 Baker, 'The field systems of Kent'.
49 Cox, 'An agricultural geography of Essex *c.* 1840'.
50 Dittmer, 'An agricultural geography of northwest Wiltshire, 1773–1840'.
51 Cox and Dittmer, 'The tithe files of the mid-nineteenth century', 1–16.
52 Cox and Dittmer, 'The tithe files of the mid-nineteenth century', 16.
53 Thomas, 'Changing land utilisation, occupation and ownership in south-west Carmarthenshire'.
54 Allison, 'The changing landscape of south-west Essex from 1600 to 1850'.
55 Mitchell, 'West Cleveland land use'.
56 R. T. Fieldhouse, 'Agriculture in Wensleydale from 1600 to the present day', *Northern History*, 16 (1980), 169–95.
57 Porter, 'Agricultural change in Cheshire during the nineteenth century', 312–13.
58 Chapman, 'Agriculture and the "waste" in Monmouthshire from 1750 to the present day'.
59 Parton, 'Town and country in Surrey *c.* 1800–1870: a study in historical geography'.
60 Kain, 'The land of Kent in the middle of the nineteenth century', 91.
61 Phillips, 'A study of farming practices and soil types in Staffordshire', 28; E. L. Jones, 'The changing basis of English agricultural prosperity, 1853–73', *Agricultural History Review*, 10 (1962), 102–19; Jones, *Agriculture and economic growth in England 1650–1815*.

62 Phillips, 'Agricultural land use, soils and the Nottinghamshire tithe surveys', 284–301.

63 Phillips, 'Agricultural land use, soils and the Nottinghamshire tithe surveys', 297–300.

64 Harriet M. E. Holt and R. J. P. Kain, 'Land use and farming in Suffolk about 1840', *Proceedings of the Suffolk Institute of Archaeology and History*, 34 (1982), 123–39.

65 J. P. Dodd, 'Norfolk agriculture in 1853–4', *Norfolk Archaeology*, 36 (1976), 253–64; Dodd, 'Hampshire agriculture in the mid-nineteenth century', *Proceedings of the Hampshire Field Club and Archaeological Society*, 35 (1979), 239–60; Dodd, 'Gloucestershire agriculture 1801–1854', *Transactions of the Bristol and Gloucestershire Archaeological Society*, 97 (1979), 101–16; Dodd, 'The West Riding crop returns for 1854', *Yorkshire Archaeological Journal*, 51 (1979), 117–29. References to Dr Dodd's earlier work with the 1854 return in Shropshire, Denbighshire and Brecknockshire are given in his West Riding paper. For the Norfolk return see also Susanna Wade Martins, *A great estate at work. The Holkham estate and its inhabitants in the nineteenth century* (Cambridge, Cambridge University Press, 1980), 19–26.

66 Dodd, 'Norfolk agriculture', 256.

67 Dodd, 'Gloucestershire agriculture', 102.

68 G. B. G. Bull, 'The changing landscape of rural Middlesex, 1500–1850', unpublished University of London Ph.D. thesis (1958).

69 Parton, 'Town and country in Surrey'; P. G. Atherall, 'The displacement of market gardening around London by urban growth from 1745–1939', unpublished University of Cambridge M.Litt. thesis (1976).

70 M. R. G. Conzen, *Alnwick, Northumberland, a study in town-plan analysis* (London, Institute of British Geographers publication, No. 27, 1960).

71 B. Winter, 'The woodlands of central Kent', unpublished University of Hull M.Sc. thesis (1966).

72 D. W. Harvey, 'Aspects of agricultural and rural change in Kent, 1800–1900', unpublished University of Cambridge Ph.D. thesis (1961), and 'Locational change in the Kentish hop industry and the analysis of land use patterns', *Transactions of the Institute of British Geographers*, 33 (1963), 123–44.

73 Giles, 'Mid-Worcestershire in the first half of the nineteenth century'; Kain, 'The land of Kent in the middle of the nineteenth century'; Phillips, 'Agricultural land use and the Herefordshire tithe surveys, *circa* 1840', 54–61.

74 D. W. Harvey, 'Fruit growing in Kent in the nineteenth century', *Archaeologia Cantiana*, 79 (1964), 95–108.

75 R. J. P. Kain, 'Compiling an atlas of agriculture in England and Wales from the tithe surveys', *Geographical Journal*, 145 (1979), 225–35 and discussion 235–41.

76 Enquiries and requests for data extracts should be addressed to The Director, ESRC Survey Archive at the University of Essex.

77 Kain and Holt, 'Agriculture and land use in Cornwall circa 1840', 139–81; Holt and Kain, 'Land use and farming in Suffolk about 1840'; R. J. P. Kain and Harriet M. E. Holt, 'Farming in Cheshire *circa* 1840: some evidence from the tithe files', *Transactions of the Lancashire and Cheshire Antiquarian Society*, 82 (1983), 22–57.

8 Farms, landowners and rural social structure

1 Mosby, *Norfolk*, 128–37, 148.
2 East, 'The form and function of settlements in relation to types of farming in England and Wales'.
3 J. T. Coppock, 'Changes in farm and field boundaries in the 19th century', *Amateur Historian*, 3 (1958), 292–8. The passage quoted is from p. 295.
4 Bennett, 'Settlement patterns and farm units in western Pembrokeshire'.
5 Grove, 'Land use changes in west Gower 1840–1950'.
6 E. Davies, 'Hendre and hafod in Caernarvonshire', *Transactions of the Caernarvonshire Historical Society*, 40 (1979), 17–46.
7 E. Davies, 'Hendre and hafod in Denbighshire', *Transactions of the Denbighshire Historical Society*, 26 (1977), 49–72; '*Hafod, hafoty* and *lluest*: their distribution, features and purpose', *Ceredigion*, 9 (1980), 1–41; the passage quoted is from p. 16.
8 Frost, 'The changing land use in the upper basin of the river Mole'.
9 Thomas, 'Changing land utilisation, occupation and ownership in south-west Carmarthenshire'.
10 Naish, 'The agricultural landscape of the Hampshire chalklands, 1700–1840'; Burrell, 'An historical geography of the Sandlings of Suffolk, 1600 to 1850'; Chapman, 'Changing agriculture and the moorland edge in the North York Moors 1750–1960'.
11 B. R. Dittmer, 'An agricultural geography of northwest Wiltshire, 1773–1840'; Gramolt, 'The coastal marshland of east Essex between the seventeenth and mid-nineteenth centuries'.
12 Chiplen, 'The rural landscape of the Blackmore Vale, *c.* 1840'.
13 M. B. Gleave, 'Dispersed and nucleated settlements in the Yorkshire Wolds, 1770–1850', *Transactions of the Institute of British Geographers*, 30 (1962), 105–18.
14 J. A. Yelling, *Common field and enclosure in England, 1450–1850* (London, Macmillan, 1977), especially chapter 7; J. Chapman, 'Parliamentary enclosure in the uplands: the case of the North York Moors', *Agricultural History Review*, 24 (1976), 1–17.
15 Thomas, 'Some enclosure patterns in central Wales, a study in landscape modification', 25–36; the passage quoted is from p. 33.
16 Powell, 'An economic geography of Montgomeryshire in the nineteenth century'.
17 Morgan, 'The effect of parliamentary enclosure on the landscape of Caernarvonshire and Merioneth'.
18 Kain, 'The land of Kent in the middle of the nineteenth century'.
19 D. J. Blair and T. H. Biss, *The measurement of shape in geography, an appraisal of methods and techniques* (Nottingham, University of Nottingham Department of Geography, Bulletin of Quantitative Data for Geographers, 11, 1967).
20 Clare T. Lukehurst, 'The Stour marshes: a study of agricultural changes 1840–1966', unpublished University of London Ph.D. thesis (1977).
21 R. J. P. Kain, 'Tithe surveys and the study of land occupation', *Local Historian*, 12 (1976), 88–92.

22 Lukehurst, 'The Stour marshes'.

23 B. M. Short, 'Agriculture in the High Weald of Kent and Sussex, 1850 to 1953 (A case study in the application of multivariate techniques in the field of historical geography)', unpublished University of London Ph.D. thesis (1973).

24 There are many examples in *VCH Essex*, Vol. 4, and *VCH Shropshire*, Vol. 8; and see, for example, Sue P. Farrant, 'Farm formation in eighteenth-century Bishopstone', *Sussex Archaeological Collections*, 114 (1976), 335–6.

25 Workers' Educational Association, King's Langley Branch, *The history of King's Langley* (King's Langley, WEA, 1963), 100–7; Sir J. Dunlop, *The pleasant town of Sevenoaks, a history* (Sevenoaks, the author, 1964), 156–8; A. Ivimey (ed.), *Westleton from the 1830s to the 1960s: a survey of a Suffolk village* (Saxmundham, WEA, 1968), 90; H. A. Lane, 'The parish of Carew, (*c.* 1938)', *Pembrokeshire Historian*, 4 (1972), 70–5; Phyllis Williams, 'Land tenure in the Bishop's manor of Whitbourne', *Transactions of the Woolhope Naturalists' Field Club*, 40 (1972), 333–55.

26 Sandell (ed.), *Abstracts of Wiltshire tithe apportionments*.

27 Skipp, *Discovering Sheldon*.

28 F. Leeson, 'The farms of Coulsdon in 1762 and 1837', *Bourne Society's Local History Records*, 7 (1968), 29–34.

29 M. A. Havinden, *Estate villages; a study of the Berkshire villages of Ardington and Lockinge* (London, Lund Humphries, 1966).

30 R. Howes, 'Joseph Pitt, landowner', in B. S. Smith (ed.), *Gloucestershire Historical Studies* (Bristol, University of Bristol Department of Extra-Mural Studies, 7, 1976), 20–4; J. D. Marshall, *Furness and the industrial revolution* (Barrow-in-Furness, Library and Museum Committee, 1958), 73–8; Sue P. Farrant, 'The management of four estates in the lower Ouse valley (Sussex) and agricultural change, 1840–1920', *Southern History*, 1 (1979), 155–70, and 'The changing structure of land ownership in the lower Ouse valley, 1780 to 1840', *Sussex Archaeological Collections*, 116 (1978), 261–8; W. K. Ford, 'Boltro Farm, Cuckfield', *Sussex Archaeological Collections*, 114 (1976), 81–96; L. W. Lloyd, 'Corsygedol, Ardudwys's principal estate', *Journal of the Merioneth Historical and Record Society*, 8 (1977–8), 27–60, 157–90; J. Weller (ed.), *Coleshill model farm Oxfordshire; past, present, future* (Architects in Agriculture Group, occasional paper 1, 1981).

31 Examples of such maps are found in Thomas, 'Changing land utilisation, occupation and ownership in south-west Carmarthenshire', and Chiplen, 'The rural landscape of the Blackmore Vale'; tithe surveys illustrating the persistence of boundaries of early manors and divisions between differing forms of customary tenure are referred to in F. A. Barnes, 'Land tenure, landscape and population in Cemlyn, Anglesey', *Transactions of the Anglesey Antiquarian Society and Field Club*, unnumbered series (1982), 15–90.

32 Carpenter, 'The value of the tithe surveys to the study of land ownership and occupancy in the mid-nineteenth century, with special reference to south Herefordshire', 48–52.

33 Postgate, 'Historical geography of the Breckland, 1600–1850', 305.

34 D. R. Mills, 'Landownership and rural population with special reference to Leicestershire in the mid-nineteenth century', unpublished University of Lei-

cester Ph.D. thesis (1963), 131–51; *Lord and peasant in nineteenth century Britain* (London, Croom Helm, 1980), 64–97.

35 Yelling, 'Open field, enclosure and farm production in east Worcestershire, 1540–1870'.

36 Ingleson, 'Settlement, agrarian systems, and field patterns in central Durham, 1600–1850: a study in historical geography'; Heather A. Fuller, 'Landownership and the Lindsey landscape', *Annals of the Association of American Geographers*, 66 (1976), 14–24, and Heather A. Clemenson, *English country houses and landed estates* (London, Croom Helm, 1982).

37 Thompson, *English landed society in the nineteenth century*, 122–7.

38 R. J. P. Kain, 'Tithe surveys and landownership', *Journal of Historical Geography*, 1 (1975), 39–48.

39 A. H. Johnson, *The disappearance of the small landowner* (Oxford, Clarendon Press, 1909); H. L. Gray, 'Yeoman farming in Oxfordshire from the sixteenth century to the nineteenth', *Quarterly Journal of Economics*, 24 (1910), 293–326; E. Davies, 'The small landowner, 1780–1832, in the light of the land tax assessments', *Economic History Review*, 1 (1927), 87–113.

40 For example, Chambers, 'Enclosure and the small landowner', 118–27; H. G. Hunt, 'Landownership and enclosure, 1750–1830', *Economic History Review*, 2nd series, 11 (1958–9), 497–505; J. M. Martin, 'The parliamentary enclosure movement and rural society in Warwickshire', *Agricultural History Review*, 15 (1967), 19–39; Barbara Kerr, *Bound to the soil: a social history of Dorset 1750–1918* (London, John Baker, 1968), 57, 256–7; M. E. Turner, *English parliamentary enclosure* (Folkestone, Dawson, 1980), 152–170; Mills, *Lord and peasant in nineteenth-century Britain*, which uses tithe surveys to analyse the size of peasant holdings and tenurial arrangements, 68–71.

41 G. E. Mingay, 'The land tax assessments and the small landowner', *Economic History Review*, 2nd series, 17 (1964), 381–8; J. M. Martin, 'Land ownership and the land tax returns', *Agricultural History Review*, 14 (1966), 96–103; J. V. Beckett and D. K. Smith, 'The land tax returns as a source for studying the English economy in the eighteenth century', *Bulletin of the Institute of Historical Research*, 54 (1981), 54–61.

42 Grigg, *The agricultural revolution in south Lincolnshire*.

43 Williams, *A west country village, Ashworthy*.

44 Thomas, 'Estate surveys as sources in historical geography', 451–68.

45 Mingay, 'The land tax assessments and the small landowner'.

46 Sarah J. Banks, 'Open and close parishes in nineteenth-century England,' unpublished University of Reading Ph.D. thesis (1982).

47 F. H. W. Sheppard, 'Sources and methods used for the Survey of London', in H. J. Dyos (ed.), *The study of urban history* (London, Edward Arnold, 1968), 131–45.

48 The discussion is printed in Dyos (ed.), *The study of urban history*, 146–53; Harley, *Maps for the local historian. A guide to the British sources*, 36.

49 T. R. Slater, 'The analysis of burgage patterns in medieval towns', *Area*, 13 (1981), 211–16.

50 M. W. Beresford and J. K. S. St Joseph, *Medieval England: an aerial survey* (Cambridge, Cambridge University Press, 1958), 154.

51 D. Ward, 'The urban plan of Leeds and the factors which have conditioned its growth', unpublished University of Leeds M.A. thesis (1960); D. Ward, 'The pre-urban cadaster and the urban pattern of Leeds', *Annals of the Association of American Geographers*, 52 (1962), 150–66.

52 M. J. Mortimore, 'Urban growth in Bradford, 1850–1950', *Transactions of the Institute of British Geographers*, 46 (1969), 105–19; R. C. W. Cox, 'Some aspects of the urban development of Croydon, 1870–1940', unpublished University of Leicester M.A. thesis (1966); Jahn, 'Railways and suburban development: outer west London 1850–1900', and 'Suburban development in outer west London, 1850–1900', in F. M. L. Thompson (ed.), *The rise of suburbia* (Leicester, Leicester University Press, 1982), 93–156; J. M. Rawcliffe, 'Bromley: Kentish market town to London suburb, 1841–81', in Thompson (ed.) *The rise of suburbia*, 27–91; R. W. Pepper, 'Urban development of Lewisham: a geographical interpretation', unpublished University of London M.A. thesis (1965).

53 D. C. D. Pocock, 'Landownership and urban growth in Scunthorpe', *East Midland Geographer*, 5 (1970), 52–61; K. L. Wallwork, 'The evolution of an industrial landscape: the Calder Darwen valley, Lancashire *c.*1740–1914', unpublished University of Leicester Ph.D. thesis (1966).

54 Jane Springett, 'Landowners and urban development: the Ramsden estate and nineteenth-century Huddersfield', *Journal of Historical Geography*, 8 (1982), 129–44.

55 H. J. Dyos, *Victorian suburb: a study of the growth of Camberwell* (Leicester, Leicester University Press, 1961), 40–1.

56 F. M. L. Thompson, *Hampstead: building a borough 1650–1964* (London, Routledge & Kegan Paul, 1974), 75–131.

57 M. J. Daunton, *House and home in the Victorian city: working-class housing, 1850–1914* (London, Edward Arnold, 1983), 74.

58 *ibid*, 78.

59 J. R. Kellett, *The impact of railways on Victorian cities* (London, Routledge & Kegan Paul, 1969), 126.

60 J. D. Marshall, 'Colonisation as a factor in the planting of towns in north-west England', in Dyos, *The study of urban history*, 215–30.

61 Witherick, 'Stages in the growth of urban settlement in central Cornwall'.

62 F. S. Ottrey, 'Geographical aspects of the development of Wirksworth from the beginning of the nineteenth century to the present', unpublished University of Nottingham M.A. thesis (1965); F. Hewitt, 'Population and urban growth in east Bristol, 1800–1914', unpublished University of Bristol Ph.D. thesis (1966); B. C. G. Nokes, 'Industrial change and settlement in north-east Worcestershire, *c.*1775–1875', unpublished University of London Ph.D. thesis (1967); R. D. F. Bromley, 'Nineteenth century economic and population change at Chulmleigh', *Reports and Transactions of the Devonshire Association*, 102 (1970), 121–40; K. A. Cowlard, 'The urban development of Wakefield 1801–1901'.

63 P. S. Richards, 'The growth of towns – a study in methodology', *Local Historian*, 9 (1970), 190–5.

64 S. Thomas, 'Land occupation, ownership and utilization in the parish of Llansantffraid', *Ceredigion*, 3 (1957), 124–55; 'The enumerators' returns as a source for a period picture of the parish of Llansantffraid, 1841–51', 408–21; 'The agricultural labour force in some south-west Carmarthenshire parishes in the mid-nineteenth century', 63–73.
65 Thomas, 'The agricultural labour force in some south-west Carmarthenshire parishes', 65.
66 G. J. Lewis, 'The demographic structure of a Welsh rural village during the mid-nineteenth century', *Ceredigion*, 5 (1966), 290–304; C. Thomas,'Rural society in nineteenth-century Wales: south Cardiganshire in 1851', *Ceredigion*, 6 (1971), 388–414.
67 A. Henstock, 'Group projects in local history – house repopulation in the mid-nineteenth century', *Bulletin of Local History, East Midlands Region*, 6 (1971), 11–20. This has been reprinted with a few amendments in *Local Population Studies*, 10 (1973), 37–52.
68 Henstock, 'Group projects in local history – house repopulation in the mid-nineteenth century', 17.
69 Gee Langdon, *The year of the map: portrait of a Wiltshire town in 1841* (Tisbury, Compton Russell, 1976).
70 D. R. Mills, 'A social and demographic study of Melbourn, Cambridgeshire, *c.*1840', *Archives*, 12 (1976), 115–20, the passage quoted is from p. 118.
71 D. R. Mills, 'The technique of house repopulation: experience from a Cambridgeshire village, 1841', *Local Historian*, 13 (1978), 86–97.
72 E. M. Yates, 'The evolution of the English village', *Geographical Journal*, 148 (1982), 182–206.
73 D. R. Mills, 'The residential propinquity of kin in a Cambridgeshire village, 1841', *Journal of Historical Geography*, 4 (1978), 265–76.

9 Summary and prospect

1 P. J. Perry, 'High farming in Victorian Britain, prospect and retrospect', *Agricultural History*, 55 (1981), 156–66.
2 H. S. A. Fox, 'Local farmers' associations and the circulation of agricultural information in nineteenth-century England', in H. S. A. Fox and R. A. Butlin (eds.), *Change in the countryside: essays on rural England, 1500–1900* (London, Institute of British Geographers, Special Publication 10, 1979), 43–63.
3 Stamp, *The land of Britain, its use and misuse*, 55 and 58.
4 Darby, *An historical geography of England before A.D. 1800*; 'An historical geography of England: twenty years after', 147–59. The passage quoted is from p. 154.
5 Darby, 'An historical geography of England: twenty years after', 154.
6 J. B. Harley, 'England *circa* 1850', in H. C. Darby (ed.), *A new historical geography of England* (Cambridge, Cambridge University Press, 1973), 527–94.
7 Gray, *English field systems*, 15.
8 Willatts, 'Changes in land utilization in the south-west of the London Basin, 1840–1932', 515–28; the passage quoted is from p. 528.

9 R. J. P. Kain, 'Tithe surveys and the rural landscape of England and Wales', *Bulletin of the Society of University Cartographers*, 11 (1977), 1–3.
10 H. C. Prince, 'The tithe surveys of the mid-nineteenth century', *Agricultural History Review*, 7 (1959), 14–26.
11 Cox and Dittmer, 'The tithe files of the mid-nineteenth century', 1–16.

Bibliography

Anon. 'Tithing customs at North Somercotes, A.D. 1588', *Lincolnshire Historian*, 10 (1952), 375 and 381.

Alcock, N. W. 'Fields and farms in an east Devon parish', *Report and Transactions of the Devonshire Association*, 107 (1975), 93–172.

Alexander, D. A. 'Settlement, field systems and landownership in Teesdale between 1600 and 1850: a study in historical geography', unpublished University of Durham M.A. thesis (1972).

Allerston, Pamela 'English village development, findings from the Pickering district of north Yorkshire', *Transactions of the Institute of British Geographers*, 51 (1970), 95–109.

Allison, R. 'The changing landscape of south-west Essex from 1600 to 1850', unpublished University of London Ph.D. thesis (1966).

Anderson, A. B. 'A study in the sociology of religious persecution: the first Quakers', *Journal of Religious History*, 9 (1977), 247–62.

Andrews, J. H. 'The Ordnance Survey in nineteenth-century Ireland', unpublished Trinity College Dublin M.Litt. thesis (1971).

A paper landscape. The Ordnance Survey in nineteenth-century Ireland, Oxford, Clarendon Press, 1975.

Armstrong, P. *The changing landscape: the history and ecology of man's impact upon the face of East Anglia*, Lavenham, Dalton, 1975.

Atherall, P. G. 'The displacement of market gardening around London by urban growth from 1745–1939', unpublished University of Cambridge M.Litt. thesis (1976).

Bainbridge, T. H. 'Land utilisation in Cumbria in the mid-nineteenth century as revealed by a study of the tithe returns', *Transactions of the Cumberland and Westmorland Antiquarian and Archaeological Society*, new series, 43 (1943), 87–95.

Baker, A. R. H. 'The field systems of Kent', unpublished University of London Ph.D. thesis (1963).

'The field system of an east Kent parish (Deal)', *Archaeologia Cantiana*, 78 (1963), 96–117.

'Open fields in Derbyshire: some reservations about recent arguments', *Derbyshire Archaeological Journal*, 83 (1963), 77–81.

'Open fields and partible inheritance on a Kent manor', *Economic History Review*, 2nd series, 17 (1964), 1–23.

'Howard Levi Gray and *English field systems*: an evaluation', *Agricultural History*, 39 (1965), 86–91.

'Field systems in the Vale of Holmesdale', *Agricultural History Review*, 14 (1966), 1–24.

Baker, A. R. H. and Butlin, R. A. (eds.) *Studies of field systems in the British Isles*, Cambridge, Cambridge University Press, 1973.

Banks, Sarah J. 'Open and close parishes in nineteenth-century England', unpublished University of Reading Ph.D. thesis (1982).

Barnes, D. G. *A history of the English Corn Laws from 1660–1846*, London, Routledge, 1930.

Barnes, F. A. 'Land tenure, landscape and population in Cemlyn, Anglesey', *Transactions of the Anglesey Antiquarian Society and Field Club*, unnumbered series (1982), 15–90.

Barratt, D. M. (ed.) *Ecclesiastical terriers of Warwick parishes*, Oxford, Dugdale Society Publications, 22, 1955.

Barton, R. M. *Life in Cornwall in the early nineteenth century*, Truro, Bradford Barton, 1970.

Barty-King, H. *Scratch a surveyor . . .*, London, Heinemann, 1975.

Beastall, T. W. *The agricultural revolution in Lincolnshire*, Lincoln, History of Lincolnshire Committee, 1978.

Beckett, J. V. and Smith, D. K. 'The land tax returns as a source for studying the English economy in the eighteenth century', *Bulletin of the Institute of Historical Research*, 54 (1981), 54–61.

Bennett, D. H. C. 'Settlement patterns and farm units in western Pembrokeshire: a study in historical geography', unpublished University of Wales M.A. thesis (1955).

Beresford, M. W. 'The lost villages of medieval England', *Geographical Journal*, 117 (1951), 129–49.

The lost villages of England, London, Lutterworth, 1954.

History on the ground: six studies in maps and landscape, London, Lutterworth, 1957.

Beresford, M. W., and St Joseph, J. K. S. *Medieval England: an aerial survey*, Cambridge, Cambridge University Press, 1958.

Best, G. F. A. *Temporal pillars*, Cambridge, Cambridge University Press, 1964.

Best, R. H. and Coppock, J. T. *The changing use of land in Britain*, London, Faber and Faber, 1962.

Billingsley, J. *General view of the agriculture of the county of Somerset*, Bath, R. Cruttwell, 1797.

Blair, D. J. and Biss, T. H. *The measurement of shape in geography: an appraisal of methods and techniques*, Nottingham University, Department of Geography, Bulletin of Quantitative Data for Geographers, 11, 1967.

Bloch, M. *French rural history, an essay on its basic characteristics* (translation of *Les caractères originaux de l'histoire rurale française*, 1931), London, Routledge and Kegan Paul, 1966.

Bonney, D. J. 'Former farms and fields at Challacombe, Manaton, Dartmoor', in

K. J. Gregory and W. L. D. Ravenhill (eds.), *Exeter essays in geography*, Exeter, University of Exeter, 1971, 83–91.

Boys, J. *General view of the agriculture of the county of Kent*, London, Sherwood, Neely and Jones, 1813.

Branch Johnson, W. 'Some sources of inn history', *Amateur Historian*, 6 (1963), 18–21.

Briault, E. W. H. *Sussex (East and West)*, Report of the Land Utilisation Survey of Great Britain, parts 83–4, 1942.

Bromley, R. D. F. 'Nineteenth century economic and population change at Chulmleigh', *Report and Transactions of the Devonshire Association*, 102 (1970), 121–40.

Brown, Gladys N. 'Scottish farmers in Hatfield', *Hertfordshire Past and Present*, 2 (1961), 41–8.

Buchanan, K. M. *Worcestershire*, Report of the Land Utilisation Survey of Great Britain, part 68, 1944.

Bull, G. B. G. 'The changing landscape of rural Middlesex, 1500–1850', unpublished University of London Ph.D. thesis (1958).

Burrell, Elizabeth D. R. 'An historical geography of the Sandlings of Suffolk 1600 to 1850', unpublished University of London M.Sc. thesis (1960).

Butlin, R. A. 'Field systems of Northumberland and Durham', in A. R. H. Baker and R. A. Butlin (eds.), *Studies of field systems in the British Isles*, Cambridge, Cambridge University Press, 1973, 93–144.

Caird, J. *High farming under liberal covenants, the best substitute for protection*, Edinburgh, Blackwood, 1849.

English agriculture in 1850–51, 2nd ed., London, Longman, Brown, Green and Longman, 1852.

Cameron, L. G. *Hertfordshire*, Report of the Land Utilisation Survey of Great Britain, part 80, 1941.

Cantor, L. M. and Hatherly, J. 'The medieval parks of England', *Geography*, 64 (1979), 71–85.

Carpenter, Aileen M. 'Changes in the agricultural geography of the south Hertfordshire plateau, 1750–1888', unpublished University of London M.A. thesis (1965).

'The value of the tithe surveys to the study of land ownership and occupancy in the mid-nineteenth century, with special reference to south Hertfordshire', *Hertfordshire Past and Present*, 7 (1967), 48–52.

Chambers, J. D. 'Enclosure and the small landowner', *Economic History Review*, 10 (1940), 118–27.

Nottinghamshire in the eighteenth century, 2nd edition, London, Frank Cass, 1966.

Chambers, J. D. and Mingay, G. E. *The agricultural revolution, 1750–1880*, London, Batsford, 1966.

Chapman, J. 'Changing agriculture and the moorland edge in the North York Moors, 1750–1960', unpublished University of London M.A. thesis (1961).

'Agriculture and the "waste" in Monmouthshire from 1750 to the present day', unpublished University of London Ph.D. thesis (1973).

'Parliamentary enclosure in the uplands: the case of the North York Moors', *Agricultural History Review*, 24 (1976), 1–17.

Chapman, Vera 'Open fields in west Cheshire', *Transactions of the Historic Society of Lancashire and Cheshire*, 104 (1952), 35–59.

Charles, B. 'The vicarage and tithes of Nevern in Pembrokeshire', *Journal of the Historical Society of the Church in Wales*, 1 (1947), 26–39.

Charlesworth, A. *Social protest in a rural society*, Historical Geography Research Series, No. 1, Norwich, Geobooks, 1979.

(ed.) *An atlas of rural protest in Britain, 1548–1900*, London, Croom Helm, 1983.

Chichester, H. M. 'Robert Kearsley Dawson', *Dictionary of National Biography*, XIV, London, Smith Elder, 1888, 228.

Chiplen, R. F. J. 'The rural landscape of the Blackmore Vale, *c.* 1840', unpublished University of Exeter M.A. thesis (1969).

Chippindall, W. H. *A history of the parish of Tunstall*, Manchester, Chetham Society, new series, 104, 1940.

Clapham, A. *A short history of the surveyor's profession*, London, Royal Institution of Chartered Surveyors, 1949.

Clapham, J. H. 'Tithe surveys as a source of agrarian history', *Cambridge Historical Journal*, 1 (1924), 201–8.

An economic history of modern Britain, 3 vols., Cambridge, Cambridge University Press, 1926–38.

Clarke, J. A. 'On the Great Level of the fens, including the fens of south Lincolnshire', *Journal of the Royal Agricultural Society of England*, 8 (1847), 80–133.

Clemenson, Heather A. *English country houses and landed estates*, London, Croom Helm, 1982.

Close, Sir Charles *The early years of the Ordnance Survey*, new edition with an introduction by J. B. Harley, Newton Abbot, David and Charles, 1969.

Clout, H. D. and Sutton, K. 'The cadastre as a source for French rural studies', *Agricultural History*, 43 (1969), 215–23.

Cobbett, W. *Rural rides*, Vol. 1, London, Everyman edition, Dent, 1912.

Coles, R. 'The historical geography of south-east Essex', unpublished University of London Ph.D. thesis (1934).

'Changes in land utilisation in three typical Essex parishes (*c.* 1840 to 1933)', in N. V. Scarfe, *Essex*, Report of the Land Utilisation Survey of Great Britain, part 82, 1942, 458.

Conzen, M. R. G. *Alnwick, Northumberland, a study in town-plan analysis*, London, Institute of British Geographers publication No. 27, 1960.

Coppock, J. T. 'The statistical assessment of British agriculture', *Agricultural History Review*, 4 (1956), 4–21 and 66–79.

'The changing arable in the Chilterns, 1875–1951', *Geography*, 43 (1957), 217–29.

'Changes in farm and field boundaries in the 19th century', *Amateur Historian*, 3 (1958), 292–8.

'Maps as sources for the study of land use in the past', *Imago Mundi*, 22 (1968), 37–49.

Cowlard, K. A. 'The urban development of Wakefield, 1801–1901', unpublished University of Leeds Ph.D. thesis (1974).

Cox, E. A. 'An agricultural geography of Essex *c.* 1840', unpublished University of London M.A. thesis (1963).

Cox, E. A. and Dittmer, B. R. 'The tithe files of the mid-nineteenth century', *Agricultural History Review*, 13 (1965), 1–16.

Cox, J. C. 'Ancient documents relating to tithes in the Peak', *Journal of the Derbyshire Archaeological and Natural History Society*, 5 (1883), 129–64.

Cox, R. C. W. 'Some aspects of the urban development of Croydon, 1870–1940', unpublished University of Leicester M.A. thesis (1966).

Cracknell, B. E. 'The alluvial marshland of the lower Thames estuary: a study in changing use patterns', unpublished University of London Ph.D. thesis (1953).

Canvey Island: the history of a marshland community, Leicester, University of Leicester, Department of English Local History, occasional paper, 12, 1959.

Cunningham, G. L. 'The changing landscape of the Dorset heathlands since 1700', unpublished University of London Ph.D. thesis (1974).

Curtler, W. H. R. *The enclosure and redistribution of our land*, Oxford, Clarendon Press, 1920.

Darby, H. C. (ed.) *An historical geography of England before A.D. 1800*, Cambridge, Cambridge University Press, 1936.

'Some early ideas on the agricultural regions of England', *Agricultural History Review*, 2 (1954), 30–47.

'An historical geography of England: twenty years after', *Geographical Journal*, 126 (1960), 147–59.

'The draining of the English claylands', *Geographische Zeitschrift*, 52 (1964), 190–201.

A new historical geography of England, Cambridge, Cambridge University Press, 1973.

The changing fenland, Cambridge, Cambridge University Press, 1983.

Daunton, M. J. *House and home in the Victorian city: working-class housing, 1850–1914*, London, Edward Arnold, 1983.

Davies, A. E. 'The New Poor Law in a rural area, 1834–1850', *Ceredigion*, 8 (1978), 246–90.

Davies, B. L. and Miller, H. *Carmarthenshire*, Report of the Land Utilisation Survey of Great Britain, part 39, 1944.

Davies, C. Stella *The agricultural history of Cheshire 1750–1850*, Manchester, Chetham Society, 3rd series, 10, 1960.

Davies, E. 'The small landowner, 1780–1832, in the light of the land tax assessments', *Economic History Review*, 1 (1927), 87–113.

'Hendre and hafod in Denbighshire', *Transactions of the Denbighshire Historical Society*, 26 (1977), 49–72.

'Hendre and hafod in Caernarvonshire', *Transactions of the Caernarvonshire Historical Society*, 40 (1979), 17–46.

'*Hafod, hafoty* and *lluest*; their distribution, features and purpose', *Ceredigion*, 9 (1980), 1–41.

Davies, I. 'The agriculture of the west midlands conurbation', unpublished University of Birmingham M.A. thesis (1955).

Davies, Margaret F. *Pembrokeshire*, Report of the Land Utilisation Survey of Great Britain, part 32, 1939.

Wales in maps, Cardiff, University of Wales, 1951.

'The open fields of Laugharne', *Geography*, 40 (1955), 169–77.

'Rhosili open fields and related south Wales field patterns', *Agricultural History Review*, 4 (1956), 80–96.

Dawson, R. K. *Plans of the cities and boroughs of England and Wales shewing their boundaries as established by the Boundaries Act, passed 11th July 1832.*

Dickinson, R. F. 'Tithing customs in west Cumberland in the eighteenth century', *Transactions of the Cumberland and Westmorland Antiquarian and Archaeological Society*, new series, 60 (1960), 130–4.

Dicks, T. R. B. 'The south-western peninsulas of England and Wales: studies in agricultural geography, 1550–1900', unpublished University of Wales Ph.D. thesis (1964).

Digby, A. 'Regional variations in land use in mid-Ribblesdale since late medieval times', unpublished University of Leeds M.A. thesis (1960).

Dilke, O. A. W. *The Roman land surveyors. An introduction to the agrimensores*, Newton Abbot, David and Charles, 1971.

Dilke, O. A. W. and Dilke, Margaret S. 'Surveyors who measured by centuries', *Geographical Magazine*, 44 (1972), 630–6.

Dittmer, B. R. 'An agricultural geography of northwest Wiltshire, 1773–1840', unpublished University of London M.A. thesis (1963).

Dodd, J. P. 'Norfolk agriculture in 1853–4', *Norfolk Archaeology*, 36 (1976), 253–64.

'Gloucestershire agriculture 1801–1854', *Transactions of the Bristol and Gloucestershire Archaeological Society*, 97 (1979), 101–16.

'The West Riding crop returns for 1854', *Yorkshire Archaeological Journal*, 51 (1979), 117–29.

'Hampshire agriculture in the mid-nineteenth century', *Proceedings of the Hampshire Field Club and Archaeological Society*, 35 (1979), 239–60.

Dodgson, J. McN. *The place-names of Cheshire*, English Place-Name Society, XLIV–XLVIII, Cambridge University Press, 1970–2.

Dunbabin, J. P. D. *Rural discontent in nineteenth-century Britain*, London, Faber, 1974.

Dunlop, Sir J. *The pleasant town of Sevenoaks, a history*, Sevenoaks, the author, 1964.

Dyer, J. F., Stygall, F., and Dony, J. *The story of Luton*, Luton, White Crescent Press, 1964.

Dymond, R. 'Devonshire fields and hedges', *Journal of the Bath and West of England Society*, 4 (1856), 132–48.

Dyos, H. J. *Victorian suburb: a study of the growth of Camberwell*, Liverpool, Liverpool University Press, 1961.

The study of urban history, London, Edward Arnold, 1968.

Eagle, W. *The acts for the commutation of tithes in England and Wales*, 3rd edition, London, Saunders and Benning, 1840.

East, Jean 'The form and function of settlements in relation to types of farming in England and Wales (with an analysis of specific examples chosen from the west midlands and elsewhere)', unpublished University of London Ph.D. thesis (1947).

Eden, F. M. *The state of the poor; or an history of the labouring classes in England*, 3 Vols., London, B. and J. White, 1797.

Edwards, J. W. 'Enclosure and agricultural improvement in the Vale of Clwyd, 1750–1875', unpublished University of London M.A. thesis (1963).

Elliott, G. 'Changing agricultural landscapes in Cumberland', unpublished University of Liverpool M.A. thesis (1956).

'Field systems of northwest England', in A. R. H. Baker and R. A. Butlin (eds.), *Studies of field systems in the British Isles,* Cambridge, Cambridge University Press, 1973, 41–92.

Emmison, F. G. *Types of open-field parishes in the Midlands*, London, Historical Association pamphlet, 108, 1937.

'Tithes, perambulations and sabbath-breach in Elizabethan Essex', in F. G. Emmison and R. Stephens (eds.), *Tribute to an antiquary: essays presented to Marc Fitch by some of his friends*, London, Leopard's Head Press, 1976, 177–215.

Evans, E. J. 'A history of the tithe system in England, 1690–1850, with special reference to Staffordshire', unpublished University of Warwick Ph.D. thesis (1970).

'Tithing customs and disputes: the evidence of glebe terriers, 1698–1850', *Agricultural History Review*, 18 (1970), 17–35.

'A nineteenth-century tithe dispute and its significance: the case of Kendal', *Transactions of the Cumberland and Westmorland Antiquarian and Archaeological Society*, new series, 74 (1974), 159–85.

'Some reasons for the growth of English rural anti-clericalism, *c.*1750–*c.*1830', *Past and Present*, 66 (1975), 84–109.

The contentious tithe. The tithe problem and English agriculture, 1750–1850, London, Routledge and Kegan Paul, 1976.

Tithes and the Tithe Commutation Act 1836, Standing Conference for Local History, London, Bedford Square Press, 1978.

Evans, J. A. 'The woodlands of the Great Bookham area 1790 to 1840', *Proceedings of the Leatherhead and District Local History Society*, 3 (1967), 27–32.

Evans, Nesta 'Tithe books as a source for the local historian', *Local Historian*, 14 (1980), 24–7.

Eyre, S. R. 'The upward limit of enclosure on the east moor of north Derbyshire', *Transactions of the Institute of British Geographers*, 23 (1957), 61–74.

Farncombe, J. 'On the farming of Sussex', *Journal of the Royal Agricultural Society of England*, 11 (1850), 75–88.

Farrant, Sue P. 'Farm formation in eighteenth-century Bishopstone', *Sussex Archaeological Collections*, 114 (1976), 335–6.

'The changing structure of land ownership in the lower Ouse Valley, 1780–1840', *Sussex Archaeological Collections*, 116 (1978), 261–8.

'The management of four estates in the lower Ouse Valley (Sussex) and agricultural change, 1840–1920', *Southern History*, 1 (1979), 155–70.

Faull, Margaret L. 'Place-names and past landscapes', *English Place-Name Society Journal*, 11 (1978–9), 24–46.

'Problems in the use of place-names', in P. Brandon and R. Millman (eds.), *Recording historic landscapes, principles and practice*, London, Polytechnic of North London, Department of Geography, 1980, 81–7.

Field, J. *English field names: a dictionary*, Newton Abbot, David and Charles, 1972.

'Progress in field name studies', *Local Historian*, 13 (1978), 388–96.

Fieldhouse, R. T. 'Agriculture in Wensleydale from 1600 to the present day', *Northern History*, 16 (1980), 169–95.

Finberg, H. P. R. 'The open field in Devon', in W. G. Hoskins and H. P. R. Finberg, *Devonshire studies*, London, Cape, 1952, 265–88.

Fitchett, C. E. *Bedfordshire*, Report of the Land Utilisation Survey of Great Britain, part 55, 1943.

Flatrès, P. *Géographie rurale de quatre contrées celtiques: Irlande, Galles, Cornwall et Man*, Rennes, Plihon, 1957.

Ford, W. K. 'Boltro Farm, Cuckfield', *Sussex Archaeological Collections*, 114 (1976), 81–96.

Fox, C. *The countryside and the law*, Newton Abbot, David and Charles, 1971.

Fox, H. S. A. 'A geographical study of the field systems of Devon and Cornwall', unpublished University of Cambridge Ph.D. thesis (1971).

'The study of field systems', *Devon Historian*, 4 (1972), 3–11.

'The chronology of enclosure and economic development in medieval Devon', *Economic History Review*, 2nd series, 28 (1975), 181–202.

'Local farmers' associations and the circulation of agricultural information in nineteenth-century England', in H. S. A. Fox and R. A. Butlin (eds.), *Change in the countryside: essays on rural England, 1500–1900*, London, Institute of British Geographers, Special Publication, 10, 1979, 43–63.

'Approaches to the adoption of the midland system', in T. Rowley (ed.), *The origins of open-field agriculture*, London, Croom Helm, 1981, 64–111.

Frost, M. J. 'The changing land use in the upper basin of the river Mole', unpublished University of London M.Sc. thesis (1964).

Fuller, Heather A. 'Landownership and the Lindsey landscape', *Annals of the Association of American Geographers*, 66 (1976), 14–24.

Gaut, R. C. *A history of Worcestershire agriculture and rural evolution*, Worcester, Littlebury, 1939.

Gawne, Elizabeth 'Field patterns in Widecombe parish and the Forest of Dartmoor', *Report and Transactions of the Devonshire Association*, 102 (1970), 49–69.

Gelling, Margaret *Signposts to the past. Place-names and the history of England*, London, Dent, 1978.

Gilbert, A. D. *Religion and society in industrial England, church, chapel and social change, 1740–1914*, London, Longman, 1976.

Giles, B. D. 'Mid-Worcestershire in the first half of the nineteenth century: the enclosure and tithe awards of five parishes', *Transactions of the Worcestershire Archaeological Society*, 3rd series, 4 (1974), 35–66.

Gleave, M. B. 'Dispersed and nucleated settlements in the Yorkshire Wolds, 1770–1850', *Transactions of the Institute of British Geographers*, 30 (1962), 105–18.

Godfrey, W. E. 'A Stavely tithe book of the Rev. James Gisborne', *Journal of the Derbyshire Archaeological and Natural History Society*, 71 (1951), 38–46.

Gonner, E. C. K. *Common land and enclosure*, London, Macmillan, 1912.

Gover, J. E. B., Mawer, A. and Stenton, F. M. *The place names of Surrey*, English Place-Name Society, XI, Cambridge, Cambridge University Press, 1934.

The place names of Middlesex apart from the City of London, English Place-Name Society XVIII, Cambridge, Cambridge University Press, 1942.

Gramolt, D. W. 'The coastal marshland of east Essex between the seventeenth and mid-nineteenth centuries', unpublished University of London M.A. thesis (1961).

Grantham, R. B. 'A description of the works for reclaiming and marling of the late Forest of Delamere in the county of Cheshire', *Journal of the Royal Agricultural Society of England*, 25 (1864), 369–80.

Gras, N. S. B. and Gras, Ethel C. *The economic and social history of an English village, Crawley, Hampshire, A.D.909–1928*, Cambridge, Mass., Harvard University Press, 1930.

Gray, H. L. 'Yeoman farming in Oxfordshire from the sixteenth century to the nineteenth', *Quarterly Journal of Economics*, 24 (1910), 293–326.

English field systems, Cambridge, Mass., Harvard University Press, 1915.

Greaves, R. W. *The corporation of Leicester, 1689–1836*, Oxford, Oxford University Press, 1970.

Griffith, D. G. 'A study of the economic development of the lower Conway valley and the Creuddyn peninsula, 1750–1914', unpublished University of Wales M.A. thesis (1954).

Grigg, D. B. *The agricultural revolution in south Lincolnshire*, Cambridge, Cambridge University Press, 1966.

Grove, H. *Alienated tithes . . .*, London, privately printed, 1896.

Grove, J. C. 'Land use changes in west Gower 1840–1950', unpublished University of Wales M.A. thesis (1956).

Gyll, G. W. J. *History of the parish of Wraysbury*, London, H. G. Bohn, 1862.

Hallam, Olive, 'Vegetation and land use on Exmoor', *Somerset Archaeology and Natural History*, 122 (1978), 37–51.

Hammond, J. L. and Hammond, Barbara *The village labourer, 1760–1832*, London, Longman, 1912.

Harley, J. B. *Maps for the local historian. A guide to the British sources*, London, National Council of Social Service, 1972.

'England *circa* 1850', in H. C. Darby (ed.), *A new historical geography of England*, Cambridge, Cambridge University Press, 1973, 527–94.

Harris, A. *The rural landscape of the East Riding of Yorkshire, 1750–1850, a study in historical geography*, Oxford, Oxford University Press, 1961.

'Changes in the early railway age: 1800–1850', in H. C. Darby (ed.), *A new historical geography of England*, Cambridge, Cambridge University Press, 1973, 465–526.

Harris, Rosemary L. 'The Ordnance Survey Memoirs', *Ulster Folklife*, 1 (1951), 43–52.

Harrison, M. J., Mead, W. R. and Pannett, D. J. 'A midland ridge-and-furrow map', *Geographical Journal*, 131 (1965), 365–9.

Hartley, F. D. 'The agricultural geography of the Chilterns, *c.* 1840', unpublished University of London M.A. thesis (1953).

Harvey, D. W. 'Aspects of agricultural and rural change in Kent, 1800–1900', unpublished University of Cambridge Ph.D. thesis (1961).

'Locational change in the Kentish hop industry and the analysis of land use patterns', *Transactions of the Institute of British Geographers*, 33 (1963), 123–44.

'Fruit growing in Kent in the nineteenth century', *Archaeologia Cantiana*, 79 (1964), 95–108.

Harvey, J. 'A short history of Bookham, Surrey – part IX', *Proceedings of the Leatherhead and District Local History Society*, 2 (1962), 187–93.

Harvey, J. H. *Sources for the history of houses*, London, British Records Association, Archives and the User, 3, 1974.

Havinden, M. A. *Estate villages; a study of the Berkshire villages of Ardington and Lockinge*, London, Lund Humphries, 1966.

Hawkes, L. R. 'A regional study of the agricultural landscape of the north Exe basin', unpublished University of London M.A. thesis (1938).

Henderson, H. C. K. 'Our changing agriculture: the distribution of arable land in the Adur basin, Sussex, from 1780 to 1931', *Journal of the Ministry of Agriculture*, 43 (1936), 625–33.

'Changes in land utilisation in Derbyshire 1837–1937', in A. H. Harris, *Derbyshire*, Report of the Land Utilisation Survey of Great Britain, part 63, 1941, 71–4.

Our changing agriculture, London, University of London inaugural lecture, 1966.

Henstock, A. 'Group projects in local history – house repopulation in the mid-nineteenth century', *Bulletin of Local History, East Midlands Region*, 6 (1971), 11–20.

'House repopulation from the census returns of 1841 and 1851', *Local Population Studies*, 10 (1973), 37–52.

Hewitt, F. 'Population and urban growth in east Bristol, 1800–1914', unpublished University of Bristol Ph.D. thesis (1966).

Hey, D. *The village of Ecclesfield*, Huddersfield, The Advertiser, 1968.

Hill, C. *Economic problems of the Church, from Archbishop Whitgift to the Long Parliament*, Oxford, Clarendon Press, 1956.

Hilton, N. 'The Land's End Peninsula: the influence of history on agriculture', *Geographical Journal*, 119 (1953), 57–72.

Hobsbawn, E. J. and Rudé, G. F. E. *Captain Swing*, London, Lawrence and Wishart, 1969.

Hockey, S. F. 'The pattern of tithes in the Isle of Wight', *Proceedings of the Hampshire Field Club and Archaeological Society*, 21 (1960), 145–55.

Holt, Harriet M. E. 'The tithe files of Norfolk', *Norfolk Research Committee Bulletin*, 23 (1980), 6–7.

'Assistant commissioners and local agents: their role in tithe commutation, 1836–1854', *Agricultural History Review* (in the press).

Holt, Harriet M. E. and Kain, R. J. P. 'Land use and farming in Suffolk about 1840', *Proceedings of the Suffolk Institute of Archaeology and History*, 34 (1982), 123–39.

Hooke, Janet M. and Kain, R. J. P. *Historical change in the physical environment: a guide to sources and techniques*, London, Butterworth, 1982.

Hooke, Janet M. and Perry, R. A. 'The planimetric accuracy of tithe maps', *Cartographic Journal*, 13 (1976), 177–83.

Hoskins, W. G. 'Three studies in family history', in W. G. Hoskins and H. P. R. Finberg, *Devonshire studies*, London, Jonathan Cape, 1952, 78–119.

The midland peasant. The economic and social history of a Leicestershire village, London, Macmillan, 1957.

Howell, D. W. *Land and people in nineteenth-century Wales*, London, Routledge and Kegan Paul, 1978.

Howell, E. J. *Shropshire*, Report of the Land Utilisation Survey of Great Britain, part 66, 1941.

'Land use and agriculture in Brecon and Radnor 150 years ago', in Rosalynde M. Whyte, *Brecon*, Report of the Land Utilisation Survey of Great Britain, part 37, 1943, 383–94.

Cardiganshire, Report of the Land Utilisation Survey of Great Britain, part 40, 1946.

Howes, R. 'Joseph Pitt, landowner', in B. S. Smith (ed.), *Gloucestershire Historical Studies*, Bristol, University of Bristol Department of Extra-Mural Studies, 7, 1976, 20–4.

Hull, F. (ed.) *Catalogue of estate maps, 1590–1840, in the Kent County Archives Office*, Maidstone, Kent County Council, 1973.

Hunt, H. G. 'Landownership and enclosure, 1750–1830', *Economic History Review*, 2nd series, 11 (1958–9), 497–505.

Hunt, N. C. *Two early political associations. The Quakers and the Dissenting Deputies in the age of Sir Robert Walpole*, Oxford, Clarendon Press, 1961.

Ingleson, J. S. 'Settlement, agrarian systems, and field patterns in central Durham, 1600–1850: a study in historical geography', unpublished University of Durham M.A. thesis (1972).

Iredale, D. 'How can I trace the history of my house?', *Amateur Historian*, 7 (1967), 182–9.

Ivimey, A. (ed.) *Westleton from the 1830s to the 1960s: a survey of a Suffolk village*, Saxmundham, Workers' Educational Association, 1968.

Jackson, J. C. 'Open field cultivation in Derbyshire', *Derbyshire Archaeological Journal*, 82 (1962), 54–72.

Jahn, M. A. 'Railways and suburban development: outer west London 1850–1900 (Acton, Chiswick, Ealing and Hanwell)', unpublished University of London M.Phil. thesis (1971).

'Suburban development in outer west London, 1850–1900', in F. M. L. Thompson (ed.), *The rise of suburbia*, Leicester, Leicester University Press, 1982, 94–156.

James, Margaret 'The political importance of the tithes controversy in the English Revolution, 1640–60', *History*, 26 (1941), 1–18.

Jarrett, M. G. and Wrathmell, S. 'Sixteenth- and seventeenth-century farmsteads: West Whelpington, Northumberland', *Agricultural History Review*, 25 (1977), 108–19.

Jarvis, J. B. 'Changes in land use in south-east Denbighshire', in E. J. Howell, *North Wales*, Report of the Land Utilisation Survey of Great Britain, parts 41–3, 1946, 734–43.

Jennings, J. N. and Lambert, Joyce M. 'The shrinkage of the Broads', *New Naturalist*, 6 (1949), 26–7.

Johnson, A. H. *The disappearance of the small landowner*, Oxford, Clarendon Press, 1909.

Johnson, H. B. *Order upon the land: the U.S. rectangular land survey and the upper Mississippi country*, New York, Oxford University Press, 1976.

Johnson, J. H. 'The Irish tithe composition applotment books as a geographical source', *Irish Geography*, 3 (1958), 254–62.

Johnson, S. A. 'Enclosure and the agricultural landscape of Lindsey from the sixteenth to the nineteenth century', unpublished University of Liverpool M.A. thesis (1957).

'Enclosure and agricultural landscapes in Lindsey', *Agricultural History Review*, 11 (1963), 95–102.

Jones, E. L. 'The changing basis of English agricultural prosperity, 1853–73', *Agricultural History Review*, 10 (1962), 102–19.

Agriculture and economic growth in England 1650–1815, London, Methuen, 1967.

The development of English agriculture, 1815–1873, London, Macmillan, 1968.

Jones, F. 'The Mathry tithe suit', *Journal of the Historical Society of the Church in Wales*, 2 (1950), 97–102.

Jones, G. R. J. 'Some medieval rural settlements in north Wales', *Transactions of the Institute of British Geographers*, 19 (1953), 51–72.

'The distribution of medieval settlement in Anglesey', *Anglesey Antiquarian Society and Field Club Transactions*, unnumbered series (1955), 27–96.

'The pattern of settlement on the Welsh border', *Agricultural History Review*, 8 (1960), 66–81.

'The tribal system in Wales: a re-assessment in the light of settlement studies', *Welsh History Review*, 1 (1961), 111–32.

'Early settlement in Arfon: the setting of Tre'r Ceiri', *Caernarvonshire Historical Society Transactions*, 24 (1963), 1–20.

'The Llanynys quillets: a measure of landscape transformation in north Wales', *Transactions of the Denbighshire Historical Society*, 13 (1964), 133–58.

'The distribution of bond settlements in north-west Wales', *Welsh History Review*, 2 (1964), 19–36.

'To the building of Kirkstall Abbey', in M. W. Beresford and G. R. J. Jones (eds.), *Leeds and its region* (Leeds, British Association for the Advancement of Science, 1967), 125.

'Field systems of north Wales', in A. R. H. Baker and R. A. Butlin (eds.), *Studies of field systems in the British Isles*, Cambridge, Cambridge University Press, 1973, 430–79.

'Early customary tenures in Wales and open-field agriculture', in T. Rowley (ed.), *The origins of open-field agriculture*, London, Croom Helm, 1981, 202–225.

Jones, P. E. 'Changes in land utilisation in Uwchgwyrfai, Caernarvonshire 1750 to 1956', unpublished University of Wales M.A. thesis (1959).

'The city of Bangor and its environs at the time of the tithe survey, 1840', *Caernarvonshire Historical Society Transactions*, 31 (1970), 64–77.

Jones, R. *Remarks on the manner in which tithe should be assessed to the poor's rate . . .*, London, Shaw and Sons, 1838.

Kain, R. J. P. 'The land of Kent in the middle of the nineteenth century', unpublished University of London Ph.D. thesis (1973).

'Contemporary opinion concerning the possible conversion of pasture to arable after tithe commutation', *Cantium*, 6 (1974), 77–9.

'The tithe commutation surveys', *Archaeologia Cantiana*, 89 (1974), 101–18.

'Tithe surveys and landownership', *Journal of Historical Geography*, 1 (1975), 39–48.

'R. K. Dawson's proposal in 1836 for a cadastral survey of England and Wales', *Cartographic Journal*, 12 (1975), 81–8.

'Tithe surveys and the study of land occupation', *Local Historian*, 12 (1976), 88–92.

'Tithe surveys and the rural landscape of England and Wales', *Bulletin of the Society of University Cartographers*, 11 (1977), 1–3.

'Compiling an atlas of agriculture in England and Wales from the tithe surveys', *Geographical Journal*, 145 (1979), 225–41.

'Tithe as an index of pre-industrial agricultural production, *Agricultural History Review*, 27 (1979), 73–81.

'Les dîmes, les relevés de dîmes et la mesure de la production agricole dans la Grande-Bretagne préindustrielle', in J. Goy and E. Le Roy Ladurie (eds.), *Prestations paysannes, dîmes, rente foncière et mouvement de la production agricole à l'époque préindustrielle*, Paris, Mouton, 1982, 713–32.

'The tithe files of mid-nineteenth century England and Wales', in M.A. Reed (ed.), *Discovering past landscapes*, London, Croom Helm, 1984, 56–84.

An atlas and index of the tithe files of mid-nineteenth century England and Wales. (Cambridge, Cambridge University Press, forthcoming).

Kain, R. J. P. and Holt, Harriet M. E. 'Agriculture and land use in Cornwall *circa* 1840', *Southern History*, 3 (1981), 139–81.

'Farming in Cheshire *circa* 1840: some evidence from the tithe files', *Transactions of the Lancashire and Cheshire Antiquarian Society*, 82 (1983), 22–57.

Kellett, J. R. *The impact of railways on Victorian cities*, London, Routledge and Kegan Paul, 1969.

Kent, N. *General view of the agriculture of the county of Norfolk*, Norwich, Norfolk Press, 1796.

Kerr, Barbara. *Bound to the soil: a social history of Dorset 1750–1918*, London, John Baker, 1968.

Kerridge, E. *The agricultural revolution*, London, Allen and Unwin, 1967.

Kiralfy, A. K. R. 'The Star Chamber litigation of vicar Richard Levitt in 1609', *Proceedings of the Leatherhead and District Local History Society*, 1 (1951), 21–3.

Ladurie, E. Le Roy and Goy, J. *Tithe and agrarian history from the fourteenth to the nineteenth centuries*, Cambridge, Cambridge University Press, 1982.

Lambert, Joyce M., Jennings, J. N., Smith, C. T., Green, C. and Hutchinson, J. N. *The making of the Broads. A reconsideration of their origin in the light of new evidence*, London, Murray, Royal Geographical Society Research Series, 3, 1960.

Lane, H. A. 'The parish of Carew, (*c.* 1838)', *Pembrokeshire Historian*, 4 (1972), 70–5.

Langdon, Gee *The year of the map: portrait of a Wiltshire town in 1841*, Tisbury, Compton Russell, 1976.

Lavergne, L. de *The rural economy of England, Scotland and Ireland*, Edinburgh and London, Blackwood, 1855.

Lavrovsky, V. 'Tithe commutation as a factor in the gradual decrease of landownership by the English peasantry', *Economic History Review*, 4 (1933), 273–89.

Laxton, P. 'Common fields and enclosure in part of central Berkshire', *Journal of the Durham University Geographical Society*, 9 (1967), 44–56.

Leeson, F. 'The farms of Coulsdon in 1762 and 1837', *Bourne Society's Local History Records*, 7 (1968), 29–34.

Lewarne, J. G. W. 'A cartographical survey of the area: 10. The Fetcham parish tithe map of 1791', *Proceedings of the Leatherhead and District Local History Society*, 2 (1965), 257–9.

Lewis, G. J. 'The demographic structure of a Welsh rural village during the mid-nineteenth century', *Ceredigion*, 5 (1966), 290–304.

Liebig, J. von *Organic chemistry in its application to agriculture and physiology*. ed. Lyon Playfair, London, Taylor and Walton, 1840.

List and Index Society *Inland Revenue tithe maps and apportionments*, London, Swift (P. and D.), 68 and 83 (1971 and 1972).

Little, A. G. 'Personal tithes', *English Historical Review*, 60 (1945), 67–88.

Lloyd, L. W. 'Corsygedol, Ardudwys's principal estate', *Journal of the Merioneth Historical and Record Society*, 8 (1977–8), 27–60 and 157–90.

Lloyd-Pritchard, M. F. 'The vicar of Mattishall and his tithes, 1781–1803', *Agricultural History*, 27 (1953), 141–7.

Lukehurst, Clare T. 'The Stour marshes: a study of agricultural changes 1840–1966', unpublished University of London Ph.D. thesis (1977).

McCulloch, J. R. *A statistical account of the British empire: exhibiting its extent, physical capacities, population, industry, and civil and religious institutions*, 2nd edition, 2 vols., London, Charles Knight, 1839.

McGregor, O. R. 'Introduction part two: after 1815', in R. E. Prothero (Lord Ernle), *English farming past and present*, 6th edition, London, Heinemann and Frank Cass, 1961, lxxix–cxlv.

McPherson, A. W. *Warwickshire*, Report of the Land Utilisation Survey of Great Britain, part 62, 1946.

Maitland, F. W. *Domesday Book and beyond: three essays in the early history of England*, Cambridge, Cambridge University Press, 1897.

Mansfield, A. J. 'An historical geography of the woodlands of the southern Chilterns, 1600–1947', unpublished University of London M.Sc. thesis (1952).

Marshall, J. D. *Furness and the industrial revolution*, Barrow-in-Furness, Library and Museum Committee, 1958.

'Colonisation as a factor in the planting of towns in north-west England', in H. J. Dyos (ed.), *The study of urban history*, London, Edward Arnold, 1968, 215–30.

Martin, J. M. 'Land ownership and the land tax returns', *Agricultural History Review*, 14 (1966), 96–103.

'The parliamentary enclosure movement and rural society in Warwickshire', *Agricultural History Review*, 15 (1967), 19–39.

Mawer, A. 'The study of field-names in relation to place-names', in J. G. Edwards, V. H. Galbraith and E. F. Jacob (eds.), *Historical essays in honour of James Tait*, Manchester, printed for the subscribers, 1933, 189–200.

May, J. and Wells, S. F. *Montgomeryshire*, Report of the Land Utilisation Survey of Great Britain, part 36, 1942.

Meekings, C. A. F. 'St Teath's tithes – 1295', *Devon and Cornwall Notes and Queries*, 32 (1972), 168–70.

Meirion-Jones, G. I. 'A contribution to the historical geography of north-east Hampshire *c.* 1600–1850', unpublished University of London M.Phil. thesis (1969).

'The use of hearth tax returns and vernacular architecture in settlement studies with examples from north-east Hampshire', *Transactions of the Institute of British Geographers*, 53 (1971), 133–60.

Meitzen, A. *Wandesungen, Anbau und Agrarrecht der Völker Europas nördlich der Alpen, erste Abteilung: Siedlung und Agrarwesen der Westgermanen und Ostgermanen, der Kelten, Römer, Finnen und Slawen*, 3 vols. and atlas, Berlin, Wilhelm Herty, 1895.

Millard, P. W. *The law relating to tithes and payments in lieu thereof*, 3rd edition, London, Butterworth, 1938.

Mills, D. R. 'Population and settlement in Kesteven (Lincolnshire) *c.*1775–*c.*1885', unpublished University of Nottingham M.A. thesis (1957).

'Landownership and rural population, with special reference to Leicestershire in the mid-nineteenth century', unpublished University of Leicester Ph.D. thesis (1963).

'A social and demographic study of Melbourn, Cambridgeshire, *c.*1840', *Archives*, 12 (1976), 115–20.

'The technique of house repopulation: experience from a Cambridgeshire village, 1841', *Local Historian*, 13 (1978), 87–97.

'The residential propinquity of kin in a Cambridgeshire village, 1841', *Journal of Historical Geography*, 4 (1978), 265–76.

Lord and peasant in nineteenth century Britain, London, Croom Helm, 1980.

Mingay, G. E. 'The land tax assessments and the small landowner', *Economic History Review*, 2nd series, 17 (1964), 381–8.

Enclosure and the small farmer in the age of the industrial revolution, London, Macmillan, 1968.

Rural life in Victorian England, London, Heinemann, 1977.

(ed.) *The agricultural revolution. Changes in agriculture, 1650–1880*, London, Black, 1977.

Mitchell, P. K. 'West Cleveland land use, *c.*1550–1850', unpublished University of Durham Ph.D. thesis (1965).

Moore, N. W., Hooper, M. D., and Davis, B. N. K. 'Hedges I. Introduction and reconnaissance studies', *Journal of Applied Ecology*, 4 (1967), 201–20.

Morgan, C. 'The effect of parliamentary enclosure on the landscape of Caernarvonshire and Merioneth', unpublished University of Wales M.Sc. thesis (1959).

Morgan, F. C. 'Bosbury tithes and oblations, 1635 to 1641', *Transactions of the Woolhope Naturalists' Field Club*, 38 (1965), 140–8.

Mortimore, M. J. 'Landownership and urban growth in Bradford and its environs in the West Riding conurbation, 1850–1950', *Transactions of the Institute of British Geographers*, 46 (1969), 105–19.

Mosby, J. E. G. *Norfolk*, Report of the Land Utilisation Survey of Great Britain, part 70, 1938.

Naish, M. C. 'The agricultural landscape of the Hampshire chalklands, 1700–1840', unpublished University of London M.A. thesis (1961).

Nightingale, M. D. 'Some evidence of open field agriculture in Kent', unpublished University of Oxford B.Litt. thesis (1952).

Nokes, B. C. G. 'Industrial change and settlement in north-east Worcestershire *c.*1775–1875', unpublished University of London Ph.D. thesis (1967).

O'Donoghue, P. 'Opposition to tithe payments in 1832–3', *Studia Hibernica*, 12 (1972), 77–108.

Olmsted, Frederick Law *Walks and talks of an American farmer in England*, Ann Arbor, University of Michigan Press, n.d.

Ordnance Survey *Account of field surveying and the preparation of the manuscript plans of the Ordnance Survey*, Southampton, Ordnance Survey, 1873.

Orwin, C. S. and Orwin, Christabel S. *The open fields*, Oxford, Clarendon Press, 1938.

Orwin, Christabel S. and Whetham, Edith H. *History of British agriculture 1846–1914*, London, Longman, 1964.

Otter, M. E. 'The land utilisation of Llanrug parish', *Transactions of the Caernarvonshire Historical Society*, 7 (1946), 55–83.

Ottrey, F. S. 'Geographical aspects of the development of Wirksworth from the beginning of the nineteenth century to the present', unpublished University of Nottingham M.A. thesis (1965).

Parton, A. G. 'Town and country in Surrey *c.*1800–1870: a study in historical geography', unpublished University of Hull Ph.D. thesis (1973).

Pemberton, W. A. 'A parson's account book', *Local Historian*, 13 (1978), 397–405.

Pepper, R. W. 'Urban development of Lewisham: a geographical interpretation', unpublished University of London M.A. thesis (1965).

Perry, P. J. (ed.) *British agriculture, 1875–1914*, London, Methuen, 1973.

'High farming in Victorian Britain, prospect and retrospect', *Agricultural History*, 55 (1981), 156–66.

Peterken, G. F. 'Development of vegetation in Staverton Park, Suffolk', *Field Studies*, 3 (1969), 1–39.

Phillips, A. D. M. 'Underdraining and the English claylands, 1850–1880: a review', *Agricultural History Review*, 17 (1969), 44–55.

'A study of farming practices and soil types in Staffordshire around 1840', *North Staffordshire Journal of Field Studies*, 13 (1973), 27–52.

'Agricultural land use, soils and the Nottinghamshire tithe surveys *circa* 1840', *East Midland Geographer*, 6 (1976), 284–301.

'Agricultural land use and the Herefordshire tithe surveys, *circa* 1840', *Transactions of the Woolhope Naturalists' Field Club*, 43 (1979), 54–61.

'Mossland reclamation in nineteenth-century Cheshire', *Transactions of the Historic Society of Lancashire and Cheshire*, 129 (1980), 93–107.

Pitt, W. *General view of the agriculture of the county of Stafford*, London, G. Nicol, 1796.

Plaisted, A. H. *The manor and parish records of Medmenham, Buckinghamshire*, London, Longmans Green, 1925.

Pocock, D. C. D. 'Landownership and urban growth in Scunthorpe', *East Midland Geographer*, 5 (1970), 52–61.

Pollard, E., Hooper, M. D. and Moore, N. W. *Hedges*, London, Collins, 1974.

Porter, G. R. *The progress of the nation*, 2nd edition, London, John Murray, 1847.

Porter, Regina E. 'Agricultural change in Cheshire during the nineteenth century', unpublished University of Liverpool Ph.D. thesis (1974).

Porter, W. *History of the Corps of the Royal Engineers*, London, Longman Green, 1889.

Portlock, J. E. *Memoir of the life of Major-General Colby*, London, Seeley, Jackson and Halliday, 1869.

Postgate, M. R. 'Historical geography of the Breckland, 1600–1850', unpublished University of London M.A. thesis (1961).

'The field systems of Breckland', *Agricultural History Review*, 10 (1962), 81–101.

'Field systems of East Anglia', in A. R. H. Baker and R. A. Butlin (eds.), *Studies of field systems in the British Isles*, Cambridge, Cambridge University Press, 1973, 281–324.

Pounds, N. J. G. 'The historical geography of Cornwall', unpublished University of London Ph.D. thesis (1945).

Powell, J. M. 'An economic geography of Montgomeryshire in the nineteenth century', unpublished University of Liverpool M.A. thesis (1962).

'Tithe surveys and schedules: some Montgomeryshire examples', *Journal of the National Library of Wales*, 16 (1969), 87–96.

Prince, H. C. 'The tithe surveys of the mid-nineteenth century', *Agricultural History Review*, 7 (1959), 14–26.

'The origin of pits and depressions in Norfolk', *Geography*, 49 (1964), 15–32.

'Victorian rural landscapes', in G. E. Mingay (ed.), *The Victorian countryside*, 2 vols., London, Routledge and Kegan Paul, 1981, Vol. 1, 17–29.

Pritchard, Constance 'Changes in the agricultural geography of the parishes of Bockleton, Kyre Magna, Tenbury township and Foreign (Worc.) and Hampton Charles (Hereford) from 1841 to 1958', unpublished University of Birmingham M.A. thesis (1965).

Prothero, R. E. (Lord Ernle) *English farming past and present*, 6th edition, London, Heinemann and Frank Cass, 1961.

Pryce, W. T. R. 'Enclosure and field pattern in the Banwy valley', *Montgomeryshire Collections*, 57 (1961–2), 23–32.

Purvis, J. S. 'A note on XVI century farming in Yorkshire', *Yorkshire Archaeological Journal*, 36 (1944–7), 435–54.

Select XVI century causes in tithe from the York Diocesan Registry, Yorkshire Archaeological Society Record Series, 114 (1949).

Pusey, P. 'On the progress of agricultural knowledge during the last four years', *Journal of the Royal Agricultural Society of England*, 3 (1842), 169–217.

'On the agricultural improvements of Lincolnshire', *Journal of the Royal Agricultural Society of England*, 4 (1843), 287–316.

'On the progress of agricultural knowledge during the last eight years', *Journal of the Royal Agricultural Society of England*, 11 (1850), 381–438.

Rackham, O. 'Documentary evidence for the historical ecologist', *Landscape History*, 1 (1979), 29–33.

Ancient woodland: its history, vegetation and uses in England, London, Edward Arnold, 1980.

Rawcliffe, J. M. 'Bromley: Kentish market town to London suburb, 1841–81', in F. M. L. Thompson (ed.), *The rise of suburbia*, Leicester, Leicester University Press, 1982, 27–91.

Reaney, P. H. *The place names of Essex*, English Place-Name Society, XII, Cambridge, Cambridge University Press, 1935.

Reay, B. 'Quaker opposition to tithes 1652–1660', *Past and Present*, 86 (1980), 98–120.

Richards, P. S. 'The growth of towns – a study in methodology', *Local Historian*, 9 (1970), 190–5.

Roberts, B. K. 'Planned villages from medieval England', in A. R. H. Baker and J. B. Harley (eds.), *Man made the land*, Newton Abbot, David and Charles, 1973, 46–58.

The green villages of County Durham: a study in historical geography, Durham, Durham County Council, 1977, 24–38.

Rural settlement in Britain, Folkestone, Dawson, 1977.

'Townfield origins: the case of Cockfield, County Durham', in T. Rowley (ed.), *The origins of open field agriculture*, London, Croom Helm, 1981, 145–61.

Robinson, D. J. and Cooke, R. U. 'Lime-kilns in Surrey: a reconstruction of a rural industry', *Surrey Archaeological Collections*, 59 (1962), 19–26.

Roden, D. 'Studies in Chiltern field systems', unpublished University of London Ph.D. thesis (1965).

'Field systems in Ibstone, a township of the south-west Chilterns, during the later middle ages', *Records of Buckinghamshire*, 18 (1966), 43–57.

'Field systems of the Chiltern Hills and their environs', in A. R. H. Baker and R. A. Butlin (eds.), *Studies of field systems in the British Isles*, Cambridge, Cambridge University Press, 1973, 325–76.

Rudé, G. F. E. 'English rural and urban disturbances on the eve of the first Reform Bill, 1830–1', *Past and Present*, 37 (1967), 87–102.

Rudge, Thomas, *General view of the agriculture of the county of Gloucester*, London, Richard Phillips, 1807.

Russell, R. C. *The enclosure of Barton-upon-Humber, 1793–1796*, Barton-upon-Humber, Workers' Educational Association, 1968.

The enclosures of East Halton, 1801–1804 and North Kelsey, 1813–1840, North Lindsey Branch of the Workers' Educational Association, 1974.

Ruston, A. G. and Witney, D. *Hooton Pagnell. The agricultural evolution of a Yorkshire village*, London, Arnold, 1934.

Rye, W. *Records and record searching: a guide to the genealogist and topographer*, 2nd edition, London, George Allen, 1897.

An account of the church and parish of Cawston, in the county of Norfolk, Norwich, privately printed, 1898.

Sandell, R. E. (ed.) *Abstracts of Wiltshire tithe apportionments*, Devizes, Wiltshire Record Society, 1975.

Secretary of the Tithe Redemption Commission 'The records of the Tithe Redemption Commission', *Journal of the Society of Archivists*, 1 (1957), 132–9.

Seebohm, F. *The English village community* . . ., London, Longman, 1883.

Shave, D. W. 'The distribution of arable land in the upper Wey basin in 1840, 1870 and 1939', in L. D. Stamp and E. C. Willatts, *Surrey*, Report of the Land Utilisation Survey of Great Britain, part 81, 1941, 392–7.

Sheail, J. 'Documentary evidence of the changes in the use, management and appreciation of the grass-heaths of Breckland', *Journal of Biogeography*, 6 (1979), 277–92.

Historical ecology: the documentary evidence, Cambridge, Institute of Terrestrial Ecology, 1980.

Shelford, L. *The acts for the commutation of tithes in England and Wales* . . ., 3rd edition, London, S. Sweet, 1842.

Sheppard, F. H. W. 'Sources and methods used for the Survey of London', in H. J. Dyos (ed.), *The study of urban history*, London, Edward Arnold, 1968, 131–45.

Sheppard, June A. 'The medieval meres of Holderness', *Transactions of the Institute of British Geographers*, 23 (1957), 75–86.

'East Yorkshire's agricultural labour force in the mid-nineteenth century', *Agricultural History Review*, 9 (1961), 43–54.

'Field systems of Yorkshire', in A. R. H. Baker and R. A. Butlin (eds.), *Studies of field systems in the British Isles*, Cambridge, Cambridge University Press, 1973, 145–87.

Short, B. M. 'Agriculture in the High Weald of Kent and Sussex, 1850 to 1953 (A case study in the application of multivariate techniques in the field of historical geography)', unpublished University of London Ph.D. thesis (1973).

Shorter, A. H. 'Landscore, stitch and quillett fields in Devon', *Devon and Cornwall Notes and Queries*, 23 (1949), 372–80.

Shorter, A. H. 'Field patterns in Brixham parish, Devon', *Report and Transactions of the Devonshire Association*, 82 (1950), 271–80.

Siegel, S. *Nonparametric statistics for the behavioral sciences*, New York, McGraw-Hill, 1956.

Simington, R. C. 'The tithe composition applotment books', *Analectica Hibernica*, 10 (1941), 295–8.

Simmonds, N. M. 'The functions and growth of the city of Exeter, 1800–1841', unpublished University of Exeter M.A. thesis (1959).

Sinfield, R. A. 'The distribution of tithe surveys in England', unpublished University College London, B. A. course paper (1969).

Skipp, V. H. T. (ed.) *Discovering Sheldon*, Birmingham, University of Birmingham Extra-Mural Department, 1960.

Slater, G. *The English peasantry and the enclosure of common fields*, London, Constable, 1907.

Slater, T. R. 'The analysis of burgage patterns in medieval towns', *Area*, 13 (1981), 211–16.

Slee, A. H. 'The open fields of Braunton. Braunton Great Field and Braunton Downs', *Report and Transactions of the Devonshire Association*, 84 (1952), 142–9.

Smalley, K. A. *Greenford – the historical geography of a north-west London parish*, Ealing Local History Society Members' Papers, 3, 1963.

Smith, W. *An economic geography of Great Britain*, London, Methuen, 1949.

Spring, D. *The English landed estate in the nineteenth century: its administration*, Baltimore, Johns Hopkins Press, 1963.

Springett, Jane 'Landowners and urban development: the Ramdsden estate and nineteenth-century Huddersfield', *Journal of Historical Geography*, 8 (1982), 129–44.

Stamp, L. D. *Devonshire*, Report of the Land Utilisation Survey of Great Britain, part 92, 1941.

Kent, Report of the Land Utilisation Survey of Great Britain, part 85, 1943.

The land of Britain, its use and misuse, 3rd edition, London, Longmans Green, 1962.

Stevenson, J. *Popular disturbances in England, 1700–1870*, London, Longman, 1979.

Street, A. G. *Farmer's glory*, London, Faber and Faber, 1932.

Sturgess, R. W. 'A study of agricultural change in the Staffordshire moorlands, 1780–1850', *North Staffordshire Journal of Field Studies*, 1 (1961), 77–85.

Swindell, K. 'The Cromford cotton mills: their site and location', *East Midland Geographer*, 3 (1965), 461–9.

Sylvester, Dorothy 'Rural settlement in Cheshire; some problems of origin and classification', *Transactions of the Historic Society of Lancashire and Cheshire*, 101 (1949), 1–37.

'Rural settlement in Anglesey', *Anglesey Antiquarian Society and Field Club Transactions*, unnumbered series (1959), 1–24.

'Settlement patterns in rural Flintshire', *Flintshire Historical Society Publications*, 15 (1954–5), 6–42.

'The rural landscape of eastern Montgomeryshire', *Montgomeryshire Collections*, 54 (1955–6), 3–26.

'The open fields of Cheshire', *Transactions of the Historic Society of Lancashire and Cheshire*, 108 (1956), 1–33.

'The common fields of the coastlands of Gwent', *Agricultural History Review*, 6 (1958), 9–26.

The rural landscape of the Welsh borderland, a study in historical geography, London, Macmillan, 1969.

Symon, J. A. *Scottish farming past and present*, Edinburgh, Oliver and Boyd, 1959.

Taylor, Bessie 'Bromley, Beckenham and Penge, Kent, since 1750: a comparative study of the changing geography of three towns on the southern fringe of the metropolis', unpublished University of London Ph.D. thesis (1966).

Taylor, C. *Fields in the English landscape*, London, Dent, 1975.

Thirsk, Joan 'Agrarian history, 1540–1950', in *Victoria History of the County of Leicester*, 2 (1954), 199–264.

Tudor enclosures, Historical Association pamphlet, 41 (1959).

Thomas, C. 'Estate surveys as sources in historical geography', *Journal of the National Library of Wales*, 14 (1966), 451–68.

'Rural society in nineteenth century Wales: south Cardiganshire in 1851', *Ceredigion*, 6 (1971) 388–414.

'Colonization, enclosure and the rural landscape', *National Library of Wales Journal*, 19 (1975), 132–46.

'Place-name studies and agrarian colonization in North Wales', *Welsh History Review*, 10 (1980), 155–71.

Thomas, D. G. 'The Gelligaer parish tithe customs', *Gelligaer*, 7 (1970), 11–17.

Thomas, J. G. 'Some enclosure patterns in central Wales, a study in landscape modification', *Geography*, 42 (1957), 25–36.

Thomas, S. 'Land occupation, ownership and utilization in the parish of Llansantffraid', *Ceredigion*, 3 (1957), 124–55.

'The enumerators' returns as a source for a period picture of the parish of Llansantffraid, 1841–51', *Ceredigion*, 4 (1963), 408–21.

'The agricultural labour force in some south-west Carmarthenshire parishes in the mid-nineteenth century', *Welsh History Review*, 3 (1966), 63–73.

Thomas, W. S. G. 'Changing land utilisation, occupation and ownership in south-west Carmarthenshire from earliest times to the present', unpublished University of London Ph.D. thesis (1965).

'Lost villages in south-west Carmarthenshire', *Transactions of the Institute of British Geographers*, 47 (1969), 191–203.

Thompson, F. M. L. *English landed society in the nineteenth century*, London, Routledge and Kegan Paul, 1963.

Chartered surveyors: the growth of a profession, London, Routledge and Kegan Paul, 1968.

Hampstead: building a borough, 1650–1964, London, Routledge and Kegan Paul, 1974.

(ed.) *The rise of suburbia*, Leicester, Leicester University Press, 1982.

Thompson, R. N. 'The working of the Poor Law Amendment Act in Cumbria, 1836–1871', *Northern History*, 15 (1979), 117–37.

Thomson, J. A. F. 'Tithe disputes in later medieval London', *English Historical Review*, 78 (1963), 1–17.

Thorpe, H. 'The geography of rural settlement in the Durham region', unpublished University of Durham M.Litt. thesis (1936).

Tuke, J. *General view of the agriculture of the North Riding of Yorkshire*, London, McMillan, 1800.

Tupling, G. H. *The economic history of Rossendale*, Manchester, University of Manchester, Economic History Series, 4, 1927.

'Terriers and tithe and enclosure awards', *Amateur Historian*, 1 (1954), 361–4.

Turner, G. *General view of the agriculture of the county of Gloucester*, London, J. Smeeton, 1794.

Turner, M. E. *English parliamentary enclosure; its historical geography and economic history*, Folkestone, Dawson, 1980.

Uhlig, H. 'Old hamlets with infield and outfield systems in western and central Europe', *Geografiska Annaler*, 43 (1961), 285–312.

Vamplew, W. 'Tithes and agriculture: some comments on commutation', *Economic History Review*, 2nd series, 34 (1981), 115–19.

Venn, J. A. 'The economy of a Norfolk parish in 1783 and at the present time', *Economic History*, 1 (1926), 76–88.

The foundations of agricultural economics, 2nd edition, Cambridge, Cambridge University Press, 1933.

Victoria History of the County of Cambridge, Vols. 4, 6; Essex, Vols. 4, 6, 7; Gloucester, Vols. 6, 8, 11; Leicester, Vol. 4; Middlesex, Vols. 3, 5; Oxford, Vols. 5, 6, 7; Shropshire, Vol. 8; Somerset, Vol. 4; Stafford, Vols. 5, 8, 17; Warwick, Vols. 3, 4, 8; Wiltshire, Vols. 4, 6, 8; Yorkshire, East Riding, Vol. 3.

Vries, B. de 'The role of the land surveyor in the development of New Zealand, 1840–76', unpublished Victoria University of Wellington M.A. thesis (1966).

Wade Martins, Susanna *A great estate at work. The Holkham estate and its inhabitants in the nineteenth century*, Cambridge, Cambridge University Press, 1980.

Wainwright, F. T. 'Field-names', *Antiquity*, 17 (1943), 57–66.

'Field-names of Amounderness Hundred', *Transactions of the Historic Society of Lancashire and Cheshire*, 97 (1945–6), 71–116.

Walker, D. *General view of the agriculture of the county of Hertford*, London, W. Bulmer, 1795.

Waller, W. C. 'Essex field names', *Transactions of the Essex Archaeological Society*, new series, 5 (1895), 144–81; 6 (1898), 60–84 and 258–77; 7 (1900), 65–92 and 285–327; 8 (1903), 76–103, 199–222 and 295–323; 9 (1903), 68–100 and 156–79.

Wallis, Helen 'The history of land use mapping', *Cartographic Journal*, 18 (1981), 45–8.

Wallwork, K. L. 'The evolution of an industrial landscape: the Calder Darwen valley, Lancashire *c.* 1740–1914', unpublished University of Leicester Ph.D. thesis (1966).

Ward, D. 'The urban plan of Leeds and the factors which have conditioned its growth', unpublished University of Leeds M.A. thesis (1960).

'The pre-urban cadaster and the urban pattern of Leeds', *Annals of the Association of American Geographers*, 52 (1962), 150–66.

Ward, M. F. 'Industrial development and location in Leeds north of the river Aire, 1775–1914', unpublished University of Leeds Ph.D. thesis (1972).

Ward, W. R. 'The tithe question in England in the early nineteenth century', *Journal of Ecclesiastical History*, 16 (1965), 67–81.

Religion and society in England, 1790–1850, London, Batsford, 1972.

Weller, J. (ed.) *Coleshill model farm Oxfordshire: past, present, future*, Architects in Agriculture Group, occasional paper, 1, 1981.

Wells, R. A. E. 'The development of the English rural proletariat and social protest, 1700–1850', *Journal of Peasant Studies*, 6 (1979), 115–39.

Whalley, G. H. *The Tithe Act, and the Tithe Amendment Act. . .*, London, Shaw and Sons, 1838.

The Tithe Act and the whole of the Tithe Amendment Acts, with explanatory notes, 2nd edition, London, Shaw and Sons, 1848, 245.

Wharham, A. 'Tithes in country life', *History Today*, 22 (1972), 426–33.

Whiteman, R. J. (ed.) *Hexton: a parish survey*, Bradford, Cummins, 1937.

Willatts, E. C. 'Changes in land utilization in the south-west of the London Basin, 1840–1932', *Geographical Journal*, 82 (1933), 515–28.

Middlesex and the London region, Report of the Land Utilisation Survey of Great Britain, part 79, 1937.

Williams, M. *The draining of the Somerset Levels*, Cambridge, Cambridge University Press, 1970.

Williams, Phyllis, 'Land tenure in the Bishop's manor of Whitbourne', *Transactions of the Woolhope Naturalists' Field Club*, 40 (1972), 333–55.

Williams, V. 'Tithing troubles. Farmers' revolt against tithes, 1747/8', *Gelligaer*, 9 (1972), 24–30.

Williams, W. M. *A west country village, Ashworthy: family, kinship and land*, London, Routledge and Kegan Paul, 1963.

Winter, B. 'The woodlands of central Kent', unpublished University of Hull M.Sc. thesis (1966).

Witherick, M. E. 'Stages in the growth of urban settlement in central Cornwall', unpublished University of Birmingham Ph.D. thesis (1963).

Woodman, A. V. 'Dunton tithe procedure', *Records of Buckinghamshire*, 16 (1960), 363–4.

Wooldridge, S. W. and Hutchings, G. E. *London's countryside*, London, Methuen, 1957.

Workers' Educational Association, King's Langley Branch, L. M. Munby (ed.), *The history of King's Langley*, King's Langley, Workers' Educational Association, 1963.

Workers' Educational Association, Redbourn Local History Tutorial Class *The story of Redbourn*, Redbourn, Workers' Educational Association, 1962.

Workman, R. 'Analysing a tithe map in depth', *Local Historian*, 14 (1981), 262–9.

Worth, R. H. 'The tenants and commoners of Dartmoor', *Report and Transactions of the Devonshire Association*, 76 (1944), 187–214.

Worthington, R. A. 'The growth of rural settlement in south-eastern Monmouthshire', unpublished University of Wales M.A. thesis (1956).

Yates, E. M. 'The evolution of the English village', *Geographical Journal*, 148 (1982), 182–206.

Yelling, J. A. 'Open field, enclosure and farm production in east Worcestershire 1540–1870', unpublished University of Birmingham Ph.D. thesis (1966).

'Changes in crop production in east Worcestershire, 1540–1867', *Agricultural History Review*, 21 (1973), 18–34.

Common field and enclosure in England 1450–1850, London, Macmillan, 1977.

Young, A. *Travels during the years 1787, 1788 and 1789 . . . with a view of ascertaining the cultivation . . . of the kingdom of France*, Bury St Edmunds, Rackham, 1792.

Index of places

General index

13361229R00202

Printed in Great Britain
by Amazon.co.uk, Ltd.,
Marston Gate.